ects

Build seven web development projects with Spring MVC, Angular 6, JHipster, WebFlux, and Spring Boot 2

Nilang Patel

BIRMINGHAM - MUMBAI

Spring 5.0 Projects

Commissioning Editor: Aaron Lazar
Acquisition Editor: Denim Pinto
Content Development Editor: Anugraha Arunagiri
Technical Editor: Abin Sebastian
Copy Editor: Safis Editing
Project Coordinator: Ulhas Kambali
Proofreader: Safis Editing
Indexer: Mariammal Chettiyar
Graphics: Tom Scaria
Production Coordinator: Aparna Bhagat

First published: February 2019

Production reference: 1280219

Published by Packt Publishing Ltd.
Livery Place
35 Livery Street
Birmingham
B3 2PB, UK.

ISBN 978-1-78839-041-5

www.packtpub.com

`mapt.io`

Mapt is an online digital library that gives you full access to over 5,000 books and videos, as well as industry leading tools to help you plan your personal development and advance your career. For more information, please visit our website.

Why subscribe?

- Spend less time learning and more time coding with practical eBooks and Videos from over 4,000 industry professionals

- Improve your learning with Skill Plans built especially for you

- Get a free eBook or video every month

- Mapt is fully searchable

- Copy and paste, print, and bookmark content

Packt.com

Did you know that Packt offers eBook versions of every book published, with PDF and ePub files available? You can upgrade to the eBook version at `www.packt.com` and as a print book customer, you are entitled to a discount on the eBook copy. Get in touch with us at `customercare@packtpub.com` for more details.

At `www.packt.com`, you can also read a collection of free technical articles, sign up for a range of free newsletters, and receive exclusive discounts and offers on Packt books and eBooks.

Contributors

About the author

Nilang Patel has over 15 years of core IT experience in leading projects, software design and development, and supporting enterprise applications using enterprise Java technologies. He is highly skilled in core Java/J2EE-based applications, and has experience in the healthcare, human resource, taxation, intranet applications, energy, and risk management domains. He contributes to different communities through various forums and his personal blog. He is also the author of *Java 9 Dependency Injection*, and acquired Liferay 6.1 Developer Certification in 2013, Brainbench Java 6 certification in 2012, and became a Sun Certified Programmer for the Java 2 Platform 1.5 (SCJP) in 2007.

About the reviewer

Krunal Patel has been working at Liferay Portal for over six years and has over ten years' experience in enterprise application development using Java and Java EE technologies. He has worked in various domains, including healthcare, hospitality, and enterprise intranet. He was awarded an ITIL Foundation certificate in IT Service Management in 2015, Liferay 6.1 Developer Certification in 2013, and was awarded a MongoDB for Java Developers certificate in 2013. He is the co author of *Java 9 Dependency Injection* book and also reviewed *Mastering Apache Solr 7.x* by *Packt Publishing*.

Packt is searching for authors like you

If you're interested in becoming an author for Packt, please visit `authors.packtpub.com` and apply today. We have worked with thousands of developers and tech professionals, just like you, to help them share their insight with the global tech community. You can make a general application, apply for a specific hot topic that we are recruiting an author for, or submit your own idea.

Table of Contents

Preface

Spring makes it simple to create RESTful applications, interact with social service, communicate with modern databases, secure your system, and make your code modular and easy to test. This book will show you how to build various projects in Spring 5.0, using its various features, as well as third-party tools.

Who this book is for

This book is for competent Spring developers who wish to understand how to develop complex yet flexible applications with Spring. You must have a good knowledge of Java programming and be familiar with the basics of Spring.

What this book covers

Chapter 1, *Creating an Application to List World Countries with their GDP*, is about kick-starting your Spring-based web application development. We will focus on creating a web application using Spring MVC, Spring Data, and the World Bank API for some statistics on different countries, and a MySQL database. The core data for the application will be from the sample world database that comes with MySQL. The UI for this application will be powered by Angular.js. We will follow the WAR model for application deployment and will deploy on the latest version of Tomcat.

Chapter 2, *Building a Reactive Web Application*, is about building a RESTful web services application purely using Spring's new WebFlux framework. Spring WebFlux is a new framework that helps create reactive applications in a functional way.

Chapter 3, *Blogpress – A Simple Blog Management System*, is about creating a simple Spring Boot-based blog management system that uses Elasticsearch as the data store. We will also implement user roles management, authentication, and authorization using Spring Security.

Chapter 4, *Building a Central Authentication Server*, is about building an application that will act as an authentication and authorization server. We will make use of the OAuth2 protocol and LDAP to build a central application that supports authentication and authorization.

Chapter 5, *Application to View Countries and Their GDP Using JHipster*, revisits the application we developed in Chapter 1, *Creating an Application to List World Countries with their GDP*, and we'll develop the same application using JHipster. JHipster helps with the development of Spring Boot and Angular.js production-ready applications, and we will explore the platform and learn about its features and functionality.

Chapter 6, *Creating an Online Bookstore*, is about creating an online store that sells books by developing a web application in a layered fashion.

Chapter 7, *Task Management System Using Spring and Kotlin*, looks at building a task management system using Spring Framework and Kotlin.

To get the most out of this book

A good understanding of Java, Git, and Spring Framework is necessary before reading this book. A deep knowledge of OOP is desired, although some key concepts are reviewed in the first two chapters.

Download the example code files

You can download the example code files for this book from your account at www.packt.com. If you purchased this book elsewhere, you can visit www.packt.com/support and register to have the files emailed directly to you.

You can download the code files by following these steps:

1. Log in or register at www.packt.com.
2. Select the **SUPPORT** tab.
3. Click on **Code Downloads & Errata**.
4. Enter the name of the book in the **Search** box and follow the onscreen instructions.

Once the file is downloaded, please make sure that you unzip or extract the folder using the latest version of:

- WinRAR/7-Zip for Windows
- Zipeg/iZip/UnRarX for Mac
- 7-Zip/PeaZip for Linux

The code bundle for the book is also hosted on GitHub
at `https://github.com/PacktPublishing/Spring 5.0 Projects`. In case there's an update
to the code, it will be updated on the existing GitHub repository.

We also have other code bundles from our rich catalog of books and videos available
at `https://github.com/PacktPublishing/`. Check them out!

Download the color images

We also provide a PDF file that has color images of the screenshots/diagrams used in this
book. You can download it here: `http://www.`
`packtpub.com/sites/default/files/downloads/9781788390415_ColorImages.pdf`.

Code in Action

Visit the following link to check out videos of the code being run: `http://bit.ly/2ED57Ss`

Conventions used

There are a number of text conventions used throughout this book.

`CodeInText`: Indicates code words in text, database table names, folder names, filenames,
file extensions, pathnames, dummy URLs, user input, and Twitter handles. Here is an
example: "The preceding line has to be added between the `<Host></Host>` tags."

A block of code is set as follows:

```
<depedency>
 <groupId>org.springframework.boot</groupId>
 <artifactId>spring-boot-starter-security</artifactId>
</dependency>
```

When we wish to draw your attention to a particular part of a code block, the relevant lines
or items are set in bold:

```
<depedency>
 <groupId>org.springframework.boot</groupId>
 <artifactId>spring-boot-starter-security</artifactId>
</dependency>
```

Any command-line input or output is written as follows:

```
$ mvn package
```

Bold: Indicates a new term, an important word, or words that you see onscreen. For example, words in menus or dialog boxes appear in the text like this. Here is an example: "Download STS, unzip it in your local folder, and open the `.exe` file to start the STS. Once started, create a new **Spring Starter Project** of the **Spring Boot** type with the following attributes."

 Warnings or important notes appear like this.

 Tips and tricks appear like this.

Get in touch

Feedback from our readers is always welcome.

General feedback: If you have questions about any aspect of this book, mention the book title in the subject of your message and email us at `customercare@packtpub.com`.

Errata: Although we have taken every care to ensure the accuracy of our content, mistakes do happen. If you have found a mistake in this book, we would be grateful if you would report this to us. Please visit `www.packt.com/submit-errata`, selecting your book, clicking on the Errata Submission Form link, and entering the details.

Piracy: If you come across any illegal copies of our works in any form on the Internet, we would be grateful if you would provide us with the location address or website name. Please contact us at `copyright@packt.com` with a link to the material.

If you are interested in becoming an author: If there is a topic that you have expertise in and you are interested in either writing or contributing to a book, please visit `authors.packtpub.com`.

Reviews

Please leave a review. Once you have read and used this book, why not leave a review on the site that you purchased it from? Potential readers can then see and use your unbiased opinion to make purchase decisions, we at Packt can understand what you think about our products, and our authors can see your feedback on their book. Thank you!

For more information about Packt, please visit `packt.com`.

1
Creating an Application to List World Countries with their GDP

Spring is an ecosystem that facilitates the development of JVM-based enterprise applications. And this is achieved using various modules provided by Spring. One of them, called Spring-core, is the heart of the framework in the Spring ecosystem, which provides support for dependency injection, web application, data access, transaction management, testing, and others.

In this chapter, we will start from scratch and use Spring Framework to develop a simple application. Familiarity with Spring Framework is not required and we will see to it that by the end of the chapter you should be confident enough to use Spring Framework.

The following are the topics covered in this chapter:

- Introduction to the application
- Understanding the database structure
- Understanding the World Bank API
- Designing the wireframes
- Creating an empty application
- Defining the model classes
- Defining the data access layer
- Defining the API controllers
- Deploying to Tomcat
- Defining the view controllers
- Defining the views

Technical requirements

All the code used in this chapter can be downloaded from the following GitHub link: `https://github.com/PacktPublishing/Spring-5.0-Projects/tree/master/chapter01`. The code can be executed on any operating system, although it has only been tested on Windows.

Introduction to the application

We will develop an application to show the GDP information of various countries. We will make use of the sample World DB (`https://dev.mysql.com/doc/world-setup/en/world-setup-installation.html`) available with MySQL to list the countries and get a detailed view to display the country information and its GDP information obtained from the World Bank API (`https://datahelpdesk.worldbank.org/knowledgebase/articles/898599-api-indicator-queries`).

The listing will make use of the countries data available in the World DB. In the detail view, we will make use of data available in the World DB to list cities and languages, and make use of the World Bank API to get additional information and the GDP information about the country.

We will also support editing basic details of the country entry, adding and deleting cities from the country entry, and adding and deleting languages from the country entry. We will use the following tools and technologies in this application:

- Spring MVC framework for implementing the MVC pattern
- The interaction with the MySQL DB will be done using the Spring JDBC template
- The interaction with the World Bank API will be done using RestTemplate
- The views will be created using a templating framework called Thymeleaf
- The frontend will be driven by jQuery and Bootstrap

Understanding the database structure

If you don't have MySQL installed, head over to the MySQL link (`https://dev.mysql.com/downloads/installer`) to install it and populate it with the world database, if it is not already available. The appendix will also guide you on how to run the queries using MySQL Workbench and MySQL command-line tool.

The world database schema is depicted in the following diagram:

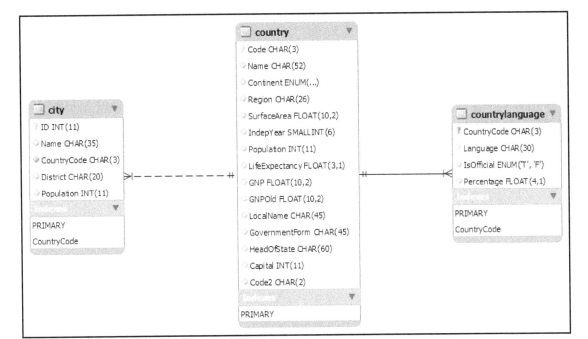

The database schema is simple, containing three tables as follows:

- **city**: List of cities mapped to the three character country coded in the country table.
- **country**: List of countries where the primary key is the three character country code. There is a column that has the ISO country code.
- **countrylanguage**: List of languages mapped to the country with one of the languages of the country marked as official.

Understanding the World Bank API

There are a lot of APIs exposed by the World Bank (http://www.worldbank.org/) and the API documentation can be found here (https://datahelpdesk.worldbank.org/knowledgebase/articles/889386-developer-information-overview). Out of the available APIs, we will use the Indicator APIs (https://datahelpdesk.worldbank.org/knowledgebase/articles/898599-api-indicator-queries), which represent information such as total population, GDP, GNI, energy use, and much more.

Using the Indicator API, we will fetch the GDP information for the countries available in the database for the last 10 years. Let's look at the API's REST URL and the data returned by the API, as follows:

```
GET
http://api.worldbank.org/countries/BR/indicators/NY.GDP.MKTP.CD?format=json
&date=2007:2017
```

The BR is a country code (*Brazil*) in this URL. The NY.GDP.MKTP.CD is the flag used by the Word Bank API internally to call Indicator API. The request parameter, date, indicates the duration of which the GDP information is required.

The excerpt from the response you will get for the preceding API is as follows:

```
[
    {
        "page": 1,
        "pages": 1,
        "per_page": "50",
        "total": 11
    },
    [
        ....// Other country data
        {
            "indicator": {
                "id": "NY.GDP.MKTP.CD",
                "value": "GDP (current US$)"
            },
            "country": {
                "id": "BR",
                "value": "Brazil"
            },
            "value": "1796186586414.45",
            "decimal": "0",
            "date": "2016"
        }
    ]
]
```

The preceding response shows the GDP indicator in US$ for Brazil for the year 2016.

Designing the wireframes of application screens

A wireframe is the basic skeleton of an application or website. It gives an idea about how the final application looks. It basically helps to decide navigation flows, understand functionality, design the user interface, and helps in setting the expectation before the application even exists. This process greatly helps developers, designers, product owners, and clients to work in a synchronous manner to avoid any gap in between. We will follow the same model and we will design various wireframes of the application as follows.

Country listing page

We will make it simple. The home page shows the country list with pagination, and allow searching by country name and filtering by continent/region. The following would be the home page of our application:

Country detail page

This screen will show details of the country such as cities, languages, and the GDP information obtained from the World Bank API. The GDP data will be visible in a graphical view. The page looks as follows:

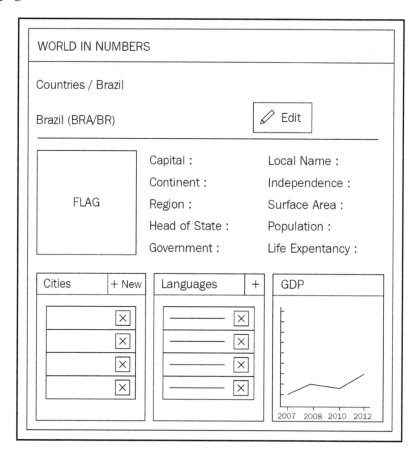

Country edit page

In country listing page, there will be one button called **Edit**. On clicking it, the system will show the country in edit mode, enabling the update of the basic details of the country. The following is the view structure for editing the basic detail of a country:

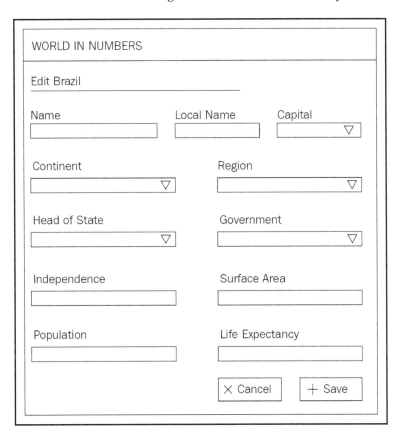

Add a new city and language

In the country detail page, two modal views, one for adding a new city and another for adding a new language, are available by clicking on the **New** button. The following is the view for the two modal dialogs used to add a new country and language. They will be opened individually:

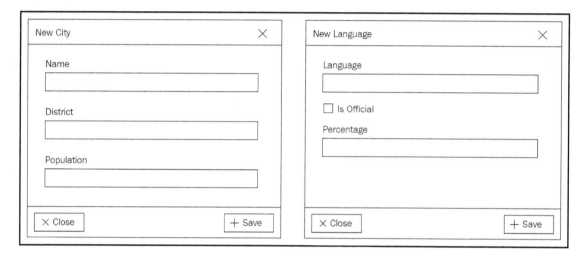

Creating an empty application

We will use Maven to generate an empty application with the structure required for Java-based web applications. If you do not have Maven installed, please follow the instructions here (https://maven.apache.org/install.html) to install Maven. Once installed, run the following command to create an empty application:

```
mvn archetype:generate -DgroupId=com.nilangpatel.worldgdp -
DartifactId=worldgdp -Dversion=0.0.1-SNAPSHOT -DarchetypeArtifactId=maven-
archetype-webapp
```

Running the preceding command will show the command-line argument values for confirmation as shown in the following screenshot:

You would have to type in Y in the Command Prompt shown in the previous screenshot to complete the empty project creation. Now you can import this project into an IDE of your choice and continue with the development activity. For the sake of simplicity, we will use Eclipse, as it is among the most popular IDEs used by the Java community today.

On successful creation of the application, you will see the folder structure, as shown in the following screenshot:

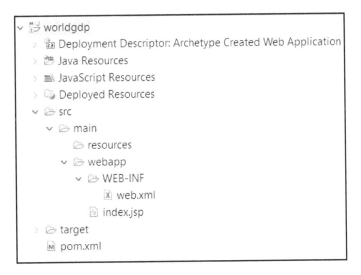

 You will see index.jsp added by default while creating the default project structure. You must delete it as, in this application, we will use Thymeleaf—another template engine to develop the landing page.

Defining the model classes

Now, let's create Java classes to model the data in the database and also the data coming from the World Bank API. Our approach is simple. We will have one Java class for each table in our database and the columns of the database will become the properties of the Java class.

In the generated application, the `java` folder is missing under the `main` directory. We will manually create the `java` folder and package the `com.nilangpatel.worldgdp`, which will be the root package for the application. Let's go ahead and implement the approach we decided on. But before that, let's see an interesting project called **Project Lombok**.

Project Lombok provides annotations for generating your getters, setters, default, and overloaded constructors, and other boilerplate code. More details on how to integrate with your IDE can be found on their project website (`https://projectlombok.org/`).

We need to update our `pom.xml` to include a dependency on Project Lombok. The following are the parts of `pom.xml` you need to copy and add to relevant locations in the XML:

```
<properties>
    <java.version>1.8</java.version>
    <lombok.version>1.16.18</lombok.version>
</properties>
<dependency>
    <groupId>org.projectlombok</groupId>
    <artifactId>lombok</artifactId>
    <optional>true</optional>
    <version>${lombok.version}</version>
</dependency>
```

All the model classes that we are going to create next belong to the `com.nilangpatel.worldgdp.model` package. The model class to represent `Country` data is given in the following code:

```
@Data
@Setter
@Getter
public class Country {
    private String code;
    private String name;
    private String continent;
    private String region;
    private Double surfaceArea;
    private Short indepYear;
```

```
    private Long population;
    private Double lifeExpectancy;
    private Double gnp;
    private String localName;
    private String governmentForm;
    private String headOfState;
    private City capital;
    private String code2;
}
```

The `City` class is not created yet, let's go ahead and create it as follows:

```
@Data
@Setter
@Getter
public class City {
    private Long id;
    private String name;
    private Country country;
    private String district;
    private Long population;
}
```

Next is to model the `CountryLanguage` class, which is the language spoken in a country, as follows:

```
@Data
@Setter
@Getter
public class CountryLanguage {
    private Country country;
    private String language;
    private String isOfficial;
    private Double percentage;
}
```

We also need a model class to map the GDP information obtained from the World Bank API. Let's go ahead and create a `CountryGDP` class as shown in the following code:

```
@Data
@Setter
@Getter
public class CountryGDP {
    private Short year;
    private Double value;
}
```

At this moment, everything works perfectly fine. But when you start calling getter and setter of these model classes into some other class, you may get a compilation error. This is because we need to do one more step to configure Lombok. After you defined the Maven dependency, you will see the JAR reference from IDE. Just right-click on it and select the **Run As | Java Application** option. Alternatively, you can execute the following command from terminal at the location where the Lombok JAR file is kept, as follows:

```
java -jar lombok-1.16.18.jar
```

Here, `lombok-1.16.18.jar` is the name of JAR file. You will see a separate window pop up as follows:

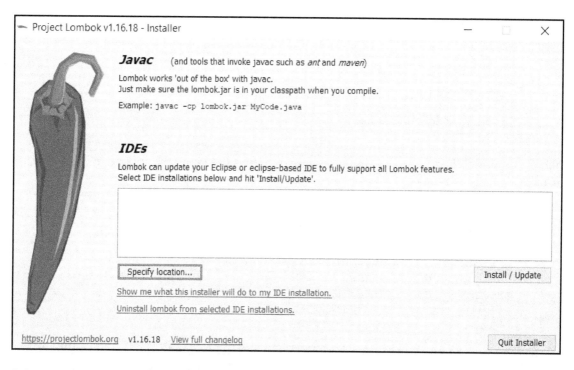

Select the location of your IDE by clicking on the **Specify location...** button. Once selected, click on the **Install / Update** button to install it. You will get a success message. Just restart the IDE and rebuild the project and you will see that just by defining `@Setter` and `@Getter`, the actual setters and getters are available to other classes. You are no longer required to add them explicitly.

Using Hibernate Validator to add validations

There are a few checks we need to add to our model classes so that the data being sent from the UI is not invalid. For this, we will make use of Hibernate Validator. You are required to add the Hibernate dependency as follows:

```
<properties>
    <java.version>1.8</java.version>
    <lombok.version>1.16.18</lombok.version>
<hibernate.validator.version>6.0.2.Final</hibernate.validator.version>
    </properties>
    <dependency>
        <groupId>org.hibernate.validator</groupId>
        <artifactId>hibernate-validator</artifactId>
        <version>${hibernate.validator.version}</version>
    </dependency>
```

Now go back to `com.nilangpatel.worldgdp.model.Country` and update it with the following:

```
@Data public class Country {

  @NotNull @Size(max = 3, min = 3) private String code;
  @NotNull @Size(max = 52) private String name;
  @NotNull private String continent;
  @NotNull @Size(max = 26) private String region;
  @NotNull private Double surfaceArea;
  private Short indepYear;
  @NotNull private Long population;
  private Double lifeExpectancy;
  private Double gnp;
  @NotNull private String localName;
  @NotNull private String governmentForm;
  private String headOfState;
  private City capital;
  @NotNull private String code2;
}
```

Next is to update the `com.nilangpatel.worldgdp.model.City` class in a similar way, as follows:

```
@Data public class City {
  @NotNull private Long id;
  @NotNull @Size(max = 35) private String name;
  @NotNull @Size(max = 3, min = 3) private String countryCode;
  private Country country;
  @NotNull @Size(max = 20) private String district;
```

```
@NotNull private Long population;
}
```

And finally, update `com.nilangpatel.worldgdp.model.CountryLanguage` class as well, as follows:

```
@Data
public class CountryLanguage {
  private Country country;
  @NotNull private String countryCode;
  @NotNull @Size(max = 30) private String language;
  @NotNull @Size(max = 1, min = 1) private String isOfficial;
  @NotNull private Double percentage;
}
```

Defining the data access layer – Spring JDBC Template

We have the model classes that reflect the structure of the data in the database that we obtained from the World Bank API. Now we need to develop a data access layer that interacts with our MySQL and populates the data stored in the database into instances of the model classes. We will use the Spring JDBC Template to achieve the required interaction with the database.

First, we need the JDBC driver to connect any Java application with MySQL. This can be obtained by adding the following dependency and version property to our `pom.xml`:

```
<properties>
    <java.version>1.8</java.version>
    <lombok.version>1.16.18</lombok.version>
<hibernate.validator.version>6.0.2.Final</hibernate.validator.version>
    <mysql.jdbc.driver.version>5.1.44</mysql.jdbc.driver.version>
</properties>
<dependency>
  <groupId>mysql</groupId>
  <artifactId>mysql-connector-java</artifactId>
  <version>${mysql.jdbc.driver.version}</version>
</dependency>
```

Wherever you see
`<something.version>1.5.6</something.version>`, it should go within the `<properties></properties>` tag. Will not mention this repeatedly. This is for keeping the versions of libraries used in one place, making it easy to maintain and look up.

Anything that comes as `<dependency></dependency>` goes within the `<dependencies></dependencies>` list.

Now we need to add a dependency to the Spring core APIs, as well as the Spring JDBC APIs (which contain the JDBC Template) to our `pom.xml`. A brief intro about these two dependencies is as follows:

1. **Spring core APIs:** It provides us with core Spring features such as dependency injection and configuration model
2. **Spring JDBC APIs:** It provides us with the APIs required to create the `DataSource` instance and interact with the database

Since this is a sample application, we aren't using Hibernate or other ORM libraries because they provide lots of functionalities apart from basic CRUD operations. Instead, we will write SQL queries and use them with JDBC Template to make things simpler.

The following code shows the `dependency` information for the two libraries:

```
<dependency>
    <groupId>org.springframework</groupId>
    <artifactId>spring-core</artifactId>
    <version>${spring.version}</version>
</dependency>
<dependency>
    <groupId>org.springframework</groupId>
    <artifactId>spring-jdbc</artifactId>
    <version>${spring.version}</version>
</dependency>
```

Along with the preceding two dependencies, we need to add a few more Spring dependencies to assist us in setting up Java-based configurations using annotations (such as `@bean`, `@Service`, `@Configuration`, `@ComponentScan`, and so on) and dependency injection using annotations (`@Autowired`). For this, we will be adding further dependencies as follows:

```
<dependency>
    <groupId>org.springframework</groupId>
```

```
      <artifactId>spring-beans</artifactId>
      <version>${spring.version}</version>
</dependency>
<dependency>
      <groupId>org.springframework</groupId>
      <artifactId>spring-context</artifactId>
      <version>${spring.version}</version>
</dependency>
```

Defining the JDBC connection properties

We will define the JDBC connection properties in an `application.properties` file and place it in `src/main/resources`. The properties we define are as follows:

```
dataSourceClassName=com.mysql.jdbc.Driver
jdbcUrl=jdbc:mysql://localhost:3306/worldgdp
dataSource.user=root
dataSource.password=test
```

The preceding properties are with the assumptions that MySQL is running on port `3306` and the database username and password are `root` and `test` respectively. You can change these properties as per your local configuration. The next step is to define a properties resolver that will be able to resolve the properties when used from within the code. We will use the `@PropertySource` annotation, along with an instance of `PropertySourcesPlaceholderConfigurer`, as shown in the following code:

```
@Configuration
@PropertySource("classpath:application.properties")
public class PropertiesWithJavaConfig {

    @Bean
    public static PropertySourcesPlaceholderConfigurer
      propertySourcesPlaceholderConfigurer() {
        return new PropertySourcesPlaceholderConfigurer();
    }
}
```

 We will follow the convention of placing all our configuration classes in `com.nilangpatel.worldgdp.config` and any root configuration will go in the `com.nilangpatel.worldgdp` package.

This class reads all the properties from the `application.properties` file stored in classpath (`src/main/resources`). Next up is to configure a `javax.sql.DataSource` object that will connect to the database using the properties defined in the `application.properties` file. We will use the HikariCP connection pooling library for creating our `DataSource` instance. This `DataSource` instance is then used to instantiate `NamedParameterJdbcTemplate`. We will use `NamedParameterJdbcTemplate` to execute all our SQL queries. At this point, we need to add a necessary dependency for the HikariCP library as follows:

```
<dependency>
    <groupId>com.zaxxer</groupId>
    <artifactId>HikariCP</artifactId>
    <version>${hikari.version}</version>
</dependency>
```

The `DBConfiguration` data source configuration class should look as follows:

```
@Configuration
public class DBConfiguration {
  @Value("${jdbcUrl}") String jdbcUrl;
  @Value("${dataSource.user}") String username;
  @Value("${dataSource.password}") String password;
  @Value("${dataSourceClassName}") String className;
  @Bean
  public DataSource getDataSource() {
    HikariDataSource ds = new HikariDataSource();
    ds.setJdbcUrl(jdbcUrl);
    ds.setUsername(username);
    ds.setPassword(password);
    ds.setDriverClassName(className);
    return ds;
  }
  @Bean
  public NamedParameterJdbcTemplate namedParamJdbcTemplate() {
    NamedParameterJdbcTemplate namedParamJdbcTemplate =
        new NamedParameterJdbcTemplate(getDataSource());
    return namedParamJdbcTemplate;
  }
}
```

Let's have a quick introduction to a few new things used in this code:

- `@Configuration`: This is to indicate to Spring Framework that this class creates Java objects that contain some configuration
- `@Bean`: This is method-level annotation, used to indicate to Spring Framework that the method returns Java objects whose life cycle is managed by Spring Framework and injected into places where its dependency is declared
- `@Value`: This is used to refer to the properties defined in the `application.properties`, which are resolved by the `PropertySourcesPlaceholderConfigurer` bean defined in the `PropertiesWithJavaConfig` class

It is always good practice to write unit test cases in JUnit. We will write test cases for our application. For that, we need to create the corresponding configuration classes for running our JUnit tests. In the next section, we will look at setting up the test environment.

Setting up the test environment

Let's adopt a test first approach here. So, before going into writing the queries and DAO classes, let's set up the environment for our unit testing. If you don't find the `src/test/java` and `src/test/resources` folders, then please go ahead and create them either from your IDE or from your OS file explorer.

The `src/test/java` folder will contain all the Java code and `src/test/resources` will contain the required property files and other resources required for test cases. After creating the required folders, the project structure looks something like that shown in the following screenshot:

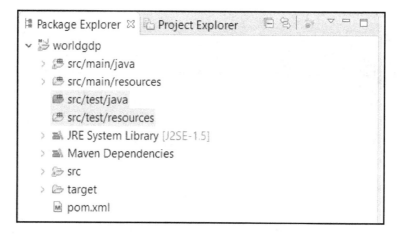

We will use the H2 database as a source of data for our testing environment. For that, we will update our Maven dependencies to add H2 and JUnit dependencies. H2 is one of the most popular embedded databases. The following is the dependency information that you need to add in your `pom.xml`:

```xml
<dependency>
    <groupId>org.springframework</groupId>
    <artifactId>spring-test</artifactId>
    <version>${spring.version}</version>
    <scope>test</scope>
</dependency>
<dependency>
    <groupId>junit</groupId>
    <artifactId>junit</artifactId>
    <version>${junit.version}</version>
    <scope>test</scope>
</dependency>
<dependency>
    <groupId>org.assertj</groupId>
    <artifactId>assertj-core</artifactId>
    <version>${assertj.version}</version>
    <scope>test</scope>
</dependency>
<dependency>
    <groupId>com.h2database</groupId>
    <artifactId>h2</artifactId>
    <version>${h2.version}</version>
</dependency>
```

We already have a property for `spring.version`, but we need version properties for the other two, as given in the following code:

```xml
<junit.version>4.12</junit.version>
<assertj.version>3.12.0</assertj.version>
<h2.version>1.4.198</h2.version>
```

The World DB schema available in MySQL will not be compatible to run with H2, but don't worry. The compatible World DB schema for H2 is available in the source code of this chapter, you can download from GitHub (`https://github.com/PacktPublishing/Spring-5.0-Projects/tree/master/chapter01`). It is kept in the `src/test/resources` folder in the project. The file name is `h2_world.sql`. We will use this file to bootstrap our H2 database with the required tables and data that will then be available in our tests.

Next up is to configure H2 and one of the things we configure is the name of the SQL script file that contains the schema and data. This SQL script file should be available on the classpath. The following is the configuration class created in the `com.nilangpatel.worldgdp.test.config` package under `src/test/java` folder:

```
@Configuration
public class TestDBConfiguration {
  @Bean
    public DataSource dataSource() {
        return new EmbeddedDatabaseBuilder()
            .generateUniqueName(true)
            .setType(EmbeddedDatabaseType.H2)
            .setScriptEncoding("UTF-8")
            .ignoreFailedDrops(true)
            .addScript("h2_world.sql")
            .build();
    }
  @Bean("testTemplate")
  public NamedParameterJdbcTemplate namedParamJdbcTemplate() {
    NamedParameterJdbcTemplate namedParamJdbcTemplate =
        new NamedParameterJdbcTemplate(dataSource());
    return namedParamJdbcTemplate;
  }
}
```

Along with the H2 configuration, we are initializing `NamedParameterJdbcTemplate` by providing it with the H2 datasource built in the other method.

 We have added few other dependencies specific to JUnit. You can refer to them by downloading the source code.

Defining the RowMapper

As we are using the JDBC Template, we need a way to map the rows of data from a database to a Java object. This can be achieved by implementing a `RowMapper` interface. We will define mapper classes for all the three entities. For `Country`, the raw mapper class looks as follows:

```
public class CountryRowMapper implements RowMapper<Country>{

  public Country mapRow(ResultSet rs, int rowNum)
                          throws SQLException {
    Country country = new Country();
```

```
    country.setCode(rs.getString("code"));
    country.setName(rs.getString("name"));
    country.setContinent(rs.getString("continent"));
    country.setRegion(rs.getString("region"));
    country.setSurfaceArea(rs.getDouble("surface_area"));
    country.setIndepYear(rs.getShort("indep_year"));
    country.setPopulation(rs.getLong("population"));
    country.setLifeExpectancy(rs.getDouble("life_expectancy"));
    country.setGnp(rs.getDouble("gnp"));
    country.setLocalName(rs.getString("local_name"));
    country.setGovernmentForm(rs.getString("government_form"));
    country.setHeadOfState(rs.getString("head_of_state"));
    country.setCode2(rs.getString("code2"));
    if ( Long.valueOf(rs.getLong("capital")) != null ) {
      City city = new City();
      city.setId(rs.getLong("capital"));
      city.setName(rs.getString("capital_name"));
      country.setCapital(city);
    }
    return country;
  }
}
```

Then we define the mapper class for `City` as follows:

```
public class CityRowMapper implements RowMapper<City>{
  public City mapRow(ResultSet rs, int rowNum)
                  throws SQLException {
    City city = new City();
    city.setCountryCode(rs.getString("country_code"));
    city.setDistrict(rs.getString("district"));
    city.setId(rs.getLong("id"));
    city.setName(rs.getString("name"));
    city.setPopulation(rs.getLong("population"));
    return city;
  }
}
```

And finally, we define `CountryLanguage` as follows:

```
public class CountryLanguageRowMapper implements
                    RowMapper<CountryLanguage> {
  public CountryLanguage mapRow(ResultSet rs, int rowNum)
                            throws SQLException {
    CountryLanguage countryLng = new CountryLanguage();
    countryLng.setCountryCode(rs.getString("countrycode"));
    countryLng.setIsOfficial(rs.getString("isofficial"));
    countryLng.setLanguage(rs.getString("language"));
```

```
        countryLng.setPercentage(rs.getDouble("percentage"));
        return countryLng;
    }
}
```

Designing the CountryDAO

Let's go ahead and define the `CountryDAO` class in the
`com.nilangpatel.worldgdp.dao` package along with the required methods, starting
with the `getCountries` method. This method will fetch the details of countries to show
them in the listing page. This method is also called while filtering the country list. Based on
listing, filtering, and paginating, we have broken up the query used in this method into the
following parts:

1. Select clause:

    ```
    private static final String SELECT_CLAUSE = "SELECT "
            + " c.Code, "
            + " c.Name, "
            + " c.Continent, "
            + " c.region, "
            + " c.SurfaceArea surface_area, "
            + " c.IndepYear indep_year, "
            + " c.Population, "
            + " c.LifeExpectancy life_expectancy, "
            + " c.GNP, "
            + " c.LocalName local_name, "
            + " c.GovernmentForm government_form, "
            + " c.HeadOfState head_of_state, "
            + " c.code2 ,"
            + " c.capital ,"
            + " cy.name capital_name "
            + " FROM country c"
            + " LEFT OUTER JOIN city cy ON cy.id = c.capital ";
    ```

2. Search where clause:

    ```
    private static final String SEARCH_WHERE_CLAUSE = " AND (
    LOWER(c.name) "
            + " LIKE CONCAT('%', LOWER(:search), '%') ) ";
    ```

3. Continent filter where clause:

    ```
    private static final String CONTINENT_WHERE_CLAUSE =
            " AND c.continent = :continent ";
    ```

4. Region filter where clause:

```
private static final String REGION_WHERE_CLAUSE =
    " AND c.region = :region ";
```

5. Pagination clause:

```
private static final String PAGINATION_CLAUSE = " ORDER BY c.code "
    + " LIMIT :size OFFSET :offset ";
```

The placeholders defined by :<<variableName>> are replaced by the values provided in the Map to the NamedParameterJdbcTemplate. This way we can avoid concatenating the values into the SQL query, thereby avoiding chances of SQL injection.
The getCountries() definition would now be as follows:

```
public List<Country> getCountries(Map<String, Object> params){
    int pageNo = 1;
    if ( params.containsKey("pageNo") ) {
      pageNo = Integer.parseInt(params.get("pageNo").toString());
    }
    Integer offset = (pageNo - 1) * PAGE_SIZE;
    params.put("offset", offset);
    params.put("size", PAGE_SIZE);
    return namedParamJdbcTemplate.query(SELECT_CLAUSE
        + " WHERE 1 = 1 "
        + (!StringUtils.isEmpty((String)params.get("search"))
           ? SEARCH_WHERE_CLAUSE : "")
        + (!StringUtils.isEmpty((String)params.get("continent"))
           ? CONTINENT_WHERE_CLAUSE : "")
        + (!StringUtils.isEmpty((String)params.get("region"))
           ? REGION_WHERE_CLAUSE : "")
        + PAGINATION_CLAUSE,
        params, new CountryRowMapper());
    }
```

Next is to implement the getCountriesCount method, which is similar to getCountries, except that it returns the count of entries matching the WHERE clause without the pagination applied. The implementation is as shown in the following code:

```
public int getCountriesCount(Map<String, Object> params) {
    return namedParamJdbcTemplate.queryForObject(
        "SELECT COUNT(*) FROM country c"
        + " WHERE 1 = 1 "
        + (!StringUtils.isEmpty((String)params.get("search"))
           ? SEARCH_WHERE_CLAUSE : "")
        + (!StringUtils.isEmpty((String)params.get("continent"))
           ? CONTINENT_WHERE_CLAUSE : "")
```

```
        + (!StringUtils.isEmpty((String)params.get("region"))
            ? REGION_WHERE_CLAUSE : ""),
        params, Integer.class);
}
```

Then we implement the `getCountryDetail` method to get the detail of the country, given its code, as follows:

```
public Country getCountryDetail(String code) {
    Map<String, String> params = new HashMap<String, String>();
    params.put("code", code);
    return namedParamJdbcTemplate.queryForObject(SELECT_CLAUSE
        +" WHERE c.code = :code", params,
        new CountryRowMapper());
}
```

In all of the previous DAO method implementations, we have made use of the `CountryRowMapper` we defined in the *Defining the RowMapper* section.

Finally, we define the method to allow editing the country information, as shown in the following code:

```
public void editCountryDetail(String code, Country country) {
    namedParamJdbcTemplate.update(" UPDATE country SET "
        + " name = :name, "
        + " localname = :localName, "
        + " capital = :capital, "
        + " continent = :continent, "
        + " region = :region, "
        + " HeadOfState = :headOfState, "
        + " GovernmentForm = :governmentForm, "
        + " IndepYear = :indepYear, "
        + " SurfaceArea = :surfaceArea, "
        + " population = :population, "
        + " LifeExpectancy = :lifeExpectancy "
        + "WHERE Code = :code ",
        getCountryAsMap(code, country));
}
```

The previous method uses a helper method that builds a `Map` object, by using the data present in the `Country` object. We need the map, as we'll be using it as a parameter source for our `namedParamJdbcTemplate`.

The helper method has a simple implementation, as shown in the following code:

```
private Map<String, Object> getCountryAsMap(String code, Country country){
    Map<String, Object> countryMap = new HashMap<String, Object>();
    countryMap.put("name", country.getName());
    countryMap.put("localName", country.getLocalName());
    countryMap.put("capital", country.getCapital().getId());
    countryMap.put("continent", country.getContinent());
    countryMap.put("region", country.getRegion());
    countryMap.put("headOfState", country.getHeadOfState());
    countryMap.put("governmentForm", country.getGovernmentForm());
    countryMap.put("indepYear", country.getIndepYear());
    countryMap.put("surfaceArea", country.getSurfaceArea());
    countryMap.put("population", country.getPopulation());
    countryMap.put("lifeExpectancy", country.getLifeExpectancy());
    countryMap.put("code", code);
    return countryMap;
}
```

Let's write our JUnit test for the `CountryDAO` class, which we haven't created yet.
Create `CountryDAOTest` class into the `com.nilangpatel.worldgdp.test.dao` package
as follows:

```
@RunWith(SpringRunner.class)
@SpringJUnitConfig( classes = {
        TestDBConfiguration.class, CountryDAO.class})
public class CountryDAOTest {

  @Autowired CountryDAO countryDao;
  @Autowired @Qualifier("testTemplate")
  NamedParameterJdbcTemplate namedParamJdbcTemplate;
  @Before
  public void setup() {
    countryDao.setNamedParamJdbcTemplate(namedParamJdbcTemplate);
  }
  @Test
  public void testGetCountries() {
    List<Country> countries = countryDao.getCountries(new HashMap<>());
    //AssertJ assertions
    //Paginated List, so should have 20 entries
    assertThat(countries).hasSize(20);
  }
  @Test
  public void testGetCountries_searchByName() {
    Map<String, Object> params = new HashMap<>();
    params.put("search", "Aruba");
    List<Country> countries = countryDao.getCountries(params);
    assertThat(countries).hasSize(1);
```

```
      }
      @Test
      public void testGetCountries_searchByContinent() {
        Map<String, Object> params = new HashMap<>();
        params.put("continent", "Asia");
        List<Country> countries = countryDao.getCountries(params);
        assertThat(countries).hasSize(20);
      }
      @Test
      public void testGetCountryDetail() {
        Country c = countryDao.getCountryDetail("IND");
        assertThat(c).isNotNull();
        assertThat(c.toString()).isEqualTo("Country(code=IND, name=India, "
            + "continent=Asia, region=Southern and Central Asia, "
            + "surfaceArea=3287263.0, indepYear=1947, population=1013662000, "
            + "lifeExpectancy=62.5, gnp=447114.0, localName=Bharat/India, "
            + "governmentForm=Federal Republic, headOfState=Kocheril Raman
Narayanan, "
            + "capital=City(id=1109, name=New Delhi, countryCode=null, "
            + "country=null, district=null, population=null), code2=IN)");
      }
      @Test public void testEditCountryDetail() {
        Country c = countryDao.getCountryDetail("IND");
        c.setHeadOfState("Ram Nath Kovind");
        c.setPopulation(13241713541);
        countryDao.editCountryDetail("IND", c);
        c = countryDao.getCountryDetail("IND");
        assertThat(c.getHeadOfState()).isEqualTo("Ram Nath Kovind");
        assertThat(c.getPopulation()).isEqualTo(13241713541);
      }
      @Test public void testGetCountriesCount() {
        Integer count = countryDao.getCountriesCount(Collections.EMPTY_MAP);
        assertThat(count).isEqualTo(239);
      }
    }
```

There are a few things to note about configuring JUnit tests using the Spring test framework from the following test, including the following:

- @RunWith is used to replace the JUnit's test runner with a custom test runner, which in this case, is Spring's SpringRunner. Spring's test runner helps in integrating JUnit with the Spring test framework.

- @SpringJUnitConfig is used to provide the list of classes that contain the required configuration to satisfy the dependencies for running the test.

Many people who choose ORM frameworks may feel that writing complicated SQL queries like this is awkward. However, from the next chapter onward, we'll start using the Spring Data framework to make an interaction with various data sources; the database is one of those accessed with the Spring Data JPA. Here, we wanted to show how the Spring JDBC offering interacts with the database.

Designing the CityDAO

The following are some of the important operations to be supported by `com.nilangpatel.worldgdp.dao.CityDAO` class:

- Get cities for a country
- Get city details for given ID
- Add a new city to a country
- Delete the given city from the country

Let's go ahead and implement each one of these functionalities starting with the `getCities`, as follows:

```
public List<City> getCities(String countryCode, Integer pageNo){
  Map<String, Object> params = new HashMap<String, Object>();
  params.put("code", countryCode);
  if ( pageNo != null ) {
    Integer offset = (pageNo - 1) * PAGE_SIZE;
    params.put("offset", offset);
    params.put("size", PAGE_SIZE);
  }
  return namedParamJdbcTemplate.query("SELECT "
      + " id, name, countrycode country_code, district, population "
      + " FROM city WHERE countrycode = :code"
      + " ORDER BY Population DESC"
      + ((pageNo != null) ? " LIMIT :offset , :size " : ""),
      params, new CityRowMapper());
}
```

We are using a paginated query to get a list of cities for a country. We will also need another overloaded version of this method where we return all the cities of a country and we will use this query to fetch all the cities while editing the country to select its capital. The overloaded version is as follows:

```
public List<City> getCities(String countryCode){
  return getCities(countryCode, null);
}
```

Next is to implement the method to get the city details, as shown in the following code:

```
public City getCityDetail(Long cityId) {
  Map<String, Object> params = new HashMap<String, Object>();
  params.put("id", cityId);
  return namedParamJdbcTemplate.queryForObject("SELECT id, "
      + " name, countrycode country_code, "
      + " district, population "
      + " FROM city WHERE id = :id",
      params, new CityRowMapper());
}
```

Then we implement the method to add a city as follows:

```
public Long addCity(String countryCode, City city) {
  SqlParameterSource paramSource = new MapSqlParameterSource(
      getMapForCity(countryCode, city));
  KeyHolder keyHolder = new GeneratedKeyHolder();
  namedParamJdbcTemplate.update("INSERT INTO city("
      + " name, countrycode, "
      + " district, population) "
      + " VALUES (:name, :country_code, "
      + " :district, :population )",
      paramSource, keyHolder);
  return keyHolder.getKey().longValue();
}
```

As we saw with adding a country, this will also make use of a helper method to return a Map from the City data, as follows:

```
private Map<String, Object> getMapForCity(String countryCode, City city){
  Map<String, Object> map = new HashMap<String, Object>();
  map.put("name", city.getName());
  map.put("country_code", countryCode);
  map.put("district", city.getDistrict());
  map.put("population", city.getPopulation());
  return map;
}
```

An important thing to notice in addCity is the use of KeyHolder and GeneratedKeyHolder to return the generated (due to auto increment) primary key that is the cityId, as follows:

```
KeyHolder keyHolder = new GeneratedKeyHolder();
//other code
return keyHolder.getKey().longValue();
```

And finally, we implement the method to delete a city from the country as shown in the following code:

```
public void deleteCity(Long cityId) {
  Map<String, Object> params = new HashMap<String, Object>();
  params.put("id", cityId);
  namedParamJdbcTemplate.update("DELETE FROM city WHERE id = :id", params);
}
```

Now let's add a test for CityDAO. Add the CityDAOTest class in com.nilangpatel.worldgdp.test.dao package under src/test/java folder as follows:

```
@RunWith(SpringRunner.class)
@SpringJUnitConfig( classes = {
  TestDBConfiguration.class, CityDAO.class})
public class CityDAOTest {

  @Autowired CityDAO cityDao;
  @Autowired @Qualifier("testTemplate")
  NamedParameterJdbcTemplate namedParamJdbcTemplate;
  @Before
  public void setup() {
    cityDao.setNamedParamJdbcTemplate(namedParamJdbcTemplate);
  }
  @Test public void testGetCities() {
    List<City> cities = cityDao.getCities("IND", 1);
    assertThat(cities).hasSize(10);
  }
  @Test public void testGetCityDetail() {
    Long cityId = 10241;
    City city = cityDao.getCityDetail(cityId);
    assertThat(city.toString()).isEqualTo("City(id=1024, name=Mumbai
(Bombay), "
      + "countryCode=IND, country=null, district=Maharashtra,
population=10500000)");
  }
  @Test public void testAddCity() {
    String countryCode = "IND";
    City city = new City();
    city.setCountryCode(countryCode);
    city.setDistrict("District");
    city.setName("City Name");
    city.setPopulation(1010101);
    long cityId = cityDao.addCity(countryCode, city);
    assertThat(cityId).isNotNull();
    City cityFromDb = cityDao.getCityDetail(cityId);
    assertThat(cityFromDb).isNotNull();
```

```
      assertThat(cityFromDb.getName()).isEqualTo("City Name");
    }
    @Test (expected = EmptyResultDataAccessException.class)
    public void testDeleteCity() {
      Long cityId = addCity();
      cityDao.deleteCity(cityId);
      City cityFromDb = cityDao.getCityDetail(cityId);
      assertThat(cityFromDb).isNull();
    }
    private Long addCity() {
      String countryCode = "IND";
      City city = new City();
      city.setCountryCode(countryCode);
      city.setDistrict("District");
      city.setName("City Name");
      city.setPopulation(1010101);
      return cityDao.addCity(countryCode, city);
    }
  }
```

Designing the CountryLanguageDAO

We will need to expose the following APIs to interact with the countrylanguage table:

- Get list of languages for a given country code
- Add a new language for a country by checking that the language doesn't already exist
- Delete a language for a country

For the sake of keeping it short, we will show the method implementations covering these three scenarios. The complete code can be found in the com.nilangpatel.worldgdp.dao.CountryLanguageDAO class available in the code downloaded for this book. The following is the code for these method implementations:

```
    public List<CountryLanguage> getLanguages(String countryCode, Integer
    pageNo){
      Map<String, Object> params = new HashMap<String, Object>();
      params.put("code", countryCode);
      Integer offset = (pageNo - 1) * PAGE_SIZE;
      params.put("offset", offset);
      params.put("size", PAGE_SIZE);
      return namedParamJdbcTemplate.query("SELECT * FROM countrylanguage"
          + " WHERE countrycode = :code"
          + " ORDER BY percentage DESC "
          + " LIMIT :size OFFSET :offset ",
```

```
      params, new CountryLanguageRowMapper());
}

public void addLanguage(String countryCode, CountryLanguage cl) {
  namedParamJdbcTemplate.update("INSERT INTO countrylanguage ( "
      + " countrycode, language, isofficial, percentage ) "
      + " VALUES ( :country_code, :language, "
      + " :is_official, :percentage ) ",
      getAsMap(countryCode, cl));
}

public boolean languageExists(String countryCode, String language) {
  Map<String, Object> params = new HashMap<String, Object>();
  params.put("code", countryCode);
  params.put("lang", language);
  Integer langCount = namedParamJdbcTemplate.queryForObject(
    "SELECT COUNT(*) FROM countrylanguage"
    + " WHERE countrycode = :code "
    + " AND language = :lang", params, Integer.class);
  return langCount > 0;
}

public void deleteLanguage (String countryCode, String language ) {
  Map<String, Object> params = new HashMap<String, Object>();
  params.put("code", countryCode);
  params.put("lang", language);
  namedParamJdbcTemplate.update("DELETE FROM countrylanguage "
      + " WHERE countrycode = :code AND "
      + " language = :lang ", params);
}

private Map<String, Object> getAsMap(String countryCode, CountryLanguage
cl){
  Map<String, Object> map = new HashMap<String, Object>();
  map.put("country_code", countryCode);
  map.put("language", cl.getLanguage());
  map.put("is_official", cl.getIsOfficial());
  map.put("percentage", cl.getPercentage());
  return map;
}
```

Designing the client for World Bank API

We need to fetch the GDP data from WorldBank API. As we discussed, it is REST end point, where we have to send few parameters and will get the response. For this, we will use RestTemplate to make REST call. The following is the definition for the `com.packt.external.WorldBankApiClient` class, which is used to invoke the World Bank API and process its response to return `List<CountryGDP>`:

```
@Service
public class WorldBankApiClient {

   String GDP_URL =
"http://api.worldbank.org/countries/%s/indicators/NY.GDP.MKTP.CD?"
      + "format=json&date=2008:2018";
   public List<CountryGDP> getGDP(String countryCode) throws ParseException
{
     RestTemplate worldBankRestTmplt = new RestTemplate();
     ResponseEntity<String> response
       = worldBankRestTmplt.getForEntity(String.format(GDP_URL,
countryCode), String.class);
     //the second element is the actual data and its an array of object
     JSONParser parser = new JSONParser();
     JSONArray responseData = (JSONArray) parser.parse(response.getBody());
     JSONArray countryDataArr = (JSONArray) responseData.get(1);
     List<CountryGDP> data = new ArrayList<CountryGDP>();
     JSONObject countryDataYearWise=null;
     for (int index=0; index < countryDataArr.size(); index++) {
       countryDataYearWise = (JSONObject) countryDataArr.get(index);
       String valueStr = "0";
       if(countryDataYearWise.get("value") !=null) {
         valueStr = countryDataYearWise.get("value").toString();
       }
       String yearStr = countryDataYearWise.get("date").toString();
       CountryGDP gdp = new CountryGDP();
       gdp.setValue(valueStr != null ? Double.valueOf(valueStr) : null);
       gdp.setYear(Short.valueOf(yearStr));
       data.add(gdp);
     }
     return data;
   }
}
```

Defining the API controllers

So far, we have written code to interact with the DB. Next up is to work on the code for the controller. We will have both types of controller—one that returns the view name (Thymeleaf template in our case) with the data for the view populated in the model object, and the other that exposes the RESTful APIs. We will need to add the following dependency to pom.xml:

```
<dependency>
    <groupId>org.springframework</groupId>
    <artifactId>spring-webmvc</artifactId>
    <version>${spring.version}</version>
</dependency>
```

Adding spring-webmvc to the dependency will automatically include spring-core, spring-beans, and spring-context dependencies. So we can remove them from the pom.xml.

Enabling Web MVC using @EnableWebMvc

To be able to make use of the Spring MVC features, we need to have one class that has been annotated with @Configuration, to be annotated with @EnableWebMvc. The @EnableWebMvc annotation, imports the Spring MVC configuration from the WebMvcConfigurationSupport class present in the Spring MVC framework. If we need to override any of the default imported configuration, we would have to implement the WebMvcConfigurer interface present in the Spring MVC framework and override the required methods.

We will create an AppConfiguration class with the following definition:

```
@EnableWebMvc
@Configuration
@ComponentScan(basePackages = "com.nilangpatel.worldgdp")
public class AppConfiguration implements WebMvcConfigurer{

  @Override
  public void addResourceHandlers(ResourceHandlerRegistry registry) {
  registry.addResourceHandler("/static/**").addResourceLocations("/static/");
  }
}
```

In the previous configuration, a few important things to note are as follows:

- `@EnableWebMvc`: This imports the Spring MVC related configuration.
- `@ComponentScan`: This is used for declaring the packages that have to be scanned for Spring components (which can be `@Configuration`, `@Service`, `@Controller`, `@Component`, and so on). If no package is defined, then it scans starting from the package where the class is defined.
- `WebMvcConfigurer`: We are going to implement this interface to override some of the default Spring MVC configuration seen in the previous code.

Configuration to deploy to Tomcat without web.xml

As we will be deploying the application to Tomcat, we need to provide the servlet configuration to the application server. We will look at how to deploy to Tomcat in a separate section, but now we will look at the Java configuration, which is sufficient to deploy the application to Tomcat or any application server without the need for an additional `web.xml`. The Java class definition is given in the following:

```
public class WorldApplicationInitializer extends
   AbstractAnnotationConfigDispatcherServletInitializer {

   @Override
   protected Class<?>[] getRootConfigClasses() {
      return null;
   }
   @Override
   protected Class<?>[] getServletConfigClasses() {
      return new Class[] {AppConfiguration.class};
   }
   @Override
   protected String[] getServletMappings() {
      return new String[] { "/" };
   }
}
```

The `AbstractAnnotationConfigDispatcherServletInitializer` abstract class is an implementation of the `WebApplicationInitializer` interface that is used to register Spring's `DispatcherServlet` instance and uses the other `@Configuration` classes to configure the `DispatcherServlet`.

We just need to override the getRootConfigClasses(), getServletConfigClasses(), and getServletMappings() methods. The first two methods point to the configuration classes that need to load into the servlet context, and the last method is used to provide the servlet mapping for DispatcherServlet.

DispatcherServlet follows the front controller pattern, where there is a single servlet registered to handle all the web requests. This servlet uses the RequestHandlerMapping and invokes the corresponding implementation based on the URL mapped to the implementation.

We need to make a small update to the Maven WAR plugin so that it doesn't fail if there is no web.xml found. This can be done by updating the <plugins> tag in the pom.xml file, as shown in the following:

```
<build>
  <finalName>worldgdp</finalName>
  <plugins>
    <plugin>
      <groupId>org.apache.maven.plugins</groupId>
      <artifactId>maven-war-plugin</artifactId>
      <executions>
        <execution>
          <id>default-war</id>
          <phase>prepare-package</phase>
          <configuration>
            <failOnMissingWebXml>false</failOnMissingWebXml>
          </configuration>
        </execution>
      </executions>
    </plugin>
  </plugins>
</build>
```

Now we are all set to implement our controllers. We will show you how to deploy to Tomcat once we have implemented all the RESTful API controllers.

Defining the RESTful API controller for country resource

Let's define the RESTful API controller for the country resource. The following is the template for the controller:

```
@RestController
@RequestMapping("/api/countries")
@Slf4j
public class CountryAPIController {
  @Autowired CountryDAO countryDao;
  @Autowired WorldBankApiClient worldBankApiClient;
  @GetMapping
  public ResponseEntity<?> getCountries(
    @RequestParam(name="search", required = false) String searchTerm,
    @RequestParam(name="continent", required = false) String continent,
    @RequestParam(name="region", required = false) String region,
    @RequestParam(name="pageNo", required = false) Integer pageNo
  ){
    //logic to fetch contries from CountryDAO
    return ResponseEntity.ok();
  }
  @PostMapping(value = "/{countryCode}",
      consumes = {MediaType.APPLICATION_JSON_VALUE})
  public ResponseEntity<?> editCountry(
    @PathVariable String countryCode, @Valid @RequestBody Country country
  ){
    //logic to edit existing country
    return ResponseEntity.ok();
  }
  @GetMapping("/{countryCode}/gdp")
  public ResponseEntity<?> getGDP(@PathVariable String countryCode){
    //logic to get GDP by using external client
    return ResponseEntity.ok();
  }
}
```

The following are a few things to note from the previous code:

- `@RestController`: This is used to annotate a class as a controller with each of the RESTful methods returning the data in the response body.
- `@RequestMapping`: This is for assigning the root URL for accessing the resources.

- @GetMapping and @PostMapping: These are used to assign the HTTP verbs that will be used to invoke the resources. The URL for the resources are passed within the annotation, along with other request headers that consume and produce information.

Let's implement each of the methods in order, starting with getCountries(), as shown in the following code:

```
@GetMapping
public ResponseEntity<?> getCountries(
  @RequestParam(name="search", required = false) String searchTerm,
  @RequestParam(name="continent", required = false) String continent,
  @RequestParam(name="region", required = false) String region,
  @RequestParam(name="pageNo", required = false) Integer pageNo
){
  try {
    Map<String, Object> params = new HashMap<String, Object>();
    params.put("search", searchTerm);
    params.put("continent", continent);
    params.put("region", region);
    if ( pageNo != null ) {
      params.put("pageNo", pageNo.toString());
    }
    List<Country> countries = countryDao.getCountries(params);
    Map<String, Object> response = new HashMap<String, Object>();
    response.put("list", countries);
    response.put("count", countryDao.getCountriesCount(params));
    return ResponseEntity.ok(response);
  }catch(Exception ex) {
    log.error("Error while getting countries", ex);
    return ResponseEntity.status(HttpStatus.INTERNAL_SERVER_ERROR)
        .body("Error while getting countries");
  }
}
```

The following are some of the things to note from the previous code:

- @RequestParam: This annotation is used to declare request parameters accepted by the controller endpoint. The parameters can be provided with a default value and can also be made mandatory.
- ResponseEntity: This class is used to return the response body, along with other response parameters such as status, headers, and so on.

Next up is the API for editing country details, as follows:

```
@PostMapping("/{countryCode}")
public ResponseEntity<?> editCountry(
  @PathVariable String countryCode, @Valid @RequestBody Country country ){
  try {
    countryDao.editCountryDetail(countryCode, country);
    Country countryFromDb = countryDao.getCountryDetail(countryCode);
    return ResponseEntity.ok(countryFromDb);
  }catch(Exception ex) {
    log.error("Error while editing the country: {} with data: {}",
        countryCode, country, ex);
    return ResponseEntity.status(HttpStatus.INTERNAL_SERVER_ERROR)
        .body("Error while editing the country");
  }
}
```

The following are a few things to note from the previous code implementation:

- `@PathVariable`: This is used to declare any variable that needs to be part of the URL path of the controller endpoint. In our case, we want the country code to be part of the URL. So the URL will be of the `/api/countries/IND` form.
- `@Valid`: This triggers the Bean Validation API to check for the restrictions on each of the class properties. If the data from the client is not valid, it returns a **400**.
- `@RequestBody`: This is used to capture the data sent in the request body and the `Jackson` library is used to convert the JSON data in the request body to the corresponding Java object.

The rest of the API implementation can be found in the `CountryAPIController` class. The tests for the API controller can be found in the `CountryAPIControllerTest` class, which is available in the source code of this book.

Defining the RESTful API controller for city resource

For the city resource we would need the following APIs:

- Get cities for a given country
- Add a new city to the country
- Delete the city from the country

The code for this controller can be found in the `CityAPIController` class and the tests for the API controller can be found in the `CityAPIControllerTest` class, which is available in the source code of this book.

Defining the RESTful API controller for country language resource

For the `CountryLanguage` resource we need the following APIs:

- Get languages for a country
- Add a language for a country
- Delete a language from the country

The code for this controller can be found in the `CountryLanguageAPIController` class and the tests for the API controller can be found in the `CountryLanguageAPIControllerTest` class, which is available in the source code of this book.

Deploying to Tomcat

Before we proceed with View and Controller for handling views, we will deploy the app developed so far to Tomcat. You can download Tomcat 8.5 from here (`https://tomcat. apache.org/download-80.cgi`). Installation is as simple as extracting the ZIP/TAR file onto your file system.

Let's create a user `admin` and `manager-gui` role in Tomcat. To do this, have to edit `apache-tomcat-8.5.23/conf/tomcat-users.xml` and add the following line:

```
<role rolename="manager-gui" />
<user username="admin" password="admin" roles="manager-gui" />
```

Starting up Tomcat is simple, as follows:

1. Navigate to `apache-tomcat-8.5.23/bin`
2. Run `startup.bat`

Navigate to `http://localhost:8080/manager/html` and enter `admin`, and `admin` for username and password respectively, to be able to view Tomcat's manager console. The initial part of the page will list the applications deployed in the current instance, and toward the later part of the page you will find an option to upload a WAR file to deploy the application, as shown in the following screenshot:

```
Deploy
Deploy directory or WAR file located on server

                           Context Path (required): [              ]
                        XML Configuration file URL: [              ]
                            WAR or Directory URL:   [                  ]
                                            [ Deploy ]

WAR file to deploy
                      Select WAR file to upload  [ Choose File ] No file chosen
                                            [ Deploy ]
```

We can either upload the WAR file generated after running `mvn package` or update the `server.xml` of the Tomcat instance to refer to the target directory of the project to be able to deploy automatically. The latter approach can be used for development, while the former that is WAR deployment can be used for production.

In a production system, you can have a continuous deployment server generate a WAR file and deploy to a remote Tomcat instance. In this scenario, we will use the latter approach of updating the Tomcat's configuration. You have to add the following line of code in the Tomcat's `server.xml` file, located at `TOMCAT_HOME/conf/server.xml`:

```
<Context path="/world" docBase="<<Directory path where you keep WAR file>>"
        reloadable="true" />
```

The preceding line has to be added between the `<Host></Host>` tags. Alternatively, you can configure Tomcat in your IDE (for example, Eclipse), which is more convenient for development purposes. We will build the project with Maven, but before that, please add following configuration to the `<properties></properties>` section of `pom.xml`:

```
<maven.compiler.target>1.8</maven.compiler.target>
<maven.compiler.source>1.8</maven.compiler.source>
```

This will make sure to choose the correct Java compiler version while building (packaging) the application with Maven from the command line. Next is to build the project using the `mvn package` and run Tomcat using `TOMCAT_HOME/bin/startup.bat`, and once the server is UP, you can visit the API `http://localhost:8080/worldgdp/api/countries` in the browser to see the following input:

```json
{
    "count": 239,
    "list": [
        { ... }, // 14 items
        { ... }, // 14 items
        {
            "code": "AGO",
            "name": "Angola",
            "continent": "Africa",
            "region": "Central Africa",
            "surfaceArea": 1246700,
            "indepYear": 1975,
            "population": 12878000,
            "lifeExpectancy": 38.29999923706055,
            "gnp": 6648,
            "localName": "Angola",
            "governmentForm": "Republic",
            "headOfState": "JosÃ© Eduardo dos Santos",
            "capital": {
                "id": 56,
                "name": "Luanda",
                "countryCode": null,
                "country": null,
                "district": null,
                "population": null
            },
            "code2": "AO"
        },
        {
            "code": "AIA",
            "name": "Anguilla",
            "continent": "North America",
```

Defining the view controller

We will have one view controller, `ViewController.java` defined in the `com.nilangpatel.worldgdp.controller.view`. The view controller will be responsible for populating the data required for the view templates and also mapping URLs to corresponding view templates.

We will be using Thymeleaf (`www.thymeleaf.org`) as the server-side template engine and Mustache.js (`https://github.com/janl/mustache.js`) as our client-side template engine. The advantage of using a client-side template engine is that any data loaded asynchronously in the form of JSON can easily be added to the DOM by generating HTML using the client-side templates. We will explore more about Thymeleaf and Mustache.js in `Chapter 3`, *Blogpress – A simple blog management system*.

There are much better ways to do this by using frameworks such as Vue.js, React.js, Angular.js, and so on. We will look at the view template in the next section. Let's continue our discussion about the view controller. The view controller should map the right view template and the data for the following scenarios:

- Listing of countries
- Viewing country detail
- Editing country detail

Let's look at the following skeletal structural definition of the `ViewController` class:

```
@Controller
@RequestMapping("/")
public class ViewController {
  @Autowired CountryDAO countryDao;
  @Autowired LookupDAO lookupDao;
  @Autowired CityDAO cityDao;
  @GetMapping({"/countries", "/"})
  public String countries(Model model,
    @RequestParam Map<String, Object> params
  ) {
    //logic to fetch country list
    return "countries";
  }
  @GetMapping("/countries/{code}")
  public String countryDetail(@PathVariable String code, Model model) {
    //Logic to Populate the country detail in model
    return "country";
  }
  @GetMapping("/countries/{code}/form")
  public String editCountry(@PathVariable String code,
```

```
    Model model) {
    //Logic to call CountryDAO to update the country
    return "country-form";
  }
}
```

The following are a few important things from the previous code:

- `@Controller`: This annotation is used to declare a controller that can return view template names to be able to render the view, as well as returning JSON/XML data in the response body.
- `@ResponseBody`: This annotation when present on the method of the controller indicates that the method is going to return the data in the response body, and hence, Spring will not use the view resolver to resolve the view to be rendered. The `@RestController` annotation by default adds this annotation to all its methods.
- `Model`: This instance is used to pass on the data required for building the view.

In case of the listing of countries, the complete HTML is rendered at the server using the Thymeleaf template engine, so we need to obtain the request parameters, if any are present in the URL, and obtain a filtered and paginated list of the countries. We also need to populate the lookups that is the data for the `<select>` controls, which will be used for filtering the data. Let's look at its implementation as follows:

```
@GetMapping({"/countries", "/"})
public String countries(Model model,
  @RequestParam Map<String, Object> params
) {
  model.addAttribute("continents", lookupDao.getContinents());
  model.addAttribute("regions", lookupDao.getRegions());
  model.addAttribute("countries", countryDao.getCountries(params));
  model.addAttribute("count", countryDao.getCountriesCount(params));
  return "countries";
}
```

The previous code is pretty straightforward. We are making use of the DAO classes to populate the required data into the `Model` instance and then returning the view name, which in this case is `countries`. Similarly, the rest of the method implementation can be found in the `ViewController` controller class.

Defining the view templates

We will be using the Thymeleaf template engine for handling server-side templates. Thymeleaf provides various dialects and conditional blocks for rendering the dynamic content within the static HTML. Let's look at some simple syntactical element of Thymeleaf, as follows:

```
<!-- Dynamic content in HTML tag -->
<div class="alert alert-info">[[${country.name}]]</div>

<!-- Dynamic attributes -->
<span th:class="|alert ${error ? 'alert-danger':
_}|">[[${errorMsg}]]</span>

<!-- Looping -->
<ol>
  <li th:each="c : ${countries}">
    [[${c.name}]]
  </li>
</ol>

<!-- Conditionals -->
<div class="alert alert-warning" th:if="${count == 0}">No results
found</div>

<!-- Custom attributes -->
<div th:attr="data-count=${count}"></div>

<!-- Form element value -->
<input type="text" th:value="${country.name}" name="name" />
```

From the previous examples, we can observe that the items to be evaluated by Thymeleaf are prefixed with th: and any content to be rendered between the tags can be done either using th:text or [[${variable}]]. The latter syntax has been introduced in Thymeleaf 3. This was a very short primer, as going in to depth on Thymeleaf is out of the scope of this book. A beautiful guide explaining different parts of the template can be found at http://www.thymeleaf.org/doc/tutorials/3.0/usingthymeleaf.html.

Configuring a Thymeleaf template engine

In order to use the Thymeleaf template engine with Spring MVC, we need to do some configuration wherein we set up the Thymeleaf template engine and update Spring's view resolver to use the template engine to resolve any views. Before moving further, we need to define required dependencies in pom.xml as follows:

```xml
<dependency>
  <groupId>org.thymeleaf</groupId>
  <artifactId>thymeleaf-spring5</artifactId>
  <version>${thymeleaf.version}</version>
</dependency>
<dependency>
  <groupId>nz.net.ultraq.thymeleaf</groupId>
  <artifactId>thymeleaf-layout-dialect</artifactId>
  <version>${thymeleaf-layout-dialect.version}</version>
</dependency>
```

Let's define the configuration view resolver in order, starting with setting up the template resolver as follows:

```java
@Bean
public ClassLoaderTemplateResolver templateResolver() {
  ClassLoaderTemplateResolver templateResolver
    = new ClassLoaderTemplateResolver();
  templateResolver.setPrefix("templates/");
  templateResolver.setSuffix(".html");
  templateResolver.setTemplateMode(TemplateMode.HTML);
  templateResolver.setCacheable(false);
  return templateResolver;
}
```

The previous configuration sets the template location that the template engine will use to resolve the template files. Next is to define the template engine, which will make use of SpringTemplateEngine and the template resolver defined earlier, as follows:

```java
@Bean
public SpringTemplateEngine templateEngine() {
  SpringTemplateEngine templateEngine = new SpringTemplateEngine();
  templateEngine.setTemplateResolver(templateResolver());
  templateEngine.addDialect(new LayoutDialect());
  return templateEngine;
}
```

In the previous configuration, we make use of the Thymeleaf Layout Dialect (`https://github.com/ultraq/thymeleaf-layout-dialect`) created by *Emanuel Rabina*. This layout dialect helps us in creating a view decorator framework wherein all the templates will be decorated with a base template and the decorated templates just provide the necessary content to complete the page. So all the headers, footers, CSS, scripts, and other common HTML can be placed in the base template. This prevents redundancy to a great extent. In our sample app, the `base.html` file present in `worldgdp/src/main/resources/templates` is the base template that is used by other templates.

Next is to define a Thymeleaf view resolver that will override Spring's default view resolver, as follows:

```
@Bean
public ViewResolver viewResolver() {
   ThymeleafViewResolver viewResolver = new ThymeleafViewResolver();
   viewResolver.setTemplateEngine(templateEngine());
   viewResolver.setCharacterEncoding("UTF-8");
   return viewResolver;
}
```

The previous configuration is available in the `com.packt.config.ViewConfiguration` class.

Managing static resources

If you look back at the `com.nilangpatel.worldgdp.AppConfiguration` class, you will see that we have overridden the `addResourceHandlers` method of `WebMvcConfigurer` interface. In the method implementation shown in the following code, we have mapped the static resources prefix URL `/static/**` to the static resources location `/static/` in the webapp directory:

```
@Override
public void addResourceHandlers(ResourceHandlerRegistry registry) {
   registry.addResourceHandler("/static/**")
     .addResourceLocations("/static/");
}
```

 We have added a few static resources (both CSS and JavaScript) in the `/src/main/webapp/static` folder of the project. Please download the code of this chapter and refer to them side by side.

Creating the base template

We mentioned before that we will be using the Thymeleaf Layout Dialect to create a base template and use the base template to decorate all other templates. The base template will contain all the CSS links, JavaScript source file links, the header, and the footer, as shown in the following code:

```
<!DOCTYPE html>
<html xmlns="http://www.w3.org/1999/xhtml"
  xmlns:th="http://www.thymeleaf.org"
  xmlns:layout="http://www.ultraq.net.nz/thymeleaf/layout">
  <head>
    <title layout:title-pattern="$CONTENT_TITLE - $LAYOUT_TITLE">World In
Numbers</title>
    <meta name="description" content=""/>
    <meta http-equiv="Content-Type" content="text/html; charset=UTF-8" />
    <!-- Include all the CSS links -->
  </head>
  <body>
    <nav class="navbar navbar-expand-lg navbar-dark bg-primary">
      <a class="navbar-brand" href="#">WORLD IN NUMBERS</a>
      <div class="collapse navbar-collapse" id="navbarColor01">
          <ul class="navbar-nav mr-auto">
          <li class="nav-item active">
            <a class="nav-link" th:href="@{/countries}">Countries</a>
          </li>
        </ul>
      </div>
    </nav>
    <div class="container">
      <div class="content">
        <div layout:fragment="page_content">
          <!-- Placeholder for content -->
        </div>
      </div>
    </div>
    <div class="modal" id="worldModal" >
    </div>
    <footer id="footer"></footer>
    <!-- /.container -->
    <!-- Include all the Javascript source files -->
    <th:block layout:fragment="scripts">
      <!-- Placeholder for page related javascript -->
    </th:block>
  </body>
</html>
```

The two main important parts of the following template are as follows:

- `<div layout:fragment="page_content"></div>`: The other templates that use the base template as decorator provide their HTML within this section. Thymeleaf Layout Dialect at runtime decorates this HTML with the content from the base template.

- `<th:block layout:fragment="scripts"></th:block>`: Similar to the HTML previous content, any page-specific JavaScript or links to any specific JavaScript source files can be added within this section. This helps in isolating page-specific JavaScript in their own pages.

Any template that wants to use the base template as the decorator will declare this attribute, `layout:decorate="~{base}"`, in the `<html>` tag. We will not go into the content of individual templates as it's mostly HTML. All the templates can be found at the location `worldgdp/src/main/resources/templates`. We have three templates:

- `countries.html`: This is for showing the countries' list with filtering and pagination

- `country-form.html`: This is for editing a country's detail

- `country.html`: This is for showing a country's detail

Logging configuration

Before we jump into the rest of the steps to develop an application, it is good practice to define a log level and format. It is, however, optional but good practice to print the logs in a desired format, along with various logging levels. For this, add an XML file called `logback.xml` with following content in it:

```xml
<?xml version="1.0" encoding="UTF-8"?>
<configuration>
  <appender name="STDOUT" class="ch.qos.logback.core.ConsoleAppender">
    <layout class="ch.qos.logback.classic.PatternLayout">
      <Pattern>
        %d{yyyy-MM-dd HH:mm:ss} [%thread] %-5level %logger{36} - %msg%n
      </Pattern>
    </layout>
  </appender>
  <logger name="com.nilangpatel.worldgdp" level="debug" additivity="false">
    <appender-ref ref="STDOUT" />
  </logger>
  <root level="debug">
    <appender-ref ref="STDOUT" />
```

```
    </root>
</configuration>
```

Logback was developed as a successor to the popular Log4j project, and is used as a logging framework for Java applications. This configuration defines the pattern, along with the logging level. To enable logback in your application, you need to add following dependencies to `pom.xml`:

```
<dependency>
    <groupId>ch.qos.logback</groupId>
    <artifactId>logback-classic</artifactId>
    <version>${logback.version}</version>
</dependency>
<dependency>
    <groupId>ch.qos.logback</groupId>
    <artifactId>logback-core</artifactId>
    <version>${logback.version}</version>
</dependency>
```

Running the application

As we have already configured the deployment to Tomcat, you should have the application running now. You can always download the source code for this book; find the source code under the `worldgdp` folder. After downloading, you have to build it using Maven, as follows:

```
$ mvn package
```

The preceding command will run the tests as well. The WAR file `worldgdp.war`, present in the `target`, can be uploaded to Tomcat through the Manager app or copied to the `TOMCAT_HOME/webapps` folder. Tomcat will then explode the archive and deploy the app.

The following are some of the screenshots of the application in action, starting with the listing page:

Next is the page that displays the country details:

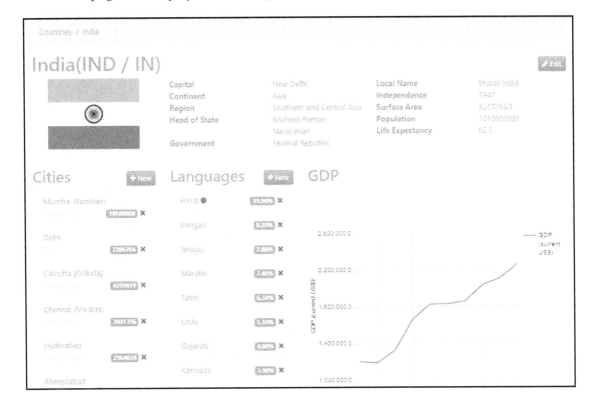

The form that is used to edit the country details is shown in the following screenshot:

Then we have popups that are used to add a new city to the country, as shown in the following screenshot:

Similarly, we have another popup to add a new country language, as shown in the following:

Summary

This chapter is designed with the aim of kick-starting your work with the Spring Framework. We have covered various topics, starting from scratch to create a project structure and design the view templates. It comprises various technologies and tools to build web-based applications in Spring.

It is always good practice to do more hands-on exercises to understand the concepts in detail. Next, you can think of enhancing the application further by adopting a few other World Bank APIs and integrate them in to this application. In this chapter, we have configured most of the things with our own.

However, Spring provides a tool called **Spring Boot**, which really helps in doing most of the configuration in an automated manner, allowing you to focus on developing the application. In subsequent chapters, we will explore how to use Spring Boot for developing web applications in Spring in more detail.

In the next chapter, we will explore another great feature called Reactive Programming in Spring Framework using WebFlux. We will learn the basics of the Reactive paradigm, what are the benefits, and explore various Reactive libraries. Spring uses `Reactor`—a library that provides implementation of Reactive Stream to develop web-based applications. So, get ready to explore all those new and exciting topics in the second chapter.

2

Building a Reactive Web Application

We began our journey by exploring some of the basics of the Spring Framework and its module system in Chapter 1, *Creating an Application to List World Countries with their GDP*. Let's leave all the new and advanced topics of Spring Framework for now and, in this chapter, look at one of the most popular topics: how to make highly scalable and responsive applications by adopting a reactive paradigm.

The world of technology is migrating from blocking, synchronous, and thread-driven implementation to non-blocking, asynchronous, and event-based systems, which are resilient and capable of managing a very large volume of data with a consistent response time. This is the core concern addressed by a reactive system.

From the perspective of the programming model, Reactive Programming has influenced the paradigm shift from an imperative style to a declarative composition of asynchronous logic. Spring Framework did this by incorporating Reactive Streams capabilities into its core framework from version 5.

In this chapter, we will discuss and explore Reactive Programming from various dimensions and angles with the following exciting topics:

- What is a reactive system
- Introduction to Reactive programming
- Reactive Programming basics, benefits, and features
- Reactive Programming in Java
- Introduction to WebFlux
- Spring supports for Reactive Programming
- A functional way of working in Reactive Programming with WebFlux
- WebSocket support in a reactive paradigm

Technical requirements

All the code used in this chapter can be downloaded from the following GitHub link: `https://github.com/PacktPublishing/Spring-5.0-Projects/tree/master/chapter02`. The code can be executed on any operating system, although it has only been tested on Windows.

Reactive system

The word reactive has become popular today and has different meanings for different people, such as lightweight, real time, asynchronous, streaming, and so on. **Reactive**, in broader terms, refers to a set of design techniques or principles, and is a way to consider the system architecture in a distributed environment. It comprises tooling, design methodologies, and implementation procedures.

The analogy of a team can be used to describe a reactive system: individual players working with each other to achieve a desired goal. The interaction between the components is the main quality that differentiates a Reactive System from other systems. Components can operate individually or still work in harmony with others to achieve the intended result as a whole system. In other words, it is the system design that allows individual sub-applications to form a single logical system, perform specific tasks, and remain aware of each other. This enables decision-making, like load balancing, scaling up and down, failover mitigation, and so on.

While talking about reactive topics, mainly in the context of software design and development, people generally use the terms **Reactive System** and **Reactive Programming** interchangeably, although they are not exactly the same. A reactive system is message-driven and associated with distributed process communication over the network, whereas Reactive Programming is generally event driven and handled locally.

A Reactive System is considered to be the same as an asynchronous message-based system by many software engineers. But as per the reactive manifesto, the Reactive System is an architectural way of developing a distributed system in a responsive style. It has the following essential characteristics:

- **Responsive:** It suggests a system should process and respond to a request in a reasonable time.

- **Resilient:** It suggests that even in case of failure, the system should remain responsive. In short, any kind of error should not put a system in a non-responsive state. All possible factors that may cause a system error must be well handled without causing a system halt.
- **Elastic:** A system should stay responsive even with a variable load. It should be flexible to scale up and down based on the load, and handle it with reasonable resource usage. To achieve this, the application must be designed in a way to avoid any central bottleneck.
- **Message-driven:** Components within a Reactive System should interact with each other with asynchronous message passing. This brings a loose coupling between components, isolation in responsibility, and transparency in location.

Among these characteristics, responsiveness, resilience, and elasticity are the standard requirements for almost every real-world application today. They look simple and straightforward, but are tricky to implement. It is the message-driven requirement that distinguishes a responsive system from others.

A Reactive System uses an asynchronous message-passing mechanism to interact among components. It also furnishes a non-blocking mechanism to control the data flow. While building a Reactive System, at all relevant points, the data processing operations are composed as stream flows. In short, a Reactive System is focused on stream processing.

Reactive Programming

Reactive Programming can be used to build a Reactive System. By definition, **Reactive Programming** is a programming practice or pattern that is aligned around the data flow and the propagation of the changes. The changes in data are automatically propagated by the underlying execution model through the data flow.

To make it simple, Reactive Programming is a way to handle asynchronous data streams in a more effective manner. In other words, it is programming dealing with an asynchronous data stream, or it can be called the subset of asynchronous programming. Reactive Programming is a way of execution where new information will push the flow forward, rather than having the flow controlled by an execution thread.

The data stream is a series of business events that happen during the system execution, such as various keyboard or mouse events, HTML field changes, HTTP requests, notification, REST API data fetch, triggering validations, changing of web component state, data updates, or anything else that can cause a change in the data stream or alter a program behavior.

In short, Reactive Programming covers a dynamic reaction in the stream that is caused by the asynchronous data flow. When the changes happen in one component, a reactive library or framework will automatically propagate those changes to other components. It is quite possible to define a static order in which the changes are propagated.

The following diagram shows how Reactive Programming is different to imperative programming:

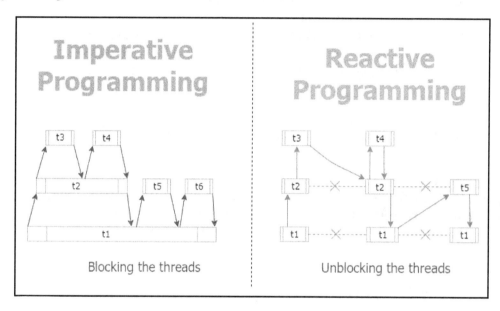

In **imperative programming**, the threads talk to each other in a synchronous way that results in blocking communication. A thread has to wait until the dependent thread of a resource is free, which can cause inefficient utilization and an easy bottleneck situation in the system. On the other hand, Reactive Programming doesn't need to wait; in fact, it is informed once the resource is available so that it can do other work in the meantime. This reduces the risk of the system hanging and makes it responsive. This effectively maintains smooth resource usage.

Reactive Programming suggests breaking down the given requirements into separate and individual steps that can be accomplished in an asynchronous, non-blocking style, and later on, combined to form a final output. In the Reactive Programming context, asynchronous means that the processing of a message or event occurs at some arbitrary time, most probably in the future.

The asynchronous and non-blocking nature of Reactive Programming is particularly useful in application environments where resources are shared; there is no need to halt the thread of execution while a resource is elsewhere engaged.

Basics of Reactive Programming

In a procedural programming model, a task is described as a series of actions executed in a sequential order. On the other hand, the Reactive Programming model facilitates the necessary arrangement to propagate the changes, which help in deciding what to do instead of how to do it.

Let's understand the concept with a very basic example, as follows:

```
int num1=3;
int num2=5;
int num3 = num1 + num2;
System.out.println("Sum is -->"+num3);
num1=6;
num2=8;
System.out.println("Sum is -->"+num3);
```

This is what we generally do in a procedural programming style. In this code, we are simply doing a summation of two numbers assigned to the third number and then printing it. In the next line, we are changing the value of the initial two numbers, but it doesn't update the third number. This is because num1 + num2 is evaluated and assigned to num3 on that line only. Now consider the same equation in an Excel sheet as follows:

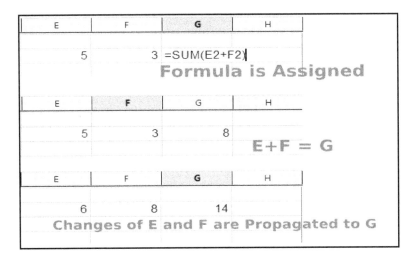

In this case, the changes of the **E** and **F** columns always listen to the **G** column. This is what Reactive Programming does. It propagates the changes to the one interested in those changes.

You might have used Reactive Programming unknowingly in your day-to-day coding practice. For example, if you have created a user registration screen where you validate the username entered by a user who is already present in the system, makes an Ajax call and shows an appropriate message saying **This username is already used**.

Another example is the listener or callback function that you define with a mouse click or keystroke on the web page. In these cases, mouse click and focus out events (for username validation) can be considered as a stream of events that you can listen to and execute appropriate action or functions on.

This is just one usage of the event stream. Reactive programming allows you to observe and react to any changes caused by the stream of events, like changes in a database, user input, property updates, data from external resources, and so on. Let's understand it by taking a real-life example.

Let's say you want to invest in mutual funds and there are many companies who provide facilities to invest on your behalf. They also produce statistics about the performance of various funds along with their history, market share, capital investment ratio, and so on. Based on this, they give some categories like moderate risk, low risk, moderately high risk, high risk, and so on. They also give a rating based on the performance of each fund.

The rating and the category will suggest that users choose a particular fund based on their requirement (short term, long term, and so on) and the type of risk they can afford. The changes happen in the rating and the category can be considered as an event (or data) stream that will cause a system to change the suggestion to the user. Another practical example of a data stream would be a social media feed, such as Facebook, Twitter, and so on.

Function reactive is a paradigm of reacting to the data stream in a functional way, providing additional features such as filters, combine, buffers, maps, and lot others. Using them, you can perform certain operations on a data stream, which help it to react in a better way. Taking the previous example of a mutual fund, the filter function can be used to suggest only those funds that are safe for investment in a real-time manner.

Reactive Programming is mainly used to build an interactive user interface and other systems that need time interaction, such as graphical applications, animations, simulations, chatbots, and so on.

Backpressure

One of the important concepts that you should know about in Reactive Programming is backpressure. It significantly improves Reactive Programming over the traditional code. What exactly is it? It is considered as one of the non-blocking regulatory mechanisms used to send asynchronous messages or feedback to the source of a stream for load regulation. Communication back to the stream sender could possibly be a request or alert to stop. However, it could also be about the receiver's intent to process more messages. The communication back to the sender has to be non-blocking. This is important.

Consider the situation where observables (source of an event) send out the data at a higher rate than the subscribers can actually handle. In this case, the subscribers would be in a stress condition, unable to handle the flow properly, and there is a high chance the system would behave unexpectedly. To avoid this situation, there must be some arrangement for conveying the speed at which the subscribers can consume the data, back to the observables.

The mechanism for notifying the source of the event saying, *Hey, I am under pressure, so don't send a further message as I can consume X amount of messages at a particular time*, is called **backpressure**. In the absence of this, the system may keep increasing the buffer size until it runs out of memory error. Backpressure is required when emission happens at a faster rate than consumption. It will make sure the system remains resilient under the load and will provide information that is used to make the decision, whether the system needs additional resources or not.

Benefits of Reactive Programming

A few years ago, the user interaction was limited to just filling in the form on a web page and submitting it to the server. It was just enough for self-sufficient applications at the time. Today, in the era of the mobile and responsive requirement, a rich user interface showing real-time information is expected to provide wide interactive possibilities.

Also, different types of apps like cloud environments, distributed apps, IoT, and real-time applications need lots of user interaction. This can be achieved by Reactive Programming. It is used to build loosely coupled, responsive, and scalable applications that are more tolerant of failure. There are many advantages of using Reactive Programming, as follows:

- **Resource utilization:** One of the essential benefits of Reactive Programming is optimizing hardware resource utilization, like the processor, memory, network, and so on. It also improves the performance by reducing serialization.

- **Enhanced user experience:** Reactive Programming provides better and improved user experience by using an asynchronous mechanism that makes the application smoother and responsive and easy to interact with.

- **Consistency:** You can design the API with lots more consistency for everything, including database call, frontend, network, computation, or anything else you may need with Reactive Programming.

- **Handle with ease:** Reactive Programming has first-class support and obvious mechanisms for asynchronous operations out of the box. Also, it makes handling UI interaction and event management easier.

- **Simple thread management:** Reactive Programming makes it simpler than regular threading mechanisms. Complex threading implementations, making the parallel work in a synchronous manner, and executing the callbacks when the function is done is easier to achieve with Reactive Programming.

- **Increased developer productivity:** In a typical imperative programming model, the developer has to do lots of work to maintain a straightforward approach to achieve an asynchronous and non-blocking computation. Reactive Programming, on the other hand, addresses the challenge by providing these features out of the box so the developer does not need explicit coordination between elements.

Reactive Programming techniques

Reactive Programming is event-based in most cases. In Reactive Programming, the APIs are exposed in the following two flavors:

- **Callback:** In this type, the anonymous routines are registered to event sources as callback functions. They will be invoked when the event is triggered by the data flow.

- **Declarative:** The events are observed through well-defined functional compositions, like a filter, map, and other stream-based operations, like count, trigger, and so on.

Reactive Programming puts the importance on data flow rather than the flow of control, so it is not uncommon to consider it as a data flow programming. There are various techniques that are used to achieve Reactive Programming as follows:

- **Futures and promise:** It is referred to as a technique to define the variable and assign its value. Though futures and promise are used interchangeably, they are not exactly the same. The future is used to describe a read-only view of a variable (or, say, define the variable), while the promise is a writable, single assignment container that is used to set the value of a variable in future.

- **Reactive Streams:** It is defined as a standard for the processing of asynchronous streams that enables non-blocking, backpressure transmutations between sources from where the events are initiated and the destination where they are observed.
- **Data flow variables:** It is a variable whose value depends on a given input, operations, and other cells, and is updated automatically when changes happen to source entities. You can think of a data flow variable as a spreadsheet cell, where a change in the value of one cell causes a ripple effect to others based on the assigned formula.

In addition to this, there are various frontend libraries available, like React.js, AngularJS, Ractive.js, Node.js, and so on, which are used to develop reactive frontend applications. Other programming languages and frameworks providing native support for reactive applications are Scala, Clojure, and GoLang, along with Java 9 and Spring 5. We will see reactive features of Spring 5 later in this chapter.

Reactive Programming in Java

An asynchronous processing approach is a perfect fit while dealing with a huge volume of data or a large set of users. It will make the system responsive and improve the overall user experience. Implementing asynchronous processing in Java with the custom code would be cumbersome and harder to implement. Reactive Programming would be beneficial in this scenario.

Java doesn't provide native support for Reactive Programming like other JVM-based programming languages such as Scala or Clojure do. However, from version 9, Java has started supporting Reactive Programming natively. Apart from native support in Java 9, there are other implementation layers that help to achieve Reactive Programming with an older version of Java (such as Java 8). We will see a few of them, as follows.

Reactive Streams

Reactive Streams is described simply as an initiative to provide a standard for asynchronous stream processing with non-blocking backpressure. It is a small and straightforward statement. However, it is essential to note that the first focus here is on the asynchronous stream processing and not just on the asynchronous programming. As discussed earlier, asynchronous systems have been around for a long time.

Before processing a stream, comes receiving the stream data. Asynchronously, this would mean managing the risk of uncertainties in the world of streams. For example, how much more data or messages could there be? Another challenge might be how to know when the stream has finished sending data. There could be a lot of questions, and we will see all of them in a little while.

Reactive Streams is used to perform Reactive Programming in Java. It is an API specification or, say, low-level contract given by the collaborations of various companies like Pivotal, Netflix, Red Hat, Twitter, Lightbend (previously known as Typesafe), Kaazing, Oracle, and many more. You can consider the Reactive Streams API to be just like JPA or JDBC. The actual implementations are provided by various vendors.

For example, JPA specifications have various vendors like Hibernate, TopLink, Apache OpenJPA that provide actual implementation. Similarly, there are many popular JVM-based libraries that support Reactive Programming like Reactor, Akka stream, Ratpack, Vert.x, and so on. They all provide an implementation of the Reactive Streams specifications, which bring interchangeability.

Reactive Streams specifications

Let's try to understand in more detail, what the specifications for Reactive Streams are. It is dealing with the asynchronous processing of a stream. Let's look at the specification available at `https://github.com/reactive-streams/reactive-streams-jvm`. It comprises the following two parts:

- **API**: This describes the specification.
- **Technology Compatibility Kit** (**TCK**): This is a criteria or standard test suite for compliance testing of implementations. In short, it will make sure the given implementation conforms to the declared specification.

Taking a closer look at the API, we find that it is rather simple and comprises just four interfaces as follows:

- **Publisher**: This interface represents an entity that acts as a supplier of an unbounded number of sequenced events or elements. It will publish the elements as per the requirement of the subscriber.
- **Subscriber:** It represents a consumer of an event from a publisher. For that, it will subscribe to the publisher.
- **Subscription:** This interface illustrates the process of subscribing or registering of a subscriber to a publisher.

- **Processor:** It is a composition of both the publisher and subscriber. It represents a processing stage that implements the contract of both.

Java 9 has started providing native support for Reactive Streams. The implementation of these interfaces is part of the Flow API in Java 9. Looking at the structure of JAR containing the Reactive Streams, we find the following structure:

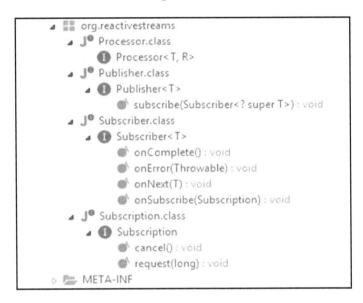

This seems rather straightforward, and implementing a set of a few interfaces shouldn't be a challenge for any developer in Java. Are we able to go to production with the implementation of these interfaces, and will it give us a stable system? Are we ready to get started with the reactive development? The answers are, *not quite yet*.

Passing the messages in an asynchronous way is the key area of focus for Reactive Streams. It ensures that it is not just the consumer that is protected from being overwhelmed by all the distributed systems. The Publisher is also safeguarded in case one or more subscribers is slow to process the messages. It primarily says that this is the way you should pass a message from thread *A* to thread *B* in a protected manner, to ensure both the publisher and the subscriber are protected.

Let's dig further into the specifications, (we will come to the TCK a little later) and see how they correspond with the original statement of the Reactive Streams manifesto. Starting with the publisher, we see that the specifications also define a set of rules that must be adhered to by the implementer of the specifications.

The rules are defined for all the four interfaces: publisher, subscriber, subscription, and processor. It won't be possible to go through all the rules here, and neither it is required, as the rules are available at: `https://github.com/reactive-streams/reactive-streams-jvm/blob/v1.0.2/README.md`.

However, in order to draw some relevance from the Reactive Streams manifesto, let's look at some of the important rules. We will analyze one or two rules each from all four interfaces to help you understand how they are laid out. Do have a look at the glossary table before reading these rules and specifications.

You should have a look at the rest of the rules, as going through them will give you a good idea about how detailed the rules are. By the time you finish reading all the rules, you will have a very good grasp of what to expect from the implementation of Reactive Streams.

Publisher rules

`Publisher` has the following interface definition:

```
public static interface Publisher<T> {
    public void subscribe(Subscriber<? super T> subscriber);
}
```

Rule number 1.1 says, the total number of `onNext` signaled by a `Publisher` to `Subscriber` must be less than, or equal to, the total number of elements requested by that `Subscriber` Subscription at all times. There are multiple facets to this definition here. Let's try to analyze them one by one:

- First and foremost, there has to be a request for a message from `Subscriber` (total number → 1 - N) to `Publisher`. Therefore, `Publisher` cannot start sending messages to unsuspecting subscribers on its own as these subscribers might still be deciding when to start receiving messages. Furthermore, some might still be performing some initial tasks in order to start receiving the message.
- Secondly, only after the request is received by `Publisher` can it begin transmitting the messages to `Subscriber`. In response to the request for messages from `Publisher`, Subscriber receives `Subscription`. Now `Subscriber` can use `Subscription` to interact with `Publisher` and vice versa. How many messages `Publisher` should send is mentioned in `Subscription` so the requested messages by `Subscribers` should be less than or equal to that number [message count <= total number].
- Thirdly, `Publisher` cannot send more messages to `Subscriber` than requested by `Subscriber`.

These three points together form a part of the backpressure we mentioned when we began with Reactive Streams.

And yes, the count requested by `Subscriber` from `Publisher` is not binding on `Publisher` as per the other rule, not binding with respect to the count of messages. `Publisher` is allowed to send less than the requested count of messages from `Subscriber`. This can be described with the following.

Subscriber rules

`Subscriber` has the following interface definition:

```
public interface Subscriber<T> {
    public void onSubscribe(Subscription s);
    public void onNext(T t);
    public void onError(Throwable t);
    public void onComplete();
}
```

Rule number 2.1 says, A `Subscriber` must signal demand via Subscription.request(long n) to receive `onNext` signals. This rule is in line with `Publisher` rule number 1.1 in the sense that it establishes the responsibility of `Subscriber` to inform when and how many messages it is able and willing to receive.

Rule number 2.4 says, `.onComplete()` and `Subscriber.onError(Throwable t)` must consider the `Subscription` cancelled after having received the signal. Here again, the design intention at play is highlighted. The design sequence of sending ensures that the process of the message being sent from `Publisher` to `Subscriber` is completely decoupled. Therefore, `Publisher` is not bound by the `Subscriber` intent to keep listening, hence ensuring a non-blocking arrangement.

As soon as `Publisher` sends out a message, it has no messages to be sent with `Subscriber.onComplete()` and the `Subscription` object is no longer valid/available. This is similar to when an exception is thrown back with `Subscriber.onError(Throwable t)`. The `Subscription` object can no longer be utilized by `Subscriber` to request more messages.

It is worthwhile mentioning another couple of rules around the same design. These are rules number 2.9 and 2.10 concerning `Subscription.request(long n)`. The rule says that a `Subscriber` can get the `onError` signal or the `onComplete` signal with or without a preceding call to `Subscription.request(long n)`.

Subscription rules

The following interface describes the `Subscription` notation:

```
public interface Subscription {
    public void request(long n);
    public void cancel();
}
```

The rule number 3.2 says, `Subscription` must allow the `Subscriber` to call `Subscription.request` synchronously from within `onNext` or `onSubscribe`. It talks about preventing both `Publisher` and `Subscriber` by restricting posting of the message only when `Publisher` gets the signal for a further request from `Subscriber`. This happens in a synchronous manner to avoid a stack overflow.

In a similar context, another rule, number 3.3, states, `Subscription.request()` must place an upper bound on possible synchronous recursion between `Publisher` and `Subscriber`. It complements rule 3.2 in a sense by deciding an upper limit in the recursive interaction between `Publisher` and `Subscriber` in the form of the `onNext()` and `request()` call. Setting the upper limit will avoid blowing out when calling a thread stack. The rules starting from number 3.5 to 3.15 describe the behavior of cancelling and completing the request.

Processor rules

`Processor` is described with the following interface definition:

```
public interface Processor<T, R> extends Subscriber<T>, Publisher<R> {
}
```

It has just two rules. The first rule talks about the contract that must be followed by both `Subscriber` and `Publisher`, while the second rule is intended to handle the error situation, either recover or propagate to `Subscriber`.

Reactive Streams TCK

Implementing the interfaces defined in Reactive Streams specification is not just suffice to build Reactive Streams. The specification comprises a set of components and rules. The components part is taken care of with four interfaces we discussed, while the rules are defined by Reactive Streams **Technology Compatibility Kit** (TCK).

The Reactive Streams TCK is a guideline to Reactive Streams implementors to verify their implementations against the rules defined in the specifications. The TCK is developed with a testing framework in Java called **TestNG** and can be used in other JVM-based programming languages, like Kotlin and Scala.

TCK covers most of the rules, but not all, defined in the specification because for some of the rules, it is not possible to construct automated test cases. So theoretically, it can't be verified fully against the specification; however, it is helpful to validate most of the important rules.

TCK comprises four TestNG test classes and contains test cases, which can be extended by implementers and provide their implementation of `Publisher`, `Subscriber`, `Subscription`, and `Processor` to validate against the specification rules. You can get it in further detail from the link: `https://github.com/reactive-streams/reactive-streams-jvm/tree/master/tck`.

RxJava

Starting with version 8, Java began supporting reactivity features as inbuilt capability, yet they were not used widely and didn't become popular among developers. However, some third party implementations of Reactive Programming in Java showed its advantages and it grew in popularity in the Java community.

There is nothing but the set of tools called **Reactive Extension** (or simply ReactiveX) allowing implementation of Reactive Programming for composing asynchronous and event-based programs using observable sequences. It is a Java VM (Virtual Machine) implementation of Reactive Extension. Initially written on Microsoft platforms, Reactive Extension offers reactive capabilities to various other programming languages, and one of the most popular among them is RxJava for the Java programming language.

It was the first Reactive Extension API specific to the Java platform. RxJava is compatible with older versions of Java and provides a facility to write asynchronous, event-based programs for both Java and Android platforms, which is very convenient. ReactiveX also covers other programming languages with Reactive Extension, like RxJs, Rx.Net, UnixRx, RxScala, RxCloujure, RxCPP, Rx.rb, and RxKotlin, along with other platforms and frameworks like RxCocoa, RxAndroid, and RxNetty.

Anatomy of RxJava

RxJava basically extends the observer pattern to support iteration on the sequence of event/data and allows the forming of sequences at the same time as abstracting away the low-level details, like threading, synchronization, concurrency, and thread safety.

At the time of writing, the current version of RxJava-2.6 has a single dependency on Reactive Streams API and provides support for Java 6 and the later versions, along with Android 2.3+. Before going deep into RxJava, let's look at the basic building blocks of ReactiveX as follows:

- `Observable`: It is basically a data stream or in other words a source of data. It can emit the data just one time or periodically in a continuous manner, based on the configuration. `Observable` can send out specific data on particular events based on the operators used with `Observable`. In short, `Observable` is the supplier of data to other components.

- `Observer`: The data stream emitted by `Observable` is consumed by Observers. For that, they need to subscribe to `Observable` using the `subscribeOn()` method. One ore more observers can be subscribed to `Observable`. When `Observable` sends the data, all registered observers receive the data with the `onNext()` callback method. Once the data is received, you can perform any operation on that. In case any error occurred during the transmission, observers will get the error data with the `onError()` callback.

- `Scheduler`: They are used for thread management to achieve asynchronous programming in ReactiveX. They will instruct `Observable` and `Observer` to choose particular thread on which they can execute the operations. For that, `Scheduler` provide the `observerOn()` and `scheduleOn()` methods for the `Observer` and `Observable` respectively.

Let's understand these concepts with a practical example. We will create a Maven project in Eclipse with settings as follows:

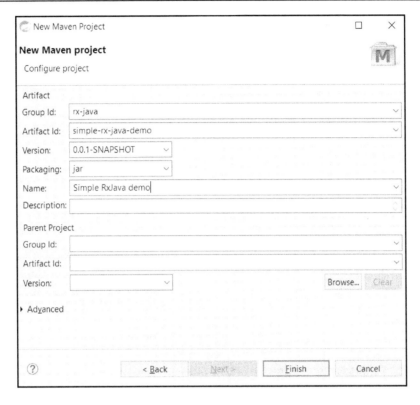

We need to give RxJava specific dependency. The current version at this moment is 2.2.6. After adding the dependency, `pom.xml` should look as follows:

```
<project xmlns="http://maven.apache.org/POM/4.0.0"
xmlns:xsi="http://www.w3.org/2001/XMLSchema-instance"
xsi:schemaLocation="http://maven.apache.org/POM/4.0.0
http://maven.apache.org/xsd/maven-4.0.0.xsd">
  <modelVersion>4.0.0</modelVersion>
  <groupId>rx-java</groupId>
  <artifactId>simple-rx-java-demo</artifactId>
  <version>0.0.1-SNAPSHOT</version>
  <name>Simple RxJava demo</name>
  <dependencies>
    <dependency>
      <groupId>io.reactivex.rxjava2</groupId>
      <artifactId>rxjava</artifactId>
      <version>2.2.6</version>
    </dependency>
  </dependencies>
</project>
```

Create a new Java class with an appropriate package and add the following code to it:

```
public class RxJavaBasics {
  public static void main(String[] args) {
    /* Observable */
    Observable<String> adminUsers =
        Observable.just("Dave",
              "John",
              "Nilang",
              "Komal",
              "David");
    /* Observer in form of lambda expression */
    adminUsers.subscribe(s -> System.out.println(s));
  }
}
```

The `adminUsers` instance is of type `Observable<String>` that pushes five strings literals (name of admin users), which is essentially a data stream or the source of data. For simplicity, we have taken String Literals, but `Observable` can push the data or events from any source, such as a database query result, social media feed, REST API response, or anything similar.

The `Observable.just()` method is used to emit a fixed set of string literals. The last line of the code describes how the `Observer` can subscribe to `Observable` with the `subscribe()` method. It is defined as a lambda expression that specifies what to do with the string it receives from `Observable`. This relation can be described in the following diagram:

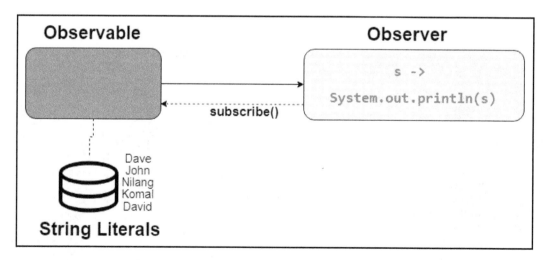

In this code, `Observer` is simply printing the string literal. RxJava provides several operators that can be used in between `Observable` and `Observer`. These operators are used to transform or manipulate each pushed data passed in between. Each operator processes the data coming from previous `Observable` and returns new `Observable`. Let's use one of the operators called `map` and update the code as follows:

```
adminUsers.map(s->s.startsWith("D") ? s:"*******")
            .subscribe(s -> System.out.println(s));
```

In this code, the data emitted by the `adminUsers` observable is passed through a map operator before being sent to `Observer`. The `map` operator here provides a lambda expression, which is used to process the submitted data from `adminUsers`. It basically prints the return string if it starts with `D` or else simply returns a string with an asterisk mark (`*`). The `map` operator returns new `Observable` that returns the data processed by the `map` operator and finally sends it to `Observer`. You will see the output, as follows:

Observer event calls

What we discussed so far is very high-level information about how we can use `Observable` in RxJava. It basically pushes (emits) the items (data or events) of a given type through a series of operators (if defined) until it reaches `Observer`. Let's dig into more details to understand which mechanism works under the hood between this interaction and how RxJava complies with Reactive Streams specifications.

`Observable` interacts with `Observers` through the following event calls:

- `onNext`: This is the call from where data/events are being sent, one at a time, down to all registered `Observers`.
- `onComplete`: This event is used to signal completion of communication to all.
- `Observers`: It simply denotes no more `onNext` calls happen.
- `onError`: In case any error occurs before an `onComplete()` call, an `onError()` event is used to signal the error from `Observable` to `Observers`. `Observable` will stop emitting the data and `Observers` will handle the error.

These events are defined as an `abstract` method in the `Observer` type, and we will see the implementation type later in this chapter. First let's see how these event calls happen during the interaction with the following code:

```
public class RxJavaCreateDemo {

    public static void main(String[] args) {
        Observable<String> daysOfWeek = Observable.create(
            sourceEmitter -> {
            try {
                sourceEmitter.onNext("Sunday");
                sourceEmitter.onNext("Monday");
                sourceEmitter.onNext("Tuesday");
                sourceEmitter.onNext("Wednesday");
                sourceEmitter.onNext("Thursday");
                sourceEmitter.onNext("Friday");
                sourceEmitter.onNext("Saturday");
                sourceEmitter.onComplete();
            }catch(Exception e) {
                sourceEmitter.onError(e);
            }
        });
        Observable<String> daysInUpperCase=
    daysOfWeek.map(day->day.toUpperCase())
    .filter(day->day.startsWith("S"));
        daysInUpperCase.subscribe(day->System.out.println("Day is -->"+day));
    }
}
```

`Observable.create()` is a factory method and used to create `Observable` with the emitter. The `onNext()` method of the emitter is used to emit (send) the data/events (one at a time) to the `Observable` chain (and finally to registered `Observers`). The `onComplete()` method is used to terminate further communication.

If you try to make an `onNext()` call after `onComplete()`, the data will not be transmitted. In case any error occurs, the `onError()` method is called. It is used to push up the error to the `Observable` chain where it is handled by `Observer`. In this code, there is no chance of any exception, but you can handle any error with `onError()`.

We have used the `map` and `filter` operators to refine the data to uppercase and starting with D respectively. Finally, they are printed by `Observer`. The flow of data will happen from `onNext()` →map→filter→Observer. Each operator will return new `Observable` class in the chain.

You notice that in the first example we used the `Observable.just()` method to emit the data. It internally invokes the `onNext()` method for each of the values pushed. On getting the last value, it will call `onComplete()`. So `Observable.just()` is equivalent to `Observable.create()` calling `onNext()` on each data and `onComplete()` on last one. The `create()` method is generally used for sources that are not reactive in nature.

Observable for iterators

`Observable` provides support to emit the data from any iterable sources, for example, lists, maps, sets, and so on. It will call `onNext()` on each item of an iterable type, and once the iterator is over, it will call `onComplete()` automatically. Iterable in Java is commonly used in collection frameworks, so `Observable` with iterable can be used while fetching data from collection classes.

Let's see how to use it as follows:

```
public class RxJavaIterableDemo {
  public static void main(String[] args) {
    List<EmployeeRating> employeeList = new ArrayList<EmployeeRating>();
    EmployeeRating employeeRating1 = new EmployeeRating();
    employeeRating1.setName("Lilly");
    employeeRating1.setRating(6);
    employeeList.add(employeeRating1);

    employeeRating1 = new EmployeeRating();
    employeeRating1.setName("Peter");
    employeeRating1.setRating(5);
    employeeList.add(employeeRating1);

    employeeRating1 = new EmployeeRating();
    employeeRating1.setName("Bhakti");
    employeeRating1.setRating(9);
    employeeList.add(employeeRating1);

    employeeRating1 = new EmployeeRating();
    employeeRating1.setName("Harmi");
    employeeRating1.setRating(9);
    employeeList.add(employeeRating1);

    Observable<EmployeeRating> employeeRatingSource =
                            Observable.fromIterable(employeeList);

    employeeRatingSource.filter(employeeRating ->
              employeeRating.getRating() >=7).subscribe(empRating ->
              System.out.println("Star Employee: " + empRating.getName()
```

```
                        + " Rating : "+empRating.getRating()));
    }
  }
```

We are populating the list of `EmployeeRating` and creating `Observable` with the `fromIterable()` method by passing this list. The class `EmployeeRating` is a simple POJO containing the `name` and `rating` attributes as follows:

```
class EmployeeRating{
  private String name;
  private int rating;
  public String getName() {
    return name;
  }
  public void setName(String name) {
    this.name = name;
  }
  public int getRating() {
    return rating;
  }
  public void setRating(int rating) {
    this.rating = rating;
  }
}
```

RxJava conforms to Reactive Streams specification by providing an implementation of interfaces. Let's recall that the `onNext()`, `onError()`, `onSubscribe()`, and `onComplete()` methods are part of the Observer interface. RxJava provides an implementation of these interfaces to handle respective events.

Custom Observers

We have seen how data emits from `Observable`, passes through a down stream of operators and eventually reaches `Observer`. Apparently, we can say that the data is transmitted from a series of `Observable` because each operator returns new `Observable`, which forms an `Observable` chain. The first `Observable` where the emission originates is called the `Observable` source. Therefore, we can say that `Observable.create()` and `Observable.just()` return the `Observable` source.

We can provide our custom implementation to handle the `Observer` events as follows:

```
public class RxJavaCustomObserverDemo {

  public static void main(String[] args) {
```

```
Observable<String> months =
    Observable.just("January", "February", "March", "April",
        "May","June","July","August");

Observer<String> customObserver = new Observer<String>() {
  @Override
  public void onSubscribe(Disposable d) {
    System.out.println(" Subscription initiated ...");
  }
  @Override
  public void onNext(String value) {
    System.out.println("The value " + value +" is received from
Observable");
  }
  @Override
  public void onError(Throwable e) {
    e.printStackTrace();
  }
  @Override
  public void onComplete() {
    System.out.println("Done!");
  }
};

months.filter(month -> month.endsWith("y"))
        .subscribe(customObserver);
  }
}
```

Like previous examples, we have defined the Observable with the list of months. We also defined custom Observers with an implementation of various methods that will be called on for a specific event. When we register the observer (customObserver in our case), Observable will call the onSubscribe() method on Observer.

Every time when Observable emits the data, it will call onNext() of registered observers, which will then be processed by observers. On sending the last data, Observable will call the onComplete() method on Observer. In case if any error occurs in between, Observable will call onError() method on Observer.

Certainly, the data will be passed through the Observable chain. In the previous case, the data emitted from the Observable source (months in this case) will be forwarded downstream to the filter operator, which will then reach the Observer or endpoint where the data is consumed and processed. By processed, we mean the data can be saved to the database, sent as a server response, written to the external document management system, composed as a structure for UI rendering, or simply printed in the console.

You will get an output as follows:

```
Subscription initiated ...
The value January is received from Observable
The value February is received from Observable
The value May is received from Observable
The value July is received from Observable
Receive all the Data !
```

 In this example, we have used an anonymous class to provide a custom implementation of Observer's methods. However, you can use a lambda expression for this purpose.

Observable types

In the examples we have seen in previous subsections of the RxJava section, the data was created within Observable. However, in the real scenario, that data comes from other sources like databases, REST APIs, and so on. The representation of any set of data/values is referred to as the producer. Observables are divided broadly into the following two categories based on where the procedure is cited.

Cold Observable

When the `Observable` itself creates the procedure or, say, `Observable` produces the data stream itself, it is said to be cold `Observable`. Generally `Observable` is lazy in nature, meaning it only emits the data when any `Observer` subscribes to it. Cold `Observable` always starts a fresh execution for each subscriber.

In other words, cold `Observable` emits separate data/event streams for individual Observers. All examples we have seen so far were of a cold `Observable` type, where we have created a data stream with the `just()` or `create()` method. Let's see how cold `Observable` works for more than one Observer subscribed, with the following example.

```
public class RxJavaColdObservable {
  public static void main(String[] args) {
    Observable<String> source =
        Observable.just("One","Two","Three","Four","Five");
    //first observer
    source.filter(data->data.contains("o"))
        .subscribe(data -> System.out.println("Observer 1 Received:" +
data));
    //second observer
```

```
      source.subscribe(data -> System.out.println("Observer 2 Received:" +
    data));
      }
    }
```

In this code, the data is created by `Observable` itself so it is called **cold Observable**. We have subscribed two different Observers. When you run this code, you will get an output as follows:

```
Observer 1 Received:Two
Observer 1 Received:Four
Observer 2 Received:One
Observer 2 Received:Two
Observer 2 Received:Three
Observer 2 Received:Four
Observer 2 Received:Five
```

Cold `Observable` provides a separate data stream for each `Observer` so when we applied the filter for first `Observer` there is no effect in the second `Observer`. Also if there are more than one `Observer`, then `Observable` will emit the sequence of data to all observers one by one.

Hot Observable

Hot `Observable`, on the other hand, has the producer created or activated outside of it. Hot `Observable` emits the stream that is shared by all observers. Let's see the example, as follows:

```
public class RxJavaHotObservable1 {
  public static void main(String args[]) {
    Observable<Long> observableInterval = Observable.interval(2,
TimeUnit.SECONDS);
    PublishSubject<Long> publishSubject = PublishSubject.create();
    observableInterval.subscribe(publishSubject);
    publishSubject.subscribe(i -> System.out.println("Observable #1 :
"+i));
    addDelay(4000);
    publishSubject.subscribe(i -> System.out.println("Observable #2 :
"+i));
    addDelay(10000);
  }
  private static void addDelay(int miliseconds) {
    try {
            Thread.sleep(miliseconds);
        } catch (InterruptedException e) {
```

```
            e.printStackTrace();
        }
    }
}
```

The `observableInterval` observable emits the event instead of data in this example. The `interval` method is used to emit sequential numbers at given intervals. We have used `PublishSubject` to make this observable as a hot type. It can be behave as either `Observable` or `Observer`. It is part of the `Observable` chain in this case. We then simply add two subscribers to `PublishSubject` with some delay in between. You will get an output as follows:

```
Observable #1 : 0
Observable #1 : 1
Observable #1 : 2
Observable #2 : 2
Observable #1 : 3
Observable #2 : 3
Observable #1 : 4
Observable #2 : 4
Observable #1 : 5
Observable #2 : 5
Observable #1 : 6
Observable #2 : 6
```

The second `Observer` is subscribed after some delay to the first `Observer`. The `Observable` emits the sequential number every two seconds. The second `Observer` starts at the fourth second. Hot `Observable` emits just a single stream, which is shared across all `Observers`. So, in the case of the second `Observer`, the actual value is started from 2 instead of 0 as it subscribes after some time.

In this sense, hot `Observable` can be compared with a subscription to a radio station. A person who starts listening will not be able to hear what was played before he subscribed, as it is common to all subscribers (or say Observers in Reactive language). There are other ways to create hot `Observable`. We will see one of them as follows:

```
public class RxJavaHotObservable2 {
  public static void main(String args[]) {
    Observable<Long> observableInt = Observable.interval(2,
TimeUnit.SECONDS);
    ConnectableObservable<Long> connectableIntObservable =
observableInt.publish();
    connectableIntObservable.subscribe(i -> System.out.println("Observable
#1 : "+i));
```

```
        connectableIntObservable.connect();
        addDelay(7000);
        connectableIntObservable.
           subscribe(i -> System.out.println("Observable #2 : "+i));
        addDelay(10000);
    }
    private static void addDelay(int miliseconds) {
        try {
                Thread.sleep(miliseconds);
            } catch (InterruptedException e) {
                e.printStackTrace();
            }
    }
}
```

In this code, hot Observable is created with `ConnectableObservable`. It will not start emitting the data until the `connect` method is called on it, making it more controllable. Soon after the `connect` method is called, it will start a single stream, which is shared across the Observers. You will get an output as follows:

```
Observable #1 : 0
Observable #1 : 1
Observable #1 : 2
Observable #1 : 3
Observable #2 : 3
Observable #1 : 4
Observable #2 : 4
Observable #1 : 5
Observable #2 : 5
Observable #1 : 6
Observable #2 : 6
Observable #1 : 7
Observable #2 : 7
```

You can see how the second Observer missed the first few items as it was subscribed with some delay. You can convert any cold Observable to `ConnectableObservable` by calling the `publish` method on it.

Other ways to get Observable

So far we have seen how to get `Observable` with `just()`, `create()`, and `interval()`. However, there are other sources to get the `Observable`. You can get full details about each source from at:`https://github.com/ReactiveX/RxJava/wiki/Creating-Observables`:

1. `range`: If you want to emit a consecutive range of integers, you can use the `Observable.range(int from, int to)` call. As its name suggests, it will start emitting a number from the start value in increments until the end count is reached.

2. `empty`: In a rare situation, you need to create `Observable` that emits nothing and calls `onComplete()`. In this case, you can use this source type with the `Observable.empty()` call.

3. `never`: It is equivalent to `empty` with the difference being that this will never make a call to `onComplete()` and keep the `Observable` waiting to emit a state. This is also used less frequently.

4. `error`: If you wish to create `Observable` that immediately calls `onError()`, you can use this source with the `Observable.error()` call. It is used for testing purposes mainly.

5. `future`: It was introduced way back and used as a placeholder for the result that is not yet produced. `Observable` is more powerful than `future` but if you are using old libraries, you can convert `Observable` to `future` with the `Observable.future()` call.

6. `defer`: This is basically used to create a separate state for each `Observer`. It is useful when the source of the stream is stateful. If you want your observers to reflect the changes happening to the `Observable` state, then you can use this source type with an `Observable.defer()` call.

7. `single`: This type of `Observable` just emits a single value and can be used with a `Single.just()` method call.

8. `maybe`: It is similar to the `single` type, the only difference that it emits zero or one data at maximum and can be used with a `Maybe.just()` call.

9. `fromCallable`: If you want to perform certain actions of computation before emitting the data, you can use this source with an `Observable.fromCallable()` call. In case any error occurs and you want to pass it to the `Observable` chain through an `onError()` call instead of throwing the error, you can use this source type.

Operators

We have seen operators like map and filter in previous examples. They are basically used to perform a specific operation on the stream of data and return new `Observable` to form an `Observable` chain. Operators themselves are `Observers` to the `Observable` they are called on.

RxJava has a rich set of operators used to perform various operations with the following categories:

- **Creating observables:** The set of operators used to create new `Observable`.
- **Transforming observables:** Operators used to transform items emitted by observables they called upon.
- **Filtering observable:** Operators used to emit selective data.
- **Combining observable:** Used to combine multiple source observables to form a single `Observable`.
- **Error handling:** Operators that are used to recover from the error condition notified from `Observable`.
- **Utility Operator:** Used to perform some miscellaneous operations with `Observable`.
- **Conditional and Boolean operators:** Used to evaluate one or more `Observable` or even emitted items.
- **Mathematical and aggregate:** Operators used to perform various operations on the entire sequence of emitted data.

It is good to visit: `http://reactivex.io/documentation/operators.html`, to get full details about each of the operators, instead of having details listed here.

Project Reactor

The Reactor can be called the reactive library on top of the JDK. Java doesn't support Reactive Programming natively, and Reactor is one of the many libraries out there. Reactor comes from the open source group Pivotal and conforms to the Reactive Streams standard. It is built on Java 8 and ReactiveX vocabulary.

It is worthwhile to note here that, although asynchronous seems to be an important attribute for Reactive Programming, the Reactor doesn't force you to go asynchronous/synchronous, as it supports both. It depends on the scheduler chosen. That choice is yours. In order to understand the Reactor in a better way, we need to understand Reactive Streams in more detail.

Reactor features

Reactor provides event-based architecture and is used to handle a large volume of requests concurrently and asynchronously, making a non-blocking and backpressure equipped system. With the Project Reactor, you have no need to implement Reactive Streams yourself as it provides a set of modules, which are embedded and interoperable. It provides the following stunning features:

Handling data stream with high volume

Project Reactor is capable of providing an API support for specific data cardinality, ranging from generating endless streams to publishing just a single data entry.

Instead of waiting for the entire data stream to process, Project Reactor enables the subscribers to handle the elements of a stream as they arrive. This makes the data processing operation more flexible and optimized by improving resource utilization. The memory required to be allocated to a subscriber is limited because data processing happens in a subset of items arriving at a particular time, rather than processing entire data streams in one go. Also, this makes the system more responsive as the results will start as soon as the first set of elements is received, instead of waiting until all items have been received and processed to deliver a final output.

Push-pull mechanism

Project Reactor has good assistance for proving a push/pull feature. There are practical scenarios where consumers intake the data at a slower rate than the producer emits them. In this case, the producer will raise the event and wait for Observers to pull it. In some situations, the consumer works faster than the producer. To handle it, consumers wait for the events to be pushed from the producer side. Project Reactor enables this flow to be dynamic in nature whenever necessary. It will be controlled by the rate of production and consumption.

Handling concurrency independently

The reactor execution paradigm is capable of handling concurrency independently, which truly makes it concurrency agnostic. The Reactor library handles the data stream in a more abstract way, rather than talking about how to execute different types of streams. The transactions happening during various operations are safe out of the box. Reactor provides a set of operators that handle different synchronous streams in different ways.

Operators

Reactor provides a set of operators that plays a vital role in the execution model by handling different synchronous streams in different ways. These operators can be used to filter, map, select, transform, and combine the data streams. They can be combined with other operators to build high-level, easy-to-operate, and highly customized data pipelines to process streams in the way you want.

Reactor sub-projects

Project reactor consists of various sub-projects as follows:

- **Reactor Core:** This project provides an implementation of Reactive Streams specification. Spring Framework 5.0 provides support for Reactive Programming with the Reactor Core sub-project as a foundation.
- **Reactor Test:** This contains necessary utilities for test verification.
- **Reactor Extra:** On top of Reactor Core, this project provides various operators to work on the data stream to perform required operations.
- **Reactor IPC:** This project provides backpressure furnished and non-blocking inter-process communication support over various network protocols, like HTTP, TCP, UDP, and web sockets. Due to this nature, this module is also helpful when building asynchronous microservice architectures.
- **Reactor Netty:** It is used to provide a reactive feature to Netty, a client server framework to develop network applications.
- **Reactive Kafka:** It is a reactive API for Apache Kakfa-based projects. It is used to communicate with Kakfa in a non-blocking and functional way.
- **Reactive RabbitMQ:** This project is used to equip RabbitMQ (a message broker system) with reactive capabilities.

Reactor types

Project Reactor is built with two core types based on the number of elements they process. They are considered as main building blocks to create a Reactive System using Reactor. They are `Flux` and `Mono`. They both implement the `Publisher<T>` interface and conform to Reactive Streams specification, and are furnished with reactive-pull and back-pressure facility. They also have several other useful methods. Let's explore the details as follows:

- `Flux`: It can be considered the equivalent of RxJava's Observable and can emit zero or more items, ending successfully or with an error signal. In short, it represents asynchronous event streams having zero or more elements.

- `Mono`: It can emit, at most, one element at a time. It is equivalent of the `Single` and `Maybe` Observable type from the RxJava side. A `Mono` type can be used for one-to-one request-response model implementation; for example, a task wish to send a completion signal can use a `Mono` type reactor.

The clear difference between the number of elements a reactor type can handle provides useful semantics and makes it an easy decision to choose which reactor type. If the model is sort of *fire and forget* then choose the `Mono` type. If execution is dealing with multiple data items or elements in the stream, then the `Flux` type is more appropriate.

Additionally, various operators play a vital role in deciding the type of reactor. For example, calling a `single()` method on a `Flux<T>` type will return `Mono<T>`, while concatenating multiple entities of type `Mono<T>` together with `concatWith()` will result in the `Flux<T>` type. The reactor type can influence which operators we can use with it. For example, some operators are applicable to either one of `Flux` or `Mono` while others can be used for both of them.

Reactor in action

Let's learn more about the reactor API with a practical example. Create a new Maven project similar to what we created in the *Anatomy of RxJava* section. The current version of the Project Reactor at the time of writing is 3.2.6. We need to provide a Maven dependency for the reactor as follows:

```
<project xmlns="http://maven.apache.org/POM/4.0.0"
   xmlns:xsi="http://www.w3.org/2001/XMLSchema-instance"
   xsi:schemaLocation="http://maven.apache.org/POM/4.0.0
             http://maven.apache.org/xsd/maven-4.0.0.xsd">
   <modelVersion>4.0.0</modelVersion>
   <groupId>reactor-demo</groupId>
   <artifactId>simple-reactor-demo</artifactId>
   <version>0.0.1-SNAPSHOT</version>
   <name>Smiple Reactor Dmo</name>
   <dependencies>
     <dependency>
       <groupId>io.projectreactor</groupId>
       <artifactId>reactor-core</artifactId>
       <version>3.2.6.RELEASE</version>
     </dependency>
   </dependencies>
</project>
```

When we define a Reactor dependency, Reactive Streams JAR will be added as a transitive dependency. Next, is to add a Java class as follows:

```
public class ReactorBasic {
  private static List<String> carModels = Arrays.asList(
          "Era","Magna","Sportz","Astha","Astha(O)");
  public static void main(String args[]) {
      Flux<String> fewWords = Flux.just("Hello", "World");
      Flux<String> manyWords = Flux.fromIterable(carModels);
      Mono<String> singleWord = Mono.just("Single value");
      fewWords.subscribe(t->System.out.println(t));
      System.out.println("--------------------------");
      manyWords.subscribe(System.out::println);
      System.out.println("--------------------------");
      singleWord.subscribe(System.out::println);
  }
}
```

We have used `Flux` and `Mono` to create various publishers. The `just()` method is used to populate the stream. We can also reach the iterable types (like `List`, `Set`, n) to form a data stream with the `fromIterable()` method. A few other methods like `from()`, `fromArray()` , and `fromStream()` are used to construct data streams from other producers, arrays, and existing Java streams, respectively, and can be used as follows:

```
public class ReactorFromOtherPublisher {
  public static void main(String[] args) {
    Flux<String> fewWords = Flux.just("One","Two");
    /* from array */
    Flux<Integer> intFlux = Flux.fromArray(new Integer[]{1,2,3,4,5,6,7});
    /* from Java 8 stream */
    Flux<String> strFlux = Flux.fromStream(Stream.of(
      "Ten", "Hundred", "Thousand", "Ten Thousands", "Lac","Ten Lac",
"Crore"));
    /* from other Publisher */
    Flux<String> fromOtherPublisherFlux = Flux.from(fewWords);
    intFlux.subscribe(System.out::println);
    strFlux.subscribe(System.out::println);
    fromOtherPublisherFlux.subscribe(System.out::println);
  }
}
```

The subscriber can be plugged with the `subscribe()` method. This is similar to what we have done with Observable in RxJava. With `Flux`, we can create a publisher with the finite or infinite stream.

We can also control to generate a stream with a value or just an empty stream. All of that can be done with a few utility methods provided by the Flux class as follows:

- Flux.empty(): It is used to generate an empty stream having no values and only executes completion events.
- Flux.error(): It is used to signal the error condition by generating an error stream with no any value but only errors.
- Flux.never(): As its name suggests, it generates a stream with no events of any type.
- Flux.defer(): It is used to construct a publisher when a subscriber makes the subscription to Flux. In short, it is lazy in nature.

Types of subscribers

The Flux and Mono classes both allow Java 8 lambda expressions as a subscriber. They also support various overloaded versions of the subscribe() method, as per the following code.

```
public class ReactorWithSubscriberWays {

  public static void main(String[] args) {
    List<String> monthList = Arrays.asList(
        "January","February","March","April","May");
    Flux<String> months = Flux.fromIterable(monthList);
/* 1) No events is consumed. */
    months.subscribe();
/* 2) Only value event is consumed */
    months.subscribe(month->System.out.println("->"+month));
/* 3) Value and Error (total 2) events are handled */
    months.subscribe(month->System.out.println("-->"+month),
            e->e.printStackTrace());
/* 4) Value, Error and Completion (total 3) events are subscribed */
    months.subscribe(month->System.out.println("--->"+month),
              e->e.printStackTrace(),
          ()->System.out.println("Finished at THIRD PLACE.. !!"));
/* 5) Value, Error, Completion and Subscription (total 4) events are
subscribed */
    months.subscribe(month->System.out.println("---->"+month),
                          e->e.printStackTrace(),
        ()->System.out.println("Finished at FOURTH PLACE ..!!"),
          s -> {System.out.println("Subscribed :");
                s.request(5L);});
  }
}
```

The `Flux` class is created with list of strings. There are five different variations of using the `subscribe()` method, and each has provision to capture various events. The detail is as follows:

- The first version does not consume any event.
- The second variant consumes the value event and it is defined with a lambda expression.
- The third `subscribe()` method listens to error events as a second argument along with the value events. We are simply printing stack-trace through lambda expressions.
- The fourth one consumes value, error, and completion events. On completion of a data stream, the completion event will be executed, which we listen to with a lambda expression.
- The fifth version consumes value, error, completion, and subscription events. The last parameter of the `Subscription` type makes this version of `subscribe()` a special case. The `Subscription` type has a method called `request()`. The publisher will not send any event until, and unless, the subscriber sends a demand signal with a `Subscription.request()` call. This is only applicable if `Subscription` is defined for the subscriber. We have to make a method call as `s.request(5L)`, meaning the publisher can only send five elements. It is less than than the total value in publisher and fires a completion event. In our case, the total elements in a data stream is five, and so it will call a completion event. If you pass fewer than five, you will not get a completion event call.

Custom subscribers

In a certain scenario, calling a `Subscribe` method on `Publisher` is not appropriate and you may want to write custom subscriber with own handling. Reactor framework provides support for defining custom subscribers by extending the `reactor.core.publisher.BaseSubscriber<T>` abstract class. You don't need to implement the `Subscribe` interface of Reactive Streams specification directly. Instead, you need to just extend this class to apply the custom implementation as follows:

```
static class CustomSubscriber extends BaseSubscriber<String>{
  @Override
  protected void hookOnSubscribe(Subscription subscription) {
  System.out.println("Fetching the values ...!!");
  subscription.request(10);
  }
  @Override
  protected void hookOnNext(String value) {
```

```
    System.out.println("Fetchig next value in hookOnNext()-->"+value);
  }
  @Override
  protected void hookOnComplete() {
  System.out.println("Congratulation, Everything is completed successfully
..!!");
  }
  @Override
  protected void hookOnError(Throwable throwable) {
  System.out.println("Opps, Something went wrong ..!!
"+throwable.getMessage());
  }
  @Override
  protected void hookOnCancel() {
  System.out.println("Oh !!, Operation has been cancelled ..!! ");
  }
  @Override
  protected void hookFinally(SignalType type) {
  System.out.println("Shutting down the operation, Bye ..!! "+type.name());
  }
}
```

The `BaseSubscriber` class provides various hook methods, which represent the corresponding event. It is a placeholder to provide a custom implementation. Implementing these methods is similar to using various versions of the `subscribe()` method that we have seen in the *Type of subscriber* section. For example, if you only implement the `hookOnNext, hookOnError` , and `hookOnComplete` methods, then it is equivalent to the fourth version of `subscribe()`.

The `hookOnSubscribe()` method facilitates a subscription event. The backpressure is provided with `subscription.request()`. You can request as many element, as you want. For example, update the code for the `hookOnSubscribe()` method as follows:

```
@Override
    protected void hookOnSubscribe(Subscription subscription) {
        System.out.println("Fetching the values ...!!");
        for(int index=0; index<6;index++) {
          try {
            Thread.sleep(1000);
          } catch (InterruptedException e) {
            e.printStackTrace();
          }
           subscription.request(1);
        }
    }
```

We are requesting records one-by-one by calling `subscription.request(1)` in a loop. To get an idea how it works, we put a two-second delay in between so you will get a record for every two requests. Once all data is completed, it will trigger the completion event and the `hookOnComplete()` method will be called. The output would be as follows:

```
Console 🔲 ⎘ Progress 🔲 Problems
<terminated> ReactorCustomSubscriber [Java Application] C:\Program Files\Java\jre1.8.0_181\bin
Fetching the values ...!!
Fetchig next value in hookOnNext()-->John
Fetchig next value in hookOnNext()-->Komal
Fetchig next value in hookOnNext()-->Harmi
Fetchig next value in hookOnNext()-->Bhakti
Fetchig next value in hookOnNext()-->Tom
Fetchig next value in hookOnNext()-->Peter
Congratulation, Everything is completed successfully ..!!
Shutting down the operation, Bye ..!! ON_COMPLETE
```

Reactor lifecycle methods

Reactor provides lifecycle methods to capture various events happening in publisher-subscriber communication. Those lifecycle methods are aligned with Reactive Streams specification. Reactor lifecycle methods can be used to hook custom implementation for a given event. Let's understand how that works with the following code:

```
public class ReactorLifecycleMethods {

  public static void main(String[] args) {
    List<String> designationList = Arrays.asList(
        "Jr Consultant","Associate Consultant","Consultant",
        "Sr Consultant","Principal Consultant");
    Flux<String> designationFlux = Flux.fromIterable(designationList);

    designationFlux.doOnComplete(
        () -> System.out.println("Operation Completed ..!!"))
    .doOnNext(
        value -> System.out.println("value in onNext() ->"+value))
    .doOnSubscribe(subscription -> {
      System.out.println("Fetching the values ...!!");
      for(int index=0; index<6;index++) {
          try {
            Thread.sleep(1000);
          } catch (InterruptedException e) {
            e.printStackTrace();
```

```
            }
            subscription.request(1);
         }
      })
   .doOnError(
      throwable-> {
         System.out.println("Opps, Something went wrong ..!! "
            +throwable.getMessage());
      })
   .doFinally(
      (signalType->
         System.out.println("Shutting down the operation, Bye ..!! "
         +signalType.name())))
   .subscribe();
}
```

We are creating the `Flux` object with data from a list and then calling various lifecycle methods, like `doOnComplete()`, `doOnNext()`, `doOnSubscribe()`, `doOnError()`, and `doOnTerminate()` in a chain. Finally, we call the `subscribe()` method, which does not consume the events, but all lifecycle methods will be executed as appropriate events are triggered.

This is similar to the custom subscriber implementation in the *Custom subscribers* section. You will see a similar output. The details of these lifecycle methods are as follows:

- `doOnComplete()`: Once all the data is received by the `Subscriber`, this method will be called.
- `doOnNext()`: This method will listen to the value event coming from the producer.
- `doOnSubscribe()`: Used to plug `Subscription`. It can control the backpressure by defining how many more elements are required with a `subscription.request()` call.
- `doOnError()`: If any error occurs, this method will be executed.
- `doOnTerminate()`: Once the operation is completed, either successfully or with error, this method will be called. It will not be considered on a manual cancellation event.
- `doOnEach()`: As the name suggests, it will be called for all `Publisher` events raised during stream processing.
- `doFinally()`: This will be called on stream closures due to error, cancellation, or successful completion of events.

Ratpack

Ratpack is set of Java libraries which are event driven, non-blocking, high performance, and asynchronous in nature to build scalable services with HTTP. It conforms to the Reactive Streams specification, meaning it comes with interoperability out of the box. It is built on Netty—a framework to build a client-server application over the network with quick and easy development.

It is a web framework to develop efficient and lightweight JVM-based applications. It has its own testing library to easily set up test cases. Spring provides support for Ratpack. You can get more information about Ratpack from its official site: `https://ratpack.io`.

Akka stream

Akka stream provides an implementation of Reactive Streams specifications on top of the Akka toolkit that uses Actor patterns for the concurrency execution model. It processes the stream of data asynchronously and in a non-blocking backpressure way with Actor. Apart from Java, Akka also works well with Scala language. Explore more about the Akka stream at the link `https://akka.io/docs`.

Vert.x

Vert.x is another tool kit provided by the Eclipse Foundation project used to build a JVM-based Reactive System. It also provides an implementation of Reactive Streams specifications similar to Ratpack. Vert.x supports and allows the use of RxJava to build a Reactive System. Needless to say, Vert.x is event based and non-blocking in nature. It supports various programming languages, like Java, JavaScript, Ruby, Groovy, Ceylon, Scala, Kotlin, and so on. You can learn more about it at: `https://vertx.io`.

Reactive support in Spring Framework

Spring is a modular framework and used to build every aspect of an application from the web to the persistence layer. Each module is considered as a sub-framework and targeted for a specific area of development. For example, to support a web layer with a servlet API, the Spring MVC module was included in the Spring Framework.

Similarly, to support a reactive stack in the web layer, Spring WebFlux was introduced in Spring Framework 5. It is fully non-blocking, backpressure, asynchronous, and compliant with Reactive Streams specifications. It can be run on Servlet 3.1+, Netty, and Undertow containers.

Spring Framework has both the stacks, Spring Web MVC and spring-WebFlux, and developers are free to use either of them, or in some scenarios to mix both of them to develop a Spring-based web application. The typical example would be using spring MVC controller with reactive WebClient; we will talk more about this in the latter part of this chapter.

Spring WebFlux

Spring 5 impressively supports creating a Reactive System with Spring WebFlux . It is a new reactive web application framework, developed based on the Project Reactor API and can also be used to build microservices. The most remarkable and direct benefit of making any application reactive is to bring asynchronous qualities to it.

Non-reactive and traditional Java-based applications use thread mechanisms for asynchronous and parallel programming. However, usage of the thread is not competent and scalable in any manner. On the other hand, Spring WebFlux encourages event loop-based programming, which is asynchronous and non-blocking in manner. This section introduces WebFlux in the context of the Spring Framework and Reactive Programming.

Spring MVC versus Spring WebFlux

Spring MVC has been part of the Spring Framework since version 2, and since then, has been a de facto standard when developing web-based applications with Spring Framework. To support Reactive Programming, Spring has introduced the WebFlux module. Therefore, it is important to understand the similarities and differences between Spring MVC and Spring WebFlux.

The Spring team has done it the hard way and kept the WebFlux syntax similar to the Spring MVC, but under the hood it has completely new technology. One of the prime differences between these two modules is the mechanism by which they handle the request. Spring MVC is based on a pure servlet API and works with a thread pool. This means that, every request has one thread from the controller to the persistence layer and may be blocked for the resources it needs.

However, Spring WebFlux is based on reactive architecture and works with the event loop mechanism, providing non-blocking support out of the box. In the event loop mechanism, everything happens as a reaction to the event. It is similar to a callback function; when any event happens, the callback function gets triggered. The concept event loop was introduced by Node.js.

Internally, WebFlux needs servlet API support, which works as an adapter layer, so that WebFlux can be deployed on both servlet and non-servlet containers. Spring MVC is built on top of a servlet API, which is synchronous (like Filter, Servlet, and so on) by nature and also performs blocking IO streams.

WebFlux, on other hand, is developed on asynchronous API (WebHandler, WebFilter, and so on) and non-blocking IO mechanisms, like `Flux` and `Mono` , which are used to handle the stream with a maximum of one value and many elements, respectively. Although Spring WebFlux is based on reactor and used by default, it also supports other reactive implementations, like Java 9 Flow API, RxJava, and Akka stream.

Both the frameworks, however, support some common features like using some annotation (like `@Controller` and `@RequestMapping`) and support for some well-known servers.

We are talking about Reactive Programming support in String with WebFlux; it does not mean Spring MVC is of no use. Both frameworks are addressing separate concern to the application. Like any framework, WebFlux may not be the best choice for all the application types.

So instead of choosing the framework by its features, you need to select it as per the requirement. There is absolutely no need to port your existing Spring MVC application completely to WebFlux if it is working perfectly well. The excellent part of WebFlux is that it can be used in conjunction with Spring MVC (if needed explicitly) without any problems.

Apart from this, if your existing Spring MVC application has a dependency on other parts that are synchronous and blocking in nature then, adapting WebFlux specific changes will obstruct from taking full benefits of reactive paradigm. You can decide, however, to pick WebFlux if your application is mainly handling the stream of data. If scalability and performance are what you are looking for then you can use WebFlux specific changes in your application.

Reactive span across Spring modules

By introducing a reactive web framework, WebFlux , Spring also made necessary changes in other modules to provide first-class support for WebFlux. Spring Boot, Spring Security, Thymeleaf, and Spring Data are among the few modules that are equipped with WebFlux capabilities. This can be described with the following diagram:

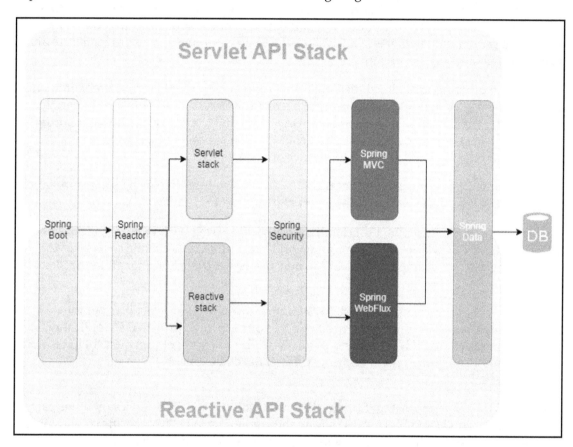

Spring Data has adopted a reactive paradigm and started supporting infinite streams from the database with the `@Tailable`annotation. Spring Data JPA is mostly associated with RDBMS, which is blocking in nature so it cannot support Reactive Programming.

Spring MVC is inherently blocking in nature; however, we can use Reactive Programming for some of the parts, which can be converted to be reactive. For example, the Spring MVC controller can be equipped with the `Flux` and `Mono` types to handle the data stream in a reactive way.

Apart from this, a few annotations like `@Controller`, `@RequestMapping`, and so on are supported in WebFlux so you can convert a Spring MVC application to WebFlux in an incremental manner. We will see more details about reactive support in Spring Framework through WebFlux by creating a sample application.

Spring WebFlux application

We will create a sample web application with the WebFlux framework. The application will simply access existing student information from a data store. Instead of making a fully fledged application, we will focus more on how to access data in a reactive manner with the WebFlux framework.

We will use Spring Boot to kickstart the development. For those who are new to Spring Boot, it is a tool and part of Spring Horizon, which is designed to speed up and simplify the bootstrapping and development of new Spring-based applications.

You might have come across bulky XML and other configurations repeatedly in Spring projects. The Spring team was well aware of this and has finally developed a tool called Spring Boot, aimed at freeing the developer from providing a boilerplate configuration, which is not only tedious but time consuming.

We will create a sample web application using MongoDB as a data store. While working with Reactive Programming, it is recommended to use non-blocking and reactive capable datastores, like MongoDB, Couchbase, Cassandra, and so on. We will use a tool called **Spring Tool Suite** (**STS**), which is an Eclipse-based IDE. It provides support for creating Spring Boot-based applications. Download it from: `https://spring.io/tools3/sts/all` and install it in your local machine.

> The STS link given here is version 3.x. At the time of writing, the current version of STS is 4.x. All the codes created in this book are with STS 3.x so the link given is version 3.x. However, you can download the latest version of STS and play with the code without any problems.

Once downloaded, open it, select the **File** | **New** | **Spring Starter Project** menu and fill the form as follows:

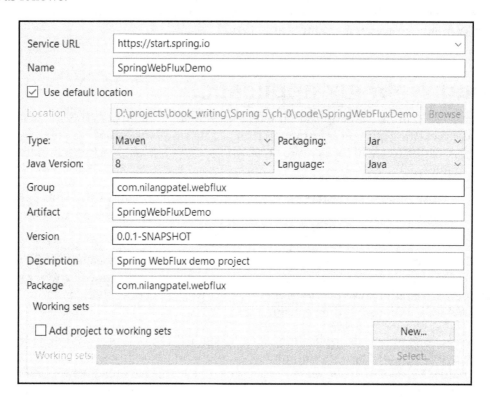

Click on the **Next** button, and you will be asked to define the dependencies. Choose the following dependencies. You can use the textbox, **Available** to search for a particular dependency:

- **Web:** Used to add Spring MVC specific dependencies.
- **Reactive Web:** To add WebFlux specific dependencies.
- **DevTools:** Helpful for development as it will auto-refresh the changes in the embedded container to see the changes quickly.
- **Reactive MongoDB:** Spring Data dependency for MongoDB that works in a reactive paradigm. Make sure you don't select MongoDB, which is a dependency to work with MongoDB in the non-reactive model.

Click on **Finish,** and you will see a project is created in the **Package Explorer** (or **Project Explorer**) section of STS. Once the project is created, we will perform the following steps.

MongoDB installation

First, you need to install MongoDB into your local machine. It is distributed as a standalone server as well as a cloud service. Download the latest version from: `https://www.mongodb.com/download-center/community`. Choose the appropriate OS from the list and install it on your machine.

MongoDB doesn't has any UI to access it. However, it provides another tool called Compass and can be downloaded from: `https://www.mongodb.com/download-center/compass`. Choose the appropriate version and target platform and download them. In most cases, it is directly executable. By default, MongoDB is accessible with the `27017` port. Just connect Compass to the MongoDB server to make sure it is running before connecting.

MongoDB data structure

Before using MongoDB, it is important to understand the schema and data structure used in it. Like a relational database, we need to first create a database in MongoDB. Along with the database, we also need to create a collection. You can consider a collection to be similar to the database table in RDBMS.

Connect the Compass (default: no credentials) and click on the **CREATE DATABASE** button, and you will see model windows as follows:

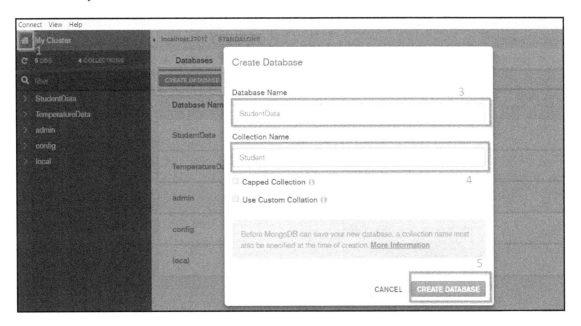

You need to give the **Database Name** and **Collection Name** and click on the **CREATE DATABASE** button from the model window. You can now insert the data for student collection into MongoDB.

Creating a Spring Data repository

Spring Data provides a consistent Spring-based programming model to access data. It abstracts away the low-level boilerplate details and can be used to access a wide variety of data stores including the SQL (relational and non-relational) database, map-reduce frameworks, cloud-based data services, and so on. The Spring Data repository basically implements the data access layer and provides abstract access to interact with the underlying data store.

We will configure the Spring Data repository to interact with MongoDB. The first step is to create an entity object (domain model). Spring Data allows accessing data in an object-oriented way, so first we need to define the entity class and provide the necessary mapping with the persistence model. An entity class can be created as follows:

```
@Document(collection="Student")
public class Student {
  @Id
  @JsonIgnore
  private String id;
  @NotNull(message="Roll no can not be empty")
  private Integer rollNo;
  @NotNull(message="Name can not be empty")
  private String name;
  @NotNull(message="Standard can not be empty")
  private Integer standard;

 //.. getter and setter
}
```

This POJO class represents the student entity in MongoDB with the `@Document` annotation. You need to give the same collection name here that we created in MongoDB. The attribute ID will be autogenerated by MongoDB and can be considered as a primary key for the `Student` entity so it is marked with the `@Id` annotation.

Next add a Spring Data repository. Spring provide repository support for specific data stores. For MongoDB, the Spring Data repository should looks as follows:

```
@Repository
public interface StudentMongoRepository extends
ReactiveMongoRepository<Student, String>{
  public Mono<Student> findByRollNo(Integer rollNo);
  public Mono<Student> findByName(String name);
}
```

Spring Data provides the `ReactiveMongoRepository` interface that can be extended to define a custom repository. It is of the `Student` type, which is an object entity type when we want to interact with MongoDB and `String`, which represent the primary key (ID in our case).

The Spring Data repository provides a nice feature called the **query** method, which is used to access data based on specific column or attribute values by following a certain naming convention. For example, `findByName(String name)` will return `StudentData` with the matching name. Spring Data provides underlying implementation of these methods out of the box. For simplicity, we kept just two methods.

To make sure the Spring application connects to MongoDB, we need to add the following properties in the `application.properties` file:

```
spring.data.mongodb.host=localhost
spring.data.mongodb.port=27017
spring.data.mongodb.database=StudentData
```

This is equivalent to defining connection properties in a database.

WebFlux programming models

Spring WebFlux is flexible enough to support different development patterns. You can create an application in WebFlux with the following two programming models:

- **Annotated controller**: This is much similar than the Spring MVC controller.
- **Functional end point**: Functional end points are used to process and route requests with functional programming features.

We will explore both these options in the sample WebFlux application that we created with the Spring Data repository and entity class. The next part is to create a controller, which can be done in the following two ways.

Annotated controller

WebFlux provides support for annotation-based configurations in a similar to the Spring MVC framework. To begin with, we will create an annotated controller class that publishes the Reactive Streams of the `Student` entity from the server side as follows:

```
@RestController
@RequestMapping("api")
public class StudentWebFluxController {

  @Autowired
  private StudentMongoRepository studentMongoRepository;
  @GetMapping("/getStudent/{rollNo}")
  public Mono<ResponseEntity<Student>> getStudent(@PathVariable("rollNo")
Integer rollNo) {
    Mono<Student> studentMonoObj =
studentMongoRepository.findByRollNo(rollNo);
    return studentMonoObj.map(student -> ResponseEntity.ok(student))
      .defaultIfEmpty(ResponseEntity.notFound().build());
  }
}
```

`StudentWebFluxController` is the annotated controller. It is similar to the Spring MVC controller. The `@RestController` annotation is used to define this controller as a REST controller. The `@RequestMapping` annotation is used to define the URL mapping for this controller.

The `studentMongoRepository` Spring Data repository supports non-blocking Reactive Streams. The `getStudent()` method will return a single `Student` object based on the `rollNo` input value. However, the return type is not just in response to `Student`; instead, it is of the `Mono` type because it returns at most one element, so the `Mono` type is more appropriate.

The repository gives `Mono<Student>` based on `rollNo`; then we call the map function to map the object of the `Mono<Student>` type to `Mono<ResponseEntity<Student>>` , which will be then taken care of by the WebFlux framework to return the student data. Add some values directly from MongoDB and try to access it with the URLs `http://localhost:8080/api/getStudent/21` (using the `8080` port, and student `rollNo` is 21) in REST client (for example, Postman), and you will get an output as follows:

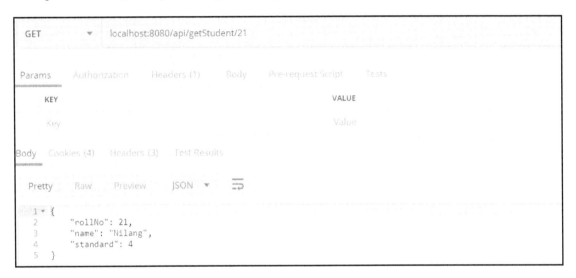

In case we want to access more than one student, we need to use the `Flux` return type as it emits 0 to N elements. Let's add one more method to the controller to fetch all the students as follows:

```
@GetMapping("/getAllStudent")
public Flux<Student> getAllStudent() {
  Flux<Student> allStudents = studentMongoRepository.findAll();
  return allStudents;
}
```

Add some more student data from MongoDB and hit the URL
`http://localhost:8080/api/getAllStudent` and you will see results as follows:

The WebFlux controller endpoint returns a Publisher in the form of either `Flux` or `Mono`. In the second method where we return all the students, it can be in the form of a **Server-Sent Event (SSE)** to the browser. For that, you need to define the return type as `text/event-stream`. The SSE is the technology allowing a browser to receive automatic updates from the server via an HTTP connection.

What does this mean? If we have a very huge stream, then the WebFlux controller will send the data as it receives from a reactive repository (from MongoDB in our case) and send it to the browser, instead of fetching all the records, which results in a blocking condition. This is how large volumes of streams are handled in Reactive Programming with Spring WebFlux.

Functional endpoint

Spring Framework 5 supports functional programming models for reactive web applications with WebFlux. This is an alternative to using the Spring MVC-style annotated controller. The functional style programming in Spring WebFlux uses the following essential components:

- `HandlerFunction`: It is used to handle the request. It is an alternative to the Spring MVC controller handler methods and works similar to it.
- `RouterFunction`: It is used to route incoming HTTP requests. `RouterFunction` is an alternative to using request mapping with the `@RequestMapping` annotation and works similar to it.

Artifacts required in functional-style Reactive Programming

Let's first understand these components. They are defined as an interface in Spring WebFlux. The `HandlerFunction` interface looks as follows:

```
@FunctionalInterface
public interface HandlerFunction<T extends ServerResponse> {
    Mono<T> handle(ServerRequest request);
}
```

This interface is similar to the `Function<T, R>` type, which takes the value (of the `T`type) and returns another value (of the `R`type). In this case, it is equivalent to `Function<ServerRequest, Mono<T>` . It is much like a servlet. The `T` type is the response type of the function that should implement the `ServerReponse` interface, which represents the server-side HTTP response.

The `handle()` method takes the `ServerRequest` object type and returns a `Mono` object type. `ServerRequest` represents the HTTP request, and we can get headers and the body of a request from this. Both `ServerRequest` and `ServerResponse` are part of the reactive API of Spring WebFlux.

You may notice that instead of putting both requests and responses in the same method call, the response is returned from the `handle()` method, which really makes it side-effect free and easy to test. Let's see what `RouterFunction` looks like. Again it is of the interface type as follows:

```
@FunctionalInterface
public interface RouterFunction<T extends ServerResponse> {
  Mono<HandlerFunction<T>> route(ServerRequest request);
  //.. other methods.
}
```

This interface has the `route()` method that returns `HandlerFunction`, which matches the given request. This method is used to create routes by applying `RequestPredicate`. When the predicate matches, it will return the handler function, which basically processes the request. `RequestPredicate` is the Java8 functional interface and part of the reactive API of Spring WebFlux. It is used to test the given `ServerRequest` for the routing and looks as follows:

```
@FunctionalInterface
public interface RequestPredicate {
  boolean test(ServerRequest request);
//Other functions
}
```

Let's create the controller in functional-style programming. We will write a controller that works exactly the same to the annotated controller but in a functional way.

Prerequisite for a functional approach in Spring WebFlux

To work in functional way, the very first thing we need to do is to make our project WebFlux aware. For that we need to add the `@EnableWebFlux` annotation to the main bootstrap class as follows:

```
@SpringBootApplication
@EnableWebFlux
public class SpringWebFluxDemoApplication {
 // other code ..
}
```

We also need to instruct Spring that the application is of the `reactive` type by adding the following property in the `application.properties` file:

```
spring.main.web-application-type=reactive
```

Defining routers and handlers

The next part is to define the router and handler for getting the student data. Let's recall that routers are used to route the request as they serve the purpose of @RequestMapping in the annotated controller, while handlers actually process the incoming request, which is similar to the Spring MVC controller handler method. The router class looks as follows:

```
@Configuration
public class StudentRouter {
    @Autowired
    private StudentHandler studentHandler;
     @Bean
      RouterFunction<ServerResponse> returnStudent() {
          return
RouterFunctions.route(RequestPredicates.GET("/api/f/getStudent/{rollNo}"),
              studentHandler::getStudent);
      }
    @Bean
      RouterFunction<ServerResponse> returnAllStudent() {
          return
RouterFunctions.route(RequestPredicates.GET("/api/f/getAllStudent"),
              studentHandler::getAllStudent);
      }
}
```

It is required to declare the router class with the @Configuration annotation so that Spring container will pick this class at the time of context loading and do the necessary configuration. We have two methods to get a single student and list of all the student data, respectively.

The router is created with the RouterFunctions.route() call. The RouterFunctions utility class has lots of useful functions. The route() method needs two parameters. The first parameter is of the RequestPredicate. type Another helper class RequestPredicates is used to define RequestPredicate with the URL pattern for each router method. The RequestPredicate class has various methods corresponding to HTTP methods.

We have used the GET method as we want to pull data from REST client with the GET method. The important thing here is to define any path variable along with the URL pattern that will be received in the handler to perform the necessary operations.

The second parameter is of the `HandlerFunction<T>` type, which is supplied by the corresponding method of the `StudentHandler` class.

The `studentHandler::getStudent` and `studentHandler::getAllStudent` double column notations will call the `getStudent()` and `getAllStudent()` methods of the `StudentHandler` class respectively. The `StudentHandler` class should look as follows:

```
@Component
public class StudentHandler {
  @Autowired
  private StudentMongoRepository studentMongoRepository;

  public Mono<ServerResponse> getStudent(ServerRequest serverRequest) {
    int rollNo = getInt(serverRequest.pathVariable("rollNo"));
    Mono<Student> studentMonoObj =
studentMongoRepository.findByRollNo(rollNo);
    return ServerResponse.ok().body(studentMonoObj, Student.class);
  }
  public Mono<ServerResponse> getAllStudent(ServerRequest serverRequest) {
    Flux<Student> allStudents = studentMongoRepository.findAll();
    return ServerResponse.ok().body(allStudents, Student.class);
  }
  private int getInt(String intStr) {
    int returnVal=0;
    if(intStr !=null !intStr.isEmpty()) {
      try {
        returnVal = Integer.parseInt(intStr);
      }catch(Exception e) {
        e.printStackTrace();
      }
    }
    return returnVal;
  }
}
```

Each handler method will have the object of `ServerRequest` as a parameter, which will be supplied by the Spring WebFlux framework while they are called from routers.

The `ServerRequest` class represents the HTTP request, and we can get parameters and body out of it.

In the `getStudent()` method, we are reading the `rollNo` path variable, and passing it to the repository method to get student data. The name of the path variable here must be the same as the path variable declared as part of the URL pattern in a router (`/api/f/getStudent/{`**`rollNo`**`}`). Finally, the `ServerResponse` class is used to construct a response and return it. To differentiate the functional endpoint, we have updated the URL pattern (added `/f/` in between to denote its functional endpoints). You will get a similar output to the annotated controller.

The handler methods are not required to be defined with the `@Bean` annotation or else you will get an error while starting the application.

Combining handler and router

We have written two different classes for the handler and router; however, we can declare the configuration that covers the functionality of both the router and handler in a single class. This can be done by combining the handler and router method pair in one single method as follows:

```
@Configuration
public class StudentRouterHandlerCombined {

    @Autowired
    private StudentMongoRepository studentMongoRepository;
    @Bean
    RouterFunction<ServerResponse> returnStudentWithCombineFun(){
        HandlerFunction<ServerResponse> studentHandler =
                serverRequest -> {
                    int rollNo = getInt(serverRequest.pathVariable("rollNo"));
                    return ServerResponse.ok().
                        body(studentMongoRepository.findByRollNo(rollNo)
                        , Student.class);
                };
        RouterFunction<ServerResponse> studentResponse =
            RouterFunctions.route(
                RequestPredicates.GET("/api/f/combine/getStudent/{rollNo}"),
                studentHandler);
        return studentResponse;
    }
    @Bean
    RouterFunction<ServerResponse> returnAllStudentWithCombineFun(){
        HandlerFunction<ServerResponse> studentHandler =
                serverRequest ->
                ServerResponse.ok().
                body(studentMongoRepository.findAll(), Student.class);
        RouterFunction<ServerResponse> studentResponse =
```

```
            RouterFunctions.route(
                RequestPredicates.GET("/api/f/combine/getAllStudent"),
                studentHandler);
        return studentResponse;
    }
    private int getInt(String intStr) {
        int returnVal=0;
        if(intStr !=null !intStr.isEmpty()) {
            try {
                returnVal = Integer.parseInt(intStr);
            }catch(Exception e) {
                e.printStackTrace();
            }
        }
        return returnVal;
    }
}
```

This class has two methods to fetch a single student and all students, respectively. In each method, we first create an instance of the handler and then pass it into the `route()` method while creating the router. The lambda expression is used to define the handler. The code is easy and straightforward. Again to make it unique, we have changed the URL pattern by adding `/combine/` in between so the endpoints of getting a single student and all students can be accessed with the URL `http://localhost:8080/api/f/combine/getStudent/21` and `http://localhost:8080/api/f/combine/getAllStudent`, respectively. You will get a similar output to when we defined handler and router separately.

You might be wondering how this works under the hood. The bean of the `RouterFunctionMapping` type scans the packages and retrieves all `RouterFunctions` at the time of starting the application. This bean is created within `WebFluxConfigurationSupport`, which is the headquarters of the Spring WebFlux configuration. All these things start happening when we define the `@EnableWebFlux` annotation to the main bootstrap class along with the `spring.main.web-application-type=reactive` property.

Composite routers

If you have lots of routers in your configuration, you can basically compose them into a chain with the `and` operator. In the previous example, we defined two routers in two different methods. This can be combined in just one method as follows:

```
@Configuration
public class StudentCompositeRoutes {

    @Autowired
```

```
private StudentMongoRepository studentMongoRepository;

@Bean
RouterFunction<ServerResponse> compositeRoutes(){

  RouterFunction<ServerResponse> studentResponse =
      RouterFunctions.route(RequestPredicates.
        GET("/api/f/composite/getStudent/{rollNo}"),
        serverRequest -> {
          int rollNo = getInt(serverRequest.pathVariable("rollNo"));
          return ServerResponse.ok().
            body(studentMongoRepository.
              findByRollNo(rollNo), Student.class);
        })
      .and(
        RouterFunctions.route(RequestPredicates.
          GET("/api/f/composite/getAllStudent"),
          serverRequest ->
        ServerResponse.ok().
        body(studentMongoRepository.findAll(), Student.class))
        );

  return studentResponse;
}
private int getInt(String intStr) {
  int returnVal=0;
  if(intStr !=null  !intStr.isEmpty()) {
    try {
      returnVal = Integer.parseInt(intStr);
    }catch(Exception e) {
      e.printStackTrace();
    }
  }
  return returnVal;
}
}
```

The and operator is used to combine two routers. Also, the second parameter of the `rout()` function, which is of the `HandlerFunction<T>` type, is defined with a lambda expression. This is how you can composite multiple routers in a single chain call with the and operator. To distinguish this feature, we again alter the endpoint URL pattern as we have added `/composite/` instead of `/combine/` to the URL pattern. Needless to say that you will get a similar output in this case as well.

WebSocket support

WebSocket is a protocol that allows full-duplex, two-way communication between a server and a client. While establishing the connection, it uses HTTP for the initial handshake. Once done, it will request a protocol upgrade. The Spring WebFlux framework supports reactive WebSocket communication between a client and server based on the Java WebSocket API. Defining WebSocket is a two-step process as follows:

- Define the handler to manage the WebSocket request
- Define mapping to access the specific handler

In WebFlux, the WebSockets are handled by implementing the `WebSocketHandler` interface. It has one method called `handle()`. It is provided with the object of `WebSocketSession` every time a connection is established to the handler. As its name suggests, `WebSocketSession` represents the connection formed by a single client.

Two separate streams accessible through the `receive()` and `send()` methods of the `Flux` type, are associated with `WebSocketSession` for handling incoming requests and outgoing messages respectively. We will first define handler mapping as follows:

```
@Autowired
SampleWebSocketHandler studentWebSocketHandler;

@Bean
public HandlerMapping webSockertHandlerMapping() {
  Map<String, WebSocketHandler> map = new HashMap<>();
  map.put("/student", studentWebSocketHandler);

  SimpleUrlHandlerMapping mapping = new SimpleUrlHandlerMapping();
  mapping.setUrlMap(map);
  return mapping;
}
@Bean
public WebSocketHandlerAdapter handlerAdapter() {
  return new WebSocketHandlerAdapter();
}
```

The `@Bean` annotated method `webSockertHandlerMapping` is used to map our custom handler with a specific URL pattern by which it can be accessible.
The `SampleWebSocketHandler` custom handler is injected with the `@Autowired` annotation and looks as follows:

```
@Component
public class SampleWebSocketHandler implements WebSocketHandler{
```

```
private ObjectMapper objMapper = new ObjectMapper();
@Autowired
StudentMongoRepository studentMongoRepository;
@Override
public Mono<Void> handle(WebSocketSession webSocketSession) {
  Flux<Student> allStudentSource = studentMongoRepository.findAll();
  System.out.println(" ****** Incoming messages ****** ");
  webSocketSession.receive().subscribe(System.out::println);
  System.out.println(" ****** Sending Student data ****** ");
  return webSocketSession.send(allStudentSource.map(student->{
    return writeValueAsSTring(student);
  }).map(webSocketSession::textMessage)
  );
}

private String writeValueAsSTring(Object obj) {
  try {
    return objMapper.writeValueAsString(obj);
  } catch (JsonProcessingException e) {
    e.printStackTrace();
  }
  return "No data";
}
}
```

The `SampleWebSocketHandler` class provides an implementation of
the `WebSocketHandler` interface with the `handle()` method. In that method, we are
simply fetching all student data from `StudentMongoRepository` and calling the `send()`
method on `WebSocketSession`. In the `send()` method, we first convert the `Student`
object to JSON string with `ObjectMapper` and finally call the `textMessage()` method
of `WebSocketSession` to convert it to `WebSocketMessage`.

Next, is to create the client. We will write client code in JavaScript and call the server from
the browser to see how the stream data is received one by one. You can create one HTML
file with the following code.

```
<html>
  <body>
    Hello
  </body>
  <script>
      var socket = new WebSocket('ws://localhost:8080/student');
      socket.addEventListener('message', function (event) {
      window.alert('message from server: ' + event.data);
      });
  </script>
</html>
```

Almost all modern browsers support WebSocket communication. Open this HTML in a browser and you will see student data one by one with a browser alert. This is how WebSocket communication happens in the reactive paradigm of Spring WebFlux.

Summary

Reactive is definitely a promising new technology that will help to build a scalable and high-performance application. Spring has done an impressive job of supporting Reactive Systems with a new framework called WebFlux. Reactive is the future of next-generation applications, and it is needed almost everywhere: datastores, middle layers, frontends, or even mobile platforms.

Through this chapter, we learned the basics of Reactive Systems and Reactive Programming followed by various techniques to achieve it. We then learned about Reactive Streams, which is one of the most popular ways of implementing a Reactive System. Starting with the Reactive Streams specifications and the basic fundamentals, we explored various JVM-based libraries that provide an implementation for a particular specification. We did some hands-on work with RxJava and Project Reactor and learned the underlying principles.

In the same direction, we have seen how the Spring Framework provides support in a reactive paradigm. We have then explored the Spring WebFlux framework by creating a Spring Boot-based web application. Apart from annotated based support for WebFlux, which is like Spring MVC, Spring also supports creating Reactive Systems with functional programming paradigms. We explored various options in functional programming with a series of examples.

To gain full advantage of the reactive capability of Spring WebFlux, the data store should also support Reactive Programming, and that was the reason we chose MongoDB as a datastore, and we learned how to configure it in a web application with the Spring Boot tool.

It has been a very exciting journey so far, and we will continue our journey in the next chapter by exploring the interesting topic of the integration of Elasticsearch with the Spring Framework. We will develop a sample application called **Blogpress**. We will also look in more detail at Spring Boot, Thymeleaf, and so on; stay tuned and ready to explore further in the next chapter.

3
Blogpress - A Simple Blog Management System

Spring supports the development of enterprise-grade applications on the Java platform. There are numerous such application that come under its purview, popular among which are Spring **Model-View-Controller** (**MVC**), Spring Security, Spring Data, Spring Batch, and Spring Cloud.

In the previous two chapters, we started exploring Spring MVC framework along with other building blocks, like Spring Data and RestTemplate, along with JavaScript frameworks like Angular, Bootstrap, and jQuery to build the web-based application. We have also seen how to build a reactive web application with the help of WebFlux, a framework for creating reactive web applications.

Creating an enterprise-ready Spring-based application requires heavy configuration, which makes the process of development quite tedious and cumbersome. On top of this, setting up the complex dependencies also needs lots of effort. Quite often, the libraries used in Spring-based web applications require common configuration to bind them together.

Considering any standard Spring-based application, you might need to perform certain repetitive tasks, specifically for configuration, for example, importing required modules and libraries to resolve dependencies; doing configuration related to various layers of application, such as data source and transaction management at the DAO layer, and view resolver and resource management at the web layer, and so on.

This is a mandated procedure that has to be followed while creating any Spring-based web application. In short, developers often resort to duplicating the configuration across application and may not following the best practices while integrating libraries.

All these factors inspired the Spring team to come up with a framework that provides integration for all the Spring libraries through auto-configuration, which basically eliminates the repetitive jobs for you. In addition to this, it provides production-ready features, such as application metrics and monitoring, and logging and deployment guidelines. This framework is known as Spring Boot.

In this chapter, we will continue our journey and look at building different components required for a blog management web application using Spring libraries and other third-party libraries all bound together with auto-configuration provided by Spring Boot and some overrides done by us to the auto-configuration.

This chapter will cover the following topics:

- Project skeleton with Spring Boot
- The main flow of the application in the Spring MVC framework
- Presentation layer with **Thymeleaf** and `Mustache.js`
- Making the application secure with Spring Security—covering authentication and authorization
- Developing the backend layer in Elasticsearch, which holds the application data and provides REST-based CRUD operations
- Developing Spring MVC REST service

Technical requirements

All the code used in this chapter can be downloaded from the following GitHub link: `https://github.com/PacktPublishing/Spring-5.0-Projects/tree/master/chapter03/blogpress`. The code can be executed on any operating system, although it has only been tested on Windows.

Application overview

Taking a real-life example is the best approach to explore and understand the concepts of a given framework context. The idea is not to show how to build the web application; instead, we will show the important components which are part of the application so that anyone can just pick one component and use it in another application. You can always find the complete working solution in the code downloaded for the book.

Let's jump into action. First, we will go through the brief about our application—blog. We will call it **Blogpress**. Please note that it will not be a full-fledged blogging application; instead, we will develop it with the following functionalities:

- Landing page—shows a list of blogs with the links to each blog.
- When a user clicks on any of the blogs, the system opens it in view mode along with all (approved) comments.
- A user can add comments to the same screen.
- Apart from this, a user can search for the blog with given search text, targeting the title or body of the blog.
- There is a login feature. Two people can log into the application—a blog user and an admin:
    - Blog user can add/update/delete the blog. He can only edit the blogs he created.
    - Admin user can perform all possible operations a blog user can do plus manage (approve or reject) the comments given by the anonymous user.
- When any user adds a comment, an email will be sent to the admin user to moderate it. Once the comment is approved, an email will be sent back to the user as a notification.

Project skeleton with Spring Boot

Spring Boot automates the process of creating the configuration which speeds up the development process. In short, Spring Boot makes the development life cycle shorter, with minimal or no configuration for building production-ready applications or services. It uses the convention-over-configuration methodology to provide rapid application development.

Spring Boot is not meant to provide any new features; instead, as it is established on top of the Spring Framework, it uses existing Spring Framework features to provide a preconfigured application skeleton out of the box, which is a getting-started mode of development.

Spring Boot has various advantages over conventional ways of creating a Spring-based application, as follows:

- Has automated configuration
- Manages dependency with ease
- Supports an embedded server to make the development process easy and straightforward
- Provides support for building the application with Maven or Gradle out of the box
- Eases integration with other Spring modules
- Speeds up the development process
- Supports command lines and IDEs to develop and test the application with ease

Configuring IDE Spring Tool Suite

Let's start developing our blog application—Blogpress. As described, we will start creating the application with Spring Boot first. Developing an application with an IDE is the most straightforward, easy, convenient, and favorable approach preferred by the majority of developers today. We use IDEs to develop our application.

Spring provides an Eclipse-based IDE called **Spring Tool Suite** (**STS**) to develop any Spring-based application with ease. Download the latest version of STS from the link `https://spring.io/tools`.

 The STS is available with Eclipse, along with Visual Studio and Atom-based code editors. You can use either of them for your convenience.

We will use the STS (an Eclipse-based IDE) to build the application in this chapter. Download STS, unzip it in your local folder, and open the `.exe` file to start the STS. Once started, create a new **Spring Starter Project** of the **Spring Boot** type with the following attributes:

- **Name:** `blogpress`
- **Type:** **Maven** (you can also select **Gradle**)
- **Packaging:** **Jar**
- **Java Version:** **8** (or above)
- **Language:** **Java**
- **Group:** This would be a Maven `groupId`, so give the appropriate value

- **Artifact**: This would be a Maven `artifactId`, so give the appropriate value
- **Version**: `0.0.1-SNAPSHOT`—the build version of our application build
- **Description**: `A simple blog management system`

 You can create a Spring Boot application from a command window as well. Spring provides a tool called Spring **command-line interface** (**CLI**) for this. Another way of creating a Spring Boot starter project is with `https://start.spring.io/`. You need to define the dependencies and it will allow users to download the entire project structure from the web.

Keeping all default options, click **Finish** to create the Spring Boot application. You will see the following dependencies in `pom.xml`:

```
<dependency>
   <groupId>org.springframework.boot</groupId>
   <artifactId>spring-boot-starter-web</artifactId>
</dependency>

<dependency>
   <groupId>org.springframework.boot</groupId>
   <artifactId>spring-boot-starter-test</artifactId>
   <scope>test</scope>
</dependency>
```

Spring Boot provides various starters, specific for each dependency so that their JARs are available in the classpath. Since we want to develop a web application (Spring MVC), we keep the starter `spring-boot-starter-web` in the previous code (in fact, it is added while creating a project in the STS).

Spring provides a set of dependencies for a specific functionality in the form of a starter. It is a convenient way of managing dependencies in a Spring Boot application. When you specify a particular starter, Spring Boot will pull all (recursive) dependencies in your application for you. For example, if you wish to add a data store to your application with JPA, simply add `spring-boot-starter-jpa` to `pom.xml` in your Spring Boot application. All dependency will be carried out by Spring Boot so that you can focus on business implementations.

You will see `spring-boot-starter-parent` in the parent element of `pom.xml`. This is the magic of Spring Boot. Your application extends all Spring Boot capabilities by this declaration, as following snippet shows:

```
<parent>
   <groupId>org.springframework.boot</groupId>
   <artifactId>spring-boot-starter-parent</artifactId>
```

```
    <version>2.1.0.BUILD-SNAPSHOT</version>
    <relativePath/>
</parent>
```

Spring Model-View-Controller web flow

The next step is to add Spring MVC capabilities. In the previous step, the required starter dependencies for the web are added to the `pom.xml` file. Next, we will define Spring MVC artifacts in our application.

Since this is a Spring Boot application, we are not required to declare everything from scratch. It is essential to define the controllers and view layer. First, we will declare a Spring MVC controller, as in the following snippet:

```
@Controller
public class BlogController {
  private Logger logger = LoggerFactory.getLogger(BlogController.class);
  @GetMapping("/")
  public String showLandingPage(Model model) {
    logger.info("This is show home page method ");
    return "home";
  }
}
```

The `@Controller` annotation describes this class as a Spring MVC controller. It basically instructs the Spring Boot application that this component will serve a web-based request. It matches the correct URL pattern to call a specific controller and its method.

In the previous declaration, we only gave the URL pattern to the controller method. However, Spring allows you to declare URL patterns for the controller as well. Since our application requires only certain functionalities, one controller is sufficient, and hence, we haven't declared the URL pattern for the controller. So, all web requests (with the `http://host/context/controllerUrlPattern` pattern) for the current application will be routed to this controller.

The `@RequestMapping("/controllerUrlPattern")` annotation is used to describe URL patterns at the controller level. In this scenario, the `http://host/context/controllerUrlPattern` pattern will reach this controller. The URL pattern of all of its methods will be appended after `http://host/context/controllerUrlPattern`.

It is always good practice to use a logger. Spring provides the
`LoggerFactory` class to get a logger instance for the current class. You
can call various methods like `info`, `debug`, `error`, and so on at
appropriate places.

The Spring MVC controller method can be mapped with a distinct URL so that it can be triggered by a matching request URL pattern. The `showLandingPage()` method is a controller method in the previous case. It is mapped with the URL / and this means the `http://localhost:8080/blogpress/` URL (considering you run the application in your local with the `8080` port and `blogpress` is the name of your application) will call this method.

This method returns a string, `home`, which represents the component from the presentation layer. Spring MVC is flexible enough to choose the desired presentation framework. So, it is absolutely unnecessary to use specific technology as your presentation layer. You can use **JavaServer Pages** (**JSP**s), Thymeleaf, or a UI framework such as Angular as your frontend for a Spring MVC web application.

In this chapter, we will use Thymeleaf to build the presentation layer.

Presentation layer with Thymeleaf

Thymeleaf is a template engine used to process various templates in XML, HTML, JavaScript, CSS, and plain TEXT on the server side. You might have a question: why Thymeleaf? We already have JSP. What are the benefits of using Thymeleaf over JSP?

The answer is, Thymeleaf is designed with a natural templating concept and provides a design prototype support without affecting the use of the template. In other words, due to its nature, Thymeleaf can be used by both developers and design teams without being locked-in or having a dependency between either of them.

Another good thing about Thymeleaf is that it is designed in accordance with web standards, mainly HTML5. This will make it easy for you to fully validate the templates if that is required.

How Thymeleaf works

For our blogging application, we will use the Thymeleaf HTML template. The very first step for working with Thymeleaf is to instruct Spring Boot so that it can make all the necessary configurations specific to Thymeleaf readily available for our application. Add the following entry in pom.xml:

```
<dependency>
  <groupId>org.springframework.boot</groupId>
  <artifactId>spring-boot-starter-Thymeleaf </artifactId>
</dependency>
```

Thymeleaf provides certain tags (a kind of JSP tags) to embed dynamic values into the template. We will first go through the bare minimum tags that we intend to use in our Blogpress application. The mechanism of inserting a dynamic value into the Thymeleaf template is different than what you might have seen in JSP tags, so it is quite vital to be familiar with it before starting to use it.

 You can see another starter for Thymeleaf. This is how Spring Boot makes the developer's life easy.

Dialects, processors, and expression objects

Dialects are a set (or group) of features that you use in your template, including pre- and post-processing logic and expression objects. Processing logic (of embedding the dynamic HTML and value in the template) is carried out by objects called a processor, while expression objects are used to describe standard expression for performing a specific operation. In short, processor objects deal with the DOM node or element, while expression objects are used to evaluate the expression.

Dialects can be used along with processors, or expression objects, or both. Let's see how a dialect can be declared and used in the template:

```
<!DOCTYPE html>
<html xmlns:th="http://www.Thymeleaf.org">

<span th:text="${name}">
```

In previous snippet, th is called the dialect prefix. It means that all attributes and tags provided by this dialect start with th:. This is a standard and out-of-the-box dialect, and it is just sufficient for most of our scenario. You can consider dialect similar to *Taglibs* in JSP.

You can define more than one dialect in your template. Additionally, you can create your own custom dialect with custom processing logic in custom processors.

The `text` attribute represents a processor that simply puts the value for the span while `${...}` describes the value expression object, which simply pulls the attribute value stored in the model. The following are the types of expression objects available in Thymeleaf:

- **Variable expression objects:** They are used to show the value of the model attribute. They are in the form of Spring **expression language** (**EL**). They can be described with the `${...}` syntax.
- **Selection expression object:** These are similar to expression objects but can only be applied to the previously selected object. They can be used with the `*{...}` syntax.
- **Message (i18n) expressions:** These are used for internationalization purposes and bringing language-specific messages. You can use the `#{...}` syntax.
- **Link (URL) expressions:** These are used to employ links dynamically. For example, form action, HREF, linking JS/CSS, or other static resources, and so on. Use the `@{...}` syntax for them.
- **Fragment expressions:** This represents a fragment of the template and can be reused in similar or other templates. They can be utilized with the `~{...}` syntax.

Next, we will see some of the processors that we are going to use in our following application. They can be used along with various expression objects listed as follows:

- `th:text`—This is used along with value expression objects to place dynamic text for HTML elements like `span`, `li`, `div`, and so on
- `th:value`—The value of the input element can be supplied with this processor
- `th:action`—This can be used to supply the action value to HTML form
- `th:href`—As its name suggests, this is used to provide an URL in the link (to import CSS) and tags in HTML
- `th:src`—This is used to provide source URL for script (and other such) elements in HTML dynamically
- `th:each`—This is used with `th:text` in the loop to construct repetitive HTML code, that is, rows of HTML tables
- **`th:if`** and `th:unless`—These are used to place dynamic values conditionally

Thymeleaf supports defining attributes and element names in HTML5 style. For example, instead of writing `th:text`, you can write `data-th-text` as an attribute in an HTML element, and it is considered a custom element in HTML5.

Why Thymeleaf is a natural template

We have seen the processors of standard dialect are placed as an attribute of HTML element. Because of this arrangement, the browser can render the Thymeleaf template as a correct HTML file, even before they are processed by the template engine.

This is quite possibly because the browser simply ignores them, considering them custom attributes, so there is no issue in displaying them. The same cannot be possible in the case of JSP. For example, the JSP with the following tag is not rendered in the browser:

```
<form:input name="name" path="name"/>
```

And if you write it with Thymeleaf, it will be as follows:

```
<input type="text" name="name" value="Nilang" th:value="${name}" />
```

The browser will display the preceding code perfectly. Additionally, Thymeleaf allows you to supply the (optional) value attribute (`Nilang` in our case), which will be displayed statically when run on the browser. When the same code is processed by the Thymeleaf template engine, the value will be substituted by evaluation of the `${name}` expression on the fly.

This is the reason why Thymeleaf is called a natural template engine. It allows the designer to work with the developer without producing dependency on either side.

Now, let's discuss which Thymeleaf templates we are going to use in our blog application. When you create a Spring Boot application, you will see a `templates` file in the `src/main/resources` folder. All our Thymeleaf templates reside there.

We are going to use following templates in our application:

- `header.html`: This template contains a common JS/CSS inclusion header, along with a navigation bar. It is included in all other templates.
- `home.html`: Shows home page content.
- `login.html`: Allows the user to login into the system.
- `user-page.html`: Once a blog user logs in, he will land on this page.
- `view-blog.html`: Opens a particular blog in read-only mode.
- `search.html`: Shows the search result.

- `new-blog.html`: A blog user or admin can create a new blog through this template.
- `manage-comments.html`: An admin user can approve/reject comments.
- `edit-blog.html`: Allows a blog user/admin user to edit the existing blog.
- `admin-page.html`: Once an admin user logs in, they will land on this page.

We will first add two templates—`home` and `header`. Before going further, let's see one more cool feature of Thymeleaf that we will use in our application. Just like JSP, you can include a template into another template. Additionally, Thymeleaf allows you to include only some portion (fragment) of the template instead of the whole template, which is not possible with JSP.

This is a great feature, as you can define common fragments in one template and include them in others. In our case, we have defined common header items in a `header.html` template as in the following snippet:

```
<!DOCTYPE html>
<html xmlns:th="http://www.Thymeleaf.org">
<head th:fragment="jscssinclude">
    <!-- Required meta tags -->
    <meta charset="utf-8">
    <meta name="viewport" content="width=device-width, initial-scale=1,
shrink-to-fit=yes">
    <!-- Bootstrap CSS -->
    <link rel="stylesheet" th:href="@{/css/bootstrap.min.css}">
    <link rel="stylesheet" th:href="@{/css/blogpress.css}">

    <script th:src="@{/js/jquery.min.js}" type="text/javascript"></script>
    <script th:src="@{/js/popper.js}" type="text/javascript"></script>
    <script th:src="@{/js/bootstrap.min.js}"
type="text/javascript"></script>

    <title th:text="${pageTitle}">Title</title>
</head>
<body>
  <div th:fragment="header_navigation">
    <div class="jumbotron text-center jumbotron-fluid"
        style="margin-bottom:0; padding:2rem 1 rem" >
        <h1>Blog Press</h1>
        <p>Let's do Blogging ..!</p>
    </div>
    <nav class="navbar navbar-expand-sm bg-dark navbar-dark">
        <button class="navbar-toggler" type="button"
            data-toggle="collapse" data-target="#collapsibleNavbar">
            <span class="navbar-toggler-icon"></span>
```

```
            </button>
            <div class="collapse navbar-collapse" id="collapsibleNavbar">
                <ul class="navbar-nav">
                    <li class="nav-item">
                        <a class="nav-link" th:href="@{/}">Home</a>
                    </li>
                </ul>
            </div>
        </nav>
      </div>
   </body>
   </html>
```

The fragment is defined by the `th:fragment` tag. You can see how Thymeleaf tags (with dialect prefix, processors, and expression objects) are used to import various static resources (JS/CSS) along, with adding a dynamic value to HTML elements (`${pageTitle}`, in our case).

We can include this header (which is defined as the fragment) in other templates. For example, in our `home.html` template, we have used it as follows:

```
<!DOCTYPE html>
<html xmlns:th="http://www.Thymeleaf.org">
  <head th:replace="header :: jscssinclude"></head>
  <body>
    <div th:replace="header :: header_navigation"></div>
    This is Home page
  </body>
</html>
```

The `th:replace` tag is used to refer the fragment code from other templates. You need to just put the name of the template (from where you are referring fragments) with two colons (`::`) and the name of the fragment (that you have defined with the `th:fragment` tag). This is how Thymeleaf allows you to refer a set of template codes as a fragment to other templates.

 We have defined another fragment, called `header_navigation`, which is referred to in the home template in the previous code snippet. It is used to show a navigation menu for our application.

At this moment, we also need to put static resources (JS/CSS) into our application. You will see a static folder in the project structure where all static resources should be placed. Spring Boot will consider everything in the static folder as a static resource. Create `css`, `img`, and `js` folders under the static folder and place the following resources in them:

- To the `css` folder, add the following:
    - `bootstrap.min.css`
- To the `js` folder, add the following:
    - `Bootstrap.min.js`
    - `Jquery.min.js`
    - `popper.js`

Now it is time to run our application to see the home page. You can build and deploy it on a server and access it with the `http://localhost:8080/blogpress` URL, and you will see the home page with a header and navigation bar. Next, we have to make our application secure with Spring security. Security is an important aspect and core concern for any application today.

Making the application secure with Spring Security

Our Blogpress application has a login functionality to access certain pages and functionalities that are not accessible by a normal (anonymous) user. It requires a good amount of effort to incorporate it if we build authentication and authorization on our own from scratch. Spring provides a feature called Spring Security, which does exactly what we need here.

Spring Security is an open source, highly comprehensive, powerful, and customizable framework used to implement authentication and authorization in J2EE-based web applications. It is a sub-project (module) of the Spring Framework.

Before talking further, it is important to understand the difference between authentication and authorization.

Authentication is the process of **validating** or determining someone or something in what it claims to be. There are several mechanisms to perform authentication. The most straightforward way of performing authentication is to provide a username and password. Other ways include through LDAP, single sign-on, OpenId, and OAuth.

On the other hand, authorization is more related to the **permission** of the actions you are allowed to do. In short, authentication means **who you are** and authorization means **what can you do** in the system.

Spring Security provides many features out of the box, including authentication, authorization, protection against CSRF attack, servlet API integration support, Spring MVC integration, remember-me features, SSO implementation support, LDAP authentication support, OpenID integration, web service security support, WebSocket security support, Spring Data integration, and many more.

Though the latest version (at the time of writing this is 5.1.0) of Spring Security supports both XML and annotation support, you still need to do a good amount of configuration if you set it on your own. But you don't have to worry, as Spring Boot is with you.

Spring Boot also supports Spring Security integration. Just like integration with other modules, you need to add a required starter for Spring Security to work with Spring Boot. Add the following dependency in the pom.xml file:

```
<dependency>
  <groupId>org.springframework.boot</groupId>
  <artifactId>spring-boot-starter-security</artifactId>
</dependency>
```

As soon as you put the previously mentioned configuration in place, Spring Security becomes active and will not allow accessing even public pages of the application without valid credentials. When you hit http://localhost:8080/blogpress, you will see a login screen.

Spring Security with its default (auto) configuration, allows you to log in with a specific credential. The username will be user and password will be generated randomly by Spring Security and printed in the server log like this:

Using generated security password: 89ca7b55-6a5d-4dd9-9d02-ae462e21df81.

You can override the username and password in a property file. In the project structure, you will see the application.properties file in the src/main/resources folder. Just add following two properties to it:

```
spring.security.user.name=nilang
spring.security.user.password=password
```

Now you can access the application with the previously mentioned credentials, but you still need authentication for accessing even public pages. By default, Spring Security is activated with the default (or auto-) configuration, which secures all the endpoints. This is not we want. So we need to instruct Spring Security which endpoints (URLs) we want to make secure and which we do not.

For this, first, we need to disable the default security (auto-) configuration. There are two possible options here.

Excluding auto-configuration

Add an `exclude` attribute to the `@SpringBootApplication` annotation for the main `bootstrap` class, as in the following snippet:

```
@SpringBootApplication(exclude = { SecurityAutoConfiguration.class })
public class BlogpressApplication {

  public static void main(String[] args) {
    SpringApplication.run(BlogpressApplication.class, args);
  }
}
```

Alternatively, you can add the following property in the `application.properties` file:

```
spring.autoconfigure.exclude=org.springframework.boot.autoconfigure.securit
y.servlet.SecurityAutoConfiguration
```

You can take either of the previously described ways to disable or exclude the security (auto-) configuration. Excluding the auto-configuration is appropriate only in certain scenarios where you need to integrate the security provided by a custom provider.

Substituting auto-configuration

Another way of disabling the auto-security configuration is to surpass it with our own custom configuration. Spring Security is a highly customizable framework and provides a fine-grained access mechanism based on URL and role.

To substitute auto-configuration with custom configuration, we need to specify the configuration class, as in the following snippet:

```
@Configuration
@EnableWebSecurity
@ComponentScan("com.nilangpatel.blogpress")
```

```
public class WebSecurityConfig extends WebSecurityConfigurerAdapter {
  .....
}
```

The `WebSecurityConfig` custom configuration class extends the `WebSecurityConfigurerAdapter` abstract class. This abstract class has certain extension points (in the form of abstract methods for which you can provide your custom implementation) and default implementation for the common tasks.

Since our class (`WebSecurityConfig`) provides custom configuration, we have to define it with the `@Configuration` and `@ComponentScan("com.nilangpatel.blogpress")` annotations. You need to give the package (where the custom configuration class resides) name into the `@ComponentScan` annotation.

The `@EnableWebSecurity` annotation is also important because we are disabling the default security configuration. Without it, our application will not start. We will now override one method of the `WebSecurityConfigurerAdapter` class that will be used to define the web configuration and add one additional method that will be used to define user details:

```
@Override
public void configure(WebSecurity web) throws Exception {
  web.ignoring().antMatchers("/js/**");
  web.ignoring().antMatchers("/css/**");
}
```

Spring Security by default applies to all requests—including static resources as well. This method is used to define an escape sequence for static resources. Spring Security will block them by default if they are not configured to be ignored here. In the absence of the previously discussed configuration, the static resource will not be loaded into the browser so you will not see any `javascript`, `css`, or `images` files. Next, we will add user's details to the same class as follows:

```
// create users and admin
@Autowired
public void configureGlobal(AuthenticationManagerBuilder auth) throws
Exception {

  BCryptPasswordEncoder encoder = passwordEncoder();
  auth.inMemoryAuthentication() .passwordEncoder(encoder)
.withUser("blogUser1").password(encoder.encode("password")).authorities("US
ER")
    .and()
.withUser("blogUser2").password(encoder.encode("password")).authorities("US
ER")
```

```
    .and()
.withUser("blogAdmin").password(encoder.encode("password")).authorities("AD
MIN");
}

@Bean
public BCryptPasswordEncoder passwordEncoder() {
    return new BCryptPasswordEncoder();
}
```

The `configureGlobal` method is used here to create a username with a password and role on the fly. It is declared with the `@Autowired` annotation so that Spring will inject the object of the `AuthenticationManagerBuilder` class in it.
The `AuthenticationManagerBuilder` class is used to provide the implementation of `AuthenticationManager`. As we have seen, Spring Security allows various mechanisms for authentication, and provides an implementation of `AuthenticationManager` for each of those mechanisms, such as in-memory authentication, LDAP authentication, JDBC authentication, OAuth authentication, and so on.

To make the thing simple, we have used in-memory authentication, which simply puts the user details in memory. This is not ideal for production, however. You are supposed to create user details in a database, and Spring Security is flexible enough to support this scenario as well.

Making the password secure is the most important, core part of any security framework, and hence Spring Security provides an encoding mechanism for this. It provides `BCryptPasswordEncoder` , which is an encoder class used to encode the password. It uses the **bcrpt** algorithm for encoding, which is a very strong password hashing routine widely used in Spring Security today.

 Spring Security also provides a class called `NoOpPasswordEncoder` in case you wish to store the password as it is (in plain text form). However, starting with version 5, Spring has decided to deprecate it and it may be removed in future releases. This is because putting passwords as plain text is not encouraged and can lead to a security breach. So you should never use the `NoOpPasswordEncoder` class (not even for any POC).

We have used a method named `configureGlobal` , but you are absolutely free to choose the one you feel appropriate.

Next, we will override one more method, which is an extension point, to provide custom security settings for each of the endpoints we have in our application, as in the following snippet:

```
@Override
protected void configure(HttpSecurity http) throws Exception {
  http.authorizeRequests()
    .antMatchers("/").permitAll()
    .antMatchers("/controlPage/")
    .hasAnyAuthority("ROLE_USER","ROLE_ADMIN")
    .and()
  .formLogin().loginPage("/login").permitAll()
    .defaultSuccessUrl("/controlPage")
    .failureUrl("/login?error=true")
    .and()
  .logout()
    .permitAll().logoutSuccessUrl("/login?logout=true");
}
```

We override the configure method (having `HttpSecurity` as a method parameter) to provide custom security configuration. If you open the original configure method of the parent class (`WebSecurityConfigurerAdapter`), it looks like the following snippet. Just putting the reference of the original method side by side will help you to understand what custom configuration we provide for our Blogpress application:

```
protected void configure(HttpSecurity http) throws Exception {
  http.authorizeRequests()
    .anyRequest().authenticated()
    .and()
    .formLogin().and()
    .httpBasic();
}
```

The default `configure` method simply authenticates all requests. It allows a user to authenticate with a form-based login and supports HTTP basic authentication. This is the reason we were getting a default login page as soon as Spring Security was activated in Spring Boot with no custom security configuration.

 In the Spring Security paradigm, `principal` refers to the username while `authorities` refers to the roles a user has. Keeping these terminologies in mind while working with Spring Security will help you understand the concepts better.

Now, let's see what customization we did in our overridden configure method as follows:

- The `antMatchers("/", "/home").permitAll()` line will allow the listed URLs without any authentication. It means the / (default URL —`http://localhost:8080/blogpress`) URL is accessible publicly. You can provide any further URLs in comma-separated lists here.
- The next `antMatchers("/controlPage").hasAnyAuthority("ROLE_USER","ROLE_ADMIN")` line makes the `/controlPage` URL accessible to any user with the ROLE_USER or ROLE_ADMIN roles.
- The next `formLogin().loginPage("/login").permitAll()` line allows us to set the login page URL. We kept the `/login` URL, but you can give any custom login URL. Since the login page should be accessible publicly, the `permitAll()` method will make the login URL accessible to all.
- Once Spring Security authenticates the user, it will send to a success page. You can configure the custom success page with `defaultSuccessUrl("/controlPage")`. In this case, the success URL is `/controlPage`.
- Similarly in case authentication fails, it should send to the error page. The `failureUrl("/login?error=true")` line will send the flow to the `/login` URL (along with parameters) on failed authentication.
- Finally, the `permitAll().logoutSuccessUrl("/login?logout=true")` line configured the logout page. Once a user logs out, the system will trigger the `/login` URL (along with parameters).

We have added our custom security configuration; now it is time to add methods in Spring MVC corresponding to each URL we mentioned in the previous Spring configuration. Add the following methods in Spring MVC:

```
@GetMapping("/")
  public String showHomePage(Model model) {
    logger.info("This is show home page method ");
    setProcessingData(model, BlogpressConstants.TITLE_HOME_PAGE);
    return "home";
  }
@GetMapping("/controlPage")
  public String showControlPage(Model model) {
    logger.info("This is control page ");
      setProcessingData(model,
BlogpressConstants.TITLE_LANDING_CONTROL_PAGE);
      return "control-page";
  }
```

```
@GetMapping("/login")
  public String showLoginPage(@RequestParam(value = "error",required =
false) String error,
      @RequestParam(value = "logout", required = false) String logout,Model
model) {
    logger.info("This is login page URL ");
    if (error != null) {
      model.addAttribute("error", "Invalid Credentials provided.");
    }
    if (logout != null) {
      model.addAttribute("message", "Logged out");
    }
    setProcessingData(model, BlogpressConstants.TITLE_LOGIN_PAGE);
    return "login";
  }
```

The `showHomePage` method is responsible for showing the home page when a user clicks on the **Home** link from navigation. It is associated with / URL and will show the `home.html` (Thymeleaf) template. In addition, this method is also called when you hit the `http://localhost:8080/blogpress` URL.

The `showControlPage` method is associated with the `/controlPage` URL and will be called on successful authentication. This method drives the user to the `control-page.html` (Thymeleaf) template, which shows administrative links based on the role. For example, a user with the `ROLE_ADMIN` role can see the links for **Manage Blogs** and **Manage Comments,** while a user with the `ROLE_USER` role will see only the **Manage Blogs** link.

The `showLoginPage` method represents the login functionality. It is associated with the `/login` URL. It stores messages based on parameter values along with the page title attribute, which is used to display a title of the page (in the `header.html` template). Finally, it opens the `login.html` template.

Apart from these methods, the following methods are added, which stores model attributes that are available in Thymeleaf templates directly using the `${}` expression:

```
@ModelAttribute("validUserLogin")
public boolean isUserLoggedIn() {
   return SecurityContextHolder.getContext().getAuthentication() != null &&
SecurityContextHolder.getContext().getAuthentication().isAuthenticated() &&
       //when Anonymous Authentication is enabled
       !(SecurityContextHolder.getContext().getAuthentication() instanceof
AnonymousAuthenticationToken);
}

@ModelAttribute("currentUserName")
```

```
public String getCurrentUserName() {
    return
SecurityContextHolder.getContext().getAuthentication().getName();
}
@ModelAttribute("hasAdminRole")
  public boolean checkIfUserHasAdminRole(){
    return checkIfUserHasRole(BlogpressConstants.ROLE_ADMIN);
  }
@ModelAttribute("hasUserRole")
  public boolean checkIfUserHasUserRole(){
    return checkIfUserHasRole(BlogpressConstants.ROLE_USER);
  }
private boolean checkIfUserHasRole(String roleName) {
    boolean hasUserRole =
SecurityContextHolder.getContext().getAuthentication().getAuthorities().str
eam()
                .anyMatch(r -> r.getAuthority().equals(roleName));
    return hasUserRole;
  }
```

The `isUserLoggedIn` method checks if any user is currently logged in. It will be called by the `${validUserLogin}` expression in the Thymeleaf template. The `getCurrentUserName` method simply provides the current logged-in username. The `checkIfUserHasUserRole` and `checkIfUserHasAdminRole` methods simply check the respective roles. You can see how the `SecurityContextHolder` class is used to fetch user login details. This class is responsible to store currently authenticated user's details, also known as principle.

We have gradually shaped up the Blogpress application, and it is now equipped with Spring MVC, Thymeleaf, and Spring Security. All this rapid development is possible with the help of Spring Boot. The next part we are going to develop is a data layer, which is the most important and crucial part of our application. As we mentioned, we will construct the data layer in **Elasticsearch**.

Storing data with Elasticsearch

Elasticsearch is a highly scalable and full-text search open source RESTful searching, indexing, and analytics engine developed on top of **Lucene**. It is one of the most popular search engines for building enterprise applications today. It can save, search, and analyze data in big volumes very quickly. Mainly, it is used for applications where complex searching is required.

It is developed in Java and provides near real-time results. It is designed to work in a distributed environment to provide high availability and scalability. It is document-oriented, stores complex entity structures in JSON format, and provides a web interface to interact with.

Elasticsearch is mainly used in applications when searching for a large amount of matching products (for example, e-Commerce), using auto-complete features for partially typed input, or analyzing the huge quantities of raw data stored in a distributed fashion.

Artifacts

It is important to understand a few terminologies that are frequently used with Elasticsearch, which will help you to understand how Elasticsearch is built and how it works. They are the core of Elasticsearch. We will look at each of them in detail.

Documents

The basic unit of information that is stored in Elasticsearch is called a **document**. You can consider a document equivalent to an entity in the **relational database management system** (**RDBMS**). For example, a document can be created for an employee, another document is for a salary, and so forth. A document will be indexed by the Elasticsearch engine, and they are presented in JSON format. Each document is associated with the document type. You can relate a document type with a **Plain Old Java Object** (**POJO**) class while a document as an object of POJO class.

Indexes

An index is a group of documents having a similar structure. You can define an **index** for employee data, another for salary data, and so on. An index can be identified by a name associated with it. An index name is used for indexing, searching along with CRUD operations for the documents it comprises. You can define as many indexes as you want. An index is always independent of another index. A group of indexes is referred to as indices in Elasticsearch.

Prior to version 6.0.0, Elasticsearch allowed the creation of multiple document types for a given index. For example, you can create document types for users and employees (or even more) for index organization. Starting with version 6, Elasticsearch put a restriction of allowing only one document type for a given index. So, you need to create a separate index for each of the document types.

Clusters and nodes

Elasticsearch is a distributed system, means it can scale horizontally and runs on more than one server to handle a huge amount of data with optimal speed. The network of such servers is called a **cluster,** where as the single server is referred to as a node.

Nodes and clusters are both identified by name. For nodes, Elasticsearch generates a default random **universally unique identifier** (**UUID**) on startup. If you wish, you can change the default name. The node name is important as it will help to administer the servers associated with the node name.

The cluster name is used by a node to join it. By default, all nodes are associated with the cluster with the `elasticsearch` name. You can create as many nodes as you want for a given cluster.

Shards and replicas

Elasticsearch stores data in the form of documents, which are grouped into an index. In the case of a huge amount of data, the number of documents in a single index may cross the limit of the underlying hardware capacity. For example, more than a trillion documents stored in a single index may need up to **100 GB** of space, which it may not be possible to store in a single node.

As a solution to this problem, Elasticsearch provides a mechanism to break the index into multiple pieces; each can be considered a separate index and can be stored in multiple nodes. The pieces of an index are called **shards**. This will also improve search performance as the search can be performed simultaneously on multiple shards.

Replica, as its name suggest, is a copy of shards. They are created for fail over; in case one shard is down or goes offline, a replica will be used to provide service and make the system highly available.

In short, an index can be divided into multiple shards; each shard can have zero or more replicas. So each index has one primary shard, along with zero or more replica shards. By default, Elasticsearch associates five primary shards for each index along with one replica (as of the latest stable version 6.4.1).

For our Blogpress application, we will keep the default values, a single node having an index with default shards and replica settings. The name of the index will be `blog`.

Interacting with Elasticsearch

Elasticsearch provides a way to interact with it for searching, indexing, and performing other CRUD operations. It provides a RESTful API for the interaction, so you can use various HTTP methods (`GET`, `POST`, `PUT`, `DELETE`, and so on) to deal with any operation on Elasticsearch.

Elasticsearch does not maintain the state of the request, and hence each request is independent, and information is exchanged in JSON format. Various HTTP methods are used to perform CRUD operations on Elasticsearch. For example, a `GET` method is used to retrieve the data, while `PUT`, `POST`, and `DELETE` are used to update or delete records.

Since Elasticsearch exposes REST APIs, you can use any REST client (for example, **Postman**) to work with it. Furthermore, to analyze and visualize the data, Elasticsearch provides another free and open source tool called **Kibana**. It provides a simple browser-based interface to perform search, view, and other CRUD operations along with rich data analysis, presented in a variety of tables, charts, and map-like memory, as well as disk utilization, indices, and document information. It also helps to manage the indices and document types, perform CRUD operations for document data, and so on.

Installation

Let's first install Elasticsearch. Download the Elasticsearch ZIP bundle from `https://www.elastic.co/downloads`. Unzip it in your local drive and run `bin/elasticsearch`. By default, it will be available on the `9200` port. Once up and running, you can access it with `http://localhost:9200`.

You can download and install Kibana from the same `https://www.elastic.co/downloads` URL. Unzip the bundle and run `bin/kibana`. You can access Kibana on the `5601` port, that is, `http://localhost:5601`.

 Elasticsearch also provides MSI Installer for Windows, which is a straightforward way to install Elasticsearch on a Windows machine.

Elasticsearch RESTful API

Next, we quickly look at some of the APIs to perform various activities on Elasticsearch. Since Elasticsearch provides REST interface to interact with, you can use any REST client, such as Postman. Alternatively, you can use **Kibana Dev Tools** to execute REST calls. There is a small difference between them.

We will understand various RESTful API by taking an example of a `student` entity. The purpose is to explain how to create a `students` index; create the `student` document type; add, update, and delete `student` data; and delete the document type and index.

Creating an index – students

With your REST client (Postman), enter the following:

- **URL:** `http://localhost:9200/students`
- **Method:** PUT
- **Type:** JSON (application/json)
- **Body:**

```
{
}
```

With Kibana, go to the **Dev Tools** option in Kibana and type the following script:

```
PUT students
{

}
```

You will see the following output:

```
2 ▾ {
3      "acknowledged": true,
4      "shards_acknowledged": true,
5      "index": "students"
6 ▴ }
```

We have created a `student` index without any explicit settings, so Elasticsearch has created the index with default settings—five shards and one replica. You can see these details in Kibana from the **Management** option. In case you wish to give the precise number of shards and replicas (instead of the default five and one), you can add the JSON setting in the body while creating the `student` index as follows:

With REST client (Postman), enter the following:

- **URL:** `http://localhost:9200/students`
- **Method: PUT**
- **Type: JSON (application/json)**
- **Body:**

```
{
    "settings" : {
        "index" : {
            "number_of_shards" : 3,
            "number_of_replicas" : 2
        }
    }
}
```

With Kibana, go to **Dev Tools** and type the following script:

```
PUT student
{
    "settings" : {
        "index" : {
            "number_of_shards" : 3,
            "number_of_replicas" : 2
        }
    }
}
```

In the previous case, the index is created with three shards and two replicas. This is how you can specify particular settings while creating an index in Elasticsearch.

Creating a document type – student

The very next thing in the sequence after creating an index is the creation of the document type. We will create a document type named `student` within the `students` index. Again, it can be done with REST client or with Kibana. We will see both options in detail.

With REST client (Postman), enter the following:

- **URL**: `http://localhost:9200/students/_mapping/student`
- **Method**: **POST**
- **Type**: **JSON (application/json)**
- **Body**:

```
{
    "properties":{
      "id":{"type":"long"},
      "name":{"type":"text"},
      "standard":{"type":"integer"},
      "division":{"type":"text"},
      "gender":{"type":"text"}
    }
}
```

With Kibana, go to **Dev Tools** option and add the following script:

```
PUT students/_mapping/student
{
  "properties": {
    "id":{"type":"long"},
    "name":{"type":"text"},
    "standard":{"type":"integer"},
    "division":{"type":"text"},
    "Gender":{"type":"text"}
    }
}
```

You can use either of these options to create the document type. We have created the `student` document type with ID, name, standard, division, and gender properties within the `students` index. Our structure is ready to add the data into Elasticsearch. Next, we will see how to insert the data for `student` type that we have defined.

 Prior to version 6, Elasticsearch allows creating multiple document types in the same index. Starting with 6, they make a restriction of creating only one document type within that index.

Adding a document (student data)

With REST client (Postman), enter the following:

- **URL**: `http://localhost:9200/students/student/1`
- **Method**: PUT
- **Type**: JSON (application/json)
- **Body**:

```
{
    "name":"Nilang",
    "standard":3,
    "division":"B",
    "gender":"M"
}
```

With Kibana, go to the **Dev Tools** option and type the following script:

```
PUT students/student/1
{
    "name":"Nilang",
    "standard":3,
    "division":"B",
    "gender":"M"
}
```

You can verify the inserted data with the following REST API.

Reading a document (student data)

With REST client, enter the following:

- **URL**: `http://localhost:9200/students/student/1`
- **Method**: GET

With Kibana, enter the following:

```
GET students/student/1
```

You will get the following JSON as an output:

```
{
    "_index": "students",
    "_type": "student",
    "_id": "1",
```

```
    "_version": 1,
    "found": true,
    "_source": {
        "name": "Nilang",
        "standard": 1,
        "division": "B",
        "gender": "M"
    }
}
```

First, it shows the index and document type. The _id attribute represents the ID that we supplied in the `http:/localhost:9200/students/student/1` URL while creating the data. If you use any existing _id, Elasticsearch will simply update that record with current values. The _version attribute represents the number of times the records are updated. The _source attribute represents the data that we supplied.

Updating a document (student data)

To update the data, the same syntax is used as an add document. While adding, the ID is not present in the system, if present, the existing data will be updated with the value provided. For example, the following command will update existing students' record having _id equal to five.

With a REST client (Postman), use the following:

- **URL**: `http://localhost:9200/students/student/5`
- **Method**: POST
- **Type**: JSON (application/json)
- **Body**:

```
{
    "name":"Robert",
    "standard":6,
    "division":"C",
    "gender":"M"
}
```

With Kibana, go to the **Dev Tools** and execute the following query:

```
PUT students/student/5
{
    "name":"Robert",
    "standard":6,
    "division":"C",
```

```
    "gender":"M"
}
```

Inserting and updating operations use similar syntax and if you try to add the record with an ID that already exists, then that record will be updated by mistake. To avoid this, you can use the `localhost:9200/students/student/1/_create` URL. This will throw an error if a record already exists with a `1` ID. Similarly, you can use `localhost:9200/students/student/1/_update` in case you wish to update the record. It will throw an error if a record does not exist while updating it.

 While adding the document record, if you do not provide `_id`, Elasticsearch will auto-generate one for you.

Deleting a document (student data)

Deleting the document is straightforward. You need to use the HTTP `DELETE` method. Just specify `_id` of the document you wish to delete, as follows.

With a REST client (Postman), do the following:

- **URL**: `http://localhost:9200/students/student/1`
- **Method**: **DELETE**

With Kibana, use the following:

```
DELETE students/student/1
```

Searching a query

Elasticsearch provides a search facility by passing `/_search` at the end of the URL. It can be applied after the server URL, the index, or the type. For example, in our case, if we want to search a student document having name equals to `nilang`, we have to use the query as follows.

With a REST client (Postman), use the following:

- **URL**:
  `http://localhost:9200/students/student/_search?q=name:nilang`
- **Method**: **GET**

With Kibana, use:

```
GET students/student/_search?q=name:nilang
```

Alternatively, you can use the following syntax for searching. It is quite useful for a complex search with multiple search criteria for multiple fields:

```
GET students/student/_search
{
   "query": {
       "match": {
         "name": "nilang"
       }
   }
}
```

Creating index and document types for Blogpress

After getting the basics of how the index and document type are created, along with inserting document data in Elasticsearch, we will create these artifacts for a Blogpress application. In this application, we need to store the data for blogs and comments. The blog and comments have a one- to-many relationship (one blog has multiple comments), we will create an index structure in such a way that multiple comments will be associated with a single blog.

Elasticsearch provides nested data types to index arrays of objects and maintains them as an independent document. We will maintain an array of comments for a single blog. We will give the index name of `blog` and set the document type, to `blog`. The following is a script you can run to create a `blog` index:

```
PUT blog
{
   "mappings":{
     "blog":{
       "properties":{
         "title":{"type":"text"},
         "body":{"type":"text"},
         "status":{"type":"text"},
         "createdBy":{"type":"text"},
         "createdDate":{"type":"date",
                 "format": "MM-dd-yyyy'T'HH:mm:ss"},
         "publishDate":{"type":"date",
                         "format": "MM-dd-yyyy'T'HH:mm:ss"},
```

```
        "comments":{
         "type":"nested",
         "properties":{
           "id":{"type":"text"},
           "parentId":{"type":"keyword"},
           "childSequence":{"type":"integer"},
           "position":{"type":"text"},
           "status":{"type":"keyword"},
           "level":{"type":"integer"},
           "user":{"type":"text"},
           "emailAddress":{"type":"text"},
           "commentText":{"type":"text"},
           "createdDate":{"type":"date",
                "format": "MM-dd-yyyy'T'HH:mm:ss"}
          }
         }
        }
       }
      }
     }
```

In the previous script, we created an index and document type together. The element next to `mappings` represents the name of the document type while the index name is with the `PUT` HTTP method (`blog` in our case). All properties are self-explanatory apart from the comments that are defined as the `nested` type, along with their properties. The format of the date can be set with a `format` attribute.

Elasticsearch integration with Spring Data

We will configure Elasticsearch as a database to provide various CRUD operations for Blogpress applications. We will use Spring Data for this integration. Spring Data provides an abstract layer for data access from various providers, such as a relational database, a non-relational database, a map-reduced framework, and cloud services.

For each of these data providers, Spring supplies a set of libraries to interact with, while maintaining the abstraction to interact with them in a symmetrical manner. Spring Data spans across various modules, including Spring Data Common, Spring Data JPA, Spring Data REST, Spring Data LDAP, Spring Data MongoDB, Spring Data JDBC, and many more. Spring Data Elasticsearch is one of them t provide data access with Elasticsearch search engines.

We will use the Spring Data Elasticsearch module for the Blogpress application. The very first thing is to make this module available in our application. Unsurprisingly, this can be done by defining a starter in `pom.xml` as follows:

```
<dependency>
    <groupId>org.springframework.boot</groupId>
    <artifactId>spring-boot-starter-data-elasticsearch</artifactId>
</dependency>
```

Elasticsearch provides a Java API to interact with it programmatically. Soon after you activate the above starter, the required JARs will be added in the classpath to access the Elasticsearch Java API. At this moment, we need to instruct the Spring Data Elasticsearch module about the cluster name, port, and hostname on which the Elasticsearch server is running. You can define these configurations in the `application.properties` file (in the `src/main/resource` folder) as follows:

```
elasticsearch.clustername=elasticsearch
elasticsearch.host=localhost
elasticsearch.port=9300
```

This is equivalent to defining a database URL, the driver class name, and credentials for database interaction with Spring Data. The next step is to define a configuration class, which basically uses the previous details and prepares the required artifacts to interact with Elasticsearch, as follows:

```
@Configuration
@EnableElasticsearchRepositories(basePackages =
"com.nilangpatel.blogpress.repository")
@ComponentScan(basePackages = { "com.nilangpatel.blogpress.config" })
public class ElasticDataConfig {

    @Value("${elasticsearch.host}")
    private String esHost;

    @Value("${elasticsearch.port}")
    private int esPort;

    @Value("${elasticsearch.clustername}")
    private String esClusterName;

    @Bean
    public Client client() throws Exception {

        TransportClientFactoryBean transportClientFactory = new
TransportClientFactoryBean();
        transportClientFactory.setClusterName(esClusterName);
        transportClientFactory.afterPropertiesSet();
```

```
        return transportClientFactory.getObject()
                .addTransportAddress(
          new TransportAddress(InetAddress.getByName(esHost), esPort));
    }

    @Bean
    public ElasticsearchTemplate elasticsearchTemplate() throws Exception
    {
        return new ElasticsearchTemplate(client());
    }

}
```

This class reads the cluster name, port, and host values defined in the
`application.properties` file with the `@Value` annotation. The `client()` method uses
the `TransactionClientFactory` object to read the configuration data and return an
object of the `TransportClient` class, which represents the client interface to interact with
Elasticsearch.

The next `elasticsearchTemplate()` method uses this client object and creates the
`ElasticsearchTemplate` object. Spring provides the data access template class for each of
the data providers. The object of the `ElasticsearchTemplate` class is initialized with the
object of the `TransportClient` class. This method is defined with the `@Bean` annotation so
that the object of `ElasticsearchTemplate` is accessible with the `@Autowired` annotation
to other classes.

This initialization happens when starting an application. The `ElasticsearchTemplate`
class is the single point of interaction of the Elasticsearch engine with Spring Data. The
`@EnableElasticsearchRepositories` annotation in this class is used to point the Spring
JPA repository package that we are going to define next. Before that, we will first define a
model class that represents a document in Elasticsearch.

Spring Data Elasticsearch model class

Spring Data facilitate the **Data Access Object** (**DAO**) layer implementation for the various
data providers. The DAO mechanism makes the system loosely coupled by providing data
access abstraction, allowing the changes in the underlying data provider without affecting
the business implementation.

It allows the interaction with the data layer in an object-oriented manner. It means you can create, read, update, and delete the data with an entity class object. This abstraction is also applicable for the Spring Data Elasticsearch module. You can access the data in the form of objects. For this, we need to define a model (entity) class that represents the data structure that we defined in Elasticsearch as follows:

```
@Document(indexName = "blog", type = "blog")
public class Blog {

  @Id
  private String _id;
  private String title;
  private String body;
  private String status;
  private String createdBy;
  @JsonFormat
     (shape = JsonFormat.Shape.STRING, pattern = "MM-dd-yyyy'T'HH:mm:ss")
  private Date createdDate;

  @JsonFormat
     (shape = JsonFormat.Shape.STRING, pattern = "MM-dd-yyyy'T'HH:mm:ss")
  private Date publishDate;
  @Field(includeInParent=true, type = FieldType.Nested)
  private List<Comment> comments;

  // Getter and setters for above properties
```

The model class is a POJO with a `@Document` annotation, which defines the index and document type name this class is associated with. The objects of the `Blog` class previously represent the document data for the `blog` index and the `blog` document in Elasticsearch. The `@Id` annotation is used to define a unique id for blog documents. You can relate it to the primary key in the relational database. The date fields are defined with the `@JsonFormat` annotation, which is used to define the desired date format.

The `@Field` annotation is used to define additional metadata about the field. For example, in the case of comments, it is defined as a `nested` type as there is no direct mapping of Elasticsearch `nested` types available in Java. For other properties, the Java types are directly mapped with Elasticsearch types. Next, we will define a DAO layer with Spring Data.

 The date format that we mentioned in the mapping script should be exactly matched with the date format defined in the POJO class with the `@JsonFormat` annotation. If not, the system will show an error while inserting the record.

Connecting Elasticsearch with Spring Data

Spring Data has a concept called a **repository** that is an abstraction of a data store. Designed to add an additional layer, it brings great power and flexibility by making the repository abstraction and providing the concrete implementation of repositories (with all boilerplate code) for each of the data providers.

For Elasticsearch, Spring Data provides a repository interface called `ElasticsearchRepository`. This interface (and its parent interface) has all the required methods to interact with Elasticsearch. To reap the benefits of Spring Data, we need to extend this interface so that Spring Data supplies concrete implementation on the fly automatically. Apparently, all the required CRUD methods are available in standard DAO out of the box.

Let's leverage Spring Data capabilities for Elasticsearch for the Blogpress application. First, let's define the custom repository interface that extends `ElasticsearchRepository<T, ID extends Serializable>`, where `T` represents an entity class and `ID` represents a unique ID in the entity class as follows:

```
public interface BlogRepository extends ElasticsearchRepository<Blog,
String>
```

The `Blog` entity class has `_Id` (a string) as a unique identifier (declared with the `@Id` annotation). Our DAO layer with all basic CRUD operations is ready. It is always a good idea to define the service class, presenting the service layer. So we will declare the `BlogService` service class as follows:

```
@Component
public class BlogService {
  @Autowired
  private BlogRepository blogRepository;
....
}
```

With the `@Autowired` annotation, Spring will inject the object of `BlogRepository` into our service class, which can be used to perform various CRUD operations. Next, we can start performing CRUD operations for blog data in Elasticsearch.

CRUD operations in Elasticsearch with Spring Data

The basic structure of DAO and the service layer is ready. We can now start performing CRUD operations. As we have seen, just by declaring a custom repository interface, Spring provides all basic CRUD operations in the DAO layer.

Adding blog data

First, we will create a new blog record. For that, add method in `BlogService` class as follows:

```
public void addUpdateBlog(Blog blog) {
    blogRepository.save(blog);
}
```

The object of `BlogRepository` is injected by Spring and can be used to perform an add operation. This service method should be called from Spring controller. Add the following methods in controller class to manage the functionality of adding (or updating) new blog:

```
@GetMapping("/showAddNew")
  public String showAddNew(Model model) {
    logger.info("This is addNew page URL ");
    setProcessingData(model, BlogpressConstants.TITLE_NEW_BLOG_PAGE);
    return "add-new";
  }
  @PostMapping("/addNewBlog")
  public String addNewBlog(@RequestParam(value = "title",required = true)
String title,
      @RequestParam(value = "body",required = true) String body,Model
model) {
    logger.info("Adding new blog with title :"+title );
    Blog blog = new Blog();
    blog.setTitle(title);
    blog.setBody(body);
    blog.setCreatedBy(getCurrentUserName());
    blog.setCreatedDate(new Date());
    blog.setPublishDate(new Date());
    blog.setStatus(BlogStatus.PUBLISHED.getStatus());
    blogService.addNewBlog(blog);
    return "home";
  }
```

The `showAddNew()` method simply opens the `add-new.html` Thymeleaf template.When a user clicks on the **Add New** link from navigation, this method will be called and will show this template where the user can add a new blog with a title and body.

The second method—addNew, which is declared with the `@PostMapping` annotation takes a `title` and `body` as request parameters, creates an object of a `Blog` type, sets those values and call the `addNewBlog()` method of service class. You can execute the following query in Kibana to see the inserted data in Elasticsearch:

```
GET blog/blog/_search
```

Reading blog data

Next is to show the blog entries on the home page in a tabular format. When a user clicks on it, the system will open the blog in am detailed view (showing the title, full body, and all comments). To list blogs on the home page, we will fetch the blog data from Elasticsearch programmatically. Add the following method in the `BlogService` class:

```
public List<Blog> getAllBlogs() {
    List<Blog> blogList = new ArrayList<Blog>();
    Iterable<Blog> blogIterable = blogRepository.findAll();
    Iterator<Blog> blogIterator = blogIterable.iterator();
    while(blogIterator.hasNext()) {
      blogList.add(blogIterator.next());
    }
    return blogList;
}
```

The `getAllBlogs()` method simply calls the `findAll()` method on `blogRepository` to get all blog entries. This service method can be called from the controller to show these data on the home page. Instead of a regular controller, we will use the REST controller to showcase how we can leverage the Spring REST controller to present the data. We will cover this in a short while, so keep reading.

 It is always advisable to use the repository method with pagination. Since the purpose of this chapter is to showcase various components and how they work, I have not used the pagination to make things simple.

Searching blog data

Since this is a blog application, search is an obvious feature. We will allow a user to search the blogs by matching the search text with blog title and body. We can search the documents by passing /_search at the end of the URL. Elasticsearch provides a Boolean query to search the data based on various conditions.

In our case, the search text should be matched with either title or body or both. It can be achieved through a Boolean search query as follows:

```
GET blog/blog/_search
{
  "query": {
    "bool": {
      "should": [
          { "match": { "title": "java" }},
          { "match": { "body": "java" }}
```

```
          ]
        }
      }
    }
```

The `should` criteria is equivalent to the *OR* condition. Elasticsearch provides the `must` criteria, in case if you want to search with the *AND* condition. You can specify as many attributes as you want. The string `java` is the search text. This query can be written programmatically in Java as follows:

```
QueryBuilder booleanQry = QueryBuilders.boolQuery()
                    .should(QueryBuilders.termQuery("title", searchTxt))
                    .should(QueryBuilders.termQuery("body", searchTxt));
    SearchResponse response =
elasticsearchTemplate.getClient().prepareSearch("blog")
            .setTypes("blog")
            .setQuery(booleanQry)
            .execute().actionGet();
```

We are creating a Boolean query and configure the search text with the title and body attribute. The search result will be returned back in JSON format with the `response` object. You can parse the JSON to get the desired output.

Adding comment data with Elasticsearch aggregation

The blog has been added to the system. Now a user can add a comment. So next, we will see how to add a comment. As discussed, the `Comment` document type is defined as a `nested` type in the blog document. It means the blog document contains an array of comment objects, making a one-to-many relationship. We also need to create a comment model class as follows:

```
public class Comment {
    private String id;
    private String blogId;
    private String parentId;
    private int childSequence;
    private String position;
    private String status;
    private int level;
    private String user;
    private String emailAddress;
    private String commentText;
    @JsonFormat
       (shape = JsonFormat.Shape.STRING, pattern = "MM-dd-yyyy'T'HH:mm:ss")
    private Date createdDate;
```

```
//Getter and Setter methods
. . . . .
}
```

Since this is nested within a blog, there is no need to define the @Document annotation as it is not directly associated with any document type. While adding the comment, there is certain metadata that needs to be taken care of, as follows:

- We are providing the comment with reply functionality. Once a user does reply to any comment, it will be added one level down, considering it as child comment. To maintain this, we use the level attribute, which simply shows at which level this comment is placed.
- The blogId attribute simply holds the ID of a blog with which this comment is associated. Since this is a nested object, in most of the cases, it is not required to have a parent document ID. But we are going to show the comment list to an admin user to moderate and reply back. To make comment administration simple, we have just added blogId in the comment.
- The parentId attribute holds the ID of parent comment, if it is placed as a reply, or else it will be zero.
- The childSequence attribute simply shows the sequence number at a particular level. For example, if there are total two replies (at the second level) and a user tries to add a third reply (at the second level), then the childSequence attribute will be three. This attribute is used to construct a value of the position attribute.
- The position attribute will be combination of level and childSequence. This is used to sort the comments so that they are displayed in the correct order for a given blog.

Since a comment is a nested type of blog, there is no such method to save only comments. Instead, we need to fetch all comments, add the new one to the associated blog, and then save the whole blog. Everything is straightforward, except getting the value of childSequence. We will see how to get maximum childSequence in a given level with the following aggregate query:

```
GET blog/blog/_search
{
  "query": {
    "match": {
      "_id": "1huEWWYB1CjEZ-A9sjir"
    }
  },
  "aggs": {
    "aggChild": {
```

```
"nested": {
  "path": "comments"
},
"aggs": {
  "filterParentId": {
    "filter": {
      "nested": {
        "path": "comments",
        "query": {
          "match": {
            "comments.parentId": "0"
          }
        }
      }
    },
    "aggs": {
      "maxChildSeq": {
        "max": {
          "field": "comments.childSequence"
        }
      }
    }
  }
}
}
}
}
```

Before we can understand the query, we need to look at what aggregation is. In Elasticsearch, an aggregation is a mechanism used to provide aggregated data on a search query. They are used to compose complex queries. They come under four categories, as follows:

- Bucketing
- Metric
- Matrix
- Pipeline

Each of these aggregation types can be used in a nested fashion, meaning it can be used as a sub-aggregation to another, to solve very complex queries. Now, let's go back to the query to find `childSequence` and understand it.

The very first `query` criteria matches the value against `blogId` (`_id`). Any attribute given to the `query` criteria in the beginning will match its value against the `blog` attribute. The next is the aggregate query that is applied to the `nested` document—`comments`. Each aggregate query has a name. The first aggregate query has the `aggChild` name.

Going further, the next aggregate query with the `filterParentId` name simply matches `parentId`, which is nothing but the parent comment ID. It is required to find `childSequence` under given a comment as a parent comment. For top-level comments, this must be zero. The last aggregate query with the `maxChildSeq` name simply finds the maximum of `childSequence`. It uses maximum criteria. Each `nested` aggregate query simply applies the search criteria to results given by the preceding aggregate query. You will get results of this query similar to the following:

```
"aggregations": {
  "aggChild": {
    "doc_count": 4,
    "filterParentId": {
      "doc_count": 2,
      "maxChildSeq": {
        "value": 3
      }
    }
  }
}
```

The query result contains other information, but we will only focus on `aggregation`. The result shows a document count at each aggregate query. The value of `maxChildSeq` is three means there are three comments at level one (top-level comment), so when a user adds a new (top-level) comment, `childSequnce` will be four.

This was the REST-based query. For the Blogpress application, we need to execute similar queries in the Java class. Elasticsearch provides Java APIs to perform anything that can be done through REST query. When we define a starter for Elasticsearch in Spring Boot, the required Elasticsearch JAR files are available in the classpath. To write the preceding query with Java APIs, we need to write a custom fetch method in our Elasticsearch repository.

Spring Data is an extensible framework, allowing us to provide customized implementation of a repository on top of what it provides out of the box. So first we will extend the Elasticsearch repository with following steps.

1. Define a custom repository interface called `BlogRepositoryCustom`.

2. The `BlogRepository` interface that we created initially should extend this interface, along with `ElasticsearchRepository<Blog, String>`, as follows:

    ```
    public interface BlogRepository extends
    ElasticsearchRepository<Blog, String>,BlogRepositoryCustom
    ```

3. Define the custom repository implementation class that implements the `BlogRepositoryCustom` interface as follows:

    ```
    @Repository
    public class BlogRepositoryCustomImpl implements
    BlogRepositoryCustom {

      private static Logger logger =
    LoggerFactory.getLogger(BlogRepositoryCustomImpl.class);
      @Autowired
      private ElasticsearchTemplate elasticsearchTemplate;
      ....
    }
    ```

This class must be declared with the `@Repository` annotation. We can define any custom method in this class. We want to write a method with an Elasticsearch Java API to find the maximum child sequence at a given level, so we will write it in this class as follows:

```
public int getCurrentChildSequence(String blogId,String parentCommentId) {
    int currentChildSeq=0;
    TermQueryBuilder termQueryBuilder = new
TermQueryBuilder("comments.parentId", parentCommentId);
    NestedAggregationBuilder aggregationBuilder =
AggregationBuilders.nested("aggChild",
"comments").subAggregation(AggregationBuilders.filter("filterParentId",
termQueryBuilder).subAggregation(AggregationBuilders.max("maxChildSeq").fie
ld("comments.childSequence")));
    TermQueryBuilder rootTermQueryBuilder = new TermQueryBuilder("_id",
blogId);
    SearchResponse response =
elasticsearchTemplate.getClient().prepareSearch("blog")
        .setTypes("blog")
        .setQuery(rootTermQueryBuilder)
        .addAggregation(aggregationBuilder)
        .execute().actionGet();
```

```
      if(response !=null) {
        if(response.getAggregations() !=null) {
          List<Aggregation> aggLst = response.getAggregations().asList();
          if(aggLst !=null) {
            Aggregation resultAgg = aggLst.get(0);
            if(resultAgg !=null) {
              //getMaxChildSequenceFromJson method parse the json to get max
  child sequence
              currentChildSeq =
  getMaxChildSequenceFromJson(resultAgg.toString());
            }
          }
        }
      }
      //Adding one to set next sequence
      currentChildSeq=currentChildSeq+1;
      return currentChildSeq;
    }
```

The `AggregationBuilders` class is used to construct an aggregate query. The Elasticsearch Java API is self-explanatory and simple. You can easily relate this Java API query with a REST query. We first create a nested aggregate query and then add a filter aggregate query as a sub-aggregation followed by a `max` aggregation.

The value of `blogId` is added with a `TermQueryBuilder` class. Finally, we get an Elasticsearch client from `elasticsearchTemplate` and initiate search by providing an index name (`blog`), a document type (`blog`), a root level query (for `blogId`), and at the end setting the aggregations. This Java API returns the aggregation JSON that we got for REST query, which you can process with a JSON API to get the desired result.

Reading comment data with Elasticsearch aggregation

Once comments are added, they must be visible when the user opens the blog. This scenario is straightforward. Since comments are nested objects of a blog, when we read a blog with the following API, all its comments are also available as part of the blog object:

```
Optional<Blog> blogObj = blogRepository.findById(blogId);
  if(blogObj.isPresent()) {
    return blogObj.get();
  }else {
    return null;
  }
```

The `findById` method is provided out of the box by a default repository implementation, available during runtime. We pass `blogId`, and it will fetch all details of the blog along with comments (as nested objects).

The second scenario for reading comment is the admin user opens the manage-comment page, where all comments are displayed for moderation purposes. In this case, the system will show all comments added to any of the blogs, so it is necessary to bring all comments from all blogs.

The first way of achieving this is to fetch all blogs, take the comments, and append them to build the comments list. But this is not an ideal solution as it requires many things to be done manually. We can use Elasticsearch aggregation queries to do this. By default, the `nested` objects cannot be fetched directly as a parent object, so it requires aggregation:

```
GET blog/blog/_search
{
   "aggs": {
     "aggChild": {
       "nested": {
         "path": "comments"
       },
       "aggs": {
         "aggSortComment": {
           "top_hits": {
             "sort": [
                {
                   "comments.createdDate": {
                     "order": "desc"
                   }
                }
             ],"from": 0,
             "size": 10
           }
         }
       }
     }
   }
}
```

This query has the `top_hits` aggregation, which simply lists all `nested` objects. We need the data in descending order of `createdDate` (recently added should be placed on top), so sorting criteria is added. The `from` and `size` criteria are used for pagination. The `from` criteria represents the offset from first record, while `size` shows the total record per page.

By default, `top_hits` will return three records if you have not provided the `size` value. Also, the maximum allowed size is 100 so while using `top_hits`, you have to use pagination.

This query returns the result. Aggregation data for full results is shown in the following snippet:

```
"aggregations": {
    "aggChild": {
      "doc_count": 7,
      "aggSortComment": {
        "hits": {
          "total": 7,
          "max_score": null,
          "hits": [
            {
              "_index": "blog",
              "_type": "blog",
              "_id": "Bsz2Y2YBksR0CLn0e37E",
              "_nested": {
                "field": "comments",
                "offset": 2
              },
              "_score": null,
              "_source": {
                "id": "e7EqiPJHsj1539275565438",
                "blogId": "Bsz2Y2YBksR0CLn0e37E",
                "parentId": "0",
                "childSequence": 2,
                "position": "1.2",
                "status": "M",
                "level": 1,
                "user": "Nilang Patel",
                "emailAddress": "nilprofessional@gmail.com",
                "commentText": "installatin of java. great blog",
                "createdDate": "10-11-2018T16:32:45"
              },
              "sort": [
                1539275565000
              ]
            },
            {
              .... Other JSON Objects, each represents comment data.
            }...
          ]
        }
    }
```

```
      }
    }
  }
```

You can write the previous query with the Elasticsearch Java API as follows:

```java
public List<Comment> getAllComments(int from, int size){

    NestedAggregationBuilder aggregation =
AggregationBuilders.nested("aggChild", "comments").
subAggregation(AggregationBuilders.topHits("aggSortComment").sort("comments
.createdDate", SortOrder.DESC).from(from).size(size));

    SearchResponse response =
elasticsearchTemplate.getClient().prepareSearch("blog")
        .setTypes("blog")
        .addAggregation(aggregation)
        .execute().actionGet();
    List<Aggregation> responseAgg = response.getAggregations().asList();
    //getAllCommentsFromJson method process the json and return desire
data.
    return getAllCommentsFromJson(responseAgg.get(0).toString());
  }
```

Again, this is self-explanatory. First, we are creating a nested aggregation query with `AggregationBuilders` and adding the sub-aggregation of the `top_hits` type, along with sorting criteria with the `from` and `size` settings. The process of getting a response is identical to what we used in the method to get the maximum child sequence.

In case we need to display comments with a specific status value, we can use the following query:

```
GET blog/blog/_search
{
  "_source": false,
  "aggs": {
    "aggChild": {
      "nested": {
        "path": "comments"
      },
      "aggs": {
        "aggStatsComment": {
          "terms": {
            "field": "comments.status",
            "include": "K"
          },
          "aggs": {
            "aggSortComment": {
```

```
                "top_hits": {
                  "sort": [
                    {
                      "comments.createdDate": {
                        "order": "desc"
                      }
                    }
                  ],
                  "from": 0,
                  "size": 10
                }
              }
            }
          }
        }
      }
    }
  }
}
```

The term aggregation query has been added which checks the value of the status field. You can use a wildcard (*) for matching criteria, for example, A* will match all statuses starting with A. The equivalent Java API appears as follows:

```
public List<Comment> getCommentsForStatus(String status,int from, int size)
{
    IncludeExclude includeExclude = new IncludeExclude(status, null);
    NestedAggregationBuilder aggregation =
AggregationBuilders.nested("aggChild", "comments").
subAggregation(AggregationBuilders.terms("aggStatsComment").
field("comments.status").includeExclude(includeExclude).
subAggregation(AggregationBuilders.topHits("aggSortComment").size(10).sort(
"com ments.createdDate", SortOrder.DESC))
    );

    SearchResponse response =
elasticsearchTemplate.getClient().prepareSearch("blog")
        .setTypes("blog")
        .addAggregation(aggregation)
        .execute().actionGet();
    List<Aggregation> responseAgg = response.getAggregations().asList();
    return getAllCommentsWithStatusFromJson(responseAgg.get(0).toString());
}
```

Updating and deleting comment data with Elasticsearch

Updating a `nested` object is straightforward. Elasticsearch does not provide a direct way to update a specific `nested` object. Instead, you need to fetch all the `nested` objects from the root document, find the particular `nested` object (possibly by some unique identifier), update it, assign the `nested` object list back to the root document, and save the root document. For example, we can update the status for specific comment (`nested`) objects of a blog with the following method. It is defined in the service class:

```
public void updateCommentStatus(String blogId,String commentId,
List<Comment> commentList, String updatedStatus) {
    if(commentList !=null) {
      for(Comment comment: commentList) {
        if(comment.getId().equals(commentId)) {
          comment.setStatus(updatedStatus);
          break;
        }
      }
        Blog blog = this.getBlog(blogId);
        blog.setComments(commentList);
        blogRepository.save(blog);
    }
}
```

Deleting of a comment is similar. Just remove the required comment object from the list and save the blog object to delete the comment.

Another way of achieving a one-to-many relationship in Elasticsearch is through the parent-child structure. However, it is slower than the `nested` objects. The only drawback with the `nested` object is whenever any `nested` object is updated, the root document needs to be re-indexed. But due to retrieval of data, this is comparatively fast, and the `nested` objects are preferred to the parent-child structure.

We have understood how to interact with Elasticsearch and fetch data. Next we will see how to display those data at the frontend.

Displaying data with RESTful web services in Spring

Spring provides RESTful web service implementations with its web MVC module. With each annotation, the creation of a REST web service is more or less like web MVC architecture. The RESTful web services can be built with the help of a REST controller. The noticeable difference between a web MVC and REST controller is the way they create the HTTP response.

A traditional web MVC uses various view technologies (such as JSP, Thymeleaf, and so on) to build a response, while the REST controller returns objects that are converted into JSON (or XML, based on the configuration), and finally sent as a HTTP response. For our Blogpress application, we will use RESTful services in the following two use cases:

- Showing blog lists on the home page
- Showing blog comments when a particular blog is open for view

To achieve this, we will write new controller class as follows:

```
@RestController
@RequestMapping("api")
public class BlogRESTController {

private Logger logger = LoggerFactory.getLogger(BlogRESTController.class);
@Autowired
private BlogService blogService;

@RequestMapping(value = "/listBlogs", method = RequestMethod.GET, produces
= MediaType.APPLICATION_JSON_VALUE)
public ResponseEntity<List<Blog>> getAllBlogJSON() {
    logger.info("getting all blog data in json format ");
    List<Blog> allBlogs = blogService.getAllBlogs();
    return new ResponseEntity<List<Blog>>(allBlogs, HttpStatus.OK);
  }
@RequestMapping(value = "/listAllComments", method = RequestMethod.GET,
produces = MediaType.APPLICATION_JSON_VALUE)
public ResponseEntity<List<Comment>> getAllCommentJSON() {
    logger.info("getting all blog data in json format ");
    List<Comment> allComments = blogService.getAllComments(0, 100);
    return new ResponseEntity<List<Comment>>(allComments, HttpStatus.OK);
  }
}
```

The REST controller must be defined with the `@RestController` annotation. Since we have two controllers now (one is the normal web MVC , and the second is the REST controller), we defined request mapping with `@RequestMapping` to differentiate the URL pattern.

The `@RequestMapping` annotation defines the method URL, HTTP method name and MIME type of the output this method produces. The `getAllBlogJSON()` method gets list of `Blog` objects and sends it with `ResponseEntity`, along with the HTTP response code. The `ResponseEntity` class represents the response body, header, and status code, and this class is used to prepare the HTTP response. To use it, the only thing required is to define it as return type of method (end point).

 Alternatively, the `@ResponseBody` annotation (at method level) can be used to produce a HTTP response. `ResponseEntity` does exactly same as `@ResponseBody` , but provides some additional features, including setting the HTTP response code so it is better.

The `ResponseEntity` type is generic, so you can send any type of object with it. Both methods return the objects of `Blog` and `Comment`, respectively. Spring automatically converts the object list into a JSON string and returns it as a HTTP body. The `MediaType` class provides various mime types. The first method is accessible with the`http://localhost:8080/api/listBlogs` URL, and the second method with `http://localhost:8080/api/listAllComments`.

Next we will see how to present this data with a presentation layer. For our Blogpress application, we used the Thymeleaf template to construct a view layer. Thymeleaf templates are processed at server side. We will use another template engine called **Mustache** for client-side processing.

Building a UI with the Mustache template

The Mustache is a web template available for many languages, like JavaScript, Ruby, PHP, Python, Perl, Android, C++, Java, and so on, with a language-specific implementation. In our Blogpress application, we will use Mustache for JavaScript, so we need to include `Mustache.js` in the Blogpress application. Let's first understand the use case where `Mustache.js` is appropriate.

Quite often, to show dynamic values in HTML, we mix the data with HTML fragments and then update the DOM markup to show the final output. The following is the sample example for this approach:

```
$("#addAddress").live('click', function(){;
        var oldAddress = "";//Assume that oldAddress value supplied from
server side.
        var newContent = "<div id='group2' class='accordion-group'>" +
                          "<input type='text' id='address' class='textbox-
input'"+ oldAddress +"/>"                        + "</div>";
        $("#accordion1").html(newContent);
   });
```

This kind of code not only creates a maintenance nightmare, but it mixes the UI and dynamic data logic together, thus causing tight coupling between them. This prevents the code being reused and breaks the separation of the concern principle.

The best solution for this kind of problem is to use some sort of HTML template. There are many client-side HTML template engines available today, Mustache.js is one of them, and we have chosen it to construct a few of the pages for our Blogpress application. Let's see how it works by taking a very simple example as follows:

```
<div id="studentSection"></div>
<script id="greeting_template" type="text/template">
    <div>
        Hello, <b><span>{{firstName}}</span></b>
<span>{{lastName}}</span>
        <div>
</script>
<script type="text/javascript">
        var template = $("#greeting_template").html();
        var student = {"firstName":"Nilang","lastName":"Patel"};
        var text = Mustache.render(template, student);
        $("#studentSection").html(text);
</script>
```

This example is self-explanatory. The template has been defined with <script> of the text/template type. With Mustache.js, we are reading the template and passing the student object. In the template, the {{...}} notation is used to insert dynamic values. This not only makes the code clear, but can accommodate any future change with ease.

`Mustache.js` is a logic-less template, which means it does not contain procedural statements such as if-else, for, and so on, but we can use tags to achieve some sort of loop and conditional. For our Blogpress application, we are using `Mustache.js` in the following two pages:

- **Home** page to show all blogs in list format with minimal information
- **Manage Comment** page where all comments are listed for moderation and reply for the admin user

First, we will deal with the home page where all blogs are shown in list format. The following is the code for the Mustache template on the home page:

```
<!-- Define the template -->
    <script id="blog_template" type="text/template">
      {{#blogs}}
       <div class="card bg-white mb-3">
         <div class="card-body">
         <h5 class="card-title">{{title}}</h5>
         <p class="card-text">{{body}}</p>
          <form th:action="@{/viewBlog}" method="post">
           <input type="hidden" name="blogId" value="{{id}}">
           <button type="submit" class="btn btn-primary">Read More
..</button>
          </form>
          </div>
          <div class="card-footer text-muted">
          By : <b>{{createdBy}}</b>    comments: <b>{{comments.length}}</b>
Published on <b>{{publishDateForDisplay}}</b>
          </div>
         </div>
        {{/blogs}}
      </script>
       <div class="container">
          <div class="blogpress-section" id="blogList">
          </div>
       </div>
    <script th:inline="javascript" type="text/javascript">
      jQuery(document).ready(function(){
        var blogData = {};
        var template = $("#blog_template").html();
        jQuery.get(/*[[@{/api/listBlogs}]]*/, function(data, status){
          blogData["blogs"] = data;
             var text = Mustache.render(template, blogData);
             $("#blogList").html(text);
          });
       });
    </script>
```

The first script tag defines the template with the `text/template` type. The `{{#blogs}}` and `{{/blogs}}` expressions are evaluated in two ways. If a blog key exists and has a false value or empty list (if it's a type of array), the HTML code in between will not be displayed. If it's true or a non-empty list (array), then it will render the in-between HTML.

In our case, we want to show the blog list with the `Mustache.js` template. The data is populated from a REST web service (which eventually calls a REST controller) through Ajax. If successful, the data is stored in the `blogData` object with `blogs` as a key. This key is used in the `Mustache.js` template (`{{#blogs}}` ....`{{/blogs}}`) to iterate the blog array. The individual attribute is placed with the `{{...}}` expression. For example, `{{body}}` will display a value of a body attribute from the blog object. `Mustache.render` takes the template and data, and produces the final output that is appended in `div` with the `blogList` ID.

We have used `th:inline` in the second script tag. This is a Thymeleaf tag. In case you need to substitute the value in the script tag, you need to define it with `th:inline`. The Thymeleaf value can be inserted with the `/*[[,,,]]*/` notation. In this case, we are passing a dynamic URL so we have used `@{/api/listBlogs}` inside `/*[ .. ]*/` (so that the final URL would be `http://localhost:8080/api/listBlogs`). This will look like the following screenshot:

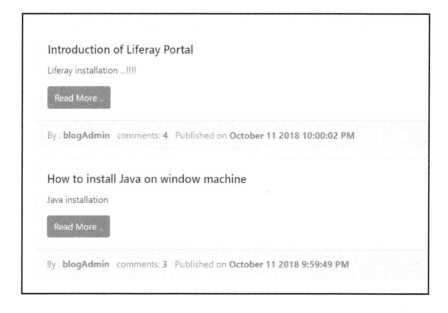

Another page is the managed comment page where the comments are displayed with the
`Mustache.js` template, as follows:

```
<script id="comment_template" type="text/template">
        {{#comments}}
         <div class="card bg-white mb-3">
           <div class="card-body">
          <div class="card-title">
            <div class="clearfix">
              <p class="mb-0">
                By <span class="float-left">{{user}}</span>
                On <span class="float-
right">{{createdDateForDisplay}}</span>
              </p>
            </div>
          </div>
          <p class="card-text">{{commentText}}</p>
           <div class="card-footer text-muted">
            {{#showApproveReject}}
             <div>
              <form th:action="@{/updateCommentStatus}" method="post"
id="updateCommentStatusFrm-{{id}}">
               <input type="hidden" name="blogId" value="{{blogId}}">
               <input type="hidden" name="commentId" value="{{id}}">
               <input type="hidden" name="commentStatus" id="commentStatus-
{{id}}" value="">
               <button type="button" class="btn btn-primary"
id="approveComment-{{id}}">Approve</button>
               <button type="button" class="btn btn-primary"
id="rejectComment-{{id}}">Reject</button>
              </form>
             </div>
            {{/showApproveReject}}
            {{#showReply}}
             <div>
                <form th:action="@{/replyComment}" method="post">
                <input type="hidden" name="blogId" value="{{blogId}}">
                <input type="hidden" name="commentId"
value="{{commentId}}">
                <button type="button" class="btn btn-
primary">Reply</button>
                </form>
             </div>
            {{/showReply}}
           </div>
          </div>
         </div>
        {{/comments}}
```

```
      </script>

        <div class="container">
          <div class="blogpress-section" id="commentList"></div>
        </div>

    <script th:inline="javascript" type="text/javascript">
      jQuery(document).ready(function(){
        var commentData = {};
        var template = $("#comment_template").html();
        jQuery.get(/*[[@{/api/listAllComments}]]*/, function(data, status){
          for (var i = 0; i < data.length; i++) {
              var comment = data[i];
              if(comment.status === 'M'){
                comment["showApproveReject"]="true";
              }
              if(comment.status === 'A'){
                comment["showReply"]="true";
              }
          }
        commentData["comments"] = data;
            var text = Mustache.render(template, commentData);
            $("#commentList").html(text);
          });
      });
    </script>
```

This template is similar to what we have seen for blog lists on the home page. The
additional thing here is the population of the showApproveReject and showReply
attributes with the true value. Since Mustache is a logic-less template, there is no direct
provision for a conditional statement, such as if-else. The only way of adding a condition is
with the {{#attribute}} ... {{/attribute}} expression, where it will check if an
attribute key is available and set to true.

In the **Manage Comment** page, each comment is listed for admin moderation. If a comment
status is **M** (moderate), the system shows buttons—**Approve** and **Reject**. If it is approved
(status **A**) then the system will show an option to **Reply** to the comment. With the
Mustache.js template, we cannot directly check the status value. So, two additional keys
(showApproveReject and showReply) are added in the comment object and set it to true,
based on the value of the status.

This will look like the following screenshot:

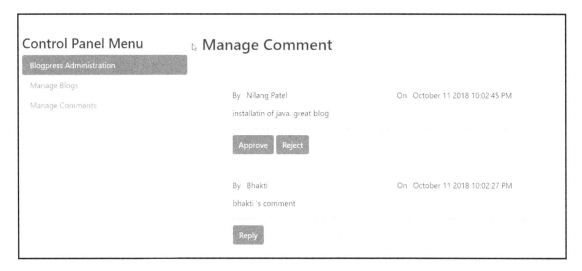

Summary

We have been on a long journey. There is no better way to build an application than taking a real-life scenario and learning about the underlying concepts, tools, and technology. In this chapter, we took a blog application and built various layers with a set of frameworks.

Taking the Spring Framework as a foundation, we began our journey with Spring Boot—a rapid tool to propel the development, with all the underlying configuration to be done with a kind of auto-mode. We framed the first layer with the Spring MVC web framework in conjunction with Thymeleaf. Being a natural template engine, Thymeleaf is another way of constructing a view layer. We built the authentication and authorization, a very important part of the application, with Spring Security.

We implemented the data source of the Blogpress application with Elasticsearch—an open source highly scalable search engine, mainly used for indexing and analyzing purposes. After exploring basic concepts, we learned how to create an index, document type, and add the document data, followed by how to search them in Elasticsearch, by taking a sample of a `student` entity.

Moving on further, we learned to create the data structure with a nested object for our Blogpress application. Inserting data into and retrieving it from the nested object with various searching and aggregation mechanisms were the main crux of the data layer we implemented in Elasticsearch.

Taking a further step to bridge the persistence layer developed in Elasticsearch with the front-facing layer in Spring MVC, we used the Spring Data module. Then we leveraged the extension capabilities of the Spring Data framework to implement customized queries with the Elasticsearch Java API. In the end, we saw how the client-side template engine `Mustache.js` is useful to solve the problem of mixing the logic of dynamic data with HTML fragments.

In the next chapter, we will focus on making the application secure with Spring Security. We will talk more about the integration of Spring Security with OAuth 2—a widely used protocol for authorization. We will also look at **Lightweight Directory Access Protocol (LDAP)** integration with Spring Security to build a central application that supports authentication and authorization.

4
Building a Central Authentication Server

Implementing security constraints is a core requirement of any application. Spring provides support to various aspects of applications, including security. One of the modules of the Spring framework, called Spring Security, was specially designed to meet security needs. It is a robust and highly adaptive framework, providing authentication and authorization out of the box.

Spring Security is the standard for securing any Spring-based application. We can see the real strength of Spring Security when integrating it with other systems. Its capabilities can be extended with ease, in order to meet custom requirements. This chapter will be devoted purely to Spring Security.

In the last chapter, we looked at the power of the Spring framework, with various modules and third-party libraries binding together in Spring Boot: a module built on top of the Spring framework, mainly designed for bootstrapping and developing a Spring-based application with auto configuration. We will continue to use it in this chapter, in order to build central authentication and authorization system.

Spring Security is a highly customizable framework, and we can integrate it with other systems that provide the data for access control. In this chapter, we will look closely at **Lightweight Directory Access Protocol** (**LDAP**) and **OAuth** integration with Spring Security.

We will cover the following interesting topics in this chapter:

- A basic understanding of LDAP and data structures
- Configuration of the LDAP server (Apache DS)
- Authentication in Spring Security with LDAP
- LDAP authorization with Spring Security
- OAuth fundamentals and various grant types

- Spring Security integration with OAuth
- Dual authentication with LDAP and OAuth in Spring Security
- OAuth implementation with a custom authorization server in Spring Security

Technical requirements

All the code used in this chapter can be downloaded from the following GitHub link: `https://github.com/PacktPublishing/Spring-5.0-Projects/tree/master/chapter04`. The code can be executed on any operating system, although it has only been tested on Windows.

LDAP

When email was introduced and started to be used in corporations, one challenge was to look up the email address of someone that had never communicated with you. It required some sort of central repository for searching the email addresses of other people within the organization.

Necessity is the mother of invention. The need for a central data depot brought companies like Microsoft, Lotus, Netscape, and IBM together, and they defined a standard called **LDAP**. It is a protocol for accessing data stored in a directory structure over the network.

The LDAP server, which holds and indexes the data in a hierarchical manner, can be accessed by LDAP-aware clients. The data can be filtered to select a particular person or group stored in a different entity. For example, imagine searching for all employees located in Chicago that are from the admin department and have been working for more than three years, and receiving their full name, designation, and email address. This is quite possible with LDAP.

Apart from contact information, LDAP can also be used to store access control data, which can then be used to perform authentication and authorization. We will start by covering the basics of LDAP and how to construct a data structure with it.

What is LDAP?

LDAP is an industry standard for accessing and managing hierarchical information stored in a directory structure over the network. LDAP has been in use for quite a long time. Nowadays, it is mainly used to build an authentication system; however, that is by no means its only purpose. LDAP can also be used to store any kind of information that needs to be accessed centrally (for example, emails or contact information in an organization).

The main motive for storing user (or any other) information, like usernames, emails, passwords, and so on, in one place, is to provide administration and maintenance support with ease. For example, rather than handling the user list for each subgroup separately in an organization, LDAP can be used to manage them as a central repository, accessible from anywhere in the network. There are certain use cases where LDAP is the perfect fit, as follows:

- Allowing a user to log in with the same credentials in multiple applications, like logging in on an intranet and on your local machine.
- Providing role-based access to a group of users; for example, accessing a specific page on the intranet site, or accessing a document in a document management system.
- Collecting user contact details and making them available globally, so that any user in the organization can access them.

LDAP is a way to access the structured information stored in directories. For this, it follows the client-server model, where data is stored on the LDAP server and the client can raise a request to access required information (through the LDAP API).

The information stored in an LDAP service is not intended to be altered upon each access, which makes that LDAP is a write once and read many times form of service. For example, LDAP would not be appropriate for maintaining the transaction records of an online shopping application, considering the fact that those records change with every operation. However, LDAP can be used to maintain data that changes less frequently, like user accounts, user addresses, and so on.

 The data stored on the LDAP server is not in a relational form; rather, it is hierarchical. However, LDAP uses the database to store the information internally, but presents it in a hierarchical manner.

Along with defining how to access the data in the directory service, LDAP also defines how the data is presented. To understand this data information model, it is essential to understand certain terms used in LDAP. This will not only help you to get a better idea of how it works, but will also illustrate how to create and search for the data in LDAP:

- **Directory information tree** (**DIT**): As we discussed, the LDAP server stores the information in a hierarchical (or a tree) form. This tree is called a directory information tree.
- **Entry**: As trees have nodes, the nodes in the DIT are called entries. The information that is stored within the entry is in the form of a key-value pair. Each entry has one parent entry (except for the root entry) and zero or more child entries. A child entry is a sibling of its parent's other child entry.
- **Root/base/suffix**: The top entry in DIT is called the root, base, or suffix.
- **Distinguished name** (**DN**): Each entry in DIT should be recognized by a unique identifier. This unique identifier is called a distinguished name. Generally, it is a string consisting of one or more comma-separated key-value pairs, which together uniquely distinguish the node (entry) in the tree. For example, the string `dc=nilangpatel, cd=com` could be the DN for the root entity.
- **Relative distinguished name** (**RDN**): A string that uniquely distinguishes the entity relative to its parent is called a relative distinguished name. The DN uniquely identifies the entity globally, while the RDN uniquely identifies the entity among its siblings.
- **Object class**: Each entity is comprised of one or more `objectClasses`. Each object class has a name and zero or more attributes. The `objectclass` is considered a container for attributes, and it will control what types of attributes can be added to the entity.
- **Attribute**: The attribute is part of the `objectclass`. It has a name and a value. It also has an abbreviation or alias.

The following is a list of a few attributes (along with their object classes) that we are going to use in this chapter:

Attribute name	Alias name	Description	Object class
dc	domainComponent	Any part of a domain name; for example, domain.com, domain, or com	dcObject
o	organizationName	Organization name	organization
ou	organisationalUnitName	Department or any subgroup	organizationUnit

cn	common name	Name of the entity	`person, organizationalPerson,` `organizationalRole, groupOfNames, applicationProcess,` `applicationEntity, posixAccount, device`
sn	surname	Surname or family name	`person`
uid	userid	Username or other unique value	`account, inetOrgPerson, posixAccount`
userPassword	–	User password for some form of access control	`organization, organizationalUnit, person, dmd,` `simpleSecurityObject, domain, posixAccount`

- **LDAP Data Interchange Format** (**LDIF**): This is an ASCII file format to describe the hierarchical tree structure of LDAP data in the form of a text file. LDAP data can be imported or exported in an LDIF file format.

Configuring Apache DS as an LDAP server

We will use **Apache Directory Server** (**Apache DS**), an extendable, modern, and embeddable LDAP server, to showcase LDAP authentication. It is written purely in Java. Apache DS comes as a standalone LDAP server. While working with it, you will need some sort of **LDAP Browser** to visualize and manipulate the data.

However, Apache provides another tool, called **Apache Directory Studio,** which is an Eclipse-based application. It ships with Apache DS and **LDAP Browser**, in a single bundle. It was designed particularly for Apache DS; however, you can use it with any LDAP server (like **OpenLDAP**).

 When you use Apache Directory Studio, you are no longer required to get another LDAP server, because it comes with Apache DS (an LDAP server).

Download Apache Directory Studio (`https://directory.apache.org/studio/`), extract it on your local machine, and double-click on the `ApacheDirectoryStudio` executable file to open it.

First, we need to add the Apache DS server. For that, go to the **LDAP Server** tab (generally placed at the bottom of the window), right-click there, select **New | New Server**, and choose the latest version of Apache DS server. Once the server has been added, right-click on it and select **Run** to start the server.

After the server is up and running, we need to create a connection. Right-click on the **Connections** tab and select **New Connection**, with the following information:

- **Connection name:** Any appropriate name.
- **Hostname**: The **localhost.**
- **Port:** The default port for any LDAP server is 389. However, the default port for Apache DS is 10389. Needless to say, that port can be changed.

Keep the rest of the options as is, and click on the **Next** button to fill in the following details:

- **Authentication Method: Simple authentication**
- **Bind DN or user:** uid=admin, ou=system
- **Bind password:** Secret

This is the default admin credential, and can be verified by clicking on the **Check Authentication** button. Click on **Finish**, and you will see the details in the **LDAP Browser** windows, as shown in the following screenshot:

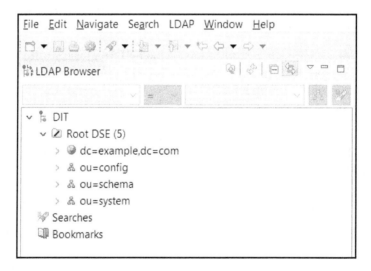

Next, we will start to create a data structure to store user details. As you have seen, LDAP can be used to store any kind of information, but we will use LDAP for authentication. LDAP stores the data in the form of a tree (DIT), so we will create a DIT structure.

Example DIT structures

Moving on, let's first look at a few data structures that are commonly used in LDAP, and then select one of them:

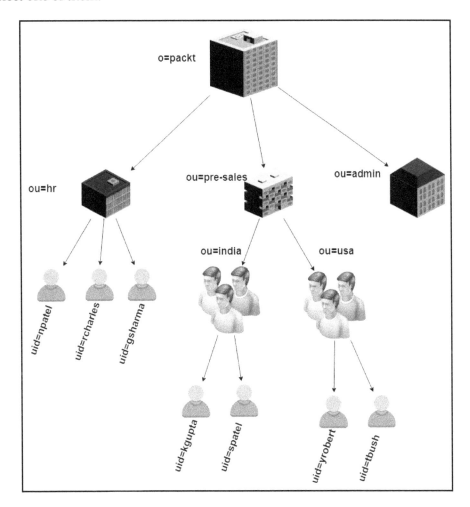

This structure starts with an organization with a name, packt (**o=packt**), followed by an organizational unit (subgroup) for each of the departments, and finally, the users. At some places, the sub-organization has a user group, followed by users.

The tree can also be arranged based on internet domain names, as follows:

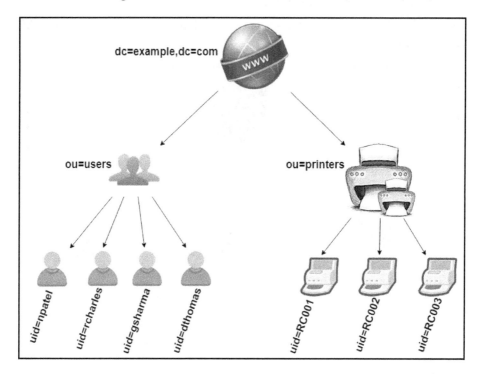

This structure has `example.com` as a domain. You can give the same attribute multiple times with different name, as previously shown. The **dc** stands for **domain component**. It is followed by subgroups for **users** and **printers** (devices), and at the end, the **users** and devices (**printers**) are listed.

Another option could be as follows:

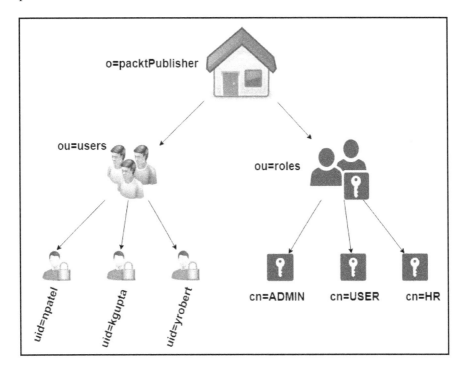

This option has an organization (**o=packtPublisher**) as the root, and two child **users** and **roles** as the **ou** (organizational unit, or subgroup). The **users** entry will have user entries, and the **roles** entry will have role entries. We will choose this option to construct a DIT in LDAP in this chapter. LDAP allows for associating the users to roles with attribute members. You will see more details about this in the *Creating roles in an LDAP server* section, later in this book.

Apache DS partitions

Apache DS has a concept called **partitions**. Every partition contains an entity tree (DIT) that is totally disconnected from the entity trees in other partitions. This means that changes that happen with entry trees in one partition will never affect entry trees in other partition. Each partition is identified by a unique ID. It also has a naming context referred to as the **partition suffix**, which can be thought of as the root (or base) for the DIT in that partition; all entries are stored beneath that.

To create a partition in Apache DS, double-click on the server instance in the **LDAP server** tab, and it will open the server configuration. Open the **Partitions** tab of the server configuration, click on the **Add** button, and give the values for the **Partition General Details** section, as follows:

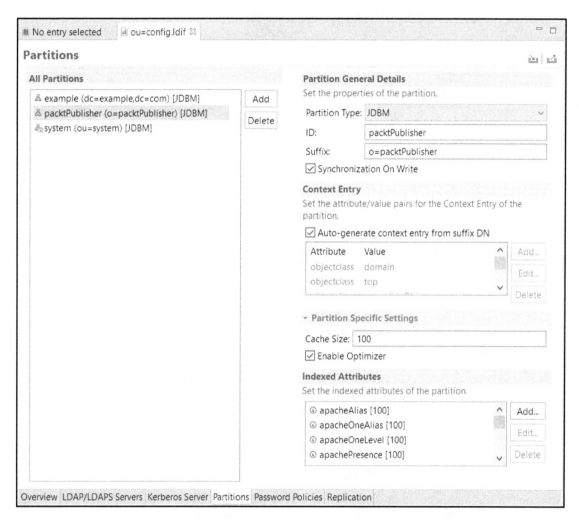

- **ID:** packtPublisher
- **Suffix:** o=packtPublisher

Keep all of the other values as the defaults, and save the configuration. Restart the server to take the partition into effect. The new partition will be available in the **LDAP Browser,** as shown in the following screenshot:

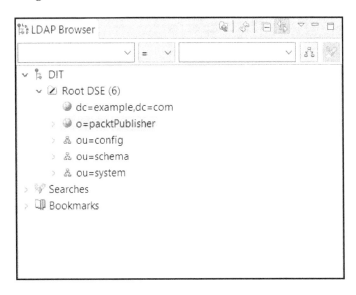

We will create an entity tree (DIT) under this partition. The partition suffix (o=packtPublisher) will be considered the base (or root) of the DIT. Next, we will create entries underneath it.

The LDAP structure

Proceeding further, we will look at the DN and RDN concept in DIT. We are targeting our DIT as per the third option that you saw in the *Example DIT structures* section. Let's recall that the RDN uniquely distinguishes the entry among its siblings. That means it is a key that makes the entry unique underneath the parent entry. We can use any attribute to declare the RDN. Additionally, at each level, the attribute used as an RDN can differ.

In our case, the RDN of the base is o=packtPublisher (which is the partition suffix). We have used the attribute o, which is the organization name. Just beneath it, there are two children, for which the ou attribute has been used as the RDN. The attribute ou stands for an organizational unit. These two children represent users and roles, respectively.

We are going to store the user information (the username and password, along with other information) under the `users` entity. So, the children of the `users` entity are the actual user entity for which the attribute `uid` is used as the RDN. The attribute `uid` stands for the **user ID**. Generally, in any organization, either the username or email ID is used for logging in; so, we can take either of them as the value of the `uid` attribute. In this case, we will give the username as `uid`.

We've gone over how the RDN works. Now, let's look at how the DN works. As we described, the DN uniquely identifies any entry in a given DIT. In other words, the DN makes the entry unique across the whole tree (DIT). The DN is a comma-separated string of the RDNs of the given entity, along with all of its parents, up till the root entity. So, the DN is automatically calculated, based on a given RDN at each level.

In the previous case, the DN of each entity (with `uid=npatel`) would be `uid=npatel`, `ou=users`, and `o=packtPublisher`. Similarly, the DN of the `users` entity is `ou=users` and `o=packtPublisher`. This is how the DN is calculated by appending the RDN at each level.

Let's create this structure in Apace DS now. Execute the following steps to expand the DIT structure in Apache Directory Studio:

1. Right-click on the partition `o=packtPublisher`, and select **New** | **New Entry**.
2. Choose an option, **Create entry from scratch**, and click on **Next**.
3. We are going to add an entity type organization unit, so choose the `organizationalUnit` object class and click on **Next**.
4. We will use `ou` (organizational unit) as an RDN and `users` as its value. The DN is automatically calculated when you give the value of the RDN. You can use more than one attribute (or the same attribute multiple times, with a different value) for the RDN. The DN will then be calculated by appending each name with a comma.
5. Click on **Next**, followed by the **Finish** button, and the entry `ou=users` will be added under `o=packtPublisher`. The updated structure will be visible in the **LDAP Browser** window.

Once the `users` entry is added, we can insert the individual user entries underneath it. The steps are as follows:

1. Right-click on the `users` entity (`ou=users`), and select **New** | **New Entry**.
2. Choose the option **Create entry from scratch** and click on **Next**.
3. We are going to add a user, so choose the `inetOrgPerson` object class, which represents a person within an organization. Click on the **Next** button.

4. We are going to add a user, so we will use the attribute uid (user ID) as the RDN. Just give the value as npatel. You can give any value that uniquely identifies the user. At this moment, the DN is calculated as uid=npatel, ou=users, o=packtPublisher.

5. Click on **Next**, and you will see a few required attributes, like cn and sn. The cn stands for **common name**, and sn means **surname**. The first name and last name can be given for cn and sn, respectively.

6. We want to authenticate a user, so there must be a password field (attribute) for a user entity. Just right-click on this screen and select **New Attribute**.

7. Give the attribute type as userPassword, and click on **Next | Finish**; a new window will pop up, in which you can give the password.

8. Give the appropriate value for the password, confirm the password, and set the **Hash** method as **SHA**; click on the **OK** button. Click on the **Finish** button from the parent window.

Add two to three such users, using the previous steps. We will look at how to add roles and create actual roles in the *LDAP authorization with Spring Security* section.

 The default configuration of Apache DS contains a data partition with the suffix dc=example, dc=com. This partition can also be used, but to understand the concept in detail, we have created a separate partition.

Congratulations! The basic step of configuring the LDAP is done. The LDAP server is ready for use. Next, we will look at how to authenticate the user against the LDAP server with Spring Security.

Spring Security integration with LDAP

In Chapter 3, *Blogpress - A Simple Blog Management System*, we provided information about Spring Boot and looked at how to create an application with it. In this chapter, we will use Spring Boot to build an app to showcase authentication and authorization in Spring Security. In the *LDAP* section, we covered the installation and setup of the LDAP server, along with its data structure. In this section, you will see how Spring Security works with LDAP.

Spring Security is a highly comprehensive and extensible framework; it provides authentication and authorization support for a J2EE-based web and REST application. We will look at how to integrate Spring Security with LDAP to perform authentication. By definition, **authentication** is a mechanism of validating or deciding whether an individual or entity is what it claims to be.

To demonstrate authentication, we will first build a web application with Spring Boot, and then we'll integrate it with LDAP.

Creating a web application with Spring Boot

We have created the data structure and have added the users, along with their credentials, in the LDAP server. Next, we will build a web application and integrate Spring Security, which will talk to the LDAP server for authentication. In the previous chapter, we built an application with Spring MVC and Thymeleaf. We will reuse the same architecture and create a web application with the following artifacts:

- Spring Boot, for creating a web application and auto configuration for other modules
- Thymeleaf, for the presentation layer
- Spring Security, to perform authentication with LDAP.

Like in the previous chapter, we will use an Eclipse-based IDE called **Spring Tool Suite (STS)** in this chapter. Create a Spring Boot application with the name `SpringAuth`, and other suitable parameters, like the group, artifact, version, description, and Java package. Make sure that the following starters are added to `pom.xml`:

```
<depedency>
  <groupId>org.springframework.boot</groupId>
  <artifactId>spring-boot-starter-security</artifactId>
</dependency>
<dependency>
  <groupId>org.springframework.boot</groupId>
  <artifactId>spring-boot-starter-thymeleaf</artifactId>
</dependency>
<dependency>
  <groupId>org.springframework.security</groupId>
  <artifactId>spring-security-ldap</artifactId>
</dependency>
```

Among the preceding entries, the `spring-security-ldap` is not a starter, but rather, a plain dependency. It provides the relevant dependencies required in the integration of Spring Security with LDAP.

We will configure the LDAP server as a data source to fetch user details and perform authentication in Spring Security. At this moment, Spring Security should know the details of how to connect with the LDAP server. These details are comprised of the URL, the base RDN, and the admin credentials. We will define these details in the `application.properties` file, as follows.

```
spring.ldap.urls=ldap://localhost:10389
spring.ldap.base=o=packtPublisher
spring.ldap.password=secret
spring.ldap.username=uid=admin,ou=system
```

The details are straightforward. The username and password represent the LDAP admin credentials. Since we are dealing with LDAP, the admin username is in the form of a DN (`uid=admin, ou=system`) instead of a direct value (like admin). We can relate these details with the information that we use to interact with a database (like the URL, port, username, and password). We will read these details and supply them to Spring Security to make a connection with LDAP. To achieve this, we will write a configuration class, as follows:

```
@Configuration
@ComponentScan(basePackages = { "com.nilangpatel.springldap.config" })
public class LdapDataConfig {
  @Value("${spring.ldap.urls}")
  private String ldapUrls;

  @Value("${spring.ldap.base}")
  private String ldapBase;

  @Value("${spring.ldap.password}")
  private String ldapManagerPwd;
  @Value("${spring.ldap.username}")
  private String ldapManagerUserName;
  @Bean("ldapAuthStructure")
  public LdapAuthStructure getLDAPAuthStructure() {
    LdapAuthStructure authStructure = new LdapAuthStructure();
    authStructure.setLdapUrl(ldapUrls);
    authStructure.setLdapBase(ldapBase);
    authStructure.setLdapManagerDn(ldapManagerUserName);
    authStructure.setLdapManagerPwd(ldapManagerPwd);
    authStructure.setUserDnPattern("uid={0},ou=users");
    authStructure.setUserSearchBase("ou=roles");
```

```
            return authStructure;
        }
    }
```

This class simply reads the LDAP connection properties with the @Value annotation, stored in the instance of the LdapAuthStructure class, and defines it as Spring Bean, so that it is available to other classes. The LdapAuthStructure is a custom class that holds LDAP configuration properties. We will use the following two additional properties for LDAP integration with Spring:

- userDnPattern: The value is uid={0}, ou=users. This is nothing but a DN pattern (relative to the entity ou=users). The {0} will be substituted with the actual value (uid, user ID) by Spring at runtime.
- userSearchBase: It represents the user base (ou=users). Basically, it represents an entity under which the users can be searched.
- groupSearchBase: It represents the group base (ou=roles). We will use this property to perform authorization in upcoming sections.

Next, we will use these properties and initialize Spring Security with the security configuration class, as follows:

```
@Configuration
@EnableWebSecurity
@ComponentScan("com.nilangpatel.springldap.security")
public class WebSecurityConfig extends WebSecurityConfigurerAdapter {
    @Autowired
    private LdapAuthStructure ldapAuthStructure;

    private Logger logger = LoggerFactory.getLogger(WebSecurityConfig.class);

    @Override
    public void configure(WebSecurity web) throws Exception {
        web.ignoring().antMatchers("/js/**");
        web.ignoring().antMatchers("/css/**");
    }

    @Override
    protected void configure(HttpSecurity http) throws Exception {
        http.authorizeRequests()
          .antMatchers("/").permitAll()
          .anyRequest().fullyAuthenticated().and()
        .formLogin().loginPage("/login").permitAll()
          .defaultSuccessUrl("/privatePage",true)
          .failureUrl("/login?error=true")
          .and()
```

```
  .logout()
    .permitAll().logoutSuccessUrl("/login?logout=true");
  logger.info("configure method is called to make the resources secure
...");
  }

@Override
protected void configure(AuthenticationManagerBuilder authManagerBuilder)
throws Exception {
    authManagerBuilder.ldapAuthentication()
    .userDnPatterns(ldapAuthStructure.getUserDnPattern())
    .userSearchBase(ldapAuthStructure.getUserSearchBase())
    .contextSource()
.url(ldapAuthStructure.getLdapUrl()+"/"+ldapAuthStructure.getLdapBase())
      .managerDn(ldapAuthStructure.getLdapManagerDn())
      .managerPassword(ldapAuthStructure.getLdapManagerPwd())
      .and()
    .passwordCompare()
      .passwordEncoder(new LdapShaPasswordEncoder())
      .passwordAttribute("userPassword");
    logger.info("configure method is called to build Authentication manager
...");
  }
}
```

The `WebSecurityConfig` is a custom class that extends
the `WebSecurityConfigurerAdapter` class. This class is a single point of configuration to
declare security-related details. The `configure(WebSecurity web)` method is used for
ignoring the requests for static resources (JS and CSS) from the security context. Without
this, not a single static resource will be loaded in the browser, because they will be filtered
by Spring Security.

 For our application, we did not use any images; if we did, the image path
(generally `/img/**`) would also need to be ignored.

The next method, `configure(HttpSecurity http)`, is used to set rules on various pages
(URLs). Our motive is to showcase authentication with LDAP; hence, to make things
simple, there are three pages with corresponding URLs, as follows:

- The home page (with the URL `/`). It is a landing page, meaning that this page will
  be opened when a user types `http://localhost:8080/springauth`
  (considering `8080` as the server port and `springauth` as the context).

- The login page (with the URL `/login`). It will show a login form, with which the user can be authenticated.
- A private page (with the URL `/privatePage`). This is a protected page and is only available to the logged in user. A user will be redirected to this page upon successful login.

The home page and login page are set to view for all, while the private page is set as a successful URL after logging in. This is a simple form login. The next method, `configure(AuthenticationManagerBuilder authManagerBuilder)`, actually does the magic. This is the place where the LDAP is being configured as an authentication mechanism.

In this class, the object of `LdapAuthStructure` is being auto-wired, which is supplied from the `LdapDataConfig` class, where we declared it with the `@Bean` annotation. Let's recall that the `LdapAuthStructure` class holds the LDAP connection data, which we are using in the `configure(AuthenticationManagerBuilder authManagerBuilder)` method. The call `ldapAuthentication()` on the `AuthenticationManagerBuilder` class will set the type of authentication as LDAP.

Further, it will set other connection data, like `userDnPattern` and `userSearchBase`. The value of `url` is supplied as a combination of the LDAP URL and the LDAP base (for example, `localhost:10389/o=packtPublisher`). In the end, the admin credential is supplied with the `managerDn()` and `managerPassword()` call. We also need to supply a password encoder. It must be the same password encoder that we used in the LDAP server, so we have used `LdapShaPasswordEncoder`. Finally, we are just mentioning the password field that we set in the LDAP server.

The LDAP authentication configuration is done. When we log in with the (same) credentials that we created in the Apache DS server, it will be successful. We have set the `uid` as `userDnPatterns`, so give `uid` as the username when logging in.

Congratulations! The LDAP integration with Spring Security has been successfully executed. The user will be authenticated against LDAP through Spring Security. If you only need to perform authentication with LDAP, the configuration that we have done so far will suffice. Next, we will look at how to interact with the LDAP server through the Spring Data repository, which we will use while working with both LDAP and OAuth later in this chapter.

Managing LDAP users with Spring Data

One part of our integration is over. The LDAP admin can configure users from the LDAP server; then, they can be authenticated from web applications created with Spring Security. However, we still have to deal with separate systems (Apache DS) to maintain the user information.

How cool would it be if an admin could directly maintain the users from a Spring web application? This is a great idea, because it will not only make the admin job easy, but a user will be able to update their profile information (like the password, first name, last name, and so on) directly in the Spring-based web application. This is quite possible with Spring Boot. We are talking about performing CRUD operations on the LDAP server from a web application.

In our application, the LDAP is used as a data store, where we are maintaining user data. Whenever we need to deal with any kind of data provider in a Spring-based application, we need to use **Spring Data**, a module of the Spring family that was specially designed to interact with the data store. Spring Data facilitates an abstract layer to interact with the underlying data provider, while providing an implementation for each of the data providers, like JPA, REST, Elasticsearch (which we used in the previous chapter), Mongo DB, and so on. Spring Data LDAP interacts with the LDAP server, and we will use it in our application.

Spring supplies a set of libraries for each of these data providers, which can be availed of by specifying the corresponding starter in the Spring Boot application. The Spring Data LDAP module can be integrated with the following starter entry in `pom.xml`:

```
<dependency>
  <groupId>org.springframework.boot</groupId>
  <artifactId>spring-boot-starter-data-ldap</artifactId>
</dependency>
```

Soon after we have defined this starter, all of the required JARs will be available in the classpath. Next, we will create the model (entity) class.

Spring Data models

The Spring Data module provides an implementation of DAO, with the aim of making data access consistent for various data providers. This brings the great flexibility of switching the underlying persistence technologies without much effort. Eventually, this will make the system loosely coupled.

Spring Data allows for exchanging the data with the persistence layer in an object-oriented manner, meaning that we can perform CRUD operations with entity class objects. Needless to say, the Spring Data LDAP module also facilitates the feature of dealing with the LDAP server in the form of the model class object. So, the first thing is to define the model (entity) class that represents the user data that we defined in the LDAP server, as follows:

```
@Entry(
   base = "ou=users",
   objectClasses = {"top", "person",
"organizationalPerson","inetOrgPerson"})
public final class LdapAuthUser implements Persistable<Name> {

   @Id
   private Name id;
   @Attribute(name = "uid")
   @DnAttribute(value="uid")
   private String userName;
   @Attribute(name = "sn")
   private String surName;
   @Attribute(name = "cn")
   private String firstName;
   @Attribute(name = "userPassword")
   private String password;
   @Transient
   private boolean isNew;

   //.. setter and getter methods
}
```

The `LdapAuthUser` class represents the LDAP user that we created in Apache DS. The `@Entity` annotation is used to map the Java class with an entity in the LDAP server. The `base` represents the base of the `users` entity (ou=users), while `objectClasses` is used to define the object class hierarchy used for creating the user entity.

The `@Attribute` annotation is used to map the instance variable with the attribute of the LDAP entity. The annotation `@DnAttribute` is used to populate the values automatically, from the distinguished names of the entries found. Special attention for `id` instance variable. It will be of the type `javax.naming.Name`.

There is no direct attribute, like `id`, in the LDAP entity, but Spring Data needs some sort of unique identifier (like `PK`, in a relational database) for each instance of the model class. So, internally, it assigns a DN relative to a `base` (in the `@Entity` annotation) defined for the model class. For example, if the `uid` of a user is `npatel`, then the `id` would be `uid=npatel, ou=users`.

Another unique point is that this model class implements the `Persistable<Name>` interface. Especially for the LDAP, at the time of adding a new entity, Spring Data does not have any way of knowing whether the entity is new or existing. So, every time Spring Data tries to search for an existing entity, it will throw an error if the entity does not exist. To avoid this, while adding a new record, we will explicitly set the `isNew` attribute to `true`, so that Spring Data will get its value with the overridden method `isNew()`.

The model class is now ready to use. Next, we will perform CRUD operations for LDAP users with Spring Data.

The Spring Data repository for LDAP

As you have seen, Spring Data provides an abstract (interface) layer while working with the persistence layer, in order to support various data stores, including relational databases, non-relational databases, map-reduce frameworks, cloud services, and so on. The abstraction starts with the `CrudRepository` interface, which provides basic CRUD operations, irrespective of the underlying data stores. This interface covers all basic CRUD operations.

Spring Data defines various interfaces, which are specific to each data provider on top of the `CrudRepository`. For LDAP support, Spring Data supplies the `LdapRepository` interface, which basically extends the `CrudRepository` interface, the one that we will extend for our custom repository. This interface has all of the required methods to perform CRUD operations. This way, by extending the specific repository interface, all basic CRUD operations for standard data access will be readily available.

Let's add Spring Data capability to LDAP in our application. The custom repository interface will be as follows:

```
@Repository
public interface LdapAuthRepository extends LdapRepository<LdapAuthUser>{

}
```

The `@Repository` annotation is used to describe that this is the repository interface. The custom interface `LdapAuthRepository` extends the `LdapRepository` with the model entity `LdapAuthUser`, which we created in the previous section. Upon declaring this interface, Spring Data provides the CRUD implementation that we can use in the service class, as follows:

```
@Component
public class LdapAuthService {
```

```java
  private Logger logger = LoggerFactory.getLogger(LdapAuthService.class);
  @Autowired
  private LdapAuthRepository ldapAuthRepository;

//Create
  public void addUser(LdapAuthUser ldapAuthUser) {
    Name dn = LdapNameBuilder
            .newInstance()
            .add("uid", ldapAuthUser.getUserName())
            .add("ou", "users")
            .build();

    boolean isExist = ldapAuthRepository.existsById(dn);
    if(isExist ==false) {
      ldapAuthRepository.save(ldapAuthUser);
    }else {
      logger.info("User with username "+ldapAuthUser.getUserName()+" is
already exist ");
    }
  }
  //Read
  public LdapAuthUser getUser(String userName) {
    Optional<LdapAuthUser> ldapAuthUserOptional = ldapAuthRepository.
            findOne(LdapQueryBuilder.query().where("uid").is(userName));
    if(ldapAuthUserOptional.isPresent()) {
      return ldapAuthUserOptional.get();
    }else {
      return null;
    }
  }
  //Update
  public void updateLdapUser(LdapAuthUser ldapUser) {
    ldapAuthRepository.save(ldapUser);
  }
//Delete
public void deleteUser(String userName) {
    Optional<LdapAuthUser> ldapAuthUserOptional = ldapAuthRepository.
            findOne(LdapQueryBuilder.query().where("uid").is(userName));
    if(ldapAuthUserOptional.isPresent()) {
      ldapAuthRepository.delete(ldapAuthUserOptional.get());
    }else {
      logger.info("User with username "+userName+" does not exist ");
    }
  }
}
```

In this service class, the object of the LdapAuthRepository class is injected with the @Autowired annotation. It is used to call the CRUD methods, as follows:

- **CREATE**: The existsById() command is used to check whether a user with the same ID already exists. The ID is of the type javax.naming.Name. The LdapNameBuilder class is used to build the ID. If a user does not exist, the save method is called on the ldapAuthRepository object, in order to create a fresh object. We can call this service method to add the record from the Spring MVC controller. We need to create the object of LdapAuthUser, set the data, and call the service method from the controller method, as follows:

```
LdapAuthUser ldapUser = new LdapAuthUser();
ldapUser.setUserName("kpatel");
ldapUser.setPassword("test1234");
ldapUser.setFirstName("Komal");
ldapUser.setSurName("Patel");
ldapUser.setIsNew(true);
Name dn = LdapNameBuilder.newInstance()
        .add("ou=users")
        .add("uid=kpatel")
        .build();
ldapUser.setId(dn);
ldapAuthService.addUser(ldapUser);
```

  - To create a new user, the object of the model class (LdapAuthUser) needs to be created first, along with its attribute.
  - Since we are creating a new user, it is required to set isNew to true, to make sure that the Spring Data module considers it a new record. Without doing this, the system will throw an error.
  - We also need to set the value of id. The LdapNameBuilder is used to create the object of the type javax.naming.Name (id). It is also required to add values like uid=kpatel (username) and ou=users in id.

- **READ**: To read the LDAP user with username, the findOne() method is used. We need to pass the LDAP query inside of this method. The LdapQueryBuilder class is used to create the LDAP query, which matches the username against the uid.

- **UPDATE**: The update operation is straightforward. The save method of ldapAuthRepository will actually update the LDAP user.

- **DELETE**: When deleting a user, first, it is required to check whether the user exists. Again, `fineOne` can be used to retrieve the existing user. The `delete` operation can only be executed if a user exists.

Additionally, we can use the following methods to perform authentication programmatically, in the service class, as follows:

```
public boolean authenticateLdapUserWithContext(String userName, String password) {
    return ldapAuthRepository.authenticateLdapUserWithContext(userName, password);
}
public boolean authenticateLdapUserWithLdapQuery(String userName, String password) {
    return ldapAuthRepository.authenticateLdapUserWithLdapQuery(userName, password);
}
```

The `authenticateLdapUserWithLdapQuery` and `authenticateLdapUserWithContext` are the custom methods defined in the `LdapAuthRepositoryCustomImpl` class, where we can define the custom method to interact with LDAP. We will discuss this topic further in the next section.

Upon successful authentication, these methods will return `true`; otherwise, they will be `false`. We need to pass the password in a plain text format for both of these methods. This is how the Spring Data repository is used to perform CRUD operations on LDAP users. Alternatively, we can use `LdapTemplate` to perform CRUD operations, as well as other complex business functions.

Performing CRUD operations with LdapTemplate

The Spring Data repository is a convenient way to interact with the underlying data provider, as it is easy to use and requires less code, because the implementation is provided by the Spring Data module out of the box. However, this simplicity comes with certain limitations. For example, with the repository programming model, we only have basic CRUD operations available to use. For more complex business needs, we need to extend this and provide our own repository implementation. This is where the Template model comes into the picture.

The template model in the Spring Data module is less handy than repository abstraction, but it is more powerful in terms of furnishing more fine-grained control for complex operations that we execute on the data store. We will look at the same CRUD operations with the Spring Data template model. Of course, the motive is to learn how to prepare the Spring Data template so that it can be used for complex business functions.

Initializing LdapTemplate

Spring Data provides templates for each of the underlying data providers, like `JdbcTemplate`, `JpaTemplate`, `MongoTemplate`, `ElasticSearchTemplate`, `CassandraTemplate`, and so on. The `LdapTemplate` is the one that is used to communicate with the LDAP server. We will first initialize `LdapTemplate`. Add the following methods to the `LdapDataConfig` class:

```
@Bean("ldapTemplate")
  public LdapTemplate getLdapTemplate() {
    return new LdapTemplate(getLdapContextSrc());
  }

  @Bean
  public ContextSource getLdapContextSrc() {
    LdapContextSource ldapContextSrc = new LdapContextSource();
    ldapContextSrc.setUrl(ldapUrls);
    ldapContextSrc.setUserDn(ldapManagerUserName);
    ldapContextSrc.setPassword(ldapManagerPwd);
    ldapContextSrc.setBase(ldapBase);
    ldapContextSrc.afterPropertiesSet();
    return ldapContextSrc;
  }
```

The `getLdapContextSrc()` method first creates an object of `LdapContextSource` and initializes it with the LDAP connection parameters that were read from `application.properties`. The `@Bean` annotation will export this object as a Spring bean. The second method, `getLdapTemplate()`, uses the object of `LdapContextSoruce` and initializes the object of the `LdapTemplate` class; then, it is exposed as a Spring bean with `id=ldapTemplate`, with the `@Bean` annotation.

Using LdapTemplate to perform CRUD operations

Now, we have initialized the `LdapTemplate` object. Next, we will use it to perform various CRUD operations. We will use `LdapTemplate` in the Spring Data repository structure. For this, we need to extend the Spring Data repository model and provide a custom implementation.

Create an interface: `LdapAuthRepositoryCustom`. This is a place where we can define customized methods that are not directly available with the repository abstraction. Update the definition of the `LdapAuthRepository` interface, as follows:

```
@Repository
public interface LdapAuthRepository extends
LdapRepository<LdapAuthUser>,LdapAuthRepositoryCustom
{

}
```

This is a glue point of the custom implementation with the Spring Data repository framework. Finally, define the `LdapAuthRepositoryCustomImpl` class that implements the `LdapAuthRepositoryCustom` interface. This is the class where the implementation of custom methods are defined, as follows:

```
@Repository
public class LdapAuthRepositoryCustomImpl implements
LdapAuthRepositoryCustom {

  private Logger logger =
LoggerFactory.getLogger(LdapAuthRepositoryCustomImpl.class);
  @Autowired
  private LdapTemplate ldapTemplate;

  ...// Custom implementation method.
```

The `LdapAuthRepositoryCustomImpl` implements the `LdapAuthRepositoryCustom` interface, which is used to declare custom repository methods. This class has an instance variable of the type `LdapTemplate`, which is injected with the `@Autowired` annotation (created in the `LdapDataConfig` class). Next, we will look at some of the methods defined in this class, as follows.

- **CREATE operation:** The following code block describes how the CREATE operation is used to add a new LDAP user, with `ldapTemplate`:

```
@Override
  public void create(LdapAuthUser ldapAuthUser) {
    ldapAuthUser.setIsNew(true);
    ldapTemplate.create(ldapAuthUser);
  }
  @Override
  public void createByBindOperation(LdapAuthUser ldapAuthUser) {
    DirContextOperations ctx = new DirContextAdapter();
    ctx.setAttributeValues("objectclass", new String[] {"top", "person",
"organizationalPerson","inetOrgPerson"});
```

```
    ctx.setAttributeValue("cn", ldapAuthUser.getFirstName());
    ctx.setAttributeValue("sn", ldapAuthUser.getSurName());
    ctx.setAttributeValue("uid", ldapAuthUser.getUserName());
    ctx.setAttributeValue("password", ldapAuthUser.getPassword());
    Name dn = LdapNameBuilder.newInstance()
            .add("ou=users")
            .add("uid=bpatel")
            .build();
    ctx.setDn(dn);
    ldapTemplate.bind(ctx);
}
```

The first method is straightforward. It uses `ldapTemplate` to create an LDAP user with the model object. We have set `isNew` to `true`, to make sure that there will not be any issues while creating the LDAP user. The second method, `createByBindOperation`, uses a low-level API to create the LDAP user. The object of `DirContextAdapter` is first initialized with various model attributes, like `objectClass`, `cn`, `sn`, `uid`, `userPassword`, and `dn`. The `LdapNameBuilder` class is used to create the DN of the LDAP user. Finally, the `bind` method of `ldapTemplate` is used to create the user. We can use either of these methods to create a user.

- **READ operation:** The following code block depicts how the READ operation is used to fetch the LDAP user, with `ldapTemplate`:

```
@Override
public LdapAuthUser findByUserName(String userName) {
    return ldapTemplate.findOne(
        LdapQueryBuilder.query().where("uid").is(userName),
LdapAuthUser.class);
}

@Override
public List<LdapAuthUser> findByMatchingUserName(String userName) {
    return ldapTemplate.find(
        LdapQueryBuilder.query().where("uid").like(userName),
LdapAuthUser.class);
}

@Override
public LdapAuthUser findByUid(String uid) {
    return
ldapTemplate.findOne(LdapQueryBuilder.query().where("uid").is(uid),
LdapAuthUser.class);
}
```

```
@Override
public List<LdapAuthUser> findAllWithTemplate() {
    return ldapTemplate.findAll(LdapAuthUser.class);
}

@Override
public List<LdapAuthUser> findBySurname(String surName) {
    return
ldapTemplate.find(LdapQueryBuilder.query().where("sn").is(surName),
LdapAuthUser.class);
}
```

These are a few methods that read the user from the LDAP server. The LdapQueryBuilder is used to construct a query that can be used to perform a search of various attributes, such as uid, and surname. It can also be used to find users with matching attributes, with the like query.

- **UPDATE operation:** The following code block shows how the UPDATE operation updates the LDAP user, with ldapTemplate:

```
@Override
  public void updateWithTemplate(LdapAuthUser ldapAuthUser) {
    ldapTemplate.update(ldapAuthUser);
  }
```

The update method is straightforward. The update() method is used to update the LDAP user with the model object.

- **DELETE operation:** The following code block describes how the DELETE operation is used to delete the LDAP user, with ldapTemplate:

```
@Override
public void deleteFromTemplate(LdapAuthUser ldapAuthUser) {
    ldapTemplate.delete(ldapAuthUser);
}
@Override
public void deleteFromTemplateWithUnbind(String userName) {
    Name dn = LdapNameBuilder.newInstance()
            .add("ou=users")
            .add("uid="+userName)
            .build();
    ldapTemplate.unbind(dn);
}
```

The first method is straightforward. It simply calls the `delete` method on the `ldapTemplate` object to delete the LDAP user. The second method first creates the user DN, and then calls the `unbind` method on `ldapTemplate`, to delete the user.

 The `delete` method on `ldapTemplate` simply calls the `unbind` method with a null check on the given entity. So, both of the methods, `delete()` and `unbind()`, are ultimately doing the same thing.

In addition to the basic CRUD operations, we can perform some other operations with `ldapTemplate`, as follows:

```
@Override
public boolean authenticateLdapUserWithLdapQuery(String userName, String
password) {
    try {
ldapTemplate.authenticate(LdapQueryBuilder.query().where("uid").is(userName
), password);
        return true;
    }catch(Exception e) {
      logger.error("Exception occuired while authenticating user with user
name "+userName,e.getMessage(),e);
    }
    return false;
  }
@Override
public boolean authenticateLdapUserWithContext(String userName, String
password) {
    DirContext ctx = null;
    try {
      String userDn = getDnForUser(userName);
      ctx = ldapTemplate.getContextSource().getContext(userDn, password);
      return true;
    } catch (Exception e) {
      // If exception occurred while creating Context, means -
authentication did not succeed
      logger.error("Authentication failed ", e.getMessage(),e);
      return false;
    } finally {
      // DirContext must be closed here.
      LdapUtils.closeContext(ctx);
    }
  }
```

The first method calls the `authenticate` method on the `ldapTemplate` by passing the `LdapQuery` and `password`. The `LdapQueryBuilder` is used to create the LDAP query for the given username. The second method calls `getContextSource().getContet()` on the `ldapTemplate` object by passing the user DN and password. The context is required to be closed at the end. The user DN is obtained for a given `userName` with the `getDnForUser()` method, as follows:

```
private String getDnForUser(String uid) {
    List<String> result = ldapTemplate.search(
        LdapQueryBuilder.query().where("uid").is(uid),
        new AbstractContextMapper<String>() {
            protected String doMapFromContext(DirContextOperations ctx) {
                return ctx.getNameInNamespace();
            }
        });
    if(result.size() != 1) {
      throw new RuntimeException("User not found or not unique");
    }
    return result.get(0);
}
```

The `search` method of `ldapTemplate` is called by passing `LdapQuery` and an implementation of `ContextMapper`, and finally, it returns a user DN (for example, `uid=npatel, ou=users, o=packtPublisher`) for the given username.

LDAP authorization with Spring Security

You saw LDAP authentication with Spring Security in the previous section. Next, we will look at how to perform authorization. Let's recall that **authorization** is a verification process of whether an entity should have access to something. In short, authorization concerns the rules that will identify who is allowed to do what. After successful authentication, a user can perform various actions, based on the authority they have.

Let's recall that authentication deals with login credentials to verify valid users. Authorization is more of a check of whether a user has the authority to perform various actions, like adding, updating, viewing, or deleting a resource. An authorization happens after the user has been successfully authenticated. In this section, we will look at how to authorize an LDAP user.

So far, you have seen that the user's details are maintained at the LDAP server, which is used by Spring Security to perform authentication. Similarly, we will set up authorization details in the LDAP server and fetch them in Spring Security to achieve authorization.

Creating roles in the LDAP server

As you saw in the previous section, we have created the `users` entity (`ou=users`) under the root entity (`o=packtPublisher`), and have kept all users under that entity in the LDAP server. Similarly, to store authorization information, we will create a new entity directly under the root entity in Apache DS, with the following steps:

1. Right-click on the partition `o=packtPublisher` and select **New** | **New Entry** from the **LDAP Browser** window.
2. Choose the option **Create entry from scratch** and click on the **Next** button.
3. We are going to add an entity type organization unit, so choose the **organizationalUnit** object class and click on the **Next** button.
4. We will use `ou` (organizational unit) as the RDN and roles as its value. The DN is automatically calculated when we give the value of the RDN. You can use more than one attribute (or the same attribute multiple times, with different values) for the RDN. The DN will then be calculated by appending each of them with a comma.
5. Click on the **Next** button, followed by the **Finish** button, and the entry `ou=roles` will be added under `o=packtPublisher`. The updated structure will be visible in the **LDAP Browser** window.

Next, we will add the actual role entries under the `ou=roles` entry. The steps are as follows:

1. Right-click on the roles entity (`ou=roles`) and select **New** | **New Entry**.
2. Choose the option **Create entry from scratch** and click on **Next**.
3. To add a role, choose `groupOfNames` as the object class that represents a role. Click on the **Next** button.
4. We are going to add a role, so we will use the attribute `cn` (common name) as the RDN. Just give the value as `ADMIN`. At this moment, the DN is calculated as `cn=ADMIN, ou=roles, o=packtPublisher`. Click on the **Next** button.
5. Since this entity has `groupOfNames` as the object class, the system will ask for the member assignment in the next window.
6. Click on the **Browse** button and choose the user that you want to assign this role, under the `o=packtPublisher` entry. Click on the **OK** button.
7. The following are the steps for assigning multiple members in the given role:
    1. Select any of the role entries from the **LDAP Browser** window. Right-click in the middle section (where the details of the selected role are visible a tabular format) and choose **New Attribute**.

2. Give the value of **Attribute type** as member, click on **Next**, and click on the **Finish** button; you will see the same window for selecting the user to assign to this role.

Execute these steps and create the following two roles under the roles entry:

- ADMIN
- USER

The role structure has been created in Apache DS. We will now import these details to perform authorization.

Importing role information to perform authorization

In the *Example DIT structures* section of this chapter, we created a role entity (ou=roles) under the root entity (o=packtPublisher). The role entity contains various roles as its child entities. We will look at how to use these roles to perform authorization with Spring Security. We have already configured Spring Security to perform authentication with LDAP. We will now add two sample pages, and configure it so that one page is only accessible by a user with the ADMIN role, and the other is accessible by a user with either the USER or ADMIN role.

To achieve this, the changes need to be done in the configure method of the WebSecurityConfig class that we created for Spring Security configuration. The updated method should look as follows:

```
@Override
protected void configure(HttpSecurity http) throws Exception {
  http.authorizeRequests()
    .antMatchers("/").permitAll()
    .antMatchers("/adminPage/").hasAnyAuthority("ADMIN")
    .antMatchers("/userPage/").hasAnyAuthority("USER")
    .anyRequest().fullyAuthenticated()
    .and()
  .formLogin().loginPage("/login").permitAll()
    .defaultSuccessUrl("/privatePage",true)
    .failureUrl("/login?error=true")
    .and()
    .logout()
    .permitAll().logoutSuccessUrl("/login?logout=true");
  logger.info("configure method is called to make the resources secure
```

```
...");
  }
```

We have added an admin page (with the URL /adminPage/) and a user page (with the URL /usePage/), and have configured them so that they can be accessed by a user with the ADMIN and USER role, respectively.

Additionally, we need to create respective Thymeleaf templates under the src/main/resources/templates folder and entries for both of these pages in the Spring MVC controller class, and update the menu structure (defined in the header template) to accommodate these pages. The full details are mentioned in the source code, which is available in GitHub (https://github.com/PacktPublishing/Spring-5.0-Projects).

Next, we will update the configure method that represents the LDAP configuration with Spring Security. This method takes an object of the type AuthenticationManagerBuilder. After making the required changes, this method will look as follows:

```
  @Override
  protected void configure(AuthenticationManagerBuilder authManagerBuilder)
throws Exception {
    authManagerBuilder.ldapAuthentication()
      .userDnPatterns(ldapAuthStructure.getUserDnPattern())
      .userSearchBase(ldapAuthStructure.getUserSearchBase())
      .groupSearchBase(ldapAuthStructure.getGroupSearchBase())
      .groupSearchFilter("member={0}").rolePrefix("")
    .contextSource()
.url(ldapAuthStructure.getLdapUrl()+"/"+ldapAuthStructure.getLdapBase())
      .managerDn(ldapAuthStructure.getLdapManagerDn())
      .managerPassword(ldapAuthStructure.getLdapManagerPwd())
      .and()
    .passwordCompare()
      .passwordEncoder(new LdapShaPasswordEncoder())
      .passwordAttribute("userPassword");
    logger.info("configure method is called to build Authentication manager
...");
  }
```

The following are the changes that we made for authorization:

- Added the groupSearchBase method call and passed the value as ou=roles, which represents the base for group search. The group search base value (ou=roles) is stored in an ldapAuthStructure object that we created to hold LDAP connection properties.

- Added a `groupSearchFilter` method call and passed the value as `member={0}`. It is used to define the pattern to search the members. The `{0}` will be substituted by the actual user DN at runtime.
- The additional method `rolePrefix("")` is placed to set the role prefix. In absence of this method call, the role name will be prepended with `ROLE_` by Spring Security. As an example, for the role `ADMIN` defined in the LDAP server, the actual role return by Spring Security would be `ROLE_ADMIN`. To avoid this, we call this method and simply pass an empty string, so that we get the exact role name that we defined in the LDAP server.

The configuration part of the authorization is over. You can create some sample users in Apache DS, assign them roles, and check whether they are able to access the pages that we have created. A user that does not have any role cannot access any of the pages (admin or user).

This was all about the integration of LDAP using Spring Security. In the next section, we will look at OAuth integration.

OAuth

A typical web application requires credentials, in the form of a username/password, to perform authentication. The HTML form is used to ask for credentials in the browser, and then send them to the server. The server then authenticates the information, creates and maintains a session at the server side, and sends the session ID back to the browser.

The session ID will be sent in each request, and the server will map the session with the session ID and pull certain information from the database to perform authorization. The browser generally stores the session ID in cookies. As long as the session is active, a user can access the restricted resources, based on the authorities assigned.

This is a quite simple and easy mechanism for client-server interaction, and hence, it is still used by many web applications and services today. However, there are certain limitations to this model, as follows:

- Generally, the cookies are stateful, so the server needs to keep track of the session and check with the database (or in the memory) for every request. This may lead to overhead on the server. Additionally, the authorization process is closely associated with the application server, which results in a tightly coupled system.
- For REST clients, like a native mobile app, cookies may not work properly.

- If the application functionality is spread across multiple domains, additional configuration may be required to maintain the cookie value.
- The cookie-based model has the limitation of granting third-party client access.

OAuth overcomes these restrictions. By definition, it is an authorization framework (or protocol, more precisely), allowing for the application to access resources within the same or different applications. In other words, OAuth 2.0 allows limited access to protected resources to a third-party application, on behalf of a resource owner. It supports authorization flows for mobile, web, and desktop applications. The current version of this protocol is OAuth 2.0. We will integrate OAuth 2.0 with Spring Security.

Even though OAuth has certain characteristics that are not available with a normal client-server mechanism with the session, the former cannot replace the latter. For example, a banking application must be implemented with a client-server mechanism. The comparison given here is to showcase how OAuth can be used to provide access to third-party applications.

OAuth roles

Before moving further, it is important that you understand certain terminologies used in OAuth. This will provide a profound understanding of its underlying concepts. They are referred to as OAuth roles, as follows:

- **Resource owner:** A person or entity that can grant access to protected resources. The OAuth protocol is not limited to a person. An application to application interaction can happen with OAuth. If the resource owner is a person (or user), it is called an end user.
- **Authorization server:** As its name suggests, it is an entity that provides authorization, in the form of a token. After the resource owner is authenticated successfully, the authorization server will issue an access token to a client.
- **Resource server:** This is the server that holds the protected resources. When a request for a protected resource comes to the resource server, it will verify the access token with the authorization server and respond accordingly.
- **Client:** An entity that initiates the request to access the protected resource in support of a resource owner is called a **client**. It can be in any form, like a mobile application asking for credentials or a web-based application that provides an alternate login functionality with social media (like Facebook or Google).

The relationships between these roles is illustrated in the following diagram:

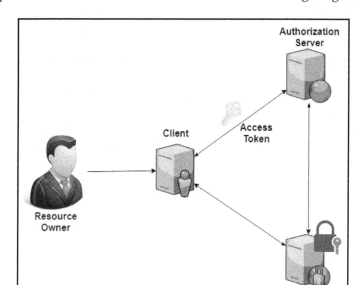

The end user, who is the **Resource owner**, interacts with an application, which acts as a **Client** here. The **Client** will talk to the **Authorization server**. The **Resource owner** provides credentials, and it will be authenticated at the **Authorization server** first. Upon successful identification, the **Authorization server** issues an access token, which is used by the **Client** to access the secure resources on the **Resource server**, in support of the **Resource owner**. The **Authorization server** is also known as an **identity provider**.

Let's look at the process of authorization in OAuth with a real-life scenario. Suppose that John has a car with a smart key. Nowadays, a vehicle with a smart key is common, wherein the vehicle cannot be operated (not even unlocked or started) without a smart key in your pocket. John has asked his friend Charles to pick him up from the airport. He already has already given him a smart key. Charles uses the smart key and starts the car.

In this analogy, the smart key gives Charles the authorization to operate John's car, as authorization involves the resources a user has access to, and what it can do with those resources. John, in this case, is the end user (**Resource owner**), whereas Charles is a **Client**. The smart key is an access token, whereas the car's security system can be considered an **Authorization server** (or identity provider) who authorizes Charles (**Client**) with a smart key (access token). The whole car is the **Resource server** (Charles can use other features of the car, like the AC, music system, and so on, as he is authorized to use the car with the access token (smart key)).

Grant types

The crux of the OAuth protocol is to provide access tokens for authorization. The way of retrieving the access token is called a **grant**. There are various ways (grants) to access and use the access token. OAuth 2.0 provides different grants for different scenarios, like the level of trust for the application, the type of the application, and so on.

OAuth 2.0 supports the following types of grants. Selecting the one that best fits an application depends on the type of that application:

- Authorization code
- Implicit
- Resource Owner Password Credentials
- Client Credentials

Let's look at each of these grant types in detail: how they work, and into which situations they fit best.

Authorization code

Being the most commonly and widely used, the authorization code grant is the best fit for server-side applications. The **Client** would be a web application. To make sure that the **Client** interacts with the **Authorization Server** properly, it is required to configure certain connection parameters, like the *Client ID* and *Client Secret*, with the **Client**. Since the **Client** is a web application, these parameters can be maintained secretly.

In this grant type, a **Client** must be able to collaborate with a **User Agent (Browser)**, because the authorization code is routed through the browser. The process of obtaining an access token for an authorization code grant can be described with the following diagram. Since the **Resource Owner** is authenticated at the **Authorization Server**, its credentials will not be shared with the **Client**:

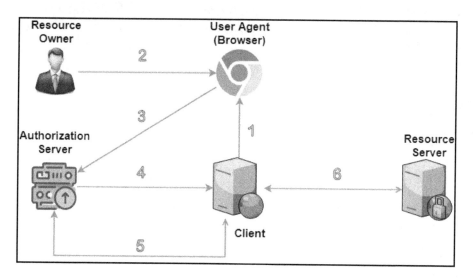

In this grant type, the access token is obtained through the following steps:

1. The **Client** is configured to establish a connection to the authorization server. It will open the link in the **User Agent (Browser)**. This link contains other information, which will be used by the authorization server to identify and respond back to the **Client**. Generally, the link opens in a separate window, and it contains a login form to authenticate a user as the first step towards authorization.

2. A user (**Resource Owner**) then enters the credentials, in the form of a username and password.

3. The browser (**User Agent**) then sends these credentials to the **Authorization Server**.

4. The **Authorization Server** verifies the credentials and sends the response back to the **Client** with the authorization code.

5. Upon receiving the authorization code, the **Client** will exchange it with the **Authorization Server** to get an access token, and optionally, a refresh token.

6. After getting an access token, the **Client** can talk to the **Resource Server** to get protected resources.

The authorization code flow can be used with web and mobile app clients. Generally, web app clients use *Client ID* and *Client Secret*, while mobile app clients use the **Proof Key for Code Exchange (PKCE)** mechanism and utilize code challenges and code verifiers.

Implicit

The implicit grant type was designed specifically for single-page JavaScript applications running in the browser. It is most similar to the authorization code flow. The only difference is in the process of exchanging the authorization code. In the implicit grant type, a client will not receive an authorization code from the **Authorization Server**, in contrast with the authorization code grant type, due to security reasons.

Alternatively, once a **User Agent** successfully sends the credentials, the **Authorization Server** issues an access token directly to the **Client**. Since the implicit flow is targeted at single-page JavaScript applications, the refresh token is also not allowed. The whole process is described in the following diagram.

Since the **Authorization Server** directly issues an access token, the round-trip of the request-response between the **Client** and **Authorization Server** is reduced, as compare to the authorization code flow:

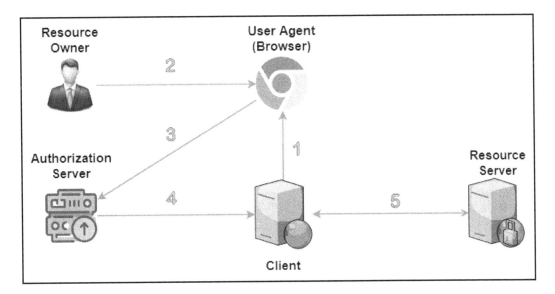

This process happens in the following sequence:

1. The **Client** will open the link in a separate window in the **User Agent** (browser), which contains a login form to authenticate a user as a first step towards authorization.
2. A user (**Resource Owner**) then enters the credentials, in the form of a username and password.
3. The browser (**User Agent**) then sends these credentials to the **Authorization Server**.
4. The **Authorization Server** verifies the credentials and sends the access token directly to the **Client**.
5. After getting the access token, the **Client** can talk to the **Resource Server** to get protected resources.

Resource Owner Password Credentials

The Resource Owner Password Credentials grant type should be used for a highly trusted client, because it handles the user credentials directly. In other words, this grant type should only be used when there is plenty of certainty and faith between the **Resource owner** and the **Client**. Mostly, the client will be a first-party application. The credentials will be used by the **Client** directly, to interact with the **Authorization Server** and get an access token. The flow can be described with the following diagram:

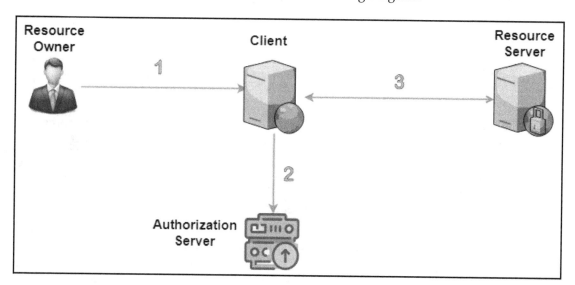

This flow can be described as follows:

1. The **Client** is highly trusted, so it will directly ask the **Resource Owner** to provide credentials. The **Client** could be a highly indulged application.
2. The credentials will be sent by the **Client** to the **Authorization Server**. The **Client** will also send its own identity to the **Authorization Server**. In response, the **Authorization Server** will send back the access token, and optionally, a refresh token.
3. The access token is used by the client to access the protected resources of the **Resource Server**.

Client Credentials

The Client Credentials grant type is similar to the Resource Owner Password Credentials flow. In the Client Credentials grant, the **Client** interacts with the **Authorization Server**, provides the identification by sending the Client ID and Client Secrets, and gets the access token. Once the access token is received, the **Client** will interact with the **Resource Server**. In this case, a refresh token should not be used. The process flow is illustrated by the following diagram:

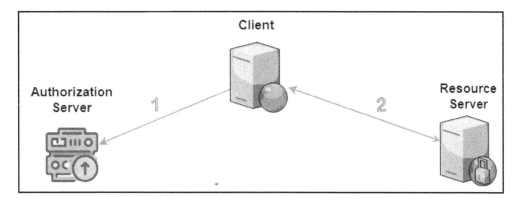

1. The Client ID and Client Secrets are configured with the **Client**. The **Client** will interact with the **Authorization Server** to get an access token.
2. After getting the access token, the **Client** can interact with the **Resource Server** to access protected resources.

Which grant type should be used?

Having seen the details about each grant type, it is important to understand the right grant type for a given application. There are various factors that play a vital role in grant type selection, like end user identification, the type of client (server-side, web-based, native, client-side), and the level of assurance between the client and resource owner.

If we are planning to build an app and allow for the access of resources to other third-party apps, then the authorization code flow is the right choice. It is a highly recommended grant type for a publicly hosted application. On the other hand, if a client is JavaScript-based and runs in a browser, we should go with the implicit grant type for a third-party client, and the resource owner password credentials grant for a first-party client.

If a client is a native (mobile) application, we can select the resource owner password credentials grant type. If the resource owner does not need the identity of the end user and the client itself behaves like a resource owner, we should use the client credentials grant type. Typically, a client credentials grant is used where the machine (and not a user) needs the authorization to access protected resources, and user permission is not required.

Spring Security integration with OAuth

Having seen the basic fundamentals of what OAuth 2.0 is and how it works, we will now look at the integration of OAuth in Spring Security. We will continue to work with the same application that we created for LDAP, and will make the necessary changes for OAuth integration.

For the OAuth demonstration, we will use readily available authorization providers. Spring Security supports Google, Facebook, Okta, and GitHub providers out of the box. Choosing one of them would only require certain configurations, and things would start to work. We will select Google as an authorization server (provider) to build OAuth for our application. The grant type that we will use in this integration is authorization code.

Every authorization provider supports some sort of mechanism that enables the clients to establish a connection with the service. This process is known as **application registration**.

Application registration

Let's register (or create) an application at Google, which provides connection access to use the authorization service. This is an essential step before start to implement OAuth. Google provides an **API console** to register an application. A valid Google account is required to access the API console. Go to `https://console.developers.google.com/apis/credentials` and follow these steps:

1. Click on the **Create credentials** button in the **Credentials** tab, and click on the **OAuth client ID** option. Select the application type as **Web Application**.

2. Give an appropriate name (like `SpringOAuthDemo`).

3. We need to set the authorized redirect URI in the Google console, which represents a path upon which users are redirected after they are successfully authorized by Google. The default implementation, provided by Spring Security for Google, has configured the redirect URI as `/login/oauth2/code/google`. Apparently, the valid redirect URI, in our case, would be `http://localhost:8080/springuath/login/oauth2/code/google` (considering `8080` as the port and `springauth` as the context name). Give this URI in **Authorized redirectURIs** in the Google console, and click on the **Create** button.

Upon successful registration of the application, Google will create client credentials in the form of the **client ID** and **client secret**, as shown in the following screenshot:

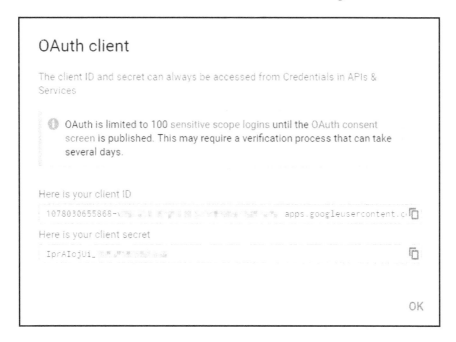

The **client ID** is a kind of public key used by the Google service API to identify the application that we have registered. It is also used to construct authorization URLs of the Google login form. The **client secret**, as its name suggests, is a kind of private key. When the application (that we registered) requests the details of a user account, at the moment the user credentials are sent, the **client secret** will be used to validate the identity of the application. Because of this, the **client secret** must be kept private between the application and the client.

Changes in the Spring Boot application

After completing the preceding requirements, we will start to make the necessary changes in the Spring Boot application that we created for LDAP authentication. The aim is to build a central authentication and authorization server that will work with both technologies (LDAP and OAuth).

When the user enters a plain username and password, the authentication and authorization will be done with LDAP. We will configure our application with Google, for OAuth. The very first step for OAuth integration is to declare the relevant starters. Spring Boot provides support for OAuth in the form of starters. Add the following starter entries in a pom.xml file:

```
<dependency>
   <groupId>org.springframework.boot</groupId>
   <artifactId>spring-boot-starter-oauth2-client</artifactId>
</dependency>
```

Upon defining this starter, Spring Boot will add the following dependencies, which are essentials for OAuth integration, automatically:

```
<dependency>
   <groupId>org.springframework.security</groupId>
   <artifactId>spring-security-oauth2-client</artifactId>
</dependency>
<dependency>
   <groupId>org.springframework.security</groupId>
   <artifactId>spring-security-oauth2-jose</artifactId>
</dependency>
<dependency>
   <groupId>org.springframework.security</groupId>
   <artifactId>spring-security-oauth2-core</artifactId>
</dependency>
```

Next, we will add properties for the client ID and client secret, along with the provider and client name, in the `application.propeties` file. These properties are prefixed with `spring.security.oauth.client.registration`, along with the provider name and property name. Set these properties with the `Client ID` and `Client Secret` that we created in the Google developer console in the previous section, as follows:

```
spring.security.oauth2.client.registration.google.provider=google
spring.security.oauth2.client.registration.google.client-name=Google
spring.security.oauth2.client.registration.google.client-
id=<GOOGLE_CLIENT_ID>
spring.security.oauth2.client.registration.google.client-
secret=<GOOGLE_SECRET>
```

The default OAuth configuration

Spring Security allows for configuring multiple OAuth clients. In addition to Google, Spring Security also supports default configurations for Facebook, GitHub, and Okta, out of the box. That means that all required classes and configurations are readily available, and we just need to define the client credentials (`Client ID` and `Client Secret`). Next, we will update the `configure(HttpSecurity http)` method of the `WebSecurityConfig` class, as follows:

```
@Override
  protected void configure(HttpSecurity http) throws Exception {
     http.authorizeRequests()
       .anyRequest().authenticated()
       .and()
         .oauth2Login();
     super.configure(http);
  }
```

The **oauth2Login()** method will initiate an OAuth call. At this moment, while executing the application, the preceding method will make an OAuth call to Google. A user will be asked for a valid Google login credential. Upon successful authentication, it will show the home page.

If we set the properties for at least one client, Spring Security will automatically enable the `Oauth2ClientAutoConfiguration` class, which will make all of the necessary arrangements to enable OAuth login, without even defining the preceding `WebSecurityConfig` class.

If more than one client is configured in the `application.properties` file, the system will show a list of those clients, with a default login (username and password) form. It will be the autogenerated login page. We can perform a login with any of those configured clients.

It is quite obvious to show the name of the user at the top, to indicate which user is currently logged in. We can get the name of the user that has been authenticated at Google with the following code snippet:

```
@ModelAttribute("currentUserName")
public String getCurrentUserName() {
  String name = "";
  if(SecurityContextHolder.getContext().getAuthentication() !=null) {
    if(SecurityContextHolder.getContext().getAuthentication()
        instanceof OAuth2AuthenticationToken) {
      OAuth2AuthenticationToken oauth2Authentication =
(OAuth2AuthenticationToken)SecurityContextHolder.getContext().getAuthentica
tion();
      name =
(String)oauth2Authentication.getPrincipal().getAttributes().get("name");
    }else {
      String userName =
SecurityContextHolder.getContext().getAuthentication().getName();
      LdapAuthUser ldapUser = ldapAuthService.getUser(userName);
      if(ldapUser !=null) {
        name = ldapUser.getFirstName()+" "+ldapUser.getSurName();
      }
    }
  }
  return name;
}
```

This method is defined with `ModelAttribute`, meaning it can be directly used in the presentation layer with the `${currentUserName}` expression. We are getting an instance of `Authentication`, and checking if it is of the type `OAuth2AuthenticationToken`. The `getPrincipal()` method will return the user details, along with the attributes. The `name` attribute returns the name of the user that logged in with Google.

The other part will be executed when we perform authentication with LDAP, which gets the `userName` from the `Authentication` object, and then calls the custom service method (`ldapAuthService.getUser()`) to fetch the LDAP user object. It is then used to get the name of the user (the first name and surname).

OAuth with a custom login page

This is how OAuth can be integrated with Spring Security. In the preceding configuration, Spring Boot provides an autogenerated login page, which may suffice for testing purposes. In real scenarios, we may need a customized login page. To build a custom login page, we need to make certain configuration changes in the `configure(HttpSecurity http)` method, as follows:

```
http.authorizeRequests()
  .antMatchers("/","/login").permitAll()
  .antMatchers("/adminPage/").hasAnyAuthority("ADMIN")
  .antMatchers("/userPage/").hasAnyAuthority("USER")
  .anyRequest().fullyAuthenticated()
    .and()
  .oauth2Login().loginPage("/login")
    .defaultSuccessUrl("/privatePage",true)
    .failureUrl("/login?error=true")
    .and()
  .logout()
    .permitAll().logoutSuccessUrl("/login?logout=true");
```

This looks similar to what we configured for LDAP. The only change is that we are using `oauth2Login()` instead of `formLogin()`. The call for `super.configure(http)` has been removed at the end, as it is no longer required. If we place it there, Spring Boot will show an autogenerated login page, so make sure to remove it at the end.

This change will show the custom login page, but the list of OAuth providers will not be visible automatically. We need to prepare the list manually, and show them in the login page. To achieve this, we will need to update the controller method, `showLoginPage()`, as follows. This method basically shows the login page:

```
@Autowired
private ClientRegistrationRepository clientRegistrationRepository;

@GetMapping("/login")
public String showLoginPage(@RequestParam(value = "error",required = false) String error,
    @RequestParam(value = "logout", required = false) String logout,Model
model) {
  logger.info("This is login page URL ");
  if (error != null) {
    model.addAttribute("error", "Invalid Credentials provided.");
  }

  if (logout != null) {
    model.addAttribute("message", "Logged out");
```

```
    }
    String authorizationRequestBaseUri = "oauth2/authorization";
    Map<String, String> oauth2AuthenticationUrls = new HashMap<String,
    String>();
    Iterable<ClientRegistration> clientRegistrations =
    (Iterable<ClientRegistration>)  clientRegistrationRepository;
    clientRegistrations.forEach(registration ->
    oauth2AuthenticationUrls.put(registration.getClientName(),
        authorizationRequestBaseUri + "/" +
registration.getRegistrationId()));
    model.addAttribute("urls", oauth2AuthenticationUrls);

    setProcessingData(model, LdapAuthConstant.TITLE_LOGIN_PAGE);
    return "login";
}
```

This is the login method that we already created at the beginning of the chapter, in order to show the login form. The changes are made specifically for OAuth. First, the instance of `ClientRegistrationRepository` is injected, which represents the repository and stores the OAuth client's primary details. It is an interface type, and Spring Boot provides the instance of the `InMemoryClientRegistrationRepository` class as a default implementation. The `InMemoryClientRegistrationRepository` maintains a map for `ClientRegistration`, a class that represents the OAuth providers.

In the preceding code, we are getting the map of `ClientRegistration` from `clientRegistrationRepository`, iterating it, and preparing the list of OAuth providers with a name and authorization URL that is prefixed with `oauth2/authorization`. We set it as a model attribute, so that it will be available to the presentation layer. After applying these changes, the login page will look as follows:

Dual authentication with OAuth and LDAP

The application will now show a custom login page, along with the list of OAuth clients that we configured. Still, when we enter the credentials manually in the login form, nothing will happen, because the Spring Security is configured for OAuth. The user, when entering credentials in a login form, should be authenticated with LDAP. To achieve this, we need to perform certain configurations specifically within LDAP.

Here, the goal is to perform manual authentication with LDAP. Spring Security provides a way to define a custom authentication provider, by implementing the AuthenticationProvider interface. First, we will write a class that implements this interface and performs LDAP authentication, as follows:

```
@Component
public class CustomLdapAuthProvider implements AuthenticationProvider{

  @Autowired
  LdapAuthService ldapAuthService;

  @Override
  public Authentication authenticate(Authentication authentication) throws
AuthenticationException {
    String userName = authentication.getPrincipal().toString();
    String password = authentication.getCredentials().toString();

    boolean isAuthenticate =
ldapAuthService.authenticateLdapUserWithContext(userName, password);

    if(isAuthenticate == true) {
      List<LdapGranntedAuthority> userRoles =
ldapAuthService.getUserAuthorities(userName);
      return new UsernamePasswordAuthenticationToken(
          userName, password, userRoles);
    }else {
      return null;
    }
  }

  @Override
  public boolean supports(Class<?> authentication) {
    return authentication.equals(
        UsernamePasswordAuthenticationToken.class);
  }
}
```

The class CustomLdapAuthProvider is defined with the @Component annotation, meaning that Spring will configure it as a bean, so that it can be available to other components with the @Autowired annotation. The AuthenticationProvider interface declares the following two methods:

- Authentication authenticate(Authentication authentication): This is the place where we can provide custom authentication.
- boolean supports(Class<?> authentication): This method indicates whether this custom authentication provider supports the indicated authenticated object.

In the authenticate method, we are first getting the username and password from an instance of Authentication. Then, we are doing manual authentication by calling the custom service method authenticateLdapUserWithContext, which we already created for LDAP authentication. If this method returns true, it means that the credentials are valid.

Along with verifying the credentials, we also need to fetch the authorities (roles) that a user has. To get them, we have defined a method in the custom repository impl class (LdapAuthRepositoryCustomImpl), as follows:

```
@Override
public List<LdapGranntedAuthority> getUserAuthorities(String userName) {
   AndFilter groupFilter = new AndFilter();
   groupFilter.and(new EqualsFilter("objectclass","groupOfNames"));
   groupFilter.and(new
EqualsFilter("member","uid="+userName+",ou=users,o=packtPublisher"));
   List<LdapGranntedAuthority> userRoleLst =
ldapTemplate.search(LdapQueryBuilder.query().
                     filter(groupFilter),new LdapRoleMapper());
   return userRoleLst;
}
```

The getUserAuthorities method takes the userName and returns the list of authorities. Let's recall that for roles, we have created a separate entity (ou=roles) in Apache DS. All of its children represent actual roles (with the attribute cn as the role name). Any LDAP user that is a member of a particular authority (role) is added with the member attribute. The aim is to fetch all the authorities of which the current user is a member.

The search method on `ldapTemplate` takes `LdapQuery` and the `ContextMapper` object and returns the list of authorities. The `LdapQuery` is built with a group filter of `objectclass` and value of member attribute. The value of `objectclass` is the same as the name of the `objectclass` that we gave to the entity (ou=roles) in LDAP. The value of the member attribute will be a valid user DN; for example, uid=npatel, ou=users, o=packtPublisher. The `ContextMapper` is a mechanism to retrieve only the required values from the `search` method. More specifically, `ContextMapper` can be used to retrieve custom results (wrap the selected value in custom POJO).

This can be done by providing the implementation for a `ContextMapper` interface. We have created a class for this implementation, as follows:

```
public class LdapRoleMapper implements
ContextMapper<LdapGranntedAuthority>{

  @Override
  public LdapGranntedAuthority mapFromContext(Object ctx) throws
NamingException {
    DirContextAdapter adapter = (DirContextAdapter) ctx;
    String role = adapter.getStringAttribute("cn");
    LdapGranntedAuthority ldapGranntedAuthority = new
LdapGranntedAuthority();
    ldapGranntedAuthority.setAuthority(role);
    return ldapGranntedAuthority;
  }
}
```

The `ContextMapper` interface is a raw type, so we have defined the type as `LdapGranntedAuthority`, which is nothing but a custom POJO. In the `mapFromContext` method, the object of `DirContextAdapter` is used to fetch the name of the role with the attribute cn. This role name is then set in the instance of `LdapGranntedAuthority`, and finally, returns it. The `LdapGranntedAuthority` class looks as follows:

```
public class LdapGranntedAuthority implements GrantedAuthority {
  String authority;
  public void setAuthority(String authority) {
    this.authority = authority;
  }
  @Override
  public String getAuthority() {
    return authority;
  }
}
```

This POJO implements the `GrantedAuthority` interface to set the name of the authority (role). Now, let's go back to the authenticate method of the `CustomLdapAuthProvider` class. After getting the authorities, we are creating the object of the `UsernamePasswordAuthenticationToken` class with the username, password, and list of authorities. The `UsernamePasswordAuthenticationToken` class basically provides an implementation of the `Authentication` interface.

Next, with the help of this custom authentication provider, we will do manual authentication. Before that, we have to change the action of the login form, since the default (`/login`) will no longer work automatically. Change the path from `/login` to `/ldapLogin` in the login form. We also need to create a corresponding controller method to handle the login flow manually, as follows:

```
@Autowired
CustomLdapAuthProvider customLdapAuthProvider;

@PostMapping("/ldapLogin")
public String ldapAuthenticate(HttpServletRequest req, @RequestParam(value =
"username", required = true) String username,
    @RequestParam(value = "password", required = true) String
password, RedirectAttributes redirectAttributes) {
  UsernamePasswordAuthenticationToken authReq
  = new UsernamePasswordAuthenticationToken(username, password);
  Authentication auth = customLdapAuthProvider.authenticate(authReq);
  if(auth !=null) {
    logger.info(" If user is authenticated .... "+auth.isAuthenticated());
    SecurityContext sc = SecurityContextHolder.getContext();
    sc.setAuthentication(auth);
    HttpSession session = req.getSession(true);
session.setAttribute(HttpSessionSecurityContextRepository.SPRING_SECURITY_C
ONTEXT_KEY, sc);

    if(auth.isAuthenticated() == true) {
      return "redirect:/privatePage";
    }else {
      redirectAttributes.addAttribute("error", "true");
      return "redirect:/login";
    }
  }else { // failed authentication - either username or password fails.
    redirectAttributes.addAttribute("error", "true");
    return "redirect:/login";
  }
}
```

The instance of `CustomLdapAuthProvider` is injected with the `@Autowired` annotation. This method is defined with the `@PostMapping` annotation, to handle the login form with the POST method. We are creating the instance of `UsernamePasswordAuthenticationToken` with the username and password that were submitted with the login form, and we pass it to the `authenticate` method of `CustomLdapAuthProvider`, which basically does authentication with LDAP and fetches the user authorities. Once the authentication is done, we will store the authentication object in the Spring Security context.

Finally, we have saved the security context in an HTTP session, so that Spring Security will create and maintain the user authentication information in the session. After performing all of these processes, we are checking whether the authentication is successful by calling the `isAuthenticated` method on the authentication object. Based on the authentication status (success or failure), we are redirecting the flow to either a private page (upon successful authentication) or a login page (upon failed authentication). This was all about using dual authentication with LDAP and OAuth. Next, we will illustrate OAuth implementation on a custom authorization server.

OAuth authorization with a custom authorization server

Now, you have seen OAuth integration with Spring using third-party providers (Google). In this section, we will build a custom authorization server (provider) and do OAuth authorization. We will also build our own resource server, and we'll access the resources once the authorization is done.

In the previous section, the authorization code grant type was used with Google. We will implement an implicit grant type in this section. Let's recall that the implicit grant type was specially designed for JavaScript applications. Since it runs in a browser, the authorization server directly sends the access token. There is no support for refresh tokens, for security purposes.

We will first develop a custom authorization server (provider) that will provide the access token. We can consider it in place of Google in the previous section, where we developed a client for authorization. For our custom authorization, we will set up a client with credentials (an ID and secret), which will be used to provide authorization (in the form of providing an access token).

We will create separate Spring Boot applications for the authorization and resource server, and we will need to run them simultaneously, in order to test the functionality. To avoid the port clashing (the default is 8080 for both applications), we need to explicitly set the port while running them. To do so, you need to give a different port with the property `server.port` in the `application.properties` file.

Authorization server configuration

We will develop a separate Spring Boot application and apply the necessary configurations to use it as an authorization server. This is our custom authorization server. Create a Spring Boot application with the name `SpringCustomAuthorization` and add the following component, which is basically an essential entry point to building a custom authorization server:

```
@Configuration
@EnableAuthorizationServer
public class CustomAuthorizationConfig extends
AuthorizationServerConfigurerAdapter{
  @Autowired
    @Qualifier("authenticationManager")
    private AuthenticationManager authenticationManager;
  @Autowired
  PasswordEncoder encoder;

  @Override
  public void configure(ClientDetailsServiceConfigurer clients)
    throws Exception {
      clients.inMemory()
        .withClient("c1")
        .authorizedGrantTypes("implicit")
        .scopes("read", "write", "trust")
        .secret(encoder.encode("123"))
        .redirectUris("http://localhost:8082/privatePage")
        .resourceIds("oauth2-server");
  }
  @Bean
  public JwtAccessTokenConverter accessTokenConverter() {
      JwtAccessTokenConverter converter = new JwtAccessTokenConverter();
      converter.setSigningKey("123");
      return converter;
  }
  @Bean
  public TokenStore tokenStore() {
      return new JwtTokenStore(accessTokenConverter());
```

```
        }

        @Override
        public void configure(
          AuthorizationServerEndpointsConfigurer endpoints)
          throws Exception {
            endpoints
              .authenticationManager(authenticationManager)
              .tokenServices(tokenServices())
              .tokenStore(tokenStore())
              .accessTokenConverter(accessTokenConverter());
        }
        @Bean("resourceServerTokenServices")
        @Primary
        public DefaultTokenServices tokenServices() {
            DefaultTokenServices defaultTokenServices = new
    DefaultTokenServices();
            defaultTokenServices.setTokenStore(tokenStore());
            defaultTokenServices.setSupportRefreshToken(false);
            defaultTokenServices.setAccessTokenValiditySeconds(120);
            defaultTokenServices.setTokenEnhancer(accessTokenConverter());
            return defaultTokenServices;
        }
    }
```

With the `@EnableAuthorizationServer` annotation, this class claims to present a configuration for the authorization server. In order to understand the concept in more detail, we will associate each step for configuring the custom authorization server with what we already did in the Google OAuth integration. The very first step in this configuration is to define a client, which basically talks to an authorization server to get an access token.

The `configure(ClientDetailsServiceConfigurer clients)` method is used to define a client with various metadata, like the client ID, grant type, scopes, secret, and redirection URI. The `resourceId` is used to make the pair with the resource server. We will configure the same `resourceId` while creating a resource server later in this chapter. The type of client that we have used here is in-memory, which is appropriate for developmental purposes.

Another type is JDBC, wherein the client details can be stored in the database. We can configure multiple clients in this method, and each can be separated with the `.and()` method call. The client is created within an authorization server. We can relate this to the client that we created in the Google developer console.

w

The `tokenStore()` method is used to construct an access token. Spring provides various mechanisms, like `InMemoryTokenStore`, `JdbcTokenStore`, `JwkTokenStore`, and `JwtTokenStore`, to create a token. Out of these, we have used `JwtTokenStore`. The `accessTokenConverter()` method is used to encode/decode the token with a signing key.

We need to use the same signing key while configuring the token store at the resource server. The `tokenServices()` method is used to configure the token service with the token store, along with a few settings. Since the grant type is implicit, the refresh token is not allowed, so we are setting `setSupportRefreshToken()` to `false`. We can also set how long the token is valid, through the `setAccessTokenValiditySeconds()` method. Since this is an implicit flow and will be used by a JavaScript application, the token should be short-lived, for security reasons.

Finally, the `configure(AuthorizationServerEndpointsConfigurer endpoints)` method is a glue point to group the things that we have configured so far together. Generally, user authentication is performed prior to authorization, and the object of `AuthenticationManager` is used to perform the authentication. After defining the authorization configuration, let's make it secure by applying security configurations, as follows:

```
@Configuration
@EnableWebSecurity
public class WebSecurityConfig extends WebSecurityConfigurerAdapter {

    @Override
    @Bean("authenticationManager")
    public AuthenticationManager authenticationManagerBean() throws
Exception {
        AuthenticationManager authenticationManager =
super.authenticationManagerBean();
        return authenticationManager;
    }
    @Override
  public void configure(WebSecurity web) throws Exception {
    web.ignoring().antMatchers("/js/**");
    web.ignoring().antMatchers("/css/**");
  }

    @Override
    protected void configure(AuthenticationManagerBuilder auth)
      throws Exception {
        auth.inMemoryAuthentication()
          .withUser("john").password(new
BCryptPasswordEncoder().encode("123")).authorities("USER");
```

```
    }

    @Override
    protected void configure(HttpSecurity http) throws Exception {
        http
            .authorizeRequests()
            .antMatchers("/oauth/authorize","/").permitAll()
            .and()
            .formLogin().loginPage("/login").permitAll();
    }

    @Bean("encoder")
    public BCryptPasswordEncoder encoder(){
        return new BCryptPasswordEncoder();
    }
}
```

With the `@EnableWebSecurity` annotation, Spring Security will be applied to the authorization server. It is a normal Spring Security configuration that you have already seen in previous sections. The `/oauth/authorize` is a default authorization endpoint. The resource server will initiate an authorization call on this path, so we have configured it in the `configure` method.

We have created an in-memory user with credentials and authority. We can associate it with the user account hold in Google, which is being asked when we initiate authorization with Google. In our case, we will provide this credential when the authorization process is initiated at the custom authorization server.

Our authorization server is now ready. It cannot be accessed directly; instead, the resource server initiates the request with certain parameters. Next, we will build the resource server.

Resource server configuration

As its name suggests, a **resource server** holds resources (in the form of data, services, files, and so on), which can be accessed by the resource owner by providing valid authorization. The process of providing authorization happens in the form of a **token sharing mechanism**.

The authorization server creates a token after authentication, which is used by a resource server to serve the restricted resources. For all incoming requests for protected resources, the resource server will check the validity of the access token with the authorization server. This is the flow of the system, in brief. Now, we will create a resource server with a separate Spring Boot application.

Spring allows for creating a resource server by declaring certain essential configurations, as follows:

```
@Configuration
@EnableResourceServer
public class ResourceServerConfig extends ResourceServerConfigurerAdapter {

private static final String RESOURCE_ID = "oauth2-server";

  @Override
  public void configure(ResourceServerSecurityConfigurer resources) {
    resources
      .tokenStore(tokenStore())
      .resourceId(RESOURCE_ID);
  }

  @Override
  public void configure(HttpSecurity http) throws Exception {
        http
            .authorizeRequests()
            .antMatchers("/api/**").authenticated()
            .and().exceptionHandling().accessDeniedHandler(new
OAuth2AccessDeniedHandler());
  }

  @Bean
    public TokenStore tokenStore() {
        return new JwtTokenStore(accessTokenConverter());
    }
  @Bean
    public JwtAccessTokenConverter accessTokenConverter() {
        JwtAccessTokenConverter converter = new JwtAccessTokenConverter();
        converter.setSigningKey("123");
        return converter;
    }

  }
```

The @EnableResourceServer annotation will instruct Spring Security to treat the component as the resource server and to authenticate incoming requests with an access token. In this configuration, we are using the same resourceId that we used in the authorization server. Also, the process of creating and converting the token, along with the signing key, is the same as what we implemented in the authorization server.

For a token of the type Jwt, we can also use the public-private key as a signing key for generating an access token. In a normal case, the signing key declared at the authorization and resource server must be the same.

The `configure(HttpSecurity http)` method of this class is a place where we can configure the path of protected resources. In our case, we are configuring /api/**, meaning that any path that starts with /api/ is considered secure. Without a valid token, the user cannot access that path. We also defined the appropriate denied handler to show an appropriate message, in the case of invalid tokens or insufficient privileges. Next, we will configure Spring Security for the resource server, as follows:

```
@Configuration
@EnableWebSecurity
public class WebSecurityConfig extends WebSecurityConfigurerAdapter{
      @Override
      protected void configure(HttpSecurity http) throws Exception {
         http
            .authorizeRequests()
            .antMatchers("/","/customAuth").permitAll()
          .anyRequest().authenticated();
      }
   }
```

This is a straightforward security configuration, where we have declared certain paths to be accessible by all. Next, we will create a Spring MVC controller, which will show the page from which we can initiate authorization, as follows:

```
@Controller
public class WebController {

  private Logger logger = LoggerFactory.getLogger(WebController.class);
  @GetMapping("/")
  public String showHomePage(Model model) {
    logger.info("This is show home page method ");
    setProcessingData(model, "Home Page");
    return "home";
  }
  @GetMapping("/privatePage")
  public String showControlPage(Model model) {
    logger.info("This is privaet page ");
      setProcessingData(model, "Private Page");
      return "private-page";
  }
  @GetMapping("/customAuth")
  public String authorizeUser(Model
```

```
model,@Value("${custom.auth.authorization-uri}") String authorizationUri,
      @Value("${custom.auth.client-id}") String clientId,
      @Value("${custom.auth.client-secret}") String clientSecret,
      @Value("${custom.auth.grant-type}") String grantType,
      @Value("${custom.auth.response-type}") String responseType) {
      UriComponentsBuilder uriBuilder =
UriComponentsBuilder.fromHttpUrl(authorizationUri)
                  .queryParam("username", clientId)
                  .queryParam("password", clientSecret)
                  .queryParam("grant_type", grantType)
                  .queryParam("response_type", responseType)
                  .queryParam("client_id", clientId);
      return "redirect:"+uriBuilder.toUriString();
  }
}
```

The first two methods show the home page and private page, respectively. We will show a link on the home page that will initiate the authorization process. This link will call the `authorizeUser()` method (with the link `/customAuth`). This method fetches the client metadata that is defined in the `application.properties` file, as follows:

```
custom.auth.authorization-uri=http://localhost:8081/oauth/authorizee
custom.auth.client-id=c1
custom.auth.client-secret=123
custom.auth.grant-type=implicit
custom.auth.response-type=token
```

In the `authorizeUser()` method, we are redirecting the flow to the authorization URI, along with the `client-id`, `client-secret`, `grant-type`, and `response-type` parameters. The `oauth/authorize` is a default authorization endpoint.

Let's recall that, while doing a client setup in the authorization server, we configured the `redirectUri` as `http://localhost:8082/privatePage`, meaning that after authorization, the flow will go back to this URL, which ultimately shows a private page, along with the access token.

Once we get the token, we can start to consume the protected resources. We have defined the path `/api/**` as protected resources in the resource server configuration. So, let's create a REST controller, as follows, which will provide the resources. For demo purpose, we will return some sample data:

```
@RestController
@RequestMapping("/api")
public class ServiceAPIController {
  private Logger logger =
LoggerFactory.getLogger(ServiceAPIController.class);
```

```
@RequestMapping("/currentUser")
public Principal getUser(Principal user) {
  return user;
}
@RequestMapping("/adminresource")
public String adminResource(Principal user) {
  return "{\"id\":\"" + user.getName() + "\",\"content\":\"Hello
World\"}";
}
@RequestMapping(value="/usergreeting", method = RequestMethod.GET,
produces = {MediaType.APPLICATION_JSON_VALUE})
  public String userResource(Principal user) {
    return "{\"id\":\"" + user.getName() + "\",\"content\":\"Hello
World\"}";
}
@RequestMapping(value = "/userlist", method = RequestMethod.GET)
public ResponseEntity<List<SampleUser>> listAllSampleUsers() {
    logger.info("Listing all users...");
    SampleUser s1 = new SampleUser();
    SampleUser s2 = new SampleUser();
    s1.setFirstName("Nilang");
    s1.setLastName("Patel");
    s2.setFirstName("Komal");
    s2.setLastName("Patel");
    List<SampleUser> users = new ArrayList<SampleUser>();
    users.add(s1);
    users.add(s2);
    return new ResponseEntity<List<SampleUser>>(users, HttpStatus.OK);
}
}
```

The REST controller is configured with path /api, meaning that all of its methods can be accessible with the valid authorization token. Now, it is time to run the application and test the flow. We will first run the resource server application (http://localhost:8082, assuming it is running on port 8082). It will show a link, which will redirect the flow to the authorization server.

Soon after the flow reaches the authorization server, it prompts a login page. This is because an authorization server required a valid authentication before even starting authorization. This makes sense, because the authorization server will authorize the given user account, and for this, a user must be logged in. We will use the in-memory credentials that we created for the authorization server.

Soon after logging in, the authorization server shows an intermediate page and asks a user to either allows or denies. Based on that, a user can access the restricted resource on the resource server, as follows:

This is similar to when we created a client in the Google developer console and did authorization with it. At that time, first, we gave Google the credentials, and after authentication, it asked for the approval of access for the client. When we authorize the client, it will redirect to the private page of the resource server with an access token.

At this moment, the access token is returned with # character in the response. To access any protected resources, we need to append the access token with ?, so that it will be supplied as a request parameter. Without this, the resource server will not allow for accessing any protected resources.

Now, we can access protected resources with the access token. The rest controller (with the path /api) will serve the resources. For example, the URL http://localhost:8082/api/ usergreeting?access_token=<token_string> will give the following output:

```
{"id":"john","content":"Hello World"}
```

It will show a token expired error if the request is made after the token validity is over. It will also throw an invalid token error if the original token is altered. Without supplying the token, it will show an error like, Full authentication is required to access this resource.

Method-level resource permissions

Now, an authorized user can access all of the resources that we have configured. How good would it be if the resources could be accessed based on user roles? It would provide for more fine-grained control over the resources. This is possible by applying method-level configurations in Spring Security. For this, first, we need to define a class that represents method-level Spring Security configurations, as follows:

```
@Configuration
@EnableGlobalMethodSecurity(prePostEnabled = true, securedEnabled = true)
public class MethodSecurityConfig extends GlobalMethodSecurityConfiguration
{

  @Override
  protected MethodSecurityExpressionHandler createExpressionHandler() {
    return new OAuth2MethodSecurityExpressionHandler();
  }
}
```

The `@EnableGlobalMethodSecurity` annotation is required to define authorization constraints at the method level. The base class, `GlobalMethodSecurityConfiguration`, provides a default implementation of method-level security configuration.

We have overridden the `createExpressionHandle` method to supply `OAuth2MethodSecurityExpressionHandler` instead of `DefaultMethodSecurityExpressionHandler`, which is provided out of the box. Spring Security uses an AOP proxy mechanism to apply method-level security configurations.

The `prePostEnabled` and `securedEnabled` options enable respective annotations at the method level, to define authorization rules. For example, `prePostEnabled` will allow for defining the Spring Security pre/post annotations `@PreAuthorize` and `@PostAuthorize`. These annotations allow for expression-based access control, meaning that we can use Spring **EL (Expression Language)** to describe the rule.

The `@PreAuthorize` will evaluate the expression before entering the method, while the `@PostAuthorize` will verify the expression after method execution has completed, and could alter the result. The `securedEnabled` option of `@EnableGlobalMethodSecurity` is used to define the `@Secured` annotation. With the `@Secuired` annotation, we can specify a list of roles on a method. Let's look at a few examples of this annotation, as follows:

```
@Secured("ROLE_USER")
public String getUserAccnt() {
. . . .
```

```
    }
    @Secured({ "ROLE_USER", "ROLE_ADMIN" })
    public String getCompanyPolicy() {
    ....
    }
```

The `getUserAccnt` method will be accessible by the user that has a role as `ROLE_USER`. The `getCompanyPolicy` method will be invoked by a user who has at least one role among `ROLE_USER` and `ROLE_ADMIN`. The `@Secuired` annotation does not allow for defining an expression with Spring EL. On the other hand, the `@PreAuthorize` and `@PostAuthorize` annotations allow for Spring EL to define the expression, meaning that we can define the more complex condition. Let's look at some examples of `@PreAuthorize`, as follows:

```
    @PreAuthorize("hasAuthority('ADMIN') and #oauth2.hasScope('read')")
    public String adminResource(Principal user) {
      ...
    }
    @PreAuthorize("hasAuthority('USER') and #oauth2.hasScope('read') or
    (!#oauth2.isOAuth() and hasAuthority('USER'))")
    public String userResource(Principal user) {
      ...
    }
    @PreAuthorize("hasAuthority('ADMIN') or #oauth2.hasScope('trust') or
    (!#oauth2.isOAuth() and hasAuthority('ADMIN'))")
    public ResponseEntity<List<SampleUser>> listAllSampleUsers() {
      ...
    }
```

The first method (`adminResource`) is accessible for the user with a `USER` role, and the client should have a `read` scope. Let's recall that for the client that we configured in the authorization server, we set three scopes: read, write, and trust. The `#oauth2` variable is provided out of the box, and is used to check the various scopes that a client has. We can utilize other methods on the `#oauth2` variable, like `clientHasRole()`, `clientHasAnyRole()`, `hasAnyScope()`, `isOAuth()`, `isUser()`, `isClient()`, and so on. They are defined in the class `OAuth2SecurityExpressionMethods`. In short, the variable `#oauth2` represents the object of this class.

The second method (`userResource`) is a bit more complex, and can be accessed under the following conditions:

- A user has a `USER` role and a client has a `read` scope
- A request is not of the OAuth type (it may be raised by a machine client) and a user has a `USER` role

The third method (`listAllSampleUsers`) is similar to the second method, and can be accessed in the following situations:

- A user has an `ADMIN` role
- A client has a `trust` scope
- A request is not of the OAuth type (it may be raised by a machine client) and a user has an `ADMIN` role

This is how the implicit grant type can be implemented with the custom authorization server. There are certain things that require attention while using the implicit grant type. Since it was designed for JavaScript applications, both the authorization and resource server should be securely accessible (with HTTPS). The second thing is, in an implicit grant type, the access token is directly returned by the authorization server to the browser, instead of at a trusted backend; it is highly recommended to configure short-lived access tokens, to mitigate the risk of the access token being leaked.

Another challenge in the implicit flow is that it does not allow refresh tokens. That means that after the short-lived token has expired, a user should be prompt to initiate the flow again; or, a better method might be to set a mechanism, like `iframe`, to get the new token without interruption.

As an exercise, you could create a few more users with different roles in the authorization server, and configure the resource methods with those roles, checking how they are accessible.

Summary

Security is an essential part of any system. How effective it is depends on various aspects, like simplicity, feature richness, ease of integration with other systems, flexibility, robustness, and so on. This whole chapter was based on Spring Security. It is a fully-fledged framework that's used to secure J2EE-based applications.

In this chapter, we explored Spring Security more closely, especially how it can be integrated with LDAP and OAuth. We started with the basics of LDAP, including its data structure and setup; we created the structure in Apache DS, which is an LDAP server. Then, we explored the required configurations with Spring Security, to integrate it with LDAP.

Along with authentication with LDAP, we explored how to manage users in LDAP from a Spring application. We used the Spring Data framework to achieve this. Next, we created a structure for the role (authority) in LDAP. In the same sequence, we fetched the role details and implemented authorization in Spring Security with LDAP.

Later in the chapter, we started to cover another mechanism, called OAuth. It is an open standard for token-based authorization. We began with the basics of OAuth roles, then explored details about various grant types; you also learned which grant should be used when. Going further, we started on Spring Security integration with OAuth. We used Google to implement the authorization code flow with Spring Security.

With the default OAuth implementation, Spring Security shows the autogenerated login page. We showed how to implement a custom login page in OAuth. Up to that point, you had only seen the two different mechanisms, LDAP and OAuth, independently. We integrated both of them together, creating dual authentication.

We then implemented OAuth with the authorization code flow. Next, we showed how to implement the implicit flow with custom authorization and the resource server. We performed a set of configurations for both the authorization and resource server, and we successfully implemented an implicit flow. Towards the end, we applied method-level authorization in Spring Security.

In next chapter, we will explore another tool, called JHipster. It is an open source application generator framework that's mainly used to develop web applications and microservices with responsive web fronts (Angular or React) and the Spring framework as a backend.

5
An Application to View Countries and their GDP using JHipster

As time has passed, changing business functions have required delivery teams to produce high-quality software products at a rapid pace. To meet this expectation, the IT industry has become focused on making the software development process streamlined and automated. As a result, many new platforms are emerging, with the aim of generating the code to prepare production-ready applications in no time.

We started our journey with a simple application developed in Spring Framework that showed the **gross domestic product** (**GDP**) information of various countries with the World Bank API, in Chapter 1, *Creating an Application to List World Countries with their GDP*. The Spring Framework provides a comprehensive way to develop an enterprise-ready application with ease.

With the birth of Spring Boot framework, development with Spring Framework has become far quicker and smarter than ever before. In subsequent chapters, we moved on to Spring Boot and explored its capabilities, specifically for integration with other Spring and third-party libraries and modules.

In this chapter, we will explore another framework, named JHipster, which is one step ahead in making Spring-based applications with just a few clicks, and makes Spring development joyful. We will utilize JHipster to develop the application from `Chapter 1`, *Creating an Application to List World Countries with their GDP*, showing the GDP information of various countries and showcasing how the development process is streamlined and automated. We will cover the following interesting topics in this chapter:

- Introducing JHipster
- Installation
- Application creation
- Modeling and creation of the entity
- Creating the GDP application
- Learn how to add customization in JHipster application
- Other features of JHipster

Technical requirements

All the code used in this chapter can be downloaded from the following GitHub link: `https://github.com/PacktPublishing/Spring-5.0-Projects/tree/master/chapter05`. The code can be executed on any operating system, although it has only been tested on Windows.

Introducing JHipster

JHipster is, in brief, a code generating tool, built on top of large collections of development, build, test, and deployment frameworks and platforms. It is a modern web application development platform, used to build all layers of a comprehensive Java-based web application, from the frontend to the database. JHipster supports various frameworks under the hood, giving the user options to choose from when starting application development.

JHipster is a free and open source platform aimed at greatly simplifying the process of generating, developing, and deploying monolithic and microservices-based applications on Spring Framework and Angular or React technologies. Before building an application in JHipster, a user will be asked various questions, in order to generate a production-ready application based on the options chosen by the user. JHipster provides the application with support for the following tools and frameworks, out of the box:

- **Build tool:** Maven, Gradle
- **Development platform:** Spring Framework
- **Security framework:** Spring Security
- **Templating:** Thymeleaf
- **Microservices:** Netflix OSS
- **RDBMS:** H2, MySQL, Oracle, PostgreSQL, MS SQL, MariaDB
- **Data streaming:** Kafka
- **DB tracker:** Liquibase
- **NoSQL:** MonboDB, Cassandra, Couchbase, Hazelcast
- **Cache implementation:** Infinispan, Ehcache
- **Search engine:** Elasticsearch and **Elasticsearch, Logstash, and Kibana** stack (**ELK**)
- **Monitoring:** Prometheus
- **ORM:** Hibernate
- **Testing framework:** Cucumber, Browsersync, Jest, Protractor test
- **Load testing:** Gatling
- **UI:** Bootstrap, HTML5, CSS3, SaaS, Redux
- **JavaScript framework:** Angular, Typescript, React, Webpack
- **Deployment:** Docker, Kubernetes, Boxfuse, Rancher
- **Cloud support:** Heroku, Cloud Foundry, AWS, OpenShift
- **CI/CD:** Jenkins, Travis CI, GitLab CI, CircleCI

The code generated by JHipster is as per industry standards, best practices, and quality compliance. Along with autogenerating application code, JHipster also supports automated testing and the continuous integration and delivery of the application in a more streamlined way. This can bring great benefits to an organization, as follows:

- Creating an application with various platforms and frameworks in a uniform and controlled way.
- Most of the boilerplate code is generated automatically, so a developer can focus on the implementation of business requirements. This will increase developer productivity and greatly improve the overall project delivery timeline.
- Easy integration of changes throughout the application, from the frontend to the database table.
- Improved code quality of the application, overall.
- Different projects in the organization can share common artifacts with ease. Consequently, the overall productivity of the project teams will be improved.

Installing JHipster

JHipster recommends that normal users install with `npm`. The `npm` is a package manager from `Node.js`, used to install various software. It is the world's largest software repository, where you will find thousands of pieces of open source software, in the form of packages. If `npm` is not installed, just go to the **Downloads** section of the Node site (`https://nodejs.org/en/download`) and install the latest 64-bit **Long Term Support** (**LTS**) version, because the non-LTS version is not supported by JHipster.

Once `npm` is installed, run the following command to install the JHipster package from the command line:

```
npm install -g generator-jhipster
```

JHipster uses another tool, named **Yeoman** (`http://yeoman.io/`), to generate the application code, which is installed along with the JHipster Node package. After creating an application, JHipster provides an option to build it with either Maven or Gradle. For this, JHipster will install the required wrappers for Maven and Gradle, so nothing is required explicitly, especially for building an app.

 Local installation of JHipster can also be done with Yarn, another package manager for installing software. The process of installing JHipster with Yarn is almost identical to that of `npm`.

Creating an application

After installing JHipster, the next step is to create an application. Create a project directory with an appropriate name in your local machine, select this directory from Command Prompt, and execute the following command. The name of the project directory is given as gdp, but it can be any valid name:

```
jhipster
```

Soon after hitting this command, JHipster will start to ask a series of questions, and will decide what has to be generated based on the answers given by the user, as follows:

1. **Which type of application would you like to create?** There are four possible options to choose from, as follows:
   - **Monolithic application:** This option is used to create a self-contained application. This is the recommended option to create a simple application, so we will choose this option.
   - **Microservice application:** If you want to design an application based on a microservices architecture, you can choose this option.
   - **Microservice gateway:** The microservice gateway is used to build a microservice-based application with the UI. By default, microservice applications do not have a UI.
   - **JHipster UAA server:** JHipster supports creating applications with **User Authentication and Authorization** (**UAA**).

2. **What is the base name of your application?** You need to give your application a name. By default, it takes the same name as the project directory. If you want, you can give it another name.

3. **What is your default Java package name?** Next, you need to give a Java package name. You can give an appropriate name (it will be considered as a base package, and all other Java source files will be generated in their respective packages relative to this package).

4. **Do you want to use the JHipster Registry to configure, monitor, and scale your application?** This question concerns using the JHipster Registry in our application. The registry is extensively used in microservice-based applications, for registering various services. For a monolithic application, we can still use it because although it is a kind of registry, it concerns the health of the application, which helps us to monitor the application. It comes as a Docker image. For simplicity, we are not going to use it, so choose **No** and go ahead.

5. **Which type of authentication would you like to use?** Next up is the authentication mechanism. It provides three options to choose from, as follows. We will select the third option (HTTP session authentication):

    1. **JWT Authentication: JSON Web Token (JWT)**, which is an open standard for transmitting information between two parties in form of JSON. Authentication is the most common use case of JWT.

    2. **OAuth2/OIDC Authentication:** JHipster provides complete support for OAuth2 with Keycloak and **OpenID Connect (OIDC)**, which is generated by default when we select this option. Keyclock is an open source identity brokering and access management solution. **Open ID Connect (OIDC)**, which is a simple identity layer on top of the OAuth2 protocol.

    3. **HTTP session authentication:** This authenticates users based on sessions. This is the most commonly used option.

6. **Which type of database would you like to use?** Next, it will ask the type of database, we would like to use in our application. JHipster supports various SQL databases. It also supports three NoSQL databases—MongoDB, Couchbase, and Cassandra, which has a Spring data backend. We will select SQL.

7. **Which production/development database would you like to use?** You will be asked separate questions to select specific databases for production and development. JHipster maintains various profiles for various environments (such as development, production, and so on). It will configure the databases based on your selected options. In our case, we will select MySQL for both production and development.

8. **Do you want to use the Spring cache abstraction?** Moving further, it will ask about the type of caching mechanism, such as Ehcache, Hazelcase, Memcached, or no cache at all; Spring cache abstraction will be used to plug any of them. We can select any of them, based on our particular business needs and the underlying hardware architecture (single node, multi-node, distributed, and so on). We will choose Ehcache (which is selected by default).

9. **Do you want to use Hibernate second level cache?** Here, we have the option to use Hibernate's second-level cache. Select **Yes** for this option.

10. **Would you like to use Maven or Gradle for building the backend?** You will be asked to choose either Maven or Gradle as a build tool. We will select **Maven**.

11. **Which other technologies would you like to use?** Towards the end, JHipster will ask to add a few additional technologies, such as Elasticsearch, WebSocket, asynchronous messaging with Kafka, and API-first development with the OpenAPI generator. API-first is an approach to designing an application with the API first, and developing web or mobile applications on top of those APIs. Nowadays, many companies are adopting this approach, and JHipster supports it out of the box. To make the thing simple and straightforward, we will not select either of them. Since this is a multiple choice selector, you can just press *Enter* to move further without selecting any of them.

12. **Which Framework would you like to use for the client?** The next question asks you to select a frontend framework, either Angular or React. Select **Angular** and press *Enter*.

13. **Would you like to enable Sass stylesheet preprocessor?** Next, it will ask you whether to use the **syntactically awesome style sheets** (**Sass**) stylesheet preprocessor. Select **Yes**.

14. **Would you like to enable internationalization support?** If you wish to add support for internationalization, select a **native language**. Select **English** as an answer.

15. **Please choose additional languages to install:** Along with your native language, you can add support for additional languages. JHipster supports around 30 languages. To make things simple, we will not add any additional language.

16. **Besides JUnit and Jest, which testing frameworks would you like to use?** You will be asked to select unit testing frameworks on this screen. JHipster supports the Gatling, Cucumber, and Protractor frameworks, as well as the default JUnit for unit testing. Select none of them and move to the next step.

17. **Would you like to install other generators from the JHipster Marketplace?** The last question will ask you whether to add additional modules from the JHipster marketplace. This is a collection of third-party generators that work on top of the core JHipster, with access to its variables and functions and acts like sub-generators. You can use them in your application by downloading them from the JHipster Marketplace (`https://www.jhipster.tech/modules/marketplace`). We will select **No** for this option.

Project structure

Now, sit back and relax, and JHipster will start to create an application based on the options we selected. At this moment, JHipster will generate the code and project structure of our application. In brief, JHipster generates the following things to make an application ready to run:

- Spring Boot application
- Angular JS application (at the frontend)
- Liquibase changelog file (used for database table **Data Definition Language (DDL)** manipulation)
- Other configuration files

We can configure an **integrated development environment** (IDE) for further development once the application has been created. JHipster supports a wide range of IDEs, including Eclipse, IntelliJ IDEA, and Visual Studio Code. You can read more about this topic at `https://www.jhipster.tech/configuring-ide`. The application structure looks as follows:

Let's look at each Java package, as follows:

- `com.nilangpatel.aop.logging`: This contains **Aspect-Oriented Programming** (**AOP**) advice for logging.
- `com.nilangpatel.config`: This package contains various configurations for properties, cache, database, profile, Liquibase, logging, Spring Security, metrics, web, locale, and so on, along with constants used across the application.
- `com.nilangpatel.config.audit`: JHipster provides auditing features out of the box. This package contains configurations specifically for auditing.
- `com.nilangpatel.domain`: This contains all of the model objects for the custom entities that we created, along with other core model objects.
- `com.nilangpatel.domain.enumeration`: This contains enumerations that we declared in the **JHipster Domain Language** (**JDL**). We will discuss JDL more in the upcoming section.
- `com.nilangpatel.repository`: Spring Data **Java Persistence API** (**JPA**) repositories for each custom and out-of-the-box entities, are stored here.
- `com.nilangpatel.security`: All security-related classes, such as constants for `Roles`, `UserDetail` service, and so on, are stored in this package.
- `com.nilangpatel.service`: This contains service-layer interfaces for out-of-the-box and custom entities.
- `com.nilangpatel.service.dto`: The **data transfer objects** (**DTOs**), used to transfer between the controller and the service, are kept here.
- `com.nilangpatel.service.mapper`: Mapper classes that are used to map model objects with DTOs will be stored in this package.
- `com.nilangpatel.service.util`: This package contains some utility classes.
- `com.nilangpatel.web.rest`: All **Representational State Transfer** (**REST**) controllers for each entity are generated under this package.
- `com.nilangpatel.web.rest.error`: Exceptions specific to REST calls are available here.
- `com.nilangpatel.web.rest.util`: This contains some utility classes that are used in REST calls.
- `com.nilangpatel.web.rest.vm`: This contains view models, which are mainly used in the **Administration** tab in the UI.

Along with Java classes and packages, JHipster also generates certain resources in the `src/main/resource` folder. The details are as follows:

- `config`: This contains various configuration files, such as `application.properties` for Spring Boot with various profiles, some Liquibase configuration files, along with `changelog` files and keystore files for importing and configuring certificates for HTTPS configuration.
- `i18`: This contains property files for various languages that we selected during application creation.
- `templates`: This folder contains various mail templates, such as activation, account creation, and password reset, along with error templates.

It is time to run an application. JHipster provides the following command to build an application with Maven. Make sure that you are at the project directory in the Command Prompt:

mvnw

Along with building an application, this command will deploy it on the embedded web server (which ships with Spring Boot by default). It can be accessed at `http://localhost:8080`, and looks as follows:

If an application needs to be deployed on any application server, JHipster provides a way to generate an executable WAR file, with the command `mvnw -Pprod package` for Maven and `gradlew -Pprod bootWar` for Gradle.

JHipster generates a set of pages and a few users accounts to start with. Click on **Account | Sign in** to login into the application. By default, `Admin` users can log in with credentials as `admin/admin`, and normal users can log in with `user/user`. The `Admin` user has access to the **Administration** menu, from where they can perform various admin functions.

Entity creation

A web application has some sort of database interaction, covering basic **Create, Read, Update, and Delete** (**CRUD**) operations, as a bare minimum. It requires a good amount of effort when done manually. The following tasks need to be completed, in this case:

- Creating database tables, along with their relations and constraints
- Constructing a model entity and building the **data access object** (**DAO**) layer to provide the data interface with the database
- Generating a service layer to encapsulate business logic
- Preparing the web controller and frontend layer, along with all validations, to store the data in the respective entity table

Apart from this, additional effort may be required to accommodate future changes on any layer. JHipster provides an ingenious solution to this problem. After creating an application, we need to build a data access layer, and JHipster makes this whole process automatic.

A concept in JHipster called **entity generation** makes this happen. Entities are the building elements of JHipster applications. The entity generation process covers various tasks, as follows:

- Creating database tables and maintaining their changes (through configuration)
- Constructing a JPA model class, along with a Spring Data JPA repository
- Creating an optional service layer to accommodate business rules
- Creating REST controllers supporting basic CRUD operations and frontend side Angular router
- Component and service along with HTML view including integration and performance tests

Isn't it cool? Let's witness the process of making an entity and generating the code automatically.

Adding an entity with the CLI

To demonstrate the process of creating an entity in JHipster, we will first create a simple entity, called **Owner**, with one attribute, called **name**. The way that JHipster allows for entity creation, along with data access, the service layer, controller, and frontend layer for that entity is identical to the process of generating application code that we saw in the previous section. Both can be done with the CLI.

For entity generation, JHipster uses the Yeoman tool internally to generate the code. Let's create our first entity. Execute the following command to create an entity:

```
jhipster entity Owner
```

The `Owner` is the name of an entity. This command will create an entity for `Owner`, and will launch a wizard that asks a few questions of the user, as follows:

1. **Do you want to add a field to your entity?** If you wish to add a field for your entity, select **y**.
2. **What is the name of your field?** You can give the name of the attribute here.
3. **What is the type of your field?** You need to provide the type of attribute. JHipster supports various attribute types, including `string`, `integer`, `long`, `float`, `double`, `BigDecimal`, and `LocalDate`.
4. **Do you want to add validation rules to your field?** This concerns whether you wish to add any constraints on an attribute of the entity. Select **y**.
5. **Which validation rules do you want to add?** JHipster also allows you to add various constraints, including `required`, `unique`, `min` value, `max` value, and regular expression patterns, to validate the input. You can select more than one constraint here.

The preceding process of adding attributes can be repeated to add further attributes to its type and constraints. We will create the `Owner` entity with the `name` attribute of the `String` type, with the `required` constraint.

JHipster also allows you to define a relation with another entity. Once we have finished adding attributes, it will ask us to add a relationship. Since we have created only the `Owner` entity, we will add the relationship after we add another entity. We will see how to add a relationship later on.

At the moment, just say no (**n**) to adding a relationship, and JHipster will show the next set of questions related to the service and controller layer, as follows:

6. **Do you want to use a separate service class for your business logic?** In this question, we have been asked if we wish to add a service layer, and the possible options are as follows. We will select the third option:

   1. No, the REST controller should use the repository directly; the REST controller will make a direct call to the repository. No service layer is added.

   2. Yes, generate a separate service class; the service layer is added with a service class only. The REST controller will call this class for any database interaction. We can write additional business logic in the service class.

   3. Yes, generate a separate service interface and implementation; in this case, the service layer is added with both interface and implementation. The clear advantage of this design is we can provide another implementation of the service interface without changing other code.

7. **Do you want to use a DTO?** The next question is related to DTO. JHipster provides an option to create a DTO for each entity. It uses MapStruct, another code generator tool used to map Java entities to generate DTOs. Basically, it is used to map the values from DTO to the model entity, and vice versa. The options for this question are as follows. We will select the second option:

   1. No, use the entity directly; an entity object is used to pass the data throughout all of the layers.

   2. Yes, generate a DTO with MapStruct; this will generate a DTO corresponding to each entity. The controller will create an instance of DTO and pass it to the service layer. The service class will map the DTO to the entity and call the repository to interact with a database.

8. **Do you want to add filtering?** This will provide a dynamic filtering option to search for specific entities. It uses a JPA static meta-model for filtering option. JHipster will create complete code, from the presentation to the DAO, if we choose **Yes**. Though it is quite useful to have the filter option, we will select **No** for this question, for the sake of simplicity.

9. **Do you want pagination on your entity?** The next question is about pagination patterns. JHipster supports the following patterns for pagination. We will select the second option:

   1. No; this will mean no pagination. All of the records will be visible in a single page. This will create performance issues for large datasets.
   2. Yes, with pagination links; this shows the pagination with links to move between pages. This is the most common pagination style.
   3. Yes, with infinite scroll; this uses infinite scroll to display the data. The scroll will serve the purpose of pagination.

Now, JHipster will start to create the entity, and will ask to override certain files wherever it finds some conflicts. This is because JHipster will start to generate the code again. Keep saying yes (**y**) and pressing *Enter* for all of the prompts, and finally, you will see a message saying that the entity has been created. Next, let's create another entity, called `Car`, with the attributes of `name`, `model`, and `manufacture year`. Follow the previous steps to create the `Car` entity.

 JHipster provides an option to build a relationship during the time of entity creation. So, if you have just added a single entity and are trying to create a relationship with another entity, you will get an error, saying something like the other entity has not been found. So, when building a relationship with another entity, make sure that it has been created first.

After step five, it will ask about adding a relationship. We already added an `Owner` entity and we want to establish a many-to-one relation (many `Cars` can be associated with one `Owner`). The following is a set of questions that will be asked specifically about the relationship, after step five:

1. **Do you want to add a relationship to another entity?** Choose **Y** here.
2. **What is the name of the other entity?** This refers to the name of the entity with which we want to set up the relationship. Give the name of the entity as `Owner` here.
3. **What is the name of the relationship?** The default is `owner` (this is the relationship name that you want to give. By default, system will give lowercase name of other side entity name. If you wish, you can change it).
4. **What is the type of the relationship?** The possible options are one-to-many, many-to-one, many-to-many, and one-to-one. They are quite straightforward. We will select many-to-one, as we are establishing a relationship with the `Car` entity.

5. **When you display this relationship on the client side, which field from** Owner **do you want to use?** This question asks whether the column name of the Owner entity should be displayed while showing or adding Car data. Internally, JHipster always uses ID columns to set the relationships between tables. Give the name as the answer to this question, as Owner has just one column(name).

6. **Do you want to add any validation rules to this relationship?** This basically adds validation to the foreign key column.

7. **Which validation rules do you want to add?** The possible validation is **required**.

After this, it will start to ask questions from the step 6. Complete it till step 9 to add the Car entity. At this moment, we have two entities—Owner and Car—with a relation between them, along with the source code of the frontend, controller, and service layers, and the DAO layer.

Now, it is time to build our application. The **mvnw** Maven command will not only build the application, but will deploy and run it on the embedded server. After generating the entities, when we build and deploy the application with this command, JHipster will create/update the database table corresponding to each entity.

 Before building the application, make sure that you set the database credentials as per your local MySQL configuration in the application-prod.yml file, in the src/main/resources/config folder. The names of the properties are spring:datasource:username and spring:datasource:password. In the absence of this, you will get an error while running the application.

Let's add some data for our entities. Log in with admin credentials (admin/admin), and go to **Entities | Owner** to add the owner data first. The **Create a new Owner** button will be used to insert an owner record. Similarly, we can add data for the Car entity. Since we have created a many-to-one relationship from Car to Owner (that is, many Car instances are associated with one Owner), you will see a field where you can select an Owner value while adding a Car entity.

The record for the `Car` entity, along with the reference to the `Owner` entity, will look as follows:

The value of the `name` attribute of the `Owner` entity is visible as a reference here, which we selected when we created the relationship. This page also shows pagination of the link type, which we selected during the `Car` entity creation, out of the box. Apart from this, you can perform CRUD operations for each individual entity without writing a single line of code yourself. This is definitely a cool feature that saves lots of development time and effort.

 By default, JHipster creates an **ID** column as the primary key for each entity table. Defining a custom column as primary key is not supported out of the box for the autogeneration of code. However, if the specific column is required as the primary key, you will need to modify the generated source code before running it with the `mvnw` command.

Modeling the entity

You have seen how JHipster speeds up development by automating many things. Modeling an entity in an application previously required many activities including table generation; the creation of the DAO, services, and a presentation layer; and validations and a user interface for each individual entity.

Although Spring Boot provides great help in terms of writing boilerplate code, the developer still has to write a lot of code to see something happening. This is a quite tedious and logically repetitive job. You have seen how JHipster greatly helps in this scenario, by providing autogenerating code to build a fully functional Spring Boot application without writing a single line of code yourself.

Designing an entity with complete working code is just a matter of providing certain information to JHipster. At first glance, this looks great, but there is another side to the coin. Think about a scenario wherein you need to incorporate more than five dozen entities with the JHipster CLI, which is quite possible when you write an enterprise application. Sometimes, the total entities reach beyond a hundred.

In this scenario, writing each entity with the CLI and providing all metadata, along with relationships with other entities, is painful. As a workaround, JHipster provides a graphical tool, where we can design all of the entities in one go. The aim is to simplify the process of defining a relationship with the visual tool, rather than doing it the classical way, with questions and answers. There are two options to visually model the entities, as follows:

- Modeling with **Unified Modeling Language** (**UML**)
- Modeling with JDL

Modeling with UML

In this option, we need to design all of the entities as a class diagram, and then import it into JHipster to generate the code for all of them in one go. So, the whole process is divided into two parts that work independently, as follows:

- Designing a class diagram of entities with a visual tool
- Exporting the class diagram and importing it into JHipster

During the early phase of application development, the class diagram is mainly used to design domain models. Showing the attributes and operations of a class, along with its relationship with other classes, the class diagram describes a static view of an application. The classes used in the class diagram are directly mapped to the object-oriented language, and are also used to model the database tables.

JHipster has provided the benefit of this process in the generation of application code. A separate tool, called JHipster UML, has been designed; it reads the class diagram to generate the entity structure. It can be installed from the Git repository, or as a separate npm package, with the following command:

```
//For Global installation
npm install -g jhipster-uml

//For local installation
npm install jhipster-uml --dev
```

Most of the tools that are available today allow for exporting the class diagram into an XMI format. JHipster UML reads XMI files and generates entities. Since this tool generates entities in JHipster from class diagrams, the attribute type selection is limited to the list of JHipster-supported types. The list of JHipster-supported attribute types, along with possible validation rules for each attribute type, is as follows:

No.	Attribute type	Possible validations
1	string	required, minlength, maxlength, pattern
2	integer	required, min, max
3	long	required, min, max
4	BigDecimal	required, min, max
5	float	required, min, max
6	double	required, min, max
7	enum	required
8	Boolean	required
9	LocalDate	required
10	ZonedDateTime	required
11	blob	required, minbytes, maxbytes
12	AnyBlob	required, minbytes, maxbytes
13	ImageBlob	required, minbytes, maxbytes
14	TextBlob	required, minbytes, maxbytes

First, we need to design the class diagram for each domain model, along with the relationships between them. JHipster recommends using the following tools to generate a class diagram:

- Modelio
- UML Designer
- GenMyModel

Out of these, the first two are completely open source, Eclipse-based graphical tools, and can be downloaded from their respective sites, while the third is a browser-based free tool and can be used directly on the web (with certain limitations). Once the class diagram is ready, export it to an XMI file and execute the following command in Command Prompt to generate the entity structure. Make sure that you are at the project directory when you execute this command:

```
jhipster-uml <class-diagram.xmi>
```

This will generate the entity structure. JHipster UML also provides various options to specify the pagination pattern, such as whether you want to use DTO or add service classes for each of your entities. It can be given along with the previous command, as follows:

```
// If you wish to use DTO. The possible values would be MapStruct
jhipster-uml <class-diagram.xmi> --dto <value>

//Type of pagination pattern.The possible values are
[pager,pagination,infinite-scroll]
jhipster-uml <class-diagram.xmi> --paginate <value>

//If you need to add service layer with class and implementation. The
values would be [serviceClass,serviceImpl]
jhipster-uml <class-diagram.xmi> --service <value>
```

Based on the options that you have provided, JHipster UML generates entities and other source code. Finally, you need to execute the `mvnw` command, so that it will create/modify the required entity tables in the database, along with the Liquibase changelog file, and deploy the application to the server. While defining the relationships between the classes in a class diagram, you need to make sure that they are allowed in JHipster. The supported relationships are as follows:

- A bidirectional one-to-many relationship
- A unidirectional many-to-one relationship
- A many-to-many relationship
- A bidirectional one-to-one relationship
- A unidirectional one-to-one relationship

Out of the box, a unidirectional one-to-many relationship is not supported by the JHipster code generator. JHipster recommends using a bidirectional one-to-many relationship instead.

Modeling with JHipster Domain Language studio

Designing the domain models as a class diagram and then generating the source code based on that is a pretty quick way to create entities in JHipster. Consequently, it saves time, compared to creating them one by one with the CLI. However, you still need to rely on third-party applications to work with JHipster. There is the chance that JHipster has very limited support for a specific version, or, in the worst case, is totally incompatible.

As a solution, JHipster provides a separate tool, called **JDL studio**. It is an online tool to create entities and build relationships between them. The clear benefit of using JDL studio is that it has been designed and maintained by the JHipster team, so there is almost no chance of version incompatibility and other issues. You can be confident when using the stable version. In case of any issues, you can easily get updates or support from the official JHipster issue tracker.

Creating entities with JDL studio is even more simple than modeling the entities with UML. **JHipster Domain Language** (**JDL**), it is a domain language that's used to construct entities with pretty simple and easy-to-use syntax in a single file (or sometimes, multiple files).

There are two ways to work with JDL. You can use either the JHipster IDE or the online JDL-Studio (`https://start.jhipster.tech/jdl-studio`). The JHipster IDE is a plugin or extension for well-known IDEs, including Eclipse, Visual Studio, and Atom. The online JDL-Studio is a browser-based IDE, with which you can construct entities and their relationship in script form, which is written in JDL. You can relate it with writing SQL script for creating a database table and their relationship.

For sake of simplicity, we will look at a simple example of creating an entity with the online JDL-Studio. While writing a definition for each entity, JDL-Studio draws the entity diagram with their relationships side by side. When opening the online JDL-Studio, you will see some sample entities, along with their relationships and other parameters, by default, to give you some ideas on how to start working with it.

Let's create `School` and `Teacher` entities, along with their relationship (one-to-many), in the online JDL-Studio. Open the URL and add the definition of these entities, as follows:

```
entity School {
  name String required
    eduType EducationType required
    noOfRooms Integer required min(5) max(99)
}
enum EducationType {
  PRIMARY, SECONDARY, HIGHER_SECONDARY
}
entity Teacher {
  name String required
    age Integer min(21) max(58)
}
// defining multiple one-to-many relationships with comments
relationship OneToMany {
  School{teacher} to Teacher{school(name) required}
}
// Set pagination options
paginate School with infinite-scroll
```

```
paginate Teacher with pagination

// Use data transfer objects (DTO)
dto * with mapstruct

// In case if DTO is not required for specific (comma separated)entities.
// dto * with mapstruct except School

// Set service options to all except few
service all with serviceImpl

// In case if service layer is not required for certain
// (comma separated) entities. Just uncomment below line
// service all with serviceImpl except School
```

Each entity can be defined with the `entity` keyword, along with its attributes and data type. We can also define certain validations on each attribute. These validations not only impose the respective constraints at the database table level, but also at the frontend side. The `maxlength` validation denotes the maximum column length of the given attribute. The `min` and `max` validations describe the minimum and maximum values to be entered. The relationship between the entities can be defined with the following syntax:

```
relationship (OneToMany | ManyToOne | OneToOne | ManyToMany) {
   <OWNER entity>[{<Relationship name>[(<Display field>)]}] to <DESTINATION
entity>[{<Relationship name>[(<Display field>)]}]
}
```

The `relationship` can be used with various options, as follows:

- `(OneToMany | ManyToOne | OneToOne | ManyToMany)`: The possible types of relationship.
- `OWNER entity`: The owner entity of the relationship. It can also be described as the source of the relationship. The owning side entity must be on the left side.
- `DESTINATION entity`: This is the other-side entity where the relationship ends, the destination.
- `Relationship name`: This is the name of the field that represents the other-side type.
- `Display field`: While adding records for the entity, JHipster shows an other-side entity drop-down menu on the screen. This attribute shows the field name of the other-side entity that would be displayed in the drop-down menu. By default, it is the ID (primary key) of the other-side entity.
- `required`: This determines whether the other-side entity is required to be selected in the drop-down menu.

The `paginate`, `dto`, and `service` keywords are used to define the configuration options for the pagination pattern, whether DTO needs to be generated, and whether a service layer with the implementation should be generated, respectively. They are quite straightforward and you can relate it to the respective options while creating the entity with the CLI. JHipster also supports mass (with `*`) and exclude options (with the `except` keyword), which are quite powerful and convenient. In short, various entity sub-generator features, like the field type, validations, relationships, DTOs, services, enumeration, and so on, are supported. JDL-Studio generates a diagram based on the definition of our entities, as follows:

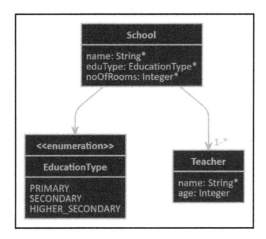

In this example, we have defined a bidirectional relationship. If a unidirectional relationship is required, you just need to remove the name or relationship on both sides. For example, the unidirectional relationship between the `School` and `Teacher` entities can be defined as follows:

```
relationship OneToMany {
  School to Teacher
}
```

JHipster does not support a unidirectional, one-to-many relationship, but this is what it looks like. While defining the relationship, you need to aware of the relationships supported by JHipster, which we discussed in the previous section.

 Along with generating the entity code, JDL is also used to create applications from scratch, along with the deployment options. So, instead of using the question-and-answer-based approach with the CLI, you can define all of the configuration options in a single JDL file and create an application in one shot.

Generating an entity using a model

We have defined the entities in JDL studio. Now, we will instruct JHipster to generate entities, along with database tables and source code. This process involves the following two tasks:

- Exporting the entity definitions
- Importing a JDL file to generate the required artifacts

From JDL-Studio, you can export the definitions as a JDL (.jh) file. JHipster provides a sub-generator that will be used to import the JDL file, with the following command:

```
jhipster import-jdl <your_jdl_file.jh>
```

Needless to say, you need to execute this command under the JHipster project directory. Upon successful build and deployment, you will see the School and Teacher entities from the **Entities** menu. You can also verify that the respective tables are generated. If an application has a large number of entities, it is quite difficult to put all of them in a single JDL file. If there is an error in one entity, the entire process of generating entities will not work properly. In the worst case, if multiple teams are working, then it will create maintenance problems.

JHipster has addressed this issue by allowing multiple JDL files, so that related entities can be grouped into individual JDL files. The import-jdl sub-generator allows importing multiple files separated by spaces. Upon executing this command for the first time, it will generate entities and all of the source code. You need to build and deploy the application with the mvnw command so that the necessary database changes will be reflected.

Second and subsequently, import-jdl will only regenerate the entities that have changed. If you wish to generate all of the entities from scratch again, you will need to add the -force option. Please be aware that this option will erase all customization applied to the entities. Certain validations are caught at the time that we build and deploy the application with the mvnw command, as follows:

- The maxlength and minlength validations are not allowed on columns of type integer, long, BigDecimal, LocalDate, Boolean, enum, double, and so on.
- If the service layer is escaped for a given entity, then JHipster shows a warning if the DTO option with mapstruct is selected for that entity. In this situation, the application may not work properly.
- While adding a single-line comment, you need to put one space after //, or else JHipster will show errors and the entities will not be generated properly.

Showing the national gross domestic product

Now that you have an idea about how to create an application and model the entities, we will start creating an application that shows the GDP of various countries with JHipster. We'll do this to showcase the ability to apply customization in auto-generated code by JHipster.

Application and entity creation

Refer to the *Create an Application* section to create a new application, naming it gdp. We are going to build an application with similar functionality to that which we created with Spring Framework in Chapter 1, *Creating an Application to List World Countries with their GDP*. To show the GDP data of various countries, we took the reference of a sample country, city and country language data from MySQL databases (https://dev.mysql.com/doc/index-other.html) and used a REST service to fetch the GDP data for a given country through the World Bank API (https://datahelpdesk.worldbank.org/knowledgebase/articles/898614-aggregate-api-queries). We will use the same reference to build an application with JHipster.

To make it simple, we will use columns which are necessary to fulfill the purpose of the application. It is important to understand the table structure first. The database tables and their relationship details will be as follows:

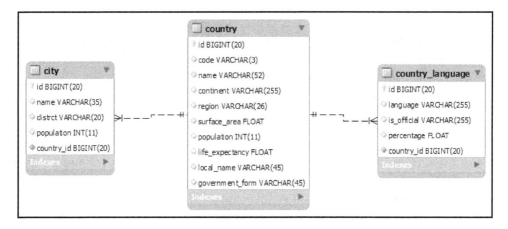

Let's define the entities first. JHipster recommends JDL for entity and code generation so we will use it to create our entity structure and generate our service layer, REST controllers, and DTO, along with a set of components for the frontend layer. The JDL script would be as follows:

```
entity Country{
  code String required maxlength(3)
    name String required maxlength(52)
    continent Continent required
    region String required maxlength(26)
    surfaceArea Float required
    population Integer required
    lifeExpectancy Float
    localName String required maxlength(45)
    governmentForm String required maxlength(45)
}
entity City{
  name String required maxlength(35)
    district String required maxlength(20)
    population Integer required
}

entity CountryLanguage{
    language String required
    isOfficial TrueFalse required
    percentage Float required
}

enum Continent {
  ASIA, EUROPE, NORTH_AMERICA, AFRICA, OCEANIA, ANTARCTICA, SOUTH_AMERICA
}

enum TrueFalse{
  T, F
}

// Set pagination options
paginate Country, City, CountryLanguage with pagination

// Use data transfer objects (DTO)
dto * with mapstruct

// Set service options. Alternatively 'Service all with sericeImpl can be used
service all with serviceImpl

relationship OneToMany{
  Country{city} to City {country(name) required}
```

```
    Country{countryLanguage} to CountryLanguage{country(name) required}
}
filter Country
```

This script contains the entity definition for respective tables, along with `enum` for `Continent` and `TrueFalse`. We also defined a pagination pattern, DTO structure, and service layer with the `Service` class and interface (`serviceImpl`), along with a type of relationship. The `Country` will have one-to-many relationships with both `City` and `CountryLanguage`.

The `country(name)` in the relationship, on the other side it will show the country name as a reference, instead of the default `ID` of the country. Give special attention to the last option—`filter`. This declares the `filter` option for the `Country` entity, which is used to apply various filtering criteria while fetching records for the entity. We will explore this in more detail in the *Developing custom screens* section. The JDL diagram should look as follows:

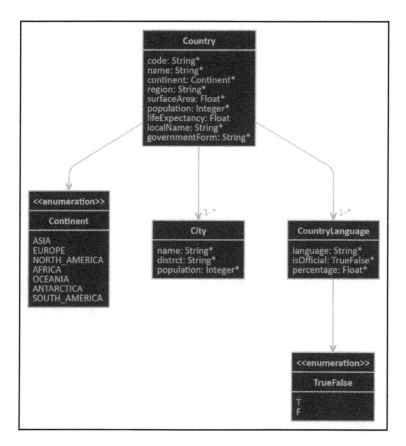

Since we have omitted a few columns in each table provided by MySQL, the required changes also need to be made in the respective insert script of these tables. You will find the modified insert script in the `download` folder of the project structure. At this moment, you have to apply the insert script before moving further.

Handling enumeration data with a database in JHipster

Next, we'll run the application and verify that JHipster has created three entities and that they are available in the **Entities** menu to perform various CRUD operations. The first time we run the application, we will get an error, as follows:

```
org.springframework.dao.InvalidDataAccessApiUsageException: Unknown name
value [Asia] for enum class [com.nilangpatel.domain.enumeration.Continent];
nested exception is java.lang.IllegalArgumentException: Unknown name value
[Asia] for enum class [com.nilangpatel.domain.enumeration.Continent] at
org.springframework.orm.jpa.EntityManagerFactoryUtils.convertJpaAccessExcep
tionIfPossible(EntityManagerFactoryUtils.java:367) ....
```

This error occurs while fetching continent data and trying to map it with the `Continent` enum data type. The root cause is that we have defined the type of the `continent` column of the `Country` entity as a `Continent` enum. The actual value in that column, which is added through an insert script (from the MySQL site) is not exactly the same as the `Continent` enum values. For example, the actual value in the database is `Asia`, while the corresponding enum is `ASIA`.

Another value of the `continent` column is `North America`, while the corresponding enum is `NORTH_AMERICA`. Because of the limitations of enum in Java, we can't put a space in the middle of the value, and that is the reason we kept the values as `NORTH_AMERICA`, `SOUTH_AMERICA`, and so on. Because of this limitation, along with the case difference, you will get the previous exception while running the application.

As a workaround, we need to provide some sort of mapping of actual values in the database column, to enum values in Java. For this, we will use the JPA attribute converter mechanism. It is basically used to define a method to convert database values to Java representations of an attribute and vice versa. Open the `Country.java` class at the `com.nilangpatel.domain` package and update the annotation declaration for the `continent` attribute as follows:

```
@NotNull
//@Enumerated(EnumType.STRING) // commented original
@Convert(converter=ContinentEnumConvertor.class) // added newly
@Column(name = "continent", nullable = false)
private Continent continent;
```

Originally, it was defined as `@Enumerated(EnumType.STRING)`, which was commented out with an added `@Convert` annotation. This annotation requires implementation of the `javax.persistence.AttributeConverter` interface. The implementation is provided by the `ContinentEnumConvertor` custom class as follows:

```
public class ContinentEnumConvertor implements
AttributeConverter<Continent, String>{
  @Override
  public String convertToDatabaseColumn(Continent continent) {
    return continent.getName();
  }
  @Override
  public Continent convertToEntityAttribute(String continentValue) {
    return Continent.getContinent(continentValue);
  }
}
```

These two methods will convert the values between the database and the corresponding enum value in Java. We also need to do necessary changes in the `Continent` enum class, as follows:

```
public enum Continent {
  ASIA("Asia"), EUROPE("Europe"), NORTH_AMERICA("North America"),
AFRICA("Africa"), OCEANIA("Oceania"), ANTARCTICA("Antarctica"),
SOUTH_AMERICA("South America");
    private String name;
  Continent(String name){
    this.name=name;
  }
  public String getName() {
    return this.name;
  }
  public static Continent getContinent(String name) {
```

```
        Continent returnContinent = null;
        switch(name){
            case "Asia": returnContinent = Continent.ASIA;break;
            case "Europe": returnContinent = Continent.EUROPE;break;
            case "North America": returnContinent =
    Continent.NORTH_AMERICA;break;
            case "Africa": returnContinent = Continent.AFRICA;break;
            case "Oceania": returnContinent = Continent.OCEANIA;break;
            case "Antarctica": returnContinent = Continent.ANTARCTICA;break;
            case "South America": returnContinent =
    Continent.SOUTH_AMERICA;break;
            default: returnContinent = null;
        }
        return returnContinent;
    }
}
```

Run the application, and you will see the entities and JHipster allows to perform CRUD operation to only logged in user. However you will still see that the continent values are rendered as enum values, such as ASIA, NORTH_AMERICA, and so on, instead of the actual database column values.

The reason for this is that, when enabling internationalization support at the time of application creation, JHipster generates the display value for various labels, error messages, and various enumerations. It nicely creates the key-value pair in a separate file for each artifact. These files are generated for each language-specific folder, under the src/main/webapp/i18n folder. For example, the language keys and their value for the Country entity are created in the src/main/webapp/i18n/en/country.json file.

Since our application only has one language, `English`, the language keys are only generated for the `English` language, under the `en` folder, as follows:

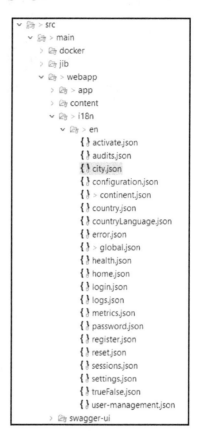

The keys and values are created in a JSON format. To understand its structure, open the `country.json` file, which looks as follows:

```
{
    "gdpApp": {
        "country": {
            "home": {
                "title": "Countries",
                "createLabel": "Create a new Country",
            },
            "created": "A new Country is created with identifier {{ param
}}",
            "delete": {
                "question": "Are you sure you want to delete Country {{ id
}}?"
```

```
        },
        "detail": {
            "title": "Country"
        },
        "code": "Code",
        "name": "Name",
        "continent": "Continent",
        ....
    }
  }
}
```

The title is accessible with the `gdpApp.country.home.title` key. This will be used in the HTML template. Open the `country.component.html` file under the `/src/main/webapp/app/entities/country` folder, and you will see the following code to use this key:

```html
<div>
    <h2 id="page-heading">
        <span jhiTranslate="gdpApp.country.home.title">Countries</span>
    ....
```

JHipster has created various modules to support validations, enums, reading and parsing JSON, and so on. One of them, `translation`, supports internationalization. These are installed during JHipster installation as a `jhipster-core` package, under the `node_modules` folder created under the project directory. If you need to add further labels, you can place the key in the respective JSON file and use `jhiTranslate` to render the value.

Now, back to our problem of showing the enum values on the screen for the `Country` entity, instead of the actual database value. This happens because the translation in `continent.json` is generated with an enum value, by default. You can change it as follows in order to show correct continent values on the screen:

```json
"ASIA": "Asia",
"EUROPE": "Europe",
"NORTH_AMERICA": "North America",
"AFRICA": "Africa",
"OCEANIA": "Oceania",
"ANTARCTICA": "Antarctica",
"SOUTH_AMERICA": "South America",
```

Everything should work as expected now. The admin is able to see all three entities, and can perform CRUD operations properly. We will now develop custom screens to show the GDP data by country.

Filter provision in service, persistence, and the REST controller layer

Let's recall that, while creating the entities with JDL, we set the **filter** option for the `Country` entity in the JDL script, at the end. Let's look at how this makes a difference to the service, persistence, and REST controller layers.

The persistence layer

When we add a filter option for any entity, JHipster makes the necessary changes to the repository interface corresponding to that entity. In our case, the `CountryRepository` is now extending the `JpaSpecificationExecutor` interface, which is used to add `Specification` capabilities to the repository, as follows:

```
public interface CountryRepository extends JpaRepository<Country, Long>,
JpaSpecificationExecutor<Country>
```

Spring Data JPA provides a `Specification` interface to execute the criteria query, which is used to retrieve values from the database with various criteria on database columns.

The service layer

In the service layer, JHipster generates a separate class as `xxxQueryService`, under the service package. For the `Country` entity, a new service class, `CountryQueryService`, is created. The purpose of this class is to retrieve the data with the filtering criteria, so it contains only fetch methods, which look as follows:

```
public Page<CountryDTO> findByCriteria(CountryCriteria criteria, Pageable
page) {
    log.debug("find by criteria : {}, page: {}", criteria, page);
    final Specification<Country> specification =
createSpecification(criteria);
    return countryRepository.findAll(specification, page)
        .map(countryMapper::toDto);
}
```

JHipster generates a **Plain Old Java Object** (**POJO**) class for each entity that is declared with the filter option. This is used to pass the filter values from the frontend to the service layer. In our case, JHipster generates a `CountryCriteria` class that serves this purpose for the `Country` entity. This class contains various filters for each corresponding field in the domain object. If filters are not applied, this will bring all of the entities.

JHipster has created various filter types, corresponding to each wrapper class type. For any custom type, it creates an inner class that extends the `io.github.jhipster.service.filter.Filter` class. The `CountryCriteria` class looks as follows:

```
public class CountryCriteria implements Serializable {
    /**
     * Class for filtering Continent
     */
    public static class ContinentFilter extends Filter<Continent> {
    }
    private static final long serialVersionUID = 1L;
    private LongFilter id;
    private StringFilter code;
    private StringFilter name;
    private ContinentFilter continent;
    private StringFilter region;
    private FloatFilter surfaceArea;
    private IntegerFilter population;
    private FloatFilter lifeExpectancy;
    private StringFilter localName;
    private StringFilter governmentForm;
    private LongFilter cityId;
    private LongFilter countryLanguageId;
  //setters and getters
}
```

The `continent` attribute in the `Country` domain class is of the enum type, so JHipster has created an inner filter class of `ContinentFilter`, and for other attributes of the type wrapper class, it uses corresponding filters. From the frontend, you need to pass search text as a request parameter in a specific way, based on the type of the attribute as follows. Consider the attribute name as `abc`:

- If attribute `abc` is of the string type:
  - `abc.contains=<seach_text>`: List down all entities where the value of `abc` contains `search_text`.
- If attribute `abc` is of any number type (float, long, double, integer) or the date:
  - `abc.greaterThan=<search_text>`: List down all entities where the value of `abc` is greater than `search_text`.
  - `abc.lessThan=<search_text>`: List down all the entities where the value of `abc` is less than `search_text`.

- abc.greaterOrEqualThan=<search_text>: List down all the entities where the value of abc is greater than or equals to search_text.
- abc.lessOrEqualThan=<search_text>: List down all the entities where the value of abc is less than or equal to search_text.
  - If attribute abc is of a custom type:
    - abc.equals=<search_text>: List down all of the entities where the value of abc is exactly similar to search_text.
    - abc.in=<comma separated search_text values>: List down all of the entities where a value of abc is within the list of search_text.
    - abc.specified=true: List down all of the entities where the value of abc is not null, which means specified.
    - abc.specified=false: List down all entities where the value of abc is null, which means not specified.

These rules can be combined for more than one attributes to form a complex query.

The REST controller layer

When applying the filter option, JHipster also makes necessary changes to the REST controller. For example, all get methods of REST controller CountryResouce for entity Country are now taking CountryCriteria as a parameter to support filtering operations, as follows:

```
@GetMapping("/countries")
@Timed
public ResponseEntity<List<CountryDTO>> getAllCountries(
    CountryCriteria criteria, Pageable pageable) {

    log.debug("REST request to get Countries by criteria: {}", criteria);
    Page<CountryDTO> page = countryQueryService.findByCriteria(criteria,
pageable);
    HttpHeaders headers = PaginationUtil.
            generatePaginationHttpHeaders(page, "/api/countries");
    return ResponseEntity.ok().headers(headers).body(page.getContent());
}
```

This is how the filter option impacts the persistence, service, and REST controller layer code generation. With single-filter configuration, JHipster makes all of the necessary changes. However, the REST controllers generated for each entity are protected with Spring Security, by default. You can verify this in the `config()` method of the `com.nilangpatel.config.SecurityConfiguration` class, as follows:

```
public void configure(HttpSecurity http) throws Exception {
    ....
    .and()
        .authorizeRequests()
        .antMatchers("/api/register").permitAll()
        .antMatchers("/api/activate").permitAll()
        .antMatchers("/api/authenticate").permitAll()
        .antMatchers("/api/account/reset-password/init").permitAll()
        .antMatchers("/api/account/reset-password/finish").permitAll()
        .antMatchers("/api/**").authenticated()
        ....
}
```

Apart from the register, activate, authenticate, and reset password operations, all other URLs (`/api/**`) are restricted to logged-in users. But, in our case, we want to show the country GDP data to regular users, without logins. For this, we need to create a custom REST controller with a different URL pattern, as follows:

```
@RestController
@RequestMapping("/api/open")
public class GenericRestResource {
  private final Logger log =
LoggerFactory.getLogger(GenericRestResource.class);
  private final CountryQueryService countryQueryService;

    public GenericRestResource(CountryQueryService countryQueryService) {
        this.countryQueryService = countryQueryService;
    }

    @GetMapping("/search-countries")
    @Timed
    public ResponseEntity<List<CountryDTO>> getAllCountriesForGdp(
            CountryCriteria criteria, Pageable pageable) {
        log.debug("REST request to get a page of Countries");
        Page<CountryDTO> page = countryQueryService.findByCriteria
            (criteria, pageable);
        HttpHeaders headers = PaginationUtil.generatePaginationHttpHeaders(
            page, "/api/open/search-countries");
        return
ResponseEntity.ok().headers(headers).body(page.getContent());
    }
```

```
    @GetMapping("/show-gdp/{id}")
    @Timed
    public ResponseEntity<CountryDTO> getCountryDetails(@PathVariable Long
id) {
        log.debug("Get Country Details to show GDP information");
        CountryDTO countryDto = new CountryDTO();
        Optional<CountryDTO> countryData = countryService.findOne(id);
        return ResponseEntity.ok().body(countryData.orElse(countryDto));
    }
}
```

The first method is similar to what it has auto-generated in `CountryResource`. The second method will be used to show the GDP data, and we will use it while creating that screen. The URL pattern map to this controller is `/api/open`. The purpose of creating a separate REST controller is to make it accessible without a login, by configuring its URL pattern with Spring Security in the `configure` method of `SecurityConfiguration`, as follows:

```
public void configure(HttpSecurity http) throws Exception {
    . . . .
    .antMatchers("/api/activate").permitAll()
    .antMatchers("/api/open/**").permitAll()
    .antMatchers("/api/authenticate").permitAll()
    . . . .
}
```

This controller is now accessible publicly. We will use the controller methods while constructing a frontend layer with Angular in the *Develop custom screens* section.

Adding a filter option to existing entities

If the entities are already generated without the filter option, and you want to add it later on, you will need to perform certain steps. The following are two possible approaches:

1. With Command Prompt, do the following:
    1. Open the entity's JSON file under the `.jhipster` folder, inside of the project directory. For example, for a `Country` entity, you will see a file named `Country.json` inside of the `.jhipster` folder.
    2. If the value of the `service` key is `no`, change it to either `serviceClass` or `serviceImpl`. The service layer option has to be enabled for the filtering option.
    3. Change the value of the key `jpaMetamodelFiltering` to `true`.
    4. Regenerate the entity with the `jhipster entity <entity_name>` command.

2. With JDL, do the following:
    1. Add a line containing `filter <entity_name>` to the JDL script file.
    2. Re-import the definition with the `jhipster jhipster-jdl <jdl_file>` command.

In both of these scenarios, the customization will be reverted while regenerating the entities, so make a proper back-up before performing this task.

Developing custom screens

By default, JHipster only shows the entities to logged-in users. The aim of our application is to show the GDP data of a given country to the end user. To achieve this, the country data must be visible publicly. In other words, it must be accessible without a login. To make it more user-friendly, we will design the flow in two different screens.

The first screen will list all the countries available in the system. Selecting any of them will show the actual GDP of that country on the second screen, with a graphical presentation. These are the custom screens that we need to develop from scratch and plug into the JHipster project structure, which we will do in this section.

The search country screen

In this screen, we will list of all of the countries available in the system with pagination. It is identical to the *Country* entity screen but available to all users (without login). For better user experience, we will add filters to find a specific country on this screen. It looks as follows:

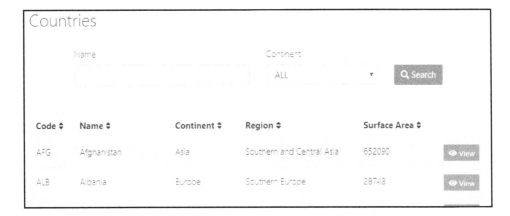

This screen has two filters. The first filter will match the search text in the country name (`contains` criteria), while the second will compare the selected continent (`equals` criteria). These filters help the user to find their desired country instantly. To make it simpler, we have added just a few columns of information about each country, which seems appropriate for this screen. At the end of each country record, the **View** button will navigate a user to the second screen, where it shows the GDP information of that country.

JHipster provides either **Angular** or **React** as an option to develop the frontend. We have chosen Angular to create this application. Consequently, all of our out-of-the-box screens are generated with the Angular framework. Since this is a custom screen, we need to use various Angular artifacts to develop it. Create a `gdp` folder inside of the `/src/webapp/app` folder, and, in the next subsection, we'll create Angular artifacts inside of it, to construct custom screens.

Creating an Angular service

Angular is a modular framework wherein we write many components, each for a specific purpose. Many times, we are in need of some common functionalities shared across multiple components. Additionally, we may need to fetch records from the database with a REST call. This is where creating an Angular service makes perfect sense. For our GDP application, we need to fetch country data in the Angular service as follows:

```
@Injectable({ providedIn: 'root'})
export class CountryGDPService {
    public searchCountryUrl = SERVER_API_URL + 'api/open/search-countries';
    public showGDPUrl = SERVER_API_URL + 'api/open/show-gdp';
    constructor(private http: HttpClient) { }
    query(req?: any): Observable<EntityArrayResponseType> {
        const options = createRequestOption(req);
        return this.http.get<ICountry[]>(this.searchCountryUrl,
            { params: options, observe: 'response' });
    }
    find(id: number): Observable<EntityResponseType> {
        return this.http.get<ICountry>(`${this.showGDPUrl}/${id}`,
            { observe: 'response' });
    }
}
```

The `query` method is used to fetch all of the countries with various request parameters sent by the `search-country` component. The second method, `find`, is used to fetch a specific country, based on a given `id` value. This service class uses the `HttpClient` module, which is provided by the Angular framework out of the box, to make a REST call to the newly created REST controller.

The `api/open/search-countries` and `api/open/show-gdp` URLs are used to make calls to the REST controller methods, `getAllCountriesForGdp()` and `getCountryDetails()`, respectively. However, the `find()` method of service component is dynamically passing the `id` value into the URL with the `${this.showGDPUrl}/${id}` expression. This service class is common for both of the screens.

Creating the Angular router

The next artifact is the Angular router. The Angular router is used to manage application navigation and routing between various components. The Angular router uses a browser URL to map it to a specific component. It does various types of processing on the browser URL, such as parsing to verify that the URL is valid; doing a redirect if that option is given; matching the component against the URL segment; validating if the given URL is accessible with the set of guards; running the associate resolves to dynamically add the data; and finally, activating the component and performing navigation. We will write the Angular router as follows:

```
@Injectable({ providedIn: 'root' })
export class CountryGDPResolve implements Resolve<ICountry> {
    constructor(private service: CountryGDPService) {}

    resolve(route: ActivatedRouteSnapshot, state: RouterStateSnapshot):
Observable<Country> {
        const id = route.params['id'] ? route.params['id'] : null;
        if (id) {
            return this.service.find(id).pipe(
                filter((response: HttpResponse<Country>) => response.ok),
                map((country: HttpResponse<Country>) => country.body)
            );
        }
        return of(new Country());
    }
}

export const countryGDPRoute: Routes = [
    {
        path: 'countries',
        component: SearchCountryComponent,
        resolve: {
            pagingParams: JhiResolvePagingParams
        },
        data: {
            defaultSort: 'name,asc',
            pageTitle: 'gdpApp.country.home.title'
```

```
        },
    },
    {
        path: 'showGDP/:id',
        component: CountryGDPComponent,

        resolve: {
            country: CountryGDPResolve
        }
    },
];
```

It comprises a `resolve` class (`CountryGDPResolve`) and a route array. The `resolve` class fetches the full country model data, based on a country ID when a user clicks on **View** button to initiate a transition to the second screen. It uses a service component to make a REST call and fetch country information. The router array holds the configuration mapping of components and the URLs by which they will be triggered. This Angular router is also common for both screens.

Angular modules

As we know, Angular is a modular framework. A module in Angular is used to group related components, pipes, directives, and services, to form an independent unit, which can be combined with other modules to form a complete application. A **module** can control which components, services, and other artifacts are hidden and visible to other modules, in much the same way that a Java class has public and private methods. We will use a single module called `CountryGDPModule`, as follows:

```
const ENTITY_STATES = [...countryGDPRoute];

@NgModule({
    imports: [GdpSharedModule, RouterModule.forChild(ENTITY_STATES)],
    declarations: [
        SearchCountryComponent,
        CountryGDPComponent,
    ],
    entryComponents: [SearchCountryComponent , CountryGDPComponent],
    schemas: [CUSTOM_ELEMENTS_SCHEMA]
})
export class CountryGDPModule {}
```

It defines all of the components and routers that are necessary to be part of this module. It is common for both screens.

Creating an Angular component to show the country list

Next, we will write a component to show the country list on the first screen. A component is a basic building block with which we create our Angular application. Every Angular application has at least one component. The component holds application data and logic to show the data in the HTML template associated with it. We will write a separate component for each of the screens in our application. For the first screen, we will write a `search-country` component, as follows:

```
@Component({
  selector: 'jhi-search-country',
  templateUrl: './search-country.component.html',
})
export class SearchCountryComponent implements OnInit {
    countries: ICountry[];
    routeData: any;
    totalItems: any;
    queryCount: any;
    itemsPerPage: any;
    page: any;
    predicate: any;
    previousPage: any;
    reverse: any;

    // variables for country name and continent filters.
    nameFilter: String;
    continentFilter: String;

  constructor(
      private countryGDPService: CountryGDPService,
      private activatedRoute: ActivatedRoute,
      private router: Router,
  ) {
      this.itemsPerPage = ITEMS_PER_PAGE;
      this.routeData = this.activatedRoute.data.subscribe(data => {
          this.page = data.pagingParams.page;
          this.previousPage = data.pagingParams.page;
          this.reverse = data.pagingParams.ascending;
          this.predicate = data.pagingParams.predicate;
      });
  }

  loadAll() {
      this.countryGDPService
          .query({
              page: this.page - 1,
              size: this.itemsPerPage,
```

```
                    sort: this.sort(),
                    'name.contains': this.nameFilter,
                    'continent.equals' : this.continentFilter
            })
            .subscribe(
                (res: HttpResponse<ICountry[]>) =>
    this.paginateCountries(res.body, res.headers),
                );
        }
     .....
    }
```

An Angular component can be created with the `@component()` decorator. The `SearchCountryComponent` class represents the `search-country` component. It is defined with certain variables that are used for pagination and filtering purposes. The object of `CountryGDPService` is injected into the component class through a constructor, which will be used in other methods to fetch country data. The constructor is initialized with pagination variables, which are used to handle pagination on the first screen.

Soon after the component class is initialized with the constructor, Angular will call the `ngOnInit()` method. In this method, we are initializing a few parameters and making a call to other methods with `loadAll()`. This method calls the `query()` method of the `countryGDPService` object to fetch the country info.

The `query()` method takes various pagination and filtering parameters. The `page`, `size`, and `sort` are pagination parameters, while `name.contains` and `continent.equals` are filtering parameters. They are eventually submitted to the REST controller through `CountryGDPService`.

The `name.contains` filtering parameter is used to filter the country data, based on the `name` attribute. Since it is of the type `String`, we have used the `contains` criteria. Similarly, the other filtering parameter, `continent.equals`, is used to filter the data for the `continent` attribute. Since it is of the type `enum`, we are using the `equals` criteria. This is what we have seen in the *Service layer* section, under the *Filter provision in service, persistence, and the REST controller layer* subsection.

The other functions, like `searchCountries()`, `trackId()`, `loadPage()`, and so on, are called from the HTML template directly associated with the `search-country` component. You can see it in the source code of the chapter from GitHub at `https://github.com/PacktPublishing/Spring-5.0-Blueprints/tree/master/chapter04`.

Angular template to show the country list

Finally, we need an HTML template to render the country data on the screen. Each Angular component has one HTML template associated with a `@Component` decorator. For our first screen to show the list of countries, the HTML template looks as follows:

```
<form name="searchCountriesForm" novalidate (ngSubmit)="searchCountries()">
    <div class="container mb-5">
        <div class="row">
            <div class="col-6">
                <label class="form-control-label"
                jhiTranslate="gdpApp.country.name"
for="nameFilter">Name</label>
                <input type="text" class="form-control"
                name="nameFilter" id="nameFilter" [(ngModel)]="nameFilter"
maxlength="52"/>
            </div>
            <div class="col-4">
                <label class="form-control-label"
jhiTranslate="gdpApp.country.continent"
                for="continentFilter">Continent</label>
                <select class="form-control" name="continentFilter"
                    [(ngModel)]="continentFilter" id="continentFilter">
                    <option value="">
                        {{'gdpApp.Continent.ALL' | translate}}</option>
                    <option value="ASIA">
                        {{'gdpApp.Continent.ASIA' | translate}}</option>
                    <option value="EUROPE">
                        {{'gdpApp.Continent.EUROPE' | translate}}</option>
                    <option value="NORTH_AMERICA">
                        {{'gdpApp.Continent.NORTH_AMERICA' |
translate}}</option>
                    <option value="AFRICA">
                        {{'gdpApp.Continent.AFRICA' | translate}}</option>
                    <option value="OCEANIA">
                        {{'gdpApp.Continent.OCEANIA' | translate}}</option>
                    <option value="ANTARCTICA">
                        {{'gdpApp.Continent.ANTARCTICA' |
translate}}</option>
                    <option value="SOUTH_AMERICA">
                        {{'gdpApp.Continent.SOUTH_AMERICA' |
translate}}</option>
                </select>
            </div>
            <div class="col-2 align-self-end">
                <label class="form-control-label" for="search-
countries"></label>
                <button type="submit" id="search-countries" class="btn btn-
```

```
primary">
                          <fa-icon [icon]="'search'"></fa-
icon><span>Search</span>
                </button>
            </div>
        </div>
    </div>
</form>
<div class="table-responsive" *ngIf="countries">
    <table class="table table-striped">
        <thead>
        <tr jhiSort [(predicate)]="predicate"
                [(ascending)]="reverse" [callback]="transition.bind(this)">
        <th jhiSortBy="code"><span jhiTranslate="gdpApp.country.code">
                Code</span> <fa-icon [icon]="'sort'"></fa-icon></th>
        <th jhiSortBy="name"><span jhiTranslate="gdpApp.country.name">
                Name</span> <fa-icon [icon]="'sort'"></fa-icon></th>
        <th jhiSortBy="continent"><span
jhiTranslate="gdpApp.country.continent">
                Continent</span> <fa-icon [icon]="'sort'"></fa-icon></th>
        <th jhiSortBy="region"><span jhiTranslate="gdpApp.country.region">
                Region</span> <fa-icon [icon]="'sort'"></fa-icon></th>
        <th jhiSortBy="surfaceArea"><span
jhiTranslate="gdpApp.country.surfaceArea">
                Area</span> <fa-icon [icon]="'sort'"></fa-icon></th>
        <th></th>
        </tr>
        </thead>
        <tbody>
        <tr *ngFor="let country of countries ;trackBy: trackId">
            <td>{{country.code}}</td>
            <td>{{country.name}}</td>
            <td jhiTranslate="{{'gdpApp.Continent.' + country.continent}}">
                {{country.continent}}</td>
            <td>{{country.region}}</td>
            <td>{{country.surfaceArea}}</td>
            <td class="text-right">
                <div class="btn-group flex-btn-group-container">
                    <button type="submit"
                            [routerLink]="['/showGDP', country.id ]"
                            class="btn btn-info btn-sm">
                        <fa-icon [icon]="'eye'"></fa-icon>
                        <span class="d-none d-md-inline"
                         jhiTranslate="entity.action.view">View GDP</span>
                    </button>
                </div>
            </td>
        </tr>
```

```
            </tbody>
        </table>
    </div>
    <div *ngIf="countries && countries.length">
        <div class="row justify-content-center">
            <jhi-item-count [page]="page" [total]="queryCount"
                [itemsPerPage]="itemsPerPage"></jhi-item-count>
        </div>
        <div class="row justify-content-center">
            <ngb-pagination [collectionSize]="totalItems"
                [(page)]="page" [pageSize]="itemsPerPage" [maxSize]="5"
[rotate]="true"
                [boundaryLinks]="true" (pageChange)="loadPage(page)"></ngb-
pagination>
        </div>
    </div>
```

The HTML `form` is used to render the filtering options, with the country name as a text field and the continent as a drop-down menu. After the filter form, it shows the countries in a tabular format, with the pagination at the bottom. The last column of each row has a **View** button, which opens the next screen using the `/showGDP` URL and passing the `id` of the current country.

Showing the GDP screen

This screen shows the basic data of a selected country, along with the GDP data, in a graphical representation. We will use the World Bank API to fetch the information in a JSON format and supply it to a chart module to render a graph of the GDP data. This screen looks as follows:

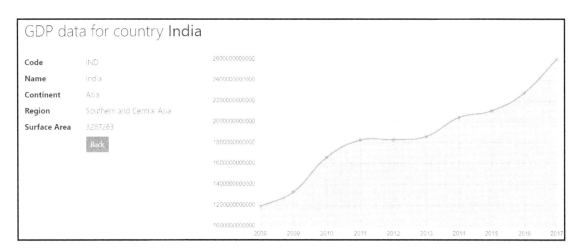

This screen uses the same service, router, and module artifacts that we created for the first screen, but will use a separate component and HTML template, as you will see in the next section.

An Angular component to show country GDP

The `show-gdp` component takes the country data from the first screen, makes a call to the World Bank API, and fetches the data in a JSON format, before finally sending it to the chart module to render the graph. This component looks as follows:

```
@Component({
  selector: 'jhi-show-gdp',
  templateUrl: './show-gdp.component.html',
  })
export class CountryGDPComponent implements OnInit {
    currentCountry: ICountry;
    data: IGdpData[];
    preGDPUrl = 'http://api.worldbank.org/v2/countries/';
    postGDPUrl = '/indicators/NY.GDP.MKTP.CD?format=json&per_page=' + 10;
    year = [];
    gdp = [];
    chart = [];
    noDataAvailale: any;
    constructor(
        private activatedRoute: ActivatedRoute,
        private httpClient: HttpClient
    ) {
        this.activatedRoute.data.subscribe(data => {
            this.currentCountry = data.country;
        });
    }
    ngOnInit() {
        const gdpUrl = this.preGDPUrl + this.currentCountry.code
                    + this.postGDPUrl;
        this.httpClient.get(gdpUrl).subscribe(res => {
            this.noDataAvailale = true;
            const gdpDataArr = res[1];
            if ( gdpDataArr ) {
                this.noDataAvailale = false;
                gdpDataArr.forEach(y => {
                    this.year.push(y.date);
                    this.gdp.push(y.value);
                });
                this.year = this.year.reverse();
                this.gdp = this.gdp.reverse();

                this.chart = new Chart('canvas', {
```

```
                    type: 'line',
                    data: {
                        labels: this.year,
                        datasets: [
                            {
                            data: this.gdp,
                            borderColor: '#3cba9f',
                            fill: true
                            }
                        ]
                    },
                    options: {
                    legend: {
                        display: false
                    },
                    scales: {
                        xAxes: [{
                            display: true
                        }],
                        yAxes: [{
                            display: true
                        }],
                    }
                    }
                });
            }
        });
    }
}
```

In the constructor of this component, we are getting the selected country from the Angular router. In the `resolve()` method of the `CountryGDPResolve` class, we are fetching the country object from the `ID` parameter in the URL, and this object is then available to this component through the router, because we have provided a resolve configuration to this component in `countryGDPRoute`, as follows:

```
{
    path: 'showGDP/:id',
    component: CountryGDPComponent,
    resolve: {
        country: CountryGDPResolve
    }
}
```

Once we get the country information, we will make our calls to the World Bank API. The URL for this is as follows:

```
http://api.worldbank.org/v2/countries/IND/indicators/NY.GDP.MKTP.CD?format=json
&per_page=10.
```

In this URL, the country code is inserted dynamically, from the country data that is given by the router. The `per_page` attribute returns the GDP data for that many numbers of years. The preceding example shows the last ten years' worth of GDP data for the country India. After getting the JSON data, we are iterating and preparing two arrays, `year` and `gdp`, and passing them to the chart module to generate a chart on the screen. The chart module can be installed as a node module, with the `npm install chart.js` command.

Angular template to show country GDP

Finally, the template for the `show-gdp` component will render the chart and show the country GDP data. The template looks as follows:

```html
<div class="container">
    <h2 id="page-heading">
        <span> GDP data for country <b>{{currentCountry.name}}</b></span>
    </h2>
    <br/>
    <div class="row">
        <div class="col-4">
            <dl class="row">
                <dt class="col-sm-4">Code</dt>
                <dd class="col-sm-8">{{currentCountry.code}}</dd>
                <dt class="col-sm-4">Name</dt>
                <dd class="col-sm-8">{{currentCountry.name}}</dd>
                <dt class="col-sm-4">Continent</dt>
                <dd class="col-sm-8">{{'gdpApp.Continent.' +
                    currentCountry.continent | translate }}</dd>
                <dt class="col-sm-4">Region</dt>
                <dd class="col-sm-8">{{currentCountry.region}}</dd>
                <dt class="col-sm-4">Surface Area</dt>
                <dd class="col-sm-8">{{currentCountry.surfaceArea}}</dd>
                <dt class="col-sm-4"></dt>
                <dd class="col-sm-8">
                    <div class="btn-group">
                        <button type="submit"
                                [routerLink]="['/countries']"
                                class="btn btn-info btn-sm">
                            <span class="d-none d-md-inline">Back</span>
                        </button>
                    </div>
```

```
                  </dd>
              </dl>
          </div>
          <div class="col-8">
              <div *ngIf="noDataAvailale">
                  GDP data for <b>{{currentCountry.name}}</b> is not
  available
              </div>
              <div *ngIf="chart">
                  <canvas id="canvas">{{ chart }}</canvas>
              </div>
          </div>
      </div>
  </div>
```

It shows a few details about the selected country, followed by a placeholder for the chart. The noDataAvailale variable is used to show a message, in the case that there is no GDP data available for the selected country. It is set in the show-gdp component while making the World Bank API call.

Hooking the GDP module into AppModule

Everything is done now. Our GDP module is ready for execution. The last step is to plug it into the JHipster project structure. You have seen that a module is comprised of multiple artifacts, such as components, pipes, services, and routers. Multiple modules are grouped together to form an application.

Every Angular application has at least one module, known as a root module, and it is used to bootstrap the application. Usually, this module is known as AppModule, by convention. Since the frontend of our application is built on top of Angular, there is an AppModule. The app.module.ts file under the /src/main/webapp/app folder represents an AppModule.

We need to configure our custom module in AppModule to make it in action. This can be achieved by adding our module to the imports declaration under @NgModule, in the app.module.ts file, as follows:

```
@NgModule({
    imports: [
        ....
        GdpHomeModule,
        GdpAccountModule,
        // jhipster-needle-angular-add-module JHipster will add new module
  here
        GdpEntityModule,
        CountryGDPModule
```

Upon adding entities into an application, JHipster generates a common module called `XXXEntityModule`, that holds the references of all the artifacts related to all entities. Soon after the entities are generated, JHipster adds this module entry to the import array inside of `@NgModule`. We have added another entry for the GDP module (`CountryGDPModule`). This is how any custom module can be plugged into `AppModule`.

Updating navigation

Our module is ready, and is also plugged into `AppModule`, to put it into action. However, one small thing is still missing, which is to locate the navigation to launch the GDP module. The best option is to put the navigation link into the navigation bar at the top of the page. JHipster provides a navigation bar as a separate module out of the box, and it shows various links. A few of them are publicly visible, and others are only for logged-in and `Admin` users.

To add the link, we need to modify the navigation template file, `navbar.component.html`, under the `/src/main/webapp/app/layouts/navbar` folder as follows:

```
<div class="navbar-collapse collapse" id="navbarResponsive"
          [ngbCollapse]="isNavbarCollapsed"
[ngSwitch]="isAuthenticated()">
      <ul class="navbar-nav ml-auto">
          <li class="nav-item" routerLinkActive="active"
              [routerLinkActiveOptions]="{exact: true}">
              <a class="nav-link" routerLink="/"
(click)="collapseNavbar()">
                  <span>
                      <fa-icon icon="home"></fa-icon>
                      <span jhiTranslate="global.menu.home">Home</span>
                  </span>
              </a>
          </li>
          <li class="nav-item" routerLinkActive="active"
              [routerLinkActiveOptions]="{exact: true}">
              <a class="nav-link" routerLink="/countries"
                  (click)="collapseNavbar()">
                  <span>
                      <fa-icon icon="list"></fa-icon>
                      <span>Countries</span>
                  </span>
              </a>
          </li>
          ....
```

We have added HTML code, highlighted in bold, to show the **Countries** menu item in the navigation bar. This looks as follows:

The path for `routerLink` is defined as **Countries**, which ultimately triggers the `t=the search-country` component to show the country list with the filter option on the first screen. This is how you can add custom screens in JHipster project.

Other JHipster features

So far, you have seen how to create fully-fledged and production-ready applications with JHipster. You have seen how to create entities and define a relationship between them. We have also added custom screens and developed various artifacts, so that you could learn how to add customized code to an application generated by the JHipster ecosystem.

These are some of the great features that not only make the developer's life easier, but also more productive, by automating lots of processes. We will look at these now.

IDE support

At the beginning of this chapter, you saw how to create an application with the JHipster CLI by answering various questions. This is more than sufficient to start working with JHipster. However, to become more productive, it is recommended to use an IDE for development. JHipster supports a wide range of IDEs, including Eclipse, Visual Studio Code, IntelliJ IDEA, and so on. While working with an IDE (or a simple text editor), you need to make sure to exclude a certain folder from doing indexing, like `node_modules`, `build`, and `target`, to reduce the initial loading time of the application.

Setting screens out of the box

JHipster provides several screens out of the box. Broadly, they can be categorized into three different groups, as follows:

- Home and login screens
- Administration
- Account management

Home and login screens

Upon starting, JHipster shows the home screen with a welcome message. This is the default home page and you can change it as per your application needs. In local development, by default, the dev profile is selected, so you will see a **development** tab at the top-left corner. On the top section of the page, you will see a navigation menu. Without have logged in, it will show the following menu items:

- **Home**: A link to show a home page.
- **Language**: This is conditional. This menu will be only visible if you have selected more than one language.
- **Account**: This shows child menu items, such as **Sign in** and **Register**.

Upon clicking on the **Sign in** option, you will see a login page, as follows:

This screen covers **Remember me**, **Did you forget forget your password?**, and **Register a new account** features. The forgotten password feature requires email verification. For this, you need to configure SMTP with JHipster in the application properties file. By default, JHipster creates the following two users:

- **Administrator**: **Username**—admin, **Password**—admin, **role**—admin.
- **User**: **Username**—user, **Password**—user, **role**—user.

Account management

JHipster facilitates login features out of the box. It also incorporates account management with this. The account screen provided by JHipster supports various actions in the form of child menus, as follows:

- **Settings**: This screen allows for updating the user account details, such as the first and last name, email address, and language. The language drop-down menu shows all available languages in the system, which are configured during the creation of the application.
- **Password**: This screen is used to update the currently logged-in user's password.
- **Registration**: This screen is used to register new users into the system. It is only available when a user is not logged in. Soon after a user is created, an activation flow will be started, with an activation email and verification. The SMTP configuration needs to be done in the application properties for sending an email. Please note that if OAuth is selected as an authentication mechanism during the application creation, JHipster will not show this screen.

Administration

Upon signing in with administrator credentials, you will see a navigation menu with the **Administration** option. It covers various modules used to manage the whole application. It is useful for development, as well as monitoring the application.

It comprises various child menus, as described in the following sections.

User management

This is a one-stop screen that's used to manage the registered users of the application. You can add a new user and modify, delete, or activate/deactivate existing users from this screen. It also shows the list of users with various attributes, such as `ID`, `username`, `email`, `Activate/Deactivate`, `Language`, `Roles`, `Created date`, `Modify by`, and `Modify date with pagination support`.

Metrics

JHipster provides various screens to analyze the performance of the application and other metrics, as follows:

- **JVM Metrics**: This shows JVM-specific statistics, like memory utilization, thread counts, thread dump, and garbage collection details.
- **HTTP requests**: Aggregated details of HTTP requests, with their status code is shown for this metric.
- **Service statistics**: Details of the execution time of various out-of-the-box and custom services are shown here. It is useful to see the usage of various services.
- **Cache statistics**: The details of the entity cache are covered in this metric.
- **DataSource statistics**: The data source details will be shown here.

The Refresh button is given to update the metrics with the latest value.

Health

This screen shows various pieces of information related to application health, such as the underlying database and disk space. It is used make decisions about data storage well in advance.

Configuration

This screen shows the current configuration applied to the application. It is especially useful for troubleshooting an application in case of any issue arising, or to check for the possibility of further performance improvement. It covers Spring Framework specific configurations, server configurations, system environment configurations, and application properties. Since this involves sensitive data, only the administrator can see it, by default.

Audit

JHipster provides an audit log for user authentication. Since authentication is done by Spring Security in JHipster, it captures security-specific events specifically for authentication, and stores them in a database at the separate Spring data repository. They are useful from a security point of view. This screen shows all of this data in tabular format, with pagination.

Logs

This screen shows, various application log levels, such as TRACE, DEBUG, INFO, WARN, ERROR, and OFF at runtime, for classes and packages. It also allows for updating the log level for individual classes and packages. This is helpful while troubleshooting the application.

API

JHipster uses Swagger, a framework used to describe the structure of APIs. As you have seen, JHipster supports entity creation, and also exposes the REST API. It uses Swagger to document the entity REST API. JHipster also provides a user interface to interact with the API using sample data, and returns the output.

Maintaining code quality

JHipster generates lots of boilerplate code while creating an application and entities. It follows best practices while generating the code, in order to maintain the quality. However, JHipster just creates the application code the first time, and the user must add custom code based on the business needs later on.

To maintain the code quality even after adding the customized code, JHipster allows analyzing the complete application code with Sonar—a tool designed specifically for monitoring code quality. The code is analyzed using **SonarCloud**—the cloud version of the Sonar. For this, you must commit the code in Git.

You also can analyze the code on a local Sonar server. For this, you must set up and run the Sonar server locally. The default port on which the Sonar server runs is 9000, so you need to make sure that the Sonar port configured in `pom.xml` (if the build type is Maven) is the same. Execute the `mvnw test sonar:sonar` command, and you will see the code analysis in Sonar, as follows:

This helps to maintain the code quality even after adding custom code to the application.

Microservice support

In this chapter, we created a monolithic application using JHipster. However, it also allows users to create microservice-based applications. The microservice-based architecture splits the whole monolithic application (both the frontend and backend) into small and independent modular services. It is a unique way of doing software development that has grown rapidly in the last couple of years.

Each modular service can interact with other services through a unique and simple API. The microservice architecture has many advantages over a monolithic design, such as independent development and deployment, managing fail-over with ease, the fact that developers can work in the independent team, making continuous delivery, and so on.

Generally, a microservice architecture does not have any frontend layer, but JHipster supports a microservice gateway with a frontend to handle web traffic. It works as a proxy microservice for the end user. In short, a user can interact with a microservice through a gateway. The JHipster microservice model is comprised of one gateway service, one registry, and at least one or more microservice applications that we can create with JHipster with a backend code, which can be accessed with an API.

Docker support

Docker is an open source software platform that supports containers, making application deployment portable and self-contained. It is used to package the entire application (including SQL and NoSQL databases, Sonar configuration, and so on) and its dependencies together as a single container image, to deploy and test on any environment.

JHipster provides support for Docker out of the box for monolithic and microservice-based applications. Docker was developed for Linux, but has separate versions for macOS and Windows. JHipster only creates a Dockerfile at the time of application generation. The Dockerfile holds the set of instructions used by Docker containers to build a Docker image.

JHipster also supports pulling Docker images from the Docker Hub. This is an online registry that's used to publish public and private Docker images. This greatly helps in using third-party tools without local installation, as Docker images can be pulled and run on a local container.

Profile management

The profile is a set of configurations for a specific environment, like development, testing, production, and so on. JHipster supports profile management, and comes with two profiles—dev and `prod`—out of the box. By default, it uses the `dev` profile. JHipster provides a separate application properties file for each profile.

In production, you need to enable the production profile with the `./mvnw -Pprod` command for Maven and the `./gradlew -Pprod` command for Gradle. If you need to export an executable WAR file in production, you can use the command `./mvnw -Pprod package` for Maven, and `./gradlew -Pprod package` for Gradle.

Live reload

One of the most challenging factors in the software development process, in terms of time management, is recompiling the code, deploying it, and restarting the server to see the changes you made. Generally, the frontend code written in JavaScript does not require compilation, and can immediately reflect the changes upon browser refresh. Nevertheless, the latest frontend frameworks require some sort of transpilation after making changes in the script file.

In this situation, for any single code change, typically, you need to build, deploy, and restart the server. This will badly impact developer productivity. To avoid this, JHipster supports a mechanism called **live reload**. JHipster generates a Spring Boot-based application with the `DevTools` module to refresh the changes on the server without doing a cold restart. This is enabled by default, so whenever any Java code changes occur, it will automatically refresh them on the server. The live reloads for any frontend code can be achieved through **BrowserSync**, which can be started with the `npm start` command, and is accessible at `http://localhost:9000`.

Testing support

Testing is an integral part of any software development process. It provides quality assurance of the application or product. While creating an application and entities, JHipster creates various automated unit test cases for both the frontend and backend (or the server side).

The server-side unit test cases are generated in the `/src/test/java` folder. They cover various layers of the application, such as the repository, service, security, REST API, and pagination. They are grouped in respective packages. You can run individual test cases from the IDE, or run all test cases from the Command Prompt with the `mvnw test` command. Make sure that you are in the application directory when you execute this command. In the case of Gradle, you will need to execute the `gradle test` command.

Frontend (or client-side) unit testing can be executed with the `npm test` command. This will execute various JavaScript test cases for the typescript residing in the `/src/test/javascript/spec` folder. JHipster also supports end-to-end client-side test cases with the Jest framework, by default. Optionally, other frameworks, such as **Gatling**, **Cucumber**, and **Protractor**, can also be used for client-side end-to-end testing.

Upgrading JHipster

Unlike other frameworks, upgrading JHipster is a painless process. A subgenerator called **JHipster upgrade** is used to upgrade an existing application for the new version, without removing any custom changes that have been added since the application was created the first time. This is quite useful, especially when a new version of JHipster is released with known bug fixes and security patches. JHipster upgrades can be executed with the following command:

```
jhipster upgrade
```

To make the whole upgrade process automated, JHipster take the help of Git with the following steps:

- The preceding command checks whether a new version of JHipster is available, unless the `--force` flag is given explicitly. If this option is given, the upgrade sub-generator will be triggered, irrespective of the latest version being installed.
- The whole upgrade process depends on Git, so if an application is not initialized with Git (if Git is not installed), JHipster will initialize Git and commit the current code to the master branch.

- JHipster will check for any uncommitted local code. The upgrade process fails if the code is not committed.
- Next, it will check if a `jhipster_upgrade` branch is available in Git. If not, this will be created. This branch is dedicated to the JHipster upgrade process, so it should never be updated manually.
- JHipster will check out the `jhipster_upgrade` branch.
- At this point, JHipster is upgraded with the latest version.
- The current project directory is cleaned and the application is generated from scratch, with the entities.
- The generated code will then be committed to the `jhipster_upgrade` branch.
- Finally, the `jhipster_upgrade` branch will be merged with the original branch from which the `jhipster_upgrade` command was launched.
- In the case of any conflicts, you will need to resolve and commit them manually.

Continuous integration support

Automated testing greatly helps in making the system bug-free, even after adding new functionalities. JHipster creates unit and integration test cases for generated code that will be helpful up to some extent. In a real scenario, we need to add further unit test cases targeted for custom business implementations; for example, you might have added few custom screens, controller and service layer for which you need to write additional unit test cases.

Also, we need to add integration test cases for newly introduced APIs. Apart from that, we also need to add client-side test cases for frontend customization.

Presently, testing and continuous integration have become an integral part of the software development process. Testing will help to produce a quality product, while continuous integration is nothing but constantly merging and testing newly introduced code changes, which assists in identifying potential bugs. This happens with the combination of executing automated units, integration, and end-to-end test cases against the code. A classic example is triggering the automated test suite on every commit on Git; or, more efficiently, running it as per a predefined schedule.

The benefits of an automated testing model can be achieved by putting a continuous integration process in place, to make sure that new code changes do not introduce regressions to the stable version. This assures the merging of new changes and deploying to production with confidence.

The continuous testing, integration, and continuous deployment results in a concept called **Continuous Integration/Continuous Deployment (CI/CD)**, which performs continuous integration, testing, and deploying the code. Continuous delivery can be achieved through various CI/CD tools. JHipster provides elegant support for well known CI/CD tools available in the market today, such as Jenkins, Travis CI, GitLab CI, and Circle CI.

Community support and documentation

No matter how good a software framework or product is, its popularity comes from how easily users can get help from documentation and the community. JHipster has very nice documentation on their official site, which is more than sufficient to start working with it.

Apart from the official GitHub forum, there are plenty of other resources and forums available, in which you can easily get help with any issue or problem while working with JHipster. Additionally, the developers provide professional help in terms of answering questions on time and providing bug fixes as a priority. This really helps to attract developers and organizations to start to work with JHipster.

The JHipster Marketplace

Who doesn't like to use reusable components or modules that fit business requirements? This would greatly save development time. As an open source software, the JHipster team not only produces a great masterpiece in the form of the framework, but also maintains a repository of reusable modules, called the **Marketplace**.

You can download various modules, as per your needs, and plug them directly in your application. You can contribute your module back to the Marketplace, so that other community users can get the benefit of that module. This is a great platform provided by JHipster to share a piece of reusable code with the community.

Summary

This has really been a great journey, exploring a new framework for building a powerful web application. JHipster is a really great tool for crafting a modern and production-ready application in no time. With lots of things happening automatically, JHipster not only makes a developer's job easier, but also improves the overall project delivery schedule.

At the beginning of this chapter, we explored the basics of JHipster as a framework, along with an installation guide. Moving forward, you learned how JHipster generates application code with a question-and-answer approach. It uses another tool, called **Yeoman**, to generate application code.

Implementing domain objects as entities and supporting complete CRUD operations is the most important part of any application. In the next step, we learned how JHipster provides support for modeling domain objects through entity generation. Entity generation can be done with three options: the classic Yeoman-based option, the UML approach, and by using JDL-Studio. We have looked at all of them in detail.

After covering these features, we started to create an application to show GDP information by country. This required us to build custom screens, and we discovered how to add customization in an application generated with JHipster. We also collected a few details of generated code in various layers, including the persistence, service, REST controller, and frontend layer, which will help us to accommodate any future customization.

Towards the end, we looked at some unseen features that demonstrate what a robust platform JHipster is, and how it allows us to build a Spring-based, enterprise-grade application with ease. In the next chapter, you will learn how to create a Spring-based application with a microservice architecture, and how this is different and can be beneficial, as compared to a monolithic application.

6
Creating an Online Bookstore

It is always beneficial to develop any web application in a layered fashion. A prominent n-tier (or sometimes 3-tier) solution is the layered architecture, which has been widely adopted as the standard pattern for designing most applications. It is not a new concept, and we have been using it for a long time.

A layered architecture separates the whole application into various layers of concerns, which are logically different from each other:

- **Presentation layer**: This layer contains the artifacts that are responsible for building a user interface or displaying the output to the end user
- **Application layer**: This layer contains business logic and interacts with the presentation and persistence layers to makeup the flow of the application
- **Persistence layer**: This layer stores the data in data stores such as databases, the filesystem, and external sources, and also retrieves it

There are numerous advantages of a layered architecture, such as increased reusability, flexibility, and consistency, because the layers are logically separated. Applications built with a layered architecture are self-contained in nature and can be executed independently of other applications. They are referred to as **monolithic applications**.

Since the beginning of this book, we have been creating a monolithic application to showcase and explore various concepts. Though logically separated as an n-tier architecture, monolithic applications face a maintenance nightmare once their size and complexity reach a certain level over a period of time. Such applications hold all the features and functionalities in one single package, which is wrapped as a single deployable unit.

Microservices, on the other hand, are a different architectural approach, adopted by organizations such as Google, Amazon, Netflix, and many others, with the aim of meeting modern business needs and developing an application that is inherently complex in nature. The microservice architecture helps to solve the various problems that arise with monolithic applications.

The concept of microservices is not new; it has come to the fore to overcome the limitations of previous architectures. In this chapter, we will closely observe the evolution of microservice architecture by developing an online bookstore application along with following topics:

- Introduction to microservice architecture
- Principles and characteristics of microservice architecture
- Various approaches to designing a microservice frontend
- Defining the structure of the database
- Exploring various Spring Cloud and Netflix OSS components to design microservices
- Making a microservice application secure

Technical requirements

All the code used in this chapter can be downloaded from the following GitHub link: `https://github.com/PacktPublishing/Spring-5.0-Projects/tree/master/chapter06`. The code can be executed on any operating system, although it has only been tested on Windows.

Microservices introduction

Microservices have emerged as a promising architecture pattern that is widely accepted as a solution to modern trends in business. Enterprises use various channels, such as mobile platforms, analytics with big data, and social media interaction, as elements to grow the business and find new customers at a rapid pace. With all these artifacts, organizations are trying to design innovations that will help them to gain a strong market share, which is a quite a difficult goal to achieve with conventional delivery methodologies.

In the past, enterprises developed single monolithic and accumulated applications for their business needs. Today, this has changed, as the goal has shifted to developing a smart solution with a short turnaround time that focuses on a specific business need.

A good example is a traveling company that executes their business with a single monolithic application. What if they want to improve the customer experience by suggesting new traveling ideas based on user searches or, more specifically, their old trips, any special occasion or festival season, user preferences, or interests?

There are many scenarios where organizations wish to implement independent solutions for each of these use cases and plug them into core business logic, instead of keeping everything together as a single application, which means they have to keep updating and testing the whole application for any future business changes, as shown in the following diagram:

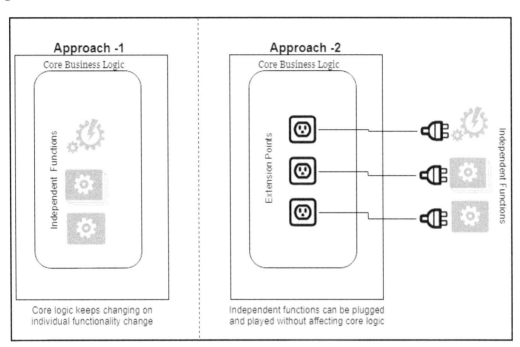

Instead of putting all these independent functionalities together with the core business logic, they can be plugged in independently. This approach is more flexible in terms of allowing new changes with a lower adoption cost. Additionally, they can be tested independently and more effectively. Any further changes can be accommodated with ease.

Such business scenarios expect an architecture that can adopt changes with minimal impact and cost, which makes it more agile. This is why the microservice approach has been developed.

Microservice architectures focus on designing an application in small parts, each of which is concerned with a specific function, instead of making the whole application a black box in a monolithic architecture.

In the last few years, the revolution in technological paradigms has completely changed the way we develop an application. This includes the frontend layer, with various popular frameworks for responsive capabilities and flexibility, such as Angular, React, Backbone, and Bootstrap, which completely change the user front.

With the introduction of cloud-aware and container mechanisms, the approach to designing and implementing the middle layer has been influenced. It also includes a change in the way we design persistence from using a relational database to NoSQL, which solved specific architectural concerns.

Microservice architecture

As time passes, architectural styles have improved significantly. Various architecture patterns, such as mainframes, client-server, n-tier, and **service-oriented architecture** (**SOA**), have been popular at various points in history. However, these architectural were all involved in developing some sort of monolithic application, either directly or indirectly.

As the revolution happened in the technology stack, microservice architecture has come to the fore as a result of improvements in all previous architectures. The aim is to provide agility, reduce the turnaround time for adopting new changes, achieve scalable performance, and take full advantage of modern tools and frameworks.

Microservice architecture breaks an application into small, independent subsystems. They also can be referred to as a system of systems, as shown in the following diagram:

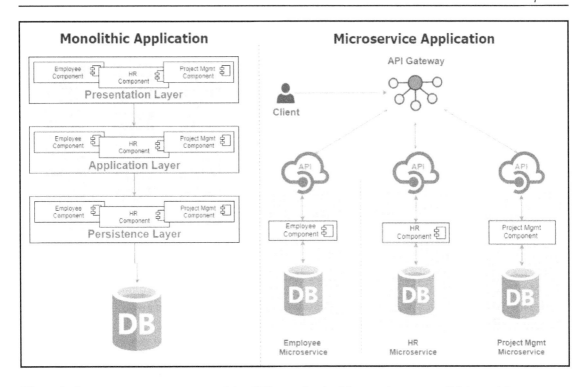

Though the components are stored in different logical layers in a monolithic architecture, they are packaged in a single application structure. On the other hand, the microservice system is a set of independent subsystems, each packaged in their own project structure and deployed as independent units. You can consider a microservice architecture as a jigsaw puzzle where each microservice is a building block of a whole application.

In short, in a monolithic system, the components are logically different but part of single physical application, whereas in a microservice architecture, the subsystems are actual physical applications that form a giant logical application.

The microservice architecture is widely used now as a set of standards to refactor monolithic applications. Emerging from a hexagonal pattern, a microservice architecture promotes the encapsulation of a business function into an individual independent unit that is isolated from other functionality.

A **Hexagonal Architecture** puts input and output on the edges of a hexagon and keeps **Business Logic** at the center. This arrangement isolates the application from outside concerns, as follows:

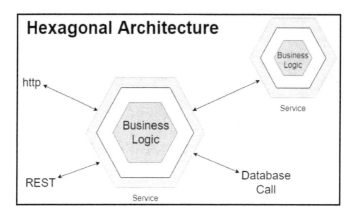

The inside part consists of **Business Logic**, whereas the outside consist of the UI, messaging, **REST**, database, and others. The outside parts can be swapped without affecting the core application functions. Each business function can be designed with the hexagonal model, which then interacts with others with a standard communication mechanism.

Let's look at the hexagonal pattern by taking an example. Consider you are developing an EMI calculator application that calculates the principal and interest amount based on total loan amount, interest rate, and tenure. This application keeps the provision of scanning the user input to calculate the loan data. The logic for taking user input is closely associated with the EMI calculator application. After a period of time, another application needs to use the EMI calculator application. In this case, the input mechanism needs to be updated.

To overcome this problem, the hexagonal pattern suggests isolating the EMI calculating logic from the input receiving mechanism by defining some sort of standard interface. This way, the EMI calculator is completely unaware of where the inputs come from. In this scenario, the interface for receiving input is referred to as a **Port**, while its implementation is known as an **Adapter**, as follows:

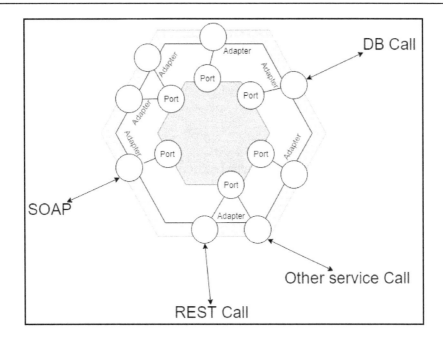

The hexagonal pattern is also referred to as the **Port** and **Adapter** pattern. The concept of the microservice architecture is derived from the hexagonal pattern, in which each hexagonal structure represents a self-contained and loosely coupled service (subsystem). Adding more hexagonal models is equivalent to adding more independent services.

That is why the microservice concept is logically compared with a honeycomb, in which multiple hexagons form a large and solid structure. Similarly, individual services (equivalent to individual hexagonal structures) form a larger application.

Microservice principles

Although there is no straight definition or standard for defining microservices, there are certain qualities, criteria, and principles that must be considered while designing microservice applications. Let's take a look at some of them in this section.

High cohesion with a single responsibility

High cohesion means a module or unit should execute a single business function. In the microservice architecture, an individual service should perform a single responsibility for a given application context. Sharing a single responsibility between multiple services should not be allowed. Also, a single service should not handle multiple responsibilities, in order to make the whole system truly modular.

This is one of the striking differences between the monolithic and microservice architectures. The components are logically separated but are still part of a single application and share some common responsibilities in the former, but they are designed as independent small applications in the latter.

While designing microservices, the goal should be the scope of the business function executed by the microservice instead of making it smaller. The term **micro** is sometimes misleading, suggesting you should make the service as small as possible. The scope should be given the highest priority, instead of the size of the service.

Service autonomy

While building a microservice application, the prime goal is to make each member (service) a standalone and independent building block. To make sure each service runs with optimal performance and provides reliable output, they must take full control over the underlying resources they use.

This can be achieved with the service autonomy principle. It recommends each service should be designed with autonomy in mind. By doing so, the control and ownership a service has over its own execution environment will be more effective, which would otherwise be difficult to achieve with shared resources in a monolithic architecture. This will greatly help in dealing with the scalability of the application.

Loose coupling

An application should be designed with microservice architecture in such a way that each unit (service) should have (ideally) zero or the bare minimum impact on other components or services. If any sort of interaction or communication is required between services, they also should be loosely coupled in nature. This is the reason synchronous calls with RESTful APIs or asynchronous calls with a messaging framework are preferable.

Hide implementation through encapsulation

Microservices must isolate underlying implementation details from the outside world and define a standard interface to interact with it. This will not only reduce complexity, but also enhance the ability to adopt new changes easily, making the whole system more flexible and robust.

Domain-driven design

Domain-driven design (**DDD**) is a way to design a system with respect to the actual domain models used in the application. The architectural style of DDD is used to develop an application in independent units, each representing a specific domain model. It also suggests the way to behave and communicate between domain models. An ideal DDD has all the qualities required to develop a modular application. Due to this, it is an ideal candidate for consideration while implementing microservice architecture.

Microservice characteristics

Here are some characteristics of a microservice architecture:

- It is a way of designing an application as a group of small services, each executed in its own procedure.
- Microservices can interact with each other internally, mostly through the HTTP API or some time-messaging mechanism such as AMQP or JMS.
- Each microservice is built to execute a specific business requirement. In other words, they are aligned to specific business needs or capabilities.
- Microservices can be deployed independently with an automated mechanism.
- Some sort of common or central process is required to manage microservices, which may or may not use the same technology stack as the individual microservices.
- Microservices manage their life cycle independently of others.
- Changes to one microservice do not impact on others as they run independently.

Microservices with Spring Cloud

Generally, microservices are designed to be deployed in a distributed system. There are certain common patterns across distributed environments. Spring Cloud provides a predefined implementation of patterns that we can use to build a microservice application quickly. They are considered Spring Cloud sub-projects. We are going to take a brief look at a few of them, and we will also see how to use them while developing our online bookstore application.

Configuration management

Configurations are part of any application, and in the Spring world they are in the form of the properties file, generally bundled with the application code. It is a tedious job to deploy the entire service any time there's a configuration change. What if a configuration can be managed outside of the application? This is a good idea because managing configurations externally allows us to reflect changes without deploying or even restarting a service. This is exactly what configuration management does. Configurations are allowed on the fly.

Service discovery

As we have seen, microservice applications are a collection of self-contained and independently deployable services that are running on the same or different physical machines, or on the cloud. Each service can be considered as an individual process that performs a specific responsibility.

Though they are separated in terms of executing different business functions, they are interconnected as a part of the whole application, and hence some sort of communication mechanism, with well-defined standards, is required.

For interprocess communication, as well as accessing a particular service, we need to know the location in terms of the port and IP of the service. Traditional monolithic applications are generally deployed and accessible with a static port and IP address. Also, they are deployed in a single package so that all the components/services are accessible with the same port and IP. The likelihood of changing the port and IP is also very low.

In contrast, microservice applications are distributed in nature and may be deployed on different machines or in the cloud. Additionally, more instances of the services may be added to improve the scalability of the system. In future, new services may be added dynamically. Due to this, the locations of microservices are dynamic.

Spring Cloud provides a **service discovery** functionality, which is actually used to locate the services in the distributed environment. Spring Cloud provides a Netflix Eureka-based discovery service out of the box. Alternatively, we can use Consul, Cloud Foundry, or Apache ZooKeeper with Spring Cloud as service discovery support.

Circuit breakers

Though microservices are designed to handle a single responsibility, they sometimes rely on other services to perform a set of actions owned by others. In this dependency channel, if one service goes down, the error will propagate to other services on the same channel. To avoid it, Spring Cloud provides a Netflix Hystrix-based fault tolerance solution, which is an implementation of the circuit breaker pattern.

Routing

Since the location of microservices can be changed dynamically, a routing mechanism is required to send the request to the specific service endpoint. Spring Cloud provides a simple and effective way to route APIs with advanced cross-cutting capabilities such as security, monitoring, filtering, and authentication through Zuul—another tool from Netflix, which is a server-side load balancer that's used for routing purposes as well. Zuul can also be used as a micro proxy, which routes the application using the proxy URL that was configured.

 Another component used for routing is Spring Cloud Gateway, which is natively developed by Spring. It is built on Spring Framework 5 and may provide a better developer experience as it's closely integrated with Spring.

Spring Cloud Security

Though microservices are accessed with standard interfaces, they need authentication and authorization in some use cases. Securing a microservice system is more complex than securing a monolithic system. Spring supports authentication with microservices through Spring Cloud Security with the Auth2 protocol to propagate the security context across the microservices in a distributed environment.

Distributed tracing service

In the microservice architecture, the application flow may pass through a chain of multiple service calls to execute a single business use case. Manually tracing the activities with the logs of multiple microservices is not an efficient solution. We may not get exactly what we want out of it. It is important to understand what is happening between the series of service call. This is quite helpful in debugging if an issue arises. Spring Cloud provides an effective way to trace the application flow in a distributed system through **Spring Cloud Sleuth**. It collects the call tracking data, which can be exported to **Zipkin**—another tool for visualizing the call trace.

Spring Cloud Stream

To handle the high volumes of data streams, we may need to work with message broker implementations such as RabbitMQ or Apache Kafka. Spring Cloud provides an easy integration of a message broker with a high-level abstraction through Spring Cloud Stream. So, instead of actually implementing the message broker, Spring Cloud Stream will handle the messages and pass them to the actual broker client at runtime, based on its configuration. This makes the code portable and loosely coupled with any message broker implementation.

Developing an online bookstore application

Now that we've looked at the microservice architecture, let's now do a practical exercise to understand the concept in more detail. We will follow the microservice pattern to develop a simple online bookstore application.

Application architecture

We need to start by designing the application's architecture first. While designing microservice-based applications, first we need to think of a single monolithic application and then derive various parts or components that are independent of each other and can be thought of as possible candidates for being individual microservices.

We will break the application into small parts based on the criteria we looked at in the previous sections, such as single responsibility, service autonomy, loose coupling, encapsulation, and DDD, as follows:

- User management
- Order management
- Catalog management
- Inventory management

They are considered independent domains or business functions. We will create individual microservices for each of them with the following high-level architecture:

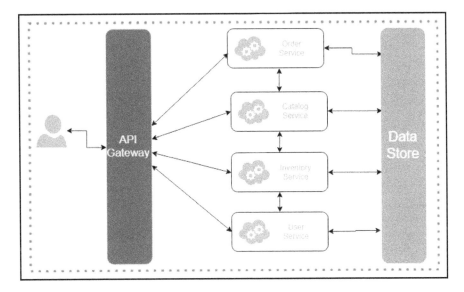

Database design

While decomposing the application to adopt the microservice architecture, we need to rethink database design as well. In a distributed environment, there are multiple options for database design.

Single monolithic database for all microservices

In this approach, though the microservices are independently designed as a separate subsystem, they still share a single monolithic database, as follows:

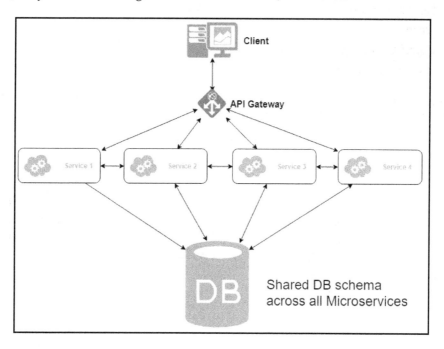

Each microservice has its own set of tables, but all are part of a single database schema. The clear benefit of this option is simplicity, as a single database can be operated with ease. Also, transactions can be carried out in a more consistent way.

However, according to best practices, microservice should be independently deployable to get better scaling optimization. Another benefit of being independently deployable is the quick adoption of changes. As soon as multiple services depend on a single monolithic data store, this flexibility is reduced to take full advantage of the distributed environment, such as high cohesion and loose coupling.

Also, multiple teams generally work on the application side. They also need to face coupling with other teams while dealing with database changes. This will slow down the development and eventually add a delay in delivery. So, this is not an ideal scenario.

Separate service to handle database interaction

In this scenario, instead of sharing a common database with all services, a separate service will be developed that will interact with the database only. All other services will talk to this service for any database operations instead of directly connecting with the database, as follows:

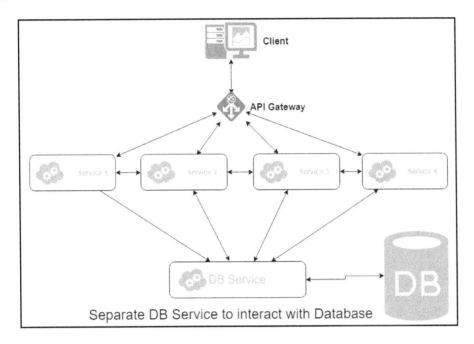

Separate DB Service to interact with Database

Though the dependency of managing database-related actions is shifted to a separate service, it is still kind of a monolithic approach and has all the limitations of the first option. So, this is also not an optimized way to design the database for a microservice architecture.

Each microservice has its own database

This option has a separate database for each individual service, as follows:

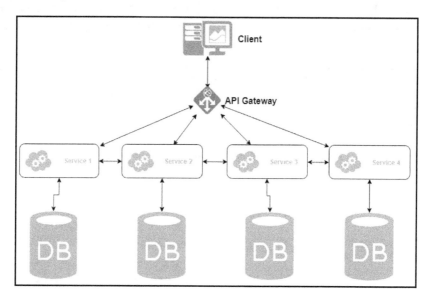

Instead of a single shared database across services, each service's database is an integral part of that service and cannot be accessed by other services directly. Another flexibility in this option is that each service is allowed to choose the type of data store that is the best fit for its capabilities. For example, if you have a search service, to perform the search in the system, you can use **Elasticsearch** as a data store.

This model has two further options:

- **Individual database schema per service:** Still use a single database server, but have a separate schema for each microservice. This option makes ownership cleaner, and it is an ideal option for most cases.
- **Individual database server per service:** Design separate database servers for each microservice. This option can be considered for services that require high throughput.

For simplicity, we will use MySQL to store the data. As per the system architecture, there will be a separate database schema for each microservice.

User schema

This schema contains the tables that store user-related data. The **user** table holds user-specific data, which will be used for authentication, while the **delivery_address** table contains delivery address information:

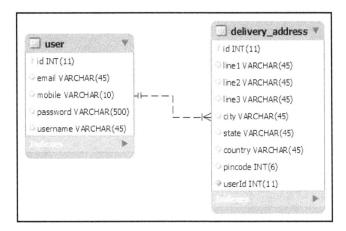

There is a *one-to-many* relationship between the **user** and **delivery_address** tables.

Order schema

This schema contains two tables, **order** and **order_item**. The relationship between them is as follows:

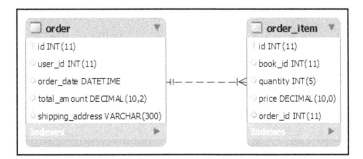

The **order** table holds the generic details of each order, such as orderId, userId, order date, total amount, and shipping address. The **order_item** table saves individual item details.

Catalog schema

This schema contains the product details. Since this is an online bookstore application, the **book** table contains details of the book. The **category** and **publisher** tables contain details about categories and publishers respectively. The relationship between these tables is as follows:

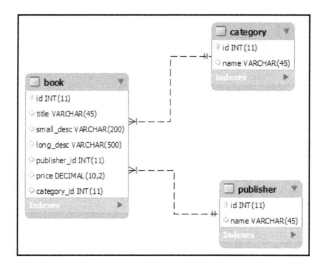

The **book** table has a *many-to-one* relationship to the **category** and **publisher** tables.

Inventory schema

Every store has an inventory. This schema stores the inventory containing information about the books. There are two tables that store this information. The **inventory** table contains the current stock of the product (books in our case), while the **inventory_history** table shows the history of adding new books into the system:

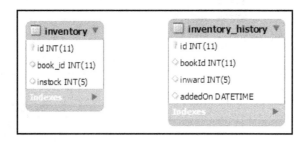

There is no relation between these tables.

Creating microservices with Spring Boot

We are going to develop an online bookstore application with an architecture of small and independently deployable microservices that can be developed by individual teams. They are expected to be developed with a quick turnaround time. This is what Spring Boot is designed for. It is a tool used to create production-grade Spring-based enterprise applications with a little configuration in no time.

We will first develop individual services with Spring Boot to develop them quickly. Spring Cloud also has solid integration capabilities with Spring Boot. While developing microservices, Spring Boot takes care of all the low-level things and allows us to concentrate on the business logic.

First, we will create Spring Boot applications for specific functionalities. Once they are created, we will then add microservice-specific capabilities to each of them:

- `user-service`: This service is intended to execute various operations related to users, such as registration, login, and user interaction
- `inventory-service`: This service performs various inventory operations performed by admin only
- `catalog-service`: This service is responsible for managing catalog information such as adding books, categories, and publisher details
- `order-service`: This service handles orders placed by a user

While creating an application with either the spring-io initializer or **Spring Tool Suite** (**STS**, an Eclipse-based IDE provided by Spring), initially we will add following dependencies:

- **DevTools**: Used to improve the development time experience by adding auto-deploy/restart capabilities as a Maven dependency.
- **JPA**: This will add a JPA-specific starter dependency, which is used to add JPA capabilities. We are going to use JPA (Hibernate implementation) to interact with the database.
- **MySQL**: This will add a MySQL connector JAR to connect to the database.
- **Web**: This is used to add Spring MVC capabilities to the application. We will use a REST controller to access individual microservice applications.

Adding microservice-specific capabilities

We have created various Spring Boot applications for each individual functionality. They all are accessible (by default) on port 8080 one by one. However, they are not ready to be executed as microservices. Now we will add microservice-specific capabilities by adding a dependencies entry in the pom.xml file of each individual Spring Boot application.

Add the following entry in the dependencies section of pom.xml:

```
<dependency>
    <groupId>org.springframework.cloud</groupId>
    <artifactId>spring-cloud-starter-netflix-eureka-client</artifactId>
</dependency>
```

You also need to add an entry for the current version of Spring Cloud next to the <java-version> entry as follows:

```
<spring-cloud.version>Greenwich.RC2</spring-cloud.version>
```

Add the following entry after the dependencies section is complete in pom.xml:

```
<dependencyManagement>
    <dependencies>
      <dependency>
        <groupId>org.springframework.cloud</groupId>
        <artifactId>spring-cloud-dependencies</artifactId>
        <version>${spring-cloud.version}</version>
        <type>pom</type>
        <scope>import</scope>
      </dependency>
    </dependencies>
  </dependencyManagement>

<repositories>
    <repository>
      <id>spring-milestones</id>
      <name>Spring Milestones</name>
      <url>https://repo.spring.io/milestone</url>
    </repository>
</repositories>
```

Make these changes in all four Spring Boot applications that we have developed. After applying these changes, they will no longer run independently as Spring Boot applications because we are now moving towards a microservice architecture.

Develop a service discovery server

The real challenge in a microservice architecture is to access particular services because they are dynamically created and destroyed, so their location keeps changing. Additionally, we also need some sort of inter-service communication to fulfill certain business use cases that span the microservices. Also, multiple instances of each microservice can be created to scale up the application's performance.

In this situation, there must be a mechanism for locating the microservices. Spring Cloud provides a Netflix Eureka-based service discovery component for this purpose. Microservices can register themselves with the discovery server so that they can be accessed and interacted with by other services. Eureka Server is basically used for discovery, self-registration, and load balancing.

Next up is to create a Eureka-based service that acts as a **service discovery server**. Creating a Eureka-based discovery service is similar to creating Spring Boot application with just a few configuration changes. Create a new Spring starter project with the following data:

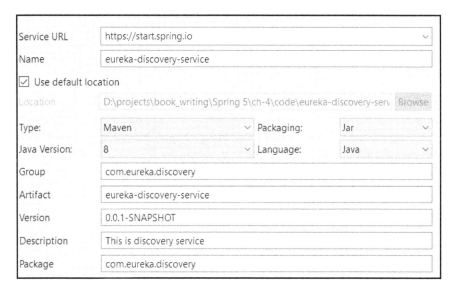

On next screen, select **Eureka Server** under the **Cloud Discovery** option as a dependency and click **Finish**. Once the project is created, open the `bootstrap` class and add the code highlighted in bold as follows:

```
@SpringBootApplication
@EnableEurekaServer
public class EurekaDiscoveryServiceApplication {

  public static void main(String[] args) {
    SpringApplication.run(EurekaDiscoveryServiceApplication.class, args);
  }
}
```

By default, the **Eureka Server** option is not enabled. The `@EnableEurekaServer` annotation is used to make it active for this application. That means this application will run as a Eureka discovery server. Next, we will add certain properties in the `application.properties` file as follows:

```
#Configure this Discovery Server
eureka.client.registerWithEureka = false
eureka.client.fetch-registry=false

#In case if Eureka port need to be changed from default 8080
server.port = 8761
```

By default, the current Eureka server is also a Eureka client and will try to register itself as a Eureka client with the Eureka server. Since we want this application to behave as a server only, we need to explicitly set the `eureka.client.registerWithEureka` property to `false`. By default, Eureka server is accessible through port `8080` and it can be changed with the `server.port` property.

Each Eureka client will fetch registry details from Eureka server. In our case, we do not want to fetch the registry details, so, we explicitly set the `eureka.client.fetch-registry` property to `false`. Now run the application, and Eureka Server is accessible through `http://localhost:8761`. It will show the server details and all registered service details, as follows:

Currently, no services are registered with our Eureka discovery server, so it shows nothing in the **Instances currently registered with Eureka** section.

 Eureka Server can be started in standalone or clustered mode. For simplicity, we have chosen standalone mode.

Next up is to register the four microservices that we have developed with the Eureka discovery server. We have already added microservice-specific dependencies to them. Now, we need to add the Eureka client configurations. Because of the way we have configured Eureka server, we need to configure the Eureka client in each of the service's bootstrap classes. For example, the Eureka client configuration for the user service's bootstrap class is highlighted in bold as follows:

```
@SpringBootApplication
@EnableDiscoveryClient
public class UserServiceApplication {
  public static void main(String[] args) {
    SpringApplication.run(UserServiceApplication.class, args);
  }
}
```

The @EnableDiscoveryClient annotation will enable client configuration. Additionally, we need to add the following properties in the application.properties file:

```
spring.application.name=user-service
server.port=8791
```

The spring.application.name property will be used to register the application with a specific name. Add client configurations and start other services, and you will see them registered with Eureka server as follows:

Instances currently registered with Eureka

Application	AMIs	Availability Zones	Status
CATALOG-SERVICE	n/a (1)	(1)	UP (1) - nil.mshome.net:catalog-service:8792
INVENTORY-SERVICE	n/a (1)	(1)	UP (1) - nil.mshome.net:inventory-service:8793
ORDER-SERVICE	n/a (1)	(1)	UP (1) - nil.mshome.net:order-service:8794
USER-SERVICE	n/a (1)	(1)	UP (1) - nil.mshome.net:user-service:8791

Another annotation, @EnableEurekaClient, can also be used for Eureka client configuration. The difference between @EnableDiscoveryClient and @EnableEurekaClient is that the former is more Spring-aware and works with discovery implementations other than Eureka, such as Consul and ZooKeeper; the latter is specific to Eureka only. So, if Eureka is present in the classpath, there is no difference between them.

Spring Cloud Eureka consists of client and server components. All the microservices are registered in the server registry, whereas each individual service behaves as a client. Any service that wants to discover other services should also be Eureka client-aware. The registration in the server happens with client identity (with its name) and URL (with its port).

The flow of communication between client and server happens as follows:

1. On starting the microservice, it reaches out to the server component and provides metadata for registration.
2. Eureka server validates the metadata and does the registration.
3. After registration, the microservice endpoint sends the ping to the server registry every 30 seconds (by default) to mark its presence.
4. The server will continuously verify the ping requests, and if no request comes for a certain period of time, it will remove the service from the registry automatically.
5. The server shares the registry information with all Eureka-aware clients, and they store it in the local cache. This information is then used by a microservice client to locate other clients in the distributed environment.
6. The server pushes the updates of registry information to all clients every 30 seconds (by default).
7. Microservices registered with a server can be grouped into a zone. In this case, the zone information can be supplied at registration.
8. When any microservice sends a request for another microservice, Eureka server will try to search service instances running in the same zone to reduce the latency.
9. The interaction between the Eureka client and server happens through REST and JSON.

Designing an API gateway

In typical microservice applications, it is quite possible that more than a hundred microservices are interacting with each other. There are certain common features that are required to be implemented for all these microservices:

- **Security**: We may need to check that authentication and authorization, or any other security policies required to make calls to microservices
- **Restrict call rate**: This allows only a certain number of calls for a specific microservice in a given time
- **Fault toleration**: If any service fails to respond, this sends an appropriate error signal
- **Monitor**: This is used to monitor for specific events or values passed across the microservices
- **Service aggregation**: This provides an aggregate response from multiple microservices in a single response, specifically in a bandwidth-restricted environment
- **Routing**: Based on certain criteria (if call forwarding is required, for example), route all the calls from a specific user to a particular region to a specific service
- **Load balancing**: This maintains the flow of calls to balance the load on the service instance

Apart from this, we may want to restrict some of the services to end users and keep them private. To achieve these goals, we need some sort of API gateway, which will intercept all the calls from end users and all inter-service communication. So, instead of microservices talking with each other directly through REST calls, they will now interact with each other through an API gateway, which will provide all the features previously listed. Since all the calls are routed from the API gateway, it can also be used for debugging and analytic purposes.

Spring Cloud provides API gateway support through another Netflix implementation called **Zuul**. Next up, let's see how to set up Zuul.

Setting up Zuul as an API gateway

We will create a Zuul proxy server as an independent Spring Boot service and register it with the Eureka discovery server. Create a new Spring starter project in Spring STS with Zuul, Eureka Discovery, and DevTool as dependencies.

Once created, open the `bootstrap` class and update it as follows:

```
@EnableZuulProxy
@EnableDiscoveryClient
@SpringBootApplication
public class ZuulApiGatewayApplication {
  public static void main(String[] args) {
    SpringApplication.run(ZuulApiGatewayApplication.class, args);
  }
}
```

The `@EnableZuulProxy` annotation will make this service a Zuul server. We also need to register it with the Eureka discovery server with the `@EnableDiscoveryClient` annotation. Every service registered with the Eureka name server needs a name (and a port). Add these details for the Zuul server in the `application.properties` file as follows:

```
spring.application.name=zuul-api-gateway
server.port=8781
```

Now the API gateway server is ready and configured, but we did not specify what to do when intercepting requests. Zuul provides request handling support through various filters. They are categories in pre, post, routing, and error filters, each targeted for specific service call life cycles. Since Zuul is a Spring Boot-based service, we can customize the API gateway programmatically. Additionally, for any special requirement, Zuul supports developing custom filters. We will see how to add custom filters and examine how requests can be intercepted with it in a short while.

 The Zuul API gateway server is also referred to as an Edge server.

Designing the UI

As we have seen, the microservice architecture is the best fit for modern applications that are big and distributed in nature. This type of architecture helps split the team that's working on a single monolithic application into a set of small and independent teams, focusing on one single module or functionality.

A microservice pattern has its own benefits, such as managing scalability and complexity, and easily adopting new changes in a short time frame. We have explored how Spring Cloud components help build a distributed application in the Spring Framework. So far, we have only talked about the middle and backend layers. This section is dedicated to an interesting topic: how to design a microservice frontend.

Unlike monolithic architectures, the frontend of a microservice application can be designed with different approaches, as follows:

- Monolithic front
- Micro front
- Composite or modular front

Monolithic front

Though the microservice pattern divides the monolithic backend into multiple independent services, this may not be straightforward for the frontend. In the monolithic front approach, we keep the whole user interface in a single big frontend application that will talk to corresponding services through REST calls to perform tasks or to show data to the end user, as per the following diagram:

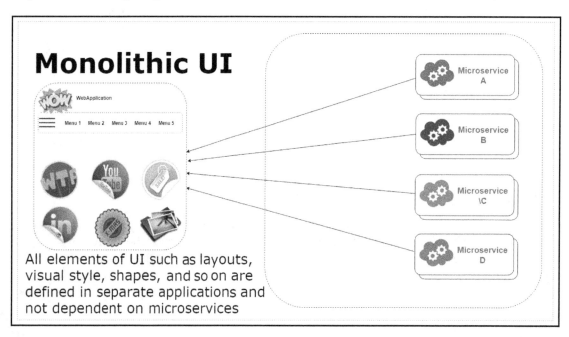

The clear benefits of this approach are an easy implementation and UI consistency across the application because everything is in a single place. On the downside, there may be a good amount of conflict regarding library versions, styling, and so on, as multiple teams are working on a single UI application.

Since everything is under one roof, it becomes harder to adopt changes as the application grows. Over a period of time, when business demand increases, it eventually becomes harder to maintain the application's UI as multiple teams spend most of their time solving problems.

Choose this approach only when you are sure that the application is divided into just a few microservices with limited scope for growth in the future.

Micro front

In this approach, each microservice has its own UI limited to the functionality it performs. So, along with the backend, the frontend is also decomposed as per the scope of the individual microservices, as follows:

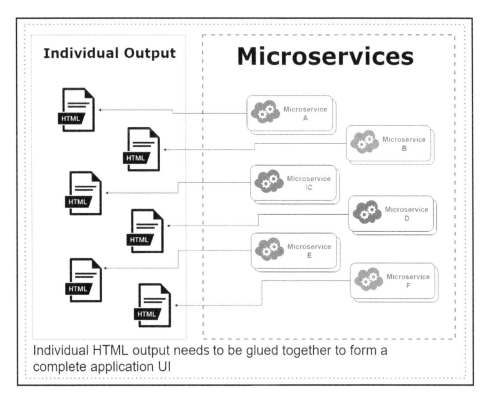

This approach eliminates all the limitations of the monolithic frontend but then introduces certain new challenges. Though microservices are split as self-contained and independent executable units, and the final frontend should be presented with a single interface. In the micro front approach, the challenge is to combine the UIs of individual microservices in a single format. There are a number of ways of doing this. Though they overcome the limitations of the first approach, they introduce certain other issues:

- **Synchronize the UI across the microservices:** In this way, just copy and paste the UI of all services to each other and use the API gateway. Though this seems simple, it produces huge maintenance issues.
- **IFrame:** Use a separate layout where the output of individual microservices can be clubbed with IFrame. However, this approach is also not brilliant because IFrame has its own limitations.
- **HTML fragments:** You can write your own JavaScript code and glue the content of the microservices through HTML fragments. However, there are some limitations, and also lots of custom script you have to write on your own. Also, there may be a chance of services' scripts and styles clashing.

Composite front

This approach is a micro font approach with the right solution to aggregate the microservice output. The layout will be created with a single UI application, whereas the business UI of individual microservices will be plugged in from of web components, as follows:

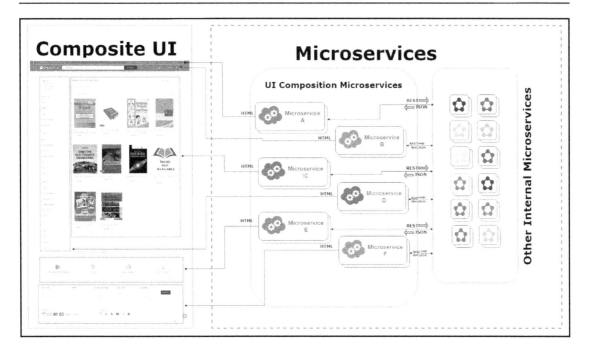

Each microservice is responsible for producing a small UI area on the page. Composite UIs can be easily designed by creating a component in popular frontend frameworks such as Angular and React. On top of this, a framework such as *single-spa* (`https://single-spa.js.org`) is designed to show aggregate output. It is basically a JavaScript library that shows a composite output of microservices as a single-page application running in a browser. Single-spa allows the coexistence of microservices developed in different frameworks.

This means that you can develop one microservice in Angular, a second in React, a third with Vue, and so on. This brings great flexibility and fulfills the aim of the microservice architecture being developed completely independently from the backend to the UI. As an enhanced version of the second approach, the composite font approach not only overcomes the limitation of the monolithic front approach but also suggests the right way to develop the front layer in a microservice architecture.

Other Spring Cloud and Netflix OSS components

Spring Cloud provides a wrapper on top of various Netflix components that are used in microservice applications extensively. We have already explored the Eureka discovery server and Zuul. In this section, we will explore a few more Netflix OSS components, along with other Spring Cloud features.

Dynamic configuration in Spring Cloud

As we know, the microservice architecture consists of a number of small and independently deployable microservices that handle end-user calls and interact with each other. Based on the project's needs, they may run in various environments, such as development, testing, staging, production, and so on. To improve the scaling capabilities of an application, there may be multiple instances of microservices configured to work with the load balancer.

Each microservice possesses a set of configurations, including database configurations, interaction with other services, message broker configurations, and custom configurations. Handling microservice configurations between various environments is one of the most challenging parts of a microservice architecture.

Maintaining each microservices configuration manually would be too complex and difficult for the operations team. The best possible solution is to separate the configuration out from each microservice and maintain them all in one central place. This way, the dependency of environments on configuration can be handled more effectively.

Spring Cloud provides a component called **Spring Cloud Config**, which is used to externalize the microservice configuration. It uses a Git repository to store all the configurations in one place, as shown in the following diagram:

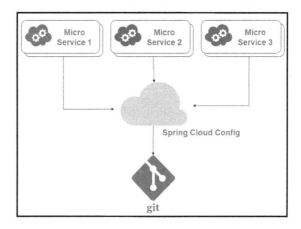

We will create a separate service for central configuration with the Spring Cloud Config feature. The next few sections explain how to do this.

Step 1 – creating a Spring Boot service for the configuration server

This is the most straightforward way of creating a component as a Spring Boot application. Create an application with STS and select the DevTool and Config server dependencies. Once the project is created, you can see the dependency in pom.xml that is responsible for adding Spring Cloud Config capabilities to the Spring Boot application, as follows:

```
<dependency>
  <groupId>org.springframework.cloud</groupId>
  <artifactId>spring-cloud-config-server</artifactId>
</dependency>
```

Next up, let's enable the Spring Cloud Config feature. Open the main bootstrap class and add the @EnableConfigServer annotation, which is used to enable external configuration:

```
@EnableConfigServer
@SpringBootApplication
public class SpringCloudConfigServerApplication {
  public static void main(String[] args) {
    SpringApplication.run(SpringCloudConfigServerApplication.class, args);
  }
}
```

Since the configuration server will also be registered with the naming server (Eureka server), we need to define certain properties in the application.properties file as follows:

```
spring.application.name=spring-cloud-config-server
server.port=8901
```

Next up, let's install and configure Git.

Step 2 – configuring Spring Cloud Config with a Git repository

The Spring Cloud Config server is ready. Now, we need to do the necessary configuration for Git repository integration. First, install the latest version of Git (https://git-scm.com/downloads) on your local machine and make sure it is available on a path. Create a directory on your local machine and initialize the Git repository with the following command:

```
git init
```

This will create an empty Git repository on the local machine. Next, add a properties file that holds the configuration details. Since the configuration server can hold configuration details for multiple microservices in Git, we need to follow a certain naming convention for the property file, as follows:

```
{microserivce-name}.properties
{microservice-name}-{active-profile}.properties
```

As we have seen, microservices' IDs (or names) are defined with the `spring.application.name` property in the `application.properties` file. So, we need to create a property file with this name in the Git repository. For example, if the microservice name is `catalog-service`, then you need to create a `catalog-service.properties` file and store all the configurations for that microservice.

For different environments, you can create a property file with an active profile appended after the microservice name. For example, the name of the property file for the development environment would be `catalog-service-dev.properties`. Once you have created the files, add the configuration details and commit them to the Git repository with the following command:

```
git add -A
git commit -m "Comment for commit"
```

The Git repository is now ready, so we need to point the configuration server to it. Open the `application.properties` file of the configuration server as follows:

```
spring.cloud.config.server.git.uri=file://D:/projects/book_writing/git_cent
ral_config
```

Since this is the local Git repository, the location of the repository folder is given with `file://` to point it to the local filesystem. The configuration server also allows configuration with a remote Git repository. In this case, you need to give the Git clone URL something like `https://github.com/<<accoun-tname>>/<<repo-name>>.git` for the `spring.cloud.config.server.git.uri` property.

We will add some sample configurations and see how they can be reflected in the corresponding microservice. Create a `service.properties` file and add the following property:

```
catalog.sample.data=Hello world !!
```

Step 3 – making each microservice Spring Cloud Config-aware using the Spring Cloud Config Client component

The last step is to make the necessary changes to the microservice (configuration client) so that the configuration will be propagated by the configuration server once it is updated in the Git repository. The important point at this moment is to create a new property file called `bootstrap.properties` and copy all the properties from the `application.properties` file, or you can directly rename `application.properties` to `bootstrap.properties`.

The reason is that Spring will process the `bootstrap.properties` file first, even before the bootstrap application and configuration server linked with it for configuration updates. You need to add a specific property in the `bootstrap.application` file, which will be used to connect the microservice with the configuration server, as follows:

```
spring.cloud.config.uri=http://localhost:8901
```

The configuration server is accessible at `http://localhost:8901`. The microservice will fetch the configuration details with this URL. Next, we will access the configuration that we declared in the Git repository in the microservice with the REST controller, as follows:

```
@RestController
@RequestMapping("/api/test")
@RefreshScope
public class TestRESTController {
  Logger logger = LoggerFactory.getLogger(this.getClass());
  @Value("${catalog.sample.data}")
  private String data;

  @GetMapping("/getSampleData")
  public String getSampleData() {
    logger.info(" sample data value is -->"+this.data);
    return this.data;
  }
}
```

In this controller, we are accessing the configuration with `catalog.sample.data` with the `@Value` annotation. This annotation is used to read the properties defined in the local `application.properties` file. The magic is that we haven't defined any such property for the category service, but it will connect to the configuration server and fetch this property value from the Git repository internally.

The @RefreshScope annotation will be used to fetch the latest configuration value whenever any change happens in the Git repository. You need to declare @RefreshScope for the component where you are reading the configuration value. When you start the catalog-service microservice, it will try to read the configuration from the configuration server, and you can verify it from the log as follows:

```
[restartedMain] c.c.c.ConfigServicePropertySourceLocator : Fetching config
from server at : http://localhost:8901
```

On startup, the catalog-service microservice will fetch the configuration from Git through the configuration server. This can be verified with the http://localhost:8792/api/test/getSampleData REST URL. When we make changes in the configuration and commit them to Git, they must be propagated to the microservice. This will not be done automatically, and you need to manually refresh it with Actuator—a tool provided by Spring Boot to monitor and manage applications. We will use the /refresh endpoint of Actuator to refresh the microservice with the latest configuration changes.

Staring with Spring Boot 2.0, certain endpoints of Actuator (including /refresh) are not enabled by default. To enable them, you need to add the following property in the bootstrap.properties file of the catalog-service microservice:

```
management.endpoints.web.exposure.include=*
```

Now, all endpoints are available, and configuration propagation can be done through a POST request to http://localhost:8792/actuator/refresh. Since this is a POST call, you need to use a REST client such as Postman. Once the refresh is completed, you will see the following output:

```
[
    "config.client.version",
    "catalog.sample.data"
]
```

This is how configuration can be applied on the fly without restarting the microservice. The whole process can be performed in a series of actions in the following order:

1. Update the files in the Git repository
2. Do the Git commit
3. Execute the refresh operation, and you will see the changes reflected in the corresponding microservice

This is a great feature of managing configuration in one central place, and it can be applied to specific microservices with ease. However, not all properties can be applied this way. For example, application name and database-specific properties cannot be applied at runtime through Spring Cloud Config. However, custom configurations can be applied dynamically.

Making RESTful calls across microservices with Feign

In microservice architecture, generally microservices interact with each other through HTTP REST web service calls. Typically, `RestTemplate` is used as a client to make REST API call programmatically in Spring-based applications. However, it requires a good amount of code to make a simple REST call. To make this simple, Spring Cloud provides Feign, another REST client that makes REST communication alot simpler than `RestTemplate`. Let's see how Feign makes calls to other services easy.

For example, `inventory-service` needs to talk with the `catalog-service` microservice to fetch book details. In this case, `inventory-service` will make a REST call to fetch a `Book` object for a given `bookId`. This would typically happen with the `RestTemplate` client as follows:

```
@GetMapping("/get-inventory/{bookId}")
  public ResponseEntity<BookDTO> getInventory(@PathVariable("bookId")
Integer bookId) {
    String url = "http://localhost:8792/api/catalog/get-book/"+bookId;
    RestTemplate restTemplate = new RestTemplate();
    ResponseEntity<BookDTO> returnValue = restTemplate.getForEntity(url,
BookDTO.class);
    return returnValue;
  }
```

We are using `RestTemplate` to call the `catalog-service` microservice to fetch the book details for the given `bookId`. Spring Cloud inherits another component, called **Feign**, from Netflix, which can be used as a declarative REST client with great simplification. It is easily integrated with Ribbon, which can be used as a client-side load-balancer; we will talk about this in the next section. To use Feign, you need to add the following starter dependency:

```
<dependency>
    <groupId>org.springframework.cloud</groupId>
    <artifactId>spring-cloud-starter-openfeign</artifactId>
</dependency>
```

Next, let's enable Feign. Open the `bootstrap` class and add a `@EnableDiscoveryClient` annotation to scan the Feign client, as follows:

```
@SpringBootApplication
@EnableDiscoveryClient
@EnableFeignClients(basePackages="com.bookstore.inventory")
public class InventoryServiceApplication {
  public static void main(String[] args) {
    SpringApplication.run(InventoryServiceApplication.class, args);
  }
}
```

Now, we will use Feign to invoke the service. We need to create a Feign proxy to talk to other services, just like we use the JPA repository to interact with the database. A Feign proxy can be created with Java as follows:

```
@FeignClient(name="catalog-service",url="http://localhost:8792",
path="/api/catalog")
public interface CatalogServiceProxy {
  @GetMapping("/get-book/{bookId}")
  public ResponseEntity<BookDTO> getInventory(@PathVariable("bookId")
Integer bookId);
}
```

The `@FeignClient` annotation is used to define the Feign proxy. The `name` attribute points to the name of the target microservice declared in the Eureka naming server (specified with the `spring.application.name` property in the `application.properties` or `bootstrap.properties` file) we want to talk to. `url` is the address at which the target microservice is accessible. The `path` attribute is used to add the path prefix used by all method-level mapping.

We have created the interface method with the same method signature that we created in the REST controller. We will use this proxy in the REST controller as follows:

```
@RestController
@RequestMapping("/api/inventory")
public class InventoryRESTController {

  @Autowired
  CatalogServiceProxy catalogServiceProxy;
  @GetMapping("/get-inventory/{bookId}")
  public ResponseEntity<BookDTO> getInventory(@PathVariable("bookId")
Integer bookId) {
    return catalogServiceProxy.getInventory(bookId);
  }
}
```

The instance of `CatalogServiceProxy` is injected by Spring through the `@Autowired` annotation. You can see how simple it is to make a RESTful web service. All the details are shifted from the controller to the Feign proxy. You will get the same output as `RestTemplate`, but the code is decoupled and simplified.

Assume the scenario where you are making more than a dozen REST calls to the `catalog-service` microservice. In this case, the Feign proxy helps us to manage all the code in one place. Other component classes do not need to know the underlying details.

Load balancing with Ribbon

In the last section, we saw how `inventory-service` can call `catalog-service` to fetch book details through Feign. However, in a distributed environment, it is quite possible that multiple instances of microservices are created to handle the enormous application load.

In a multi-instance environment, a mechanism is required to balance and divide a load of input requests seamlessly to send them to available instances. The system becomes fault tolerant. It also increases throughput, reduces response time, and optimizes resource utilization by avoiding single instances being overloaded. This will make the system more reliable and highly available.

Netflix provides a component called Ribbon, which works as a client-side load balancer that provides lots of flexibility and control while making HTTP and TCP calls. The term **client-side** refers to an individual microservice as Ribbon can be used to balance the flow of calls a microservice makes to other services.

Eureka can be easily integrated with Ribbon; however, we can configure Ribbon without Eureka. We will see how to configure Ribbon with and without Eureka.

Configuring Ribbon without Eureka

We are going to configure Ribbon while making calls from `inventory-service` to `catalog-service`, so if you have configured Eureka server, just remove it for the time being while we learn how Ribbon works without Eureka. The very first thing is to add the Ribbon starter dependency. Since we want to handle the call initiated from `inventory-service`, and add the dependency in `inventory-service` as follows:

```
<dependency>
    <groupId>org.springframework.cloud</groupId>
    <artifactId>spring-cloud-starter-netflix-ribbon</artifactId>
</dependency>
```

In the previous section, we configured the Feign client to handle REST calls. We will use Ribbon along with the Feign client. Open the proxy class that we created in the previous section and add the Ribbon configuration as follows:

```
@FeignClient(name="catalog-service", path="/api/catalog" )
@RibbonClient(name="catalog-service")
public interface CatalogServiceProxy {
  @GetMapping("/get-book/{bookId}")
  public ResponseEntity<BookDTO> getInventory(@PathVariable("bookId")
Integer bookId);
}
```

The @RibbonClient annotation is used to declare the Ribbon configuration with the name attribute pointing to the application on which we want to implement load balancing. The URL that we have configured with FeignClient is now removed and can be defined in the application.properties file as follows:

```
catalog-
service.ribbon.listOfServers=http://localhost:8792,http://localhost:8799
```

The property name will start with the name of the application that we have used with the @RibbonClient annotation. We need to define comma-separated URLs, each pointing to an individual instance of the catalog-service microservice. As per this configuration, the Ribbon client will handle the call from invoice-service to catalog-service, which has two instances running on ports 8792 and 8799.

We will make the call to the Feign client on inventory-service, which eventually triggers the call to catalog-service. We will observe that the requests are divided into two instances of the catalog-service microservice. To verify which instance the request comes from, we will add the current server port in BookDTO, which will be shown in the response. The current server port can be obtained as follows:

```
@Autowired
private Environment env;

@GetMapping("/get-book/{bookId}")
  public ResponseEntity<BookDTO> getBook(@PathVariable("bookId") Integer
bookId) {
    ......
      bookDto.setSmallDesc(bookObject.getSmallDesc());
      bookDto.setTitle(bookObject.getTitle());
      bookDto.setPort(env.getProperty("local.server.port"));
    ......
}
```

Spring injects the instance of the `Environment` class, which can be used to get current environment details. The current port is accessible with the `local.server.port` property. Next up, we will run two instances of the `catalog-service` microservice on these ports.

To start the Spring Boot application on a specific port, you need to right-click on the microservice project, select **Run As | Run Configurations**, and add the port in the **Arguments** tab with the **-Dserver.port** argument. You can also append the port in **Name** so that it can be easily identified as follows:

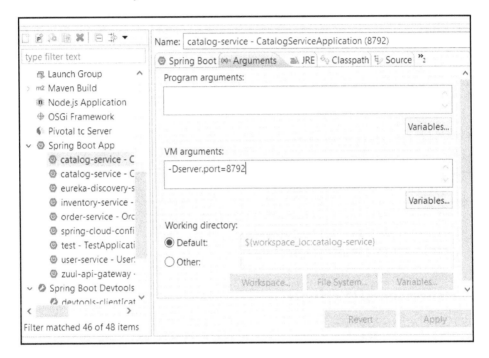

To add another instance, you need to right-click on the same instance of `catalog-service` created in the previous window, select **Duplicate**, and follow the same steps. The second time, use port `8799` as follows:

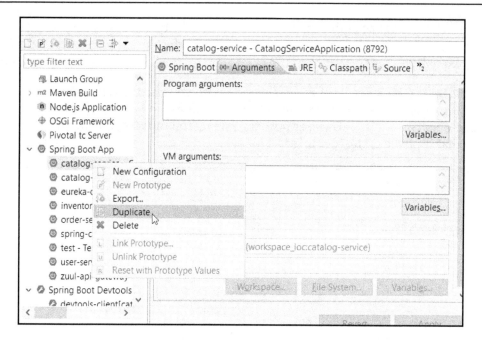

Run these two instances along with `inventory-service`. When you access `http://localhost:8793/api/inventory/get-inventory/3`, you will see the port is 8792 in the first request and 8799 in the second request. This is how the request is routed to a specific instance turn by turn.

Configuring Ribbon with Eureka

The problem in the first approach is that we still have to define the instance URLs manually. With Eureka, we can use its ability to resolve the microservice name dynamically and no more hardcore URLs are required. With Eureka, things are more straightforward. The Ribbon and Feign configuration will be changed as follows:

```
@FeignClient(name="catalog-service", path="/api/catalog" )
@RibbonClient(name="catalog-service")
public interface CatalogServiceProxy {
  @GetMapping("/get-book/{bookId}")
  public ResponseEntity<BookDTO> getInventory(@PathVariable("bookId")
Integer bookId);
}
```

No more `url` attributes are required for the `@FeignClient` annotation. Also, you can remove the `catalog-service.ribbon.listOfServers` property from the `application.properties` file of the `inventory-service` microservice. Start two instances of `catalog-service` along with `inventory-service` and make sure Eureka is running before you do. You will see two instances of `catalog-service` running in the Eureka console, as follows:

Instances currently registered with Eureka			
Application	**AMIs**	**Availability Zones**	**Status**
CATALOG-SERVICE	n/a (2)	(2)	UP (2) - nil.mshome.net:catalog-service:8792 , nil.mshome.net:catalog-service:8799
INVENTORY-SERVICE	n/a (1)	(1)	UP (1) - nil.mshome.net:inventory-service:8793

When you go to `http://localhost:8793/api/inventory/get-inventory/3`, you will get the same behavior. Once the request reaches the instance on port `8792`, the second is on `8799`, and the third is also on `8792`. This is how Ribbon is configured with Feign to achieve load balancing. You can try creating a few more instances and check the behavior. Also, if any of the instances are down, Ribbon will stop sending requests to them, which makes the system fault tolerant.

Load balancing using RestTemplate

Spring Cloud also supports the implementation of load balancing using `RestTemplate`. In this case, you need to expose the `RestTemplate` instance with load balancing capabilities instead of using it directly, as follows:

```
@LoadBalanced
@Bean
RestTemplate restTemplate() {
    return new RestTemplate();
}

@Autowired
RestTemplate restTemplate;
```

In the previous case, the @LoadBalanced annotation will do the magic of balancing the load between the instances of other services to which we make a REST call. You need to inject this object in your controller and make the call with it.

Configuring the API gateway

In previous sections, we saw how to define Zuul as an API gateway. In subsequent sections, we explored other Netflix components, such as Feign and Ribbon, to make RESTful calls for inter-service communication. However, the interaction that we created happened directly between services. Though we have configured an API gateway with Zuul, we have not used it as a central point of the request flow. In this section, we will make the necessary configuration changes so that every request passes through our API gateway.

The very first thing we will learn is to implement a custom filter and configure it to the API gateway to trace the request and print it in the log. For simplicity, we will capture a few details about the current request. Open the Spring Boot application that we created for Zuul and add a filter class as follows:

```
@Component
public class CustomPreFilter extends ZuulFilter {
   private static Logger _logger =
LoggerFactory.getLogger(ZuulFilter.class);
   @Override
   public boolean shouldFilter() {
     return true;
   }
   @Override
   public Object run() throws ZuulException {
     HttpServletRequest request = RequestContext.
               getCurrentContext().getRequest();
     _logger.info("********** REQUEST STARTED ******************");
     _logger.info("Port :"+ request.getLocalPort());
     _logger.info("HTTP Method :"+ request.getMethod());
     return null;
   }
   @Override
   public String filterType() {
     return "pre";
   }
   @Override
   public int filterOrder() {
     return 0;
   }
}
```

For any custom filter, you need to extend an abstract class, `ZuulFilter`, which is provided by Netflix. There are certain abstract methods that we need to provide the implementation, as follows:

- `shouldFilter()`: We apply this filter or not based on the return value of this method.
- `filterType()`: As we have seen, Zuul supports various filters type such as `pre`, `post`, `error`, and so on. The `pre` filter will be executed after the request reaches Zuul and before it is routed to other microservices. Similarly, the `post` filter will be executed once the response returns from other microservices, and the `error` filter type will be triggered when an error happens in between.
- `filterOrder()`: We can define as many filters as we want. This method defines their order of priority.
- `run()`: This method is the placeholder where you can write your filter logic.

We use will another filter that will be triggered once the response comes back, filter type `post`, as follows:

```
@Component
public class CustomPostFilter extends ZuulFilter {
  private static Logger _logger =
LoggerFactory.getLogger(ZuulFilter.class);
  @Override
  public boolean shouldFilter() {
    return true;
  }
  @Override
  public Object run() throws ZuulException {
    _logger.info("********* REQUEST ENDED *************");
    return null;
  }
  @Override
  public String filterType() {
    return "post";
  }
  @Override
  public int filterOrder() {
    return 0;
  }
}
```

Next, let's see how to access microservices through our API gateway. We have exposed a REST API for `inventory-service` as `http://localhost:8793/api/inventory/get-inventory/3`, and we will now update this URL to route the request from the API gateway. The pattern for the API gateway URL would be as follows:

```
http://<API_Gateway_Host>:<API_Gateway_Port>/{service-name}/{uri}
```

The Zuul API gateway will use the Eureka naming server to connect to the desired microservice. The service name in the previous pattern is the name (with the `spring.application.name` property in the `application.properties` or `bootstrap.properties` file) of the service registered in the Eureka naming server. The API gateway is accessible with `http://localhost:8781`, so to access the `inventory-service` URL with the API gateway, the new URL would be `http://localhost:8781/inventory-service/api/inventory/get-inventory/3`. You will get the request details in the Zuul log as follows:

```
o.s.web.servlet.DispatcherServlet : Completed initialization in 9 ms
com.netflix.zuul.ZuulFilter : ******************** REQUEST STARTED
***********
com.netflix.zuul.ZuulFilter : Port :8781
com.netflix.zuul.ZuulFilter : HTTP Method :GET
.........
com.netflix.zuul.ZuulFilter : ******************** REQUEST ENDED
*************
```

This is how we can trace the request with various filters with the Zuul API gateway. However, the call is forwarded from `inventory-service` to `catalog-service` with Feign, which is still bypassing the API gateway and making a direct call to the microservice. Now, let's see how to configure Feign so that the call is routed through the Zuul API gateway. The original Feign proxy was as follows:

```
@FeignClient(name="catalog-service", path="/api/catalog")
@RibbonClient(name="catalog-service")
public interface CatalogServiceProxy {
...
}
```

The updated Feign proxy interface would be as follows:

```
@FeignClient(name="zuul-api-gateway", path="y/api/catalog")
@RibbonClient(name="catalog-service")
public interface CatalogServiceProxy {
....
}
```

The change happened in the service name of the `@FeignClient` annotation. Previously, it was directly pointing to `catalog-service`, but now it is pointing to the Zuul API gateway service. `zuul-api-gateway` is the name of the Zuul API gateway service defined with the `spring.application.name` property in the `application.properties` file.

Run the URL again, and you will see the logs are printed twice. The loges are printed first, when the request reaches `inventory-service`, and second when the request is routed from `inventory-service` to `catalog-service` through Feign. This is how Zuul is configured to trace every request made across the microservices.

Securing an application

In a typical monolithic application, when the user logs in, an HTTP session will be created to hold user-specific information, which will be then used until the session expires. The session will be maintained by a common security component on the server side and all the requests are passed through it. So, it is straightforward to handle user authentication and authorization in a monolithic application.

If we want to follow the same pattern for microservice architecture, we need to implement a security component at every microservice level as well as in a central place (the gateway API) from where all the requests are routed. This is because microservices interact over the network, so the approach of applying security constraints is different.

Using Spring Security is a standard practice to meet the security needs of Spring-based Java applications. For microservices, Spring Cloud Security (another component from Spring Cloud) provides a one-stop solution to integrate Spring Security features with various components of the microservice architecture, such as the gateway proxy, a configuration server, load balancers, and so on.

In a microservice environment, security concerns can be addressed through widely used standard security protocols such as OAuth2 and OpenID Connect. In `Chapter 4`, *Building a Central Authentication Server*, we talked about OAuth2 in detail. Now, we will see how it can be used to meet security needs in a microservice architecture.

Let's see how the OAuth security system works in a microservice architecture. The high-level flow of authorization looks as follows:

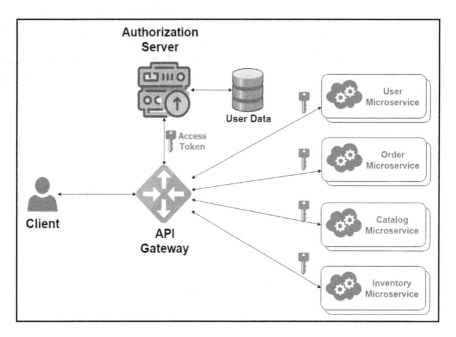

To understand the series of actions, let's take a use case of an order being placed by a user of the online bookstore. The whole process happens in the following steps:

1. A user tries to access the order page through the Zuul proxy server (API gateway) and does not have a session or an access token.
2. The Zuul proxy then redirects a user to an authorization server with pre-configured parameters such as grant type, client ID, token URL, and authorization URL.
3. If the user does not log in, the authorization server redirects to the login page.
4. Once the user does log in with valid credentials, the authorization server generates a token and sends it back to the API gateway.
5. On receiving the token, the API gateway (the Zuul proxy server) propagates the token downstream to the microservices it is proxying.
6. For restricted resources, the system will check whether a valid token exists. If not, the user will be redirected to the login page (or the token will be refreshed based on the grant type configured in the system).

The authentication server will be implemented as a separate microservice and registered in the Eureka discovery server. It can be created as a Spring Boot application with security-specific starter dependencies as follows:

```
<dependency>
  <groupId>org.springframework.cloud</groupId>
  <artifactId>spring-cloud-starter-oauth2</artifactId>
</dependency>
<dependency>
  <groupId>org.springframework.cloud</groupId>
  <artifactId>spring-cloud-starter-security</artifactId>
</dependency>
```

Spring Cloud Security has different starters for OAuth and standard Spring Security for the microservice architecture. Next, we will add the required configurations to make this application an authorization server, as follows:

```
@Configuration
@EnableAuthorizationServer
public class CustomAuthorizationConfig extends
AuthorizationServerConfigurerAdapter {

  @Autowired
  @Qualifier("authenticationManager")
  private AuthenticationManager authenticationManager;
  @Override
  public void configure(ClientDetailsServiceConfigurer clients) throws
Exception {
    clients.inMemory()
    .withClient("testClientId")
    .secret(new BCryptPasswordEncoder().encode("test123"))
    .authorizedGrantTypes("authorization_code", "refresh_token",
"implicit", "password", "client_credentials")
    .scopes("registeredUser","admin")
.redirectUris("http://localhost:8781/inventory-test/api/inventory/home")
    .resourceIds("oauth2-server");
  }
  @Bean
  public JwtAccessTokenConverter accessTokenConverter() {
    JwtAccessTokenConverter converter = new JwtAccessTokenConverter();
    converter.setSigningKey("123");
    return converter;
  }
  @Bean
  public TokenStore tokenStore() {
    return new JwtTokenStore(accessTokenConverter());
  }
  @Override
```

```
    public void configure(
        AuthorizationServerEndpointsConfigurer endpoints)
            throws Exception {
      endpoints
      .authenticationManager(authenticationManager)
      .tokenServices(tokenServices())
      .tokenStore(tokenStore())
      .accessTokenConverter(accessTokenConverter());
    }
    @Bean("resourceServerTokenServices")
    @Primary
    public DefaultTokenServices tokenServices() {
      DefaultTokenServices defaultTokenServices = new
          DefaultTokenServices();
      defaultTokenServices.setTokenStore(tokenStore());
      defaultTokenServices.setSupportRefreshToken(false);
      defaultTokenServices.setAccessTokenValiditySeconds(120);
      defaultTokenServices.setTokenEnhancer(accessTokenConverter());
      return defaultTokenServices;
    }
  }
```

The `@EnableAuthorizationServer` annotation is used to declare the component as an authorization server. OAuth can be done with various third-party clients, and Spring Security provides support for Google, Facebook, Okta, and GitHub out of the box. In our case, we will define a custom authorization server.

The `configure(ClientDetailsServiceConfigurer clients)` method of this class is used to define configuration for the custom authorization client. It initializes the client with various configurations, such as `ClientId`, secret (a kind of client password), possible authorization grant types you want the client to support, various scopes that can be used to fine-tune access control, and user authority and `resourceId`.

Spring OAuth is flexible enough to allow various mechanisms to generate the access token, and JWT is one of them. The `tokenStore()` and `tokenService()` methods are used to apply the required configuration for JWT. The `configure(AuthorizationServerEndpointsConfigurer endpoints)` method is used to configure tokens, along with the authentication manager. The `AuthenticationManager` object is injected from the `WebSecurityConfig` class as follows:

```
@Configuration
@EnableWebSecurity
public class WebSecurityConfig extends WebSecurityConfigurerAdapter{

  @Override
```

```
@Bean("authenticationManager")
public AuthenticationManager authenticationManagerBean() throws
Exception {
    AuthenticationManager authenticationManager =
        super.authenticationManagerBean();
    return authenticationManager;
}
@Override
public void configure(WebSecurity web) throws Exception {
    web.ignoring().antMatchers("/js/**");
    web.ignoring().antMatchers("/css/**");
}
@Override
protected void configure(AuthenticationManagerBuilder auth)
    throws Exception {
    auth.inMemoryAuthentication()
    .withUser("john").password(
        encoder().encode("999")).authorities("USER");
}
@Override
protected void configure(HttpSecurity http) throws Exception {
    http
    .authorizeRequests()
    .antMatchers("/oauth/authorize","/oauth/token","/").permitAll()
    .and()
    .formLogin().loginPage("/login").permitAll();
}
@Bean("encoder")
public BCryptPasswordEncoder encoder(){
    return new BCryptPasswordEncoder();
}
}
```

This class is responsible for configuring various endpoints, static resources, and the login page, along with the authentication mechanism. This is all about authorization server configuration. As we know, all requests are routed through the Zuul proxy server (an API Gateway), so we must configure it to route the requests for restricted resources to the authorization server.

The authorization server provides an access token that will be routed along with the request (in the header). When other microservices read it, they will verify the access token with the authorization server to allow the user to access restricted resources. In short, access tokens will be routed to various microservices. This requires some sort of SSO implementation, and with Spring Cloud Security, we can do it.

Additionally, particular functionality (for example, placing an order) initiated by a user will eventually involve interaction with other microservices along with the Zuul proxy server, so they are considered resource servers in OAuth terminology. First, add the `@EnableOAuth2Sso` annotation to a `bootstrap` class of the Zuul proxy application, as follows:

```
@EnableZuulProxy
@EnableOAuth2Sso
@EnableDiscoveryClient
@SpringBootApplication
public class ZuulApiGatewayApplication {
...
}
```

This annotation allows the Zuul proxy server to forward the access token generated by the authorization server downstream to other services involved in processing the request. The resource server configuration for the Zuul proxy server, as well as other microservices, should be as follows:

```
@EnableResourceServer
public class ResourceServerConfig extends ResourceServerConfigurerAdapter{

    private static final String RESOURCE_ID = "oauth2-server";
    @Override
    public void configure(ResourceServerSecurityConfigurer resources) {
        resources
        .tokenStore(tokenStore())
        .resourceId(RESOURCE_ID);
    }
    @Override
    public void configure(HttpSecurity http) throws Exception {
        http
        .requestMatcher(new RequestHeaderRequestMatcher("Authorization"))
        .authorizeRequests()
        // Microservice specific end point configuration will go here.
        .antMatchers("/**").authenticated()
        .and().exceptionHandling().accessDeniedHandler(new
            OAuth2AccessDeniedHandler());
    }
    @Bean
    public TokenStore tokenStore() {
        return new JwtTokenStore(accessTokenConverter());
    }
    @Bean
    public JwtAccessTokenConverter accessTokenConverter() {
        JwtAccessTokenConverter converter = new JwtAccessTokenConverter();
        converter.setSigningKey("123");
```

```
        return converter;
    }
}
```

The `@EnableResourceServer` annotation will enable the component as a resource server. `resourceId` should be the same as we configured in the authorization server. Also, we are using the same JWT token configuration that we set in the authorization server. The `configure` method is used to set the configuration for individual microservice endpoints.

We also need to set certain properties in the `application.properties` file, which will be used by the resource server to interact with the authorization server as follows:

```
#security.oauth2.sso.login-path=/login
security.oauth2.client.access-token-uri=http://localhost:9999/oauth/token
security.oauth2.client.user-authorization-
uri=http://localhost:9999/oauth/authorize
security.oauth2.client.client-id=testClientId
security.oauth2.client.client-secret=test123
security.oauth2.client.scope=registeredUser,admin,openid
security.oauth2.client.grant-type=implicit
security.oauth2.resource.id=oauth2-server
security.oauth2.resource.jwt.key-value=123
```

The authorization server is configured to access `localhost:9999`. The resource server configuration, along with previous properties, need to be placed with every microservice that we want to access securely through OAuth.

Summary

Unlike other chapters and applications that we have seen so far in this book, this chapter introduced a new type of application development in a distributed environment. The term **microservice** has existed since 2011. It has emerged as an enhancement of previous architectures.

With the introduction of Spring Cloud, developers can provide an implementation of various common patterns in a distributed environment. Starting with Spring Boot, creating a microservice application just takes a few configurations.

At the beginning of this chapter, we have explored what a microservice is and how it differs from the monolithic architecture, followed by various principles and criteria that need to be adhered to if you want to develop a microservice system. We then explored various Spring Cloud components and other Netflix OSS components in brief.

We have also learned how to create a microservice application by building a real-life example—an online bookstore application. We started with the application's architecture and the database design. We looked at creating microservices as Spring Boot applications with the required configurations.

We then saw practical examples of how to build various Netflix OSS and Spring Cloud components, such as a Eureka discovery server, a Zuul proxy server, a Feign client, Ribbon, and Spring Cloud Config. These components are the building blocks for developing a distributed application. We also saw various options and approaches to building a microservice frontend. Finally, we secured the application with Spring Cloud Security.

Java was the only de facto programming language for building Spring-based applications for quite a long time. However, the team at Pivotal (the company behind Spring) has started to support other functional programming languages, such as Scala. Starting with version 5, Spring announced support for Kotlin, a JVM-based language mainly used for Android applications. In the next chapter, we will dive into an altogether new way of building Spring applications with Kotlin.

7
Task Management System Using Spring and Kotlin

In the chapters so far, we have explored various topics and concepts in depth. Starting with the pure Spring Framework and moving onto Spring Boot, we learned how quickly and easily we can create an enterprise-grade application with Spring Boot.

We also learned about the integration of the Spring Framework with other tools and technologies, such as Elasticsearch, LDAP, and OAuth, within the purview of the Spring Boot context. We then learned a new way of creating an application with Spring as a backend and Angular as a frontend with a tool called **JHipster**.

Then, we discovered how to create an application with modern architecture in the dimension of the distributed environment called **microservice**. In this chapter, we go further and explore a completely different dimension of the Spring Framework, looking at how it is supported by a new programming language called **Kotlin**.

As a programming language, Kotlin has quickly become popular among developers and companies. The first stable version of Kotlin was released officially in 2016. The very next year Google officially declared Kotlin as a supported language for mobile development on an Android platform. This greatly increased the popularity and adoption rate of Kotlin.

Starting with version 5, Spring announced support for Kotlin to develop enterprise applications on a Spring Framework. In this chapter, we will explore how to develop a Spring-based application with Kotlin. We will build an application called Task Management with Spring Boot and Kotlin, and will cover the following:

- Introduction to Kotlin
- Basic features of Kotlin as a programming language
- Kotlin versus Java
- Spring support for Kotlin
- Developing a Task Management application in Spring with Kotlin

Technical requirements

All the code used in this chapter can be downloaded from the following GitHub link: `https://github.com/PacktPublishing/Spring-5.0-Projects/tree/master/chapter07`. The code can be executed on any operating system, although it has only been tested on Windows.

Introducing Kotlin

Kotlin is a language for **Java Virtual Machine** (**JVM**) and hence can be used in place of Java. Be it server side, mobile, or web, you can use Kotlin everywhere Java is used at present. It is sponsored by a company called **JetBrains**; it is open source, and you can download the source code from GitHub (`https://github.com/jetbrains/kotlin`). They plan to roll out Kotlin for embedded and iOS platforms in the near future.

Kotlin provides good support as a functional programming language. The term functional programming is used to describe a declarative paradigm where the program is created by an expression or declaration rather than by the execution of commands. The functional programming model inherently brings certain qualities to the application, such as more compressed and predicted code, easy testing ability, reusability, and so on. Kotlin brings a functional paradigm in the form of inbuilt features.

There are many similarities between Java and Kotlin, and so the question arises, why do we need another programming language when Java has been widely used and very popular for more than two decades. The answer lies in some of the cool features Kotlin has, which make it the better choice for developing JVM-based applications.

Interoperability

One of the most promising features of Kotlin is its interoperable capabilities. Kotlin is 100% interoperable with Java. The application can combine both the languages. The call to Java libraries can be made from Kotlin without any conversion or fuss. Similarly, code written in Kotlin can also be called from Java with ease. This greatly helps Java developers to migrate from Java to Kotlin without any difficulty.

Migrating a code from one programming language to another is a quite tedious and time-consuming task, especially when those programming languages are incompatible, in terms of rules, syntax, features, and so on. Although there are a bunch of features available in Kotlin that are not present directly or indirectly in Java, it is the interoperability of Kotlin that allows running the code with both programming languages simultaneously. You do not have to migrate all Java code to Kotlin. Kotlin's **Interoperability** is shown in the following diagram:

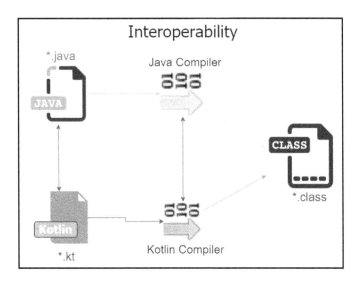

On top of this, the Kotlin standard library is dependent on the Java Class Library, which enables reusing the dependencies, and no code refactoring is required in any of the places. For example: Kotlin's collection framework is built on top of Java's collection API.

Concise yet powerful

While working with Kotlin, you will find another good quality is how concise it is. The Kotlin syntax is easy to read and interpret even without prior knowledge of any programming language. Kotlin has certain features that make it a truly concise language, such as type interface, data classes, properties, smart casts, and a lot more. We will see more detail about each of them later in this chapter.

With these features, the code written with Kotlin is compact without losing its capabilities. Kotlin is more concise than Java in many aspects, and because of this we can implement the same functionality with fewer lines of code. This greatly improves legibility and ease of use. Developers can easily read, code, and update the program, even when it has been written by others.

Furthermore, Kotlin enables the speeding up of day-to-day development tasks with various features such as default parameters, extension functions, and object declarations. Your code is more compact and yet robust, without raising any maintainability concerns. This will reduce the possibility of bugs in the system.

Kotlin evolved as an enhancement to Java rather than as a completely new language. So the skills and knowledge you have with Java can be applied to Kotlin, making it an easy language to learn.

Safety feature

Another reason you will love Kotlin is its safety feature. The code written in Kotlin is far safer than that written in Java. Kotlin is designed in a way to shield it from the common programming flaws, which results in a more stable system with fewer crashes and failures.

For any programming language that allows the null reference will create a runtime exception, such as `NullPointerException`, during the execution of the application. Improper handling of such a scenario may result in an abrupt system collision. If you have prior experience of Java, you might have experienced such scenarios.

Kotlin was designed with this in mind and defines the reference types in two categories: those that are nullable and those that are not. By default, Kotlin does not allow the reference with the null value and forces the developer to handle them in a specific manner. This greatly reduces the possibility of problems caused by `NullPointerException`.

IDE Support

JetBrains, the company behind Kotlin, is well known for its **integrated development environment (IDE)** called **IntelliJ IDEA**, and obviously has first-class support for Kotlin. As far as the IDE is concerned, Eclipse is also one of the most favored among Java developers, and so JetBrains also offers a Kotlin plugin for Eclipse.

In the very early days when Java had just evolved, there was no IDE in the initial stage and developers had to use text editors to do coding. It was difficult working without the safety and convenience of an IDE. When Eclipse came onto the market, developers quickly adopted it and since then it has become popular and widely accepted among Java developers.

Kotlin, on the other hand, was lucky enough to get IDE support from day one. This quickly boosted the popularity of Kotlin. It was really convenient and easy to learn. Developers were able to produce good quality code quickly, improving the software development life cycle.

Needless to say, Kotlin allows coding with text editors. Also, you can use Command Prompt to build Kotlin applications. Additionally, if you are an Android developer, it has its own IDE called **Android Studio** developed on top of IntelliJ IDEA IDE.

Kotlin features

Kotlin was designed not to compete with Java, but rather to be a good JVM language with added features not present in Java. Kotlin, as a language, has lots of new and exciting features, compared to Java, that increase code readability and maintainability.

It is vital to understand the basic features of Kotlin. In this section, we will explore a few of them that are essential for building an application in Kotlin.

The concept of a function

By definition, a function is a set or group of related statements that perform a specific task. It is a basic building block of any program. You can equate the function in Kotlin with the method in Java; however, there are certain differences. The function in Kotlin can be defined at the top level, meaning it is not required to be enclosed in a class. The function can be part of a class as well as defined within another function.

In Kotlin, the functions get first-class support, meaning it supports all the operations and can be stored into a variable and data structure, passed as an argument to other function as well as being returned from other (top-level) functions, it can be defined as an expression, and lots more. All these features bring a great amount of flexibility and make Kotlin really concise. We will see the following uses of functions in Kotlin.

Function as an expression

While writing the function, you need to put the code in a function body. However, in Kotlin, you can define a function as an expression. For example: you want to find the minimum between two numbers and you wrote a function called `min()` as follows:

```
fun main(args: Array<String>) {
    print(min(4,7))
}
fun min(numberA: Int, numberB:Int) : Int {
    if(numberA < numberB){
        return numberA
    }else{
        return numberB
    }
}
```

This will return the minimum number out of two given numbers. This function can be written as an expression style as follows:

```
fun min(numberA: Int, numberB:Int) : Int = if(numberA < numberB){ numberA
}else{ numberB }
```

This is how the code looks expressive and compact. Also, notice that we have removed the `return` keyword, as Kotlin is smart enough to return the last value without explicitly specifying the `return` keyword. This is what is called a **single line** or **one line** function. However, for a complex function, you can write it in multiple lines as follows:

```
fun min(numberA: Int, numberB:Int) : Int
  =  if(numberA < numberB){
            numberA
        }else{
            numberB
        }
```

This looks more compact and expressive.

Default function arguments

Often, the amount of data that we supply to functions or constructors varies in different use cases. The system should be flexible enough to produce the desired result even if we don't provide the values of all the parameters.

If you want to achieve this in Java, you need to write a couple of overloaded functions or constructors as per your need. You will end up writing the same method multiple times with a different set of input parameters and calling other constructors or methods with default values. This quickly results in verbose code—writing code again and again for the same thing.

Kotlin provides an intuitive solution to this scenario with the feature called the default function argument. This is as simple as it sounds. You need to define a default value to those function arguments that you feel may not be provided with the value at the time of executing the function.

For example: let's say we wrote the function to find the volume of the cube as follows:

```
fun getVolume(length:Int, width:Int,height:Int):Int{
    return length * width * height;
}
```

While calling this function, you need to pass all three parameters or else the compiler will signal the error. Now, assume that we want the system to take the default height as 10 if it is not provided explicitly. It can be written as follows:

```
fun getVolume(length:Int, width:Int,height:Int =10):Int{
    return length * width * height;
}
```

This function can be called as `getVolume(2,4)` and `10` will be substituted as a default value to `height`.

Extension functions

If you need to extend a class with a set of new functionalities, you need to update the Java source code. However, if you are using third-party libraries, you may not have the source. A class needs to be extended to accommodate other functions. You also can use various design patterns such as decorator and strategy for this purpose.

However, Kotlin allows the straightforward adding of extra functions to an existing class with the feature called an **extension function**. As its name implies, an extension function extends the functionality of the class without touching its source code. In other words, you are no longer required to inherit the class to be extended. This sounds really interesting. It behaves just like other member functions but is declared outside of the class.

Assume that you need to convert the given string into camel case. The Kotlin `String` class does not provide the functionality to convert a given string into camel case out of the box. We will the use extension function to define a separate function that, will actually do this job as follows:

```
fun String.camelCase():String{
    var camelCaseStr = StringBuffer()
    var wordLst : List<String> = this.trim().split(" ")
    for(word in wordLst){
        camelCaseStr.append(word.replaceFirst(word[0],
word[0].toUpperCase())).append(" ")
    }
    return camelCaseStr.trim().toString()
}
```

The `camelCase()` function is the extension function on the `String` class, which returns the string. The custom logic resides in the body of this function. You can call the `camelCase()` function on any string literal as follows:

```
fun main(args: Array<String>) {
    print("this is just for sample".camelCase())
 // This will print as—This Is Just For Sample
}
```

The `camelCase()` function is our custom function so you can use any other name you feel appropriate. Let's see one more example of an extension function. Suppose you want to find the square of a given integer. Again, Kotlin does not provide a direct function for that but we can write the extension function as follows:

```
fun Int.square():Int{
    return this * this
}
```

The `square()` extension function can be called in an integer literal as follows:

```
fun main(args: Array<String>) {
    print(3.square())
}
```

This is an extraordinary feature that we can use to extend functionalities without updating the code or inheriting the base class.

Lambda expression or function literal

Every programming language has a provision for defining the literals, such as string, integer, double, and so on. They can be defined in a specific manner such as string literal as `Hello`, double literal as `34.23`, and so on. Kotlin allows us to define a function as a literal by enclosing the code in braces as follows:

```
//This is functional literal
{ println(" This is function literal ")}
```

This function can be declared in a normal way as follows:

```
fun printMsg(message:String){
    println(message)
}
```

It is essentially the same thing as a function literal. But the functional literal looks pretty compact yet expressive. A function literal can be assigned to a variable and called at a later point of the code as follows:

```
//Functional literal assigned to variable
var greetingMsg = { println("Hello World ...!!!")}

//Calling the function through literal
greetingMsg()
```

The function literal can be assigned to a variable as in the first line. Just like other functions, the function literal can be invoked with a variable (with parenthesis) as shown in the second line. There are certain characteristics of the function literal as follows:

- It represents the block or body of the function that does not have any name.
- It is not associated with or bound to any entity such as class, interface, or object, and hence an access modifier is not allowed.
- Since it does not have a name, it is called **anonymous.**
- It can be passed to other functions (mainly high-order functions) as an argument.
- It is generally surrounded by curly braces and without the `fun` keyword.
- It is also known as a lambda expression.

Kotlin also allows passing parameters to a function literal or lambda expression as follows:

```
//Lambda with parameter
var showWarning = {message : String -> println(message)}

//Calling Lambda expression with parameter
showWarning(" Warning 1 occurred ..!!!")
showWarning(" Warning 2 occurred ..!!!")
```

The lambda expression is divided into two parts by an arrow (->). The left part is the parameter section, while the right part is the lambda or function body. Multiple parameters are allowed with comma-separated lists and without enclosing them in parentheses as follows:

```
//Multiple parameters
var addition = { num1: Int, num2: Int ->
        println("sum of $num1 and $num2 is ..${num1+num2}")
    }
addition(3, 5)
```

We can write this code in a slightly different way as follows:

```
var addition2 : (Int,Int)-> Unit = { num1, num2 ->
    println("sum of $num1 and $num2 is ..${num1+num2}")
}
addition2(3, 5)
```

In this code, the declaration of a parameter is moved out from the lambda expression. The Unit function in Kotlin is equivalent to void in Java. This feature makes Kotlin a truly functional language. The function literal can also be the parameter of another function.

Passing lambda to another function

Kotlin allows us to pass a function to other (higher-order) functions as a parameter, using the lambda expression. Such a function can accept as a parameter a lambda expression or an anonymous function. Before discussing this topic further, let us first understand what a function type is.

Kotlin is a statically typed language and the functions also need to have a type. It is called a **function type**. We will see a few examples of how to define them as follows:

- `()->Int`: The function type that returns an integer type and takes no argument.
- `(Int)->Unit`: The function type that takes an integer parameter and returns nothing.
- `()->(Int)->String`: The function type that returns another function, which eventually returns a string. The latter function takes an integer as a parameter.

Now, let's see how we can define a function type as an input parameter to the outer function. Consider a scenario where you are designing an application for a bank loan. You need to check the eligibility criteria and decide whether a loan is applicable. The function that does this job should look as follows:

```kotlin
data class Applicant(
                    var applicantId: Int,
                    var name: String,
                    var age: Int,
                    var gender: String)

fun isEligibleForLoan (mobileNo:String,
eligibilityScore:(applicantId:Int)->Double) : Boolean{
    //Business logic to fetch applicant details from given mobileNo
    var applicant = Applicant(12,"Nilang",38,"M");
    var score = eligibilityScore(applicant.applicantId);
    return score >80
}
```

The `isEligibleForLoan()` function is a higher-order function that takes two parameters. The first parameter is the applicant's mobile number from which it will fetch the applicant's details. The second parameter is a function type, which we can consider as a sort of interface type. It simply calculates the eligibility score based on a given applicant ID. The actual implementation of the function type will be provided when the `isEligibleForLoan()` function is called as follows:

```kotlin
var isEligible = isEligibleForLoan("9998789671",{
    applicantId -> //Write logic to calculate the
                    //eligibility of candidate and return the score
    85.23 // This is sample value
})
println(" isEligibile: $isEligible ")
```

We need to pass a lambda expression in the second parameter. It is nothing but an anonymous function that takes the application ID as an input parameter and calculates an eligibility score. The score will be returned back to the `isEligibleForLoan()` function from where, based on the score, we return whether a loan is applicable or not.

If the function type is the last parameter, then Kotlin allows to call it in a slightly different way. The preceding function can be called alternatively as follows:

```
var isEligible2 = isEligibleForLoan("9998789671"){
        applicantId -> //Write logic to calculate the eligibility
                       //of candidate and return the score
    75.23 // This is sample value
}
```

In this way, the lambda expression is placed outside of the parenthesis, which is more expressive. But this is only possible when a function type is declared at the last parameter. Passing a lambda expression as a function type is useful, especially for an Ajax call where we want to update the page element once we get the data from the response without freezing the UI. The function that is injected through the lambda expression will work as a callback function.

Returning a function from another function

We have seen how function type can be defined as a parameter while calling another function. With the help of a lambda expression, it becomes even more straightforward. One step further, Kotlin allows the returning of a function from another function. Let's understand how that works.

Suppose we have one interface called `WildAnimal` that is implemented by three classes as follows:

```
interface WildAnimal{
    fun setName(name:String)
    fun bark():String
}

class Dog : WildAnimal{
    private var dogName: String = ""
    override fun bark(): String {
        print(" Bhao bhao ...")
        return "${dogName} Dog is barking ..."
    }
    override fun setName(name: String) {
        this.dogName = name
    }
```

```
}
class Fox : WildAnimal{
    private var foxName: String = ""
    override fun bark(): String {
        print(" Haaaaoooooo...")
        return "${foxName} Fox is barking ..."
    }
    override fun setName(name: String) {
        this.foxName = name
    }
}
class Lion : WildAnimal{
    private var lionName: String = ""
    override fun bark(): String {
        print(" HHHHHAAAAAAAAAAA...")
        return "${lionName} Lion is Barking ..."
    }
    override fun setName(name: String) {
        this.lionName = name
    }
}
```

Each class implements two methods—setName() and bark() that will set the animal and show a barking voice respectively. We will create an instance of each of the class, set its name, and call the bark() function to print the barking voice and also print the name of the animal. To achieve this, we will write a function as follows:

```
fun getAnimalVoiceFun(animal: WildAnimal):(String) -> String{
    return {
        animal.setName(it)
        animal.bark()
    }
}
```

The getAnimalVoiceFun function takes the implementation of WildAnimal as a parameter and returns the function that takes String as a parameter and returns String as an output. The code written inside the { } braces in the body of the getAnimalVoiceFun function denotes the function that is returning from it. The it parameter points to the String parameter of the enclosing function.

The animal.bark() function, which actually returns the string, will be ultimately returned from an enclosed function. This function can be written in a slightly different way as follows:

```
fun getAnimalVoiceFun(animal: WildAnimal):(name:String) -> String{
    return {
```

```
                animal.setName(name=it)
                animal.bark()
        }
    }
```

The difference is we are declaring the name of the parameter—name of the type string and using it as a `name=it` expression in the enclosing function. In both of the previous ways, the parenthesis represents the function, so the `fun` keyword is silent. However, you can declare it as follows:

```
fun getAnimalVoiceFun(animal: WildAnimal):(String) -> String{
    return fun(name:String):String {
        animal.setName(name)
        return animal.bark()
    }
}
```

In this way, we are explicitly using the `fun` keyword for enclosing function. Also, you have to explicitly mention the `return` keyword in the enclosing function. You can use either of these ways to declare the `getAnimalVoiceFun` function. You can call this function as follows:

```
println(getAnimalVoiceFun(Lion())("Jake"))
println(getAnimalVoiceFun(Dog())("Boomer"))
println(getAnimalVoiceFun(Fox())("Lilli"))
```

We are calling the `getAnimalVoiceFun` function with an instance of the respective class. You can see how the second string parameter included in separate parenthesis will be provided to a function defined within the function—`getAnimalVoiceFun`. You will get an output as follows:

```
HHHHHAAAAAAAAAAAA...Jake Lion is Barking ...
Bhao bhao ...Boomer Dog is barking ...
Haaaaoooooo...Lilli Fox is barking ...
```

In Kotlin, the function can be defined as a type. We can use the function type to declare the preceding function as follows:

```
val getAnimalVoice: (WildAnimal) ->(String)-> String = {
        animal:WildAnimal -> {
                animal.setName(it)
                animal.bark()
        }
    }
```

The `getAnimalVoice` variable is defined as a function type, which takes the `WildAnimal` object and returns another function, which takes `String` as an input parameter (with the `it` keyword) and returns a `String` output (by calling `animal.bark()`). The lambda expression is used to define this function. This can be called as follows:

```
println(getAnimalVoice(Lion())("Lio"))
println(getAnimalVoice(Dog())("Tommy"))
println(getAnimalVoice(Fox())("Chiku"))
```

And the output would be as follows:

```
HHHHHAAAAAAAAAAA...Lio Lion is Barking ...
Bhao bhao ...Tommy Dog is barking ...
Haaaaoooooo...Chiku Fox is barking ...
```

There may be other straightforward ways to set the animal name and print the barking voice. However, we have just seen how it can be possible by returning the function from another function. You can write some common logic that is applicable to multiple functions, and returning common code as a separate function would be an ideal scenario to use the function as a return type of another function. This is how flexible and concise Kotlin is.

Null safety

While working with Java, when the program executes and tries to access the variables set to null and then not initialized with a proper value, it will crash the system and produce the classic exception called `NullPointerException`.

As we know, Kotlin is a statically typed language so everything is defined as a type, including null values. The nullability is a type in Kotlin. By default, a Kotlin compiler does not allow a null value to any type. Generally, when we define variables, we set their values at the time of declaration.

But, in some exceptional cases, you don't want to initialize the variable at the time of declaration. In this case, while using those variables, the Kotlin compiler will raise the concern. For example: the following code will give an error signal in Kotlin:

```
var msg:String = "Sample Message !!"
msg = null
var anotherMsg :String = null
```

The variable initialized with some value is not allowed to be reassigned with the null value. Also, any variable defined with type (`String`, in our case) is not allowed to initialize with null. The Kotlin compiler has this restriction to avoid `NullPointerException`, so it will catch this at compile time rather than causing a runtime error which results in an abrupt system collision.

Kotlin wants us to initialize the typed variable at the time of declaration. As we said, there are situations where we have to initialize variables with null and Kotlin allows it in a different way, as follows:

```
var nullableMsg : String? = " I have some value ..!! "
println(nullableMsg)
nullableMsg=null
```

The nullable variable can be defined with a question mark with a type of variable called a **safe call operator**. You can now assign null value. However, when we define a nullable variable and try to call its method, the compiler will show an error as follows:

```
var nullableMsg2 : String? = " I have some value ..!! "
println(nullableMsg2.length) // Compiler will show an error here.
```

The reason for this is Kotlin will not allow calling methods on a nullable type without either explicitly checking for null or calling the method in a safe way. The previous code can be rewritten to avoid a compilation error in the following ways:

```
//Correct ways to call nullable variable
if(nullableMsg2 !=null){
    println(nullableMsg2.length) // Option 1
}
println(nullableMsg2?.length) // Option 2
```

The `nullableMsg2?` method is the safe way to call a nullable variable. If the variable is null, Kotlin will silently bypass that call and return a null value. This is a more concise way for a safe null check in Kotlin. But if you want to make sure the value is returned, even if it is null, then you can use another approach as follows:

```
println(nullableMsg2?.length ?: -1)
```

The additional question mark and colon (`?:`) is called the **Elvis operator**. It is basically similar to the if-else block and returns the length if not null. If it is null, then it will return -1. This is basically the short form of a ternary operator, such as `if(a) ? b : c`, but cleaner and more compact. This will prevent any accidental `NullPointerException` at runtime.

Data classes

You might have created a class that is a simple data container without specific business logic or functionality. Such a scenario happens while following the value object or the data transfer object pattern. Typically, such classes look as follows:

```java
// Java code
public class StudentVOJava {
    private String name;
    private int age;
    private int standard;
    private String gender;
    public StudentVO(String name, int age, int standard, String gender) {
        this.name = name;
        this.age = age;
        this.standard = standard;
        this.gender = gender;
    }
    public String getName() {
        return name;
    }
    public void setName(String name) {
        this.name = name;
    }
    public int getAge() {
        return age;
    }
    public void setAge(int age) {
        this.age = age;
    }
    public int getStandard() {
        return standard;
    }
    public void setStandard(int standard) {
        this.standard = standard;
    }
    public String getGender() {
        return gender;
    }
    public void setGender(String gender) {
        this.gender = gender;
    }
    @Override
    public boolean equals(Object o) {
        if (this == o) return true;
        if (o == null || getClass() != o.getClass()) return false;
        StudentVO studentVO = (StudentVO) o;
```

```
            return age == studentVO.age &&
                    standard == studentVO.standard &&
                    Objects.equals(name, studentVO.name) &&
                    Objects.equals(gender, studentVO.gender);
        }
        @Override
        public int hashCode() {
            return Objects.hash(name, age, standard, gender);
        }
        @Override
        public String toString() {
            return "StudentVO{" +
                    "name='" + name + '\'' + ", age=" + age +
                    ", standard=" + standard +
                    ", gender='" + gender + '\'' +
                    '}';
        }
    }
}
```

There is nothing special in this class, just a few properties, getters, setters, constructor, and the implementation of `hashCode()`, `equals()`, and `toString()`. Lots of boilerplate code would really distract any business functionality. Due to this, the code becomes less readable, searchable, and verbose.

With the help of modern IDEs, it is just a matter of a few clicks to generate this code, but still it has a readability issue. The same code written in Kotlin is not only much cleaner on the first view but also helps with focusing on the important part out of the boring boilerplate stuff, as follows:

```
data class StudentVOKotlin(var name: String, var age: Int,
                           var standard: Int, var gender: String)
```

Everything is covered in just a single line of code, and it is also more readable. A declaration such as this will create setters, getters, constructor, and the implementation of the `toString()`, `hashCode()`, and `equals()` methods along with other useful functionalities behind the curtain by Kotlin. If you want to make your class immutable, just declare the properties with `val` instead of `var` as follows:

```
data class StudentVOKotlin(val name: String, val age: Int,
                           val standard: Int, val gender: String)
```

Immutable variables can be defined with `val` in Kotlin. You can now call only getters on the object of the `StudentVOKotlin` class. We can use this class as follows:

```
fun main(args: Array<String>) {
    var student = StudentVOKotlin("Nilang",10,5,"M")
```

```
    println("Student is  $student") // This will call toString()
    //This will call getter of respective properties
    println("age of ${student.name} is ${student.age}")
}
```

This really makes the code compact and readable.

Interoperability

As we have seen, Kotlin is fully interoperable with Java so that you can write Java and Kotlin functions altogether in the same project and call them from each other. Let's understand how that magic happens. Before that, let's look at how things happen behind the scenes.

For example, you wrote a Kotlin function in the `CheckOperability.kt` file as follows:

```
fun greeting(name: String){
    print(" Hello $name !!!")
}
```

This code will be compiled by the Kotlin compiler and converted into byte code. The generated Java class file will be as follows:

```
public final class CheckInterOperabilityKt
{
  public static final void greeting(@NotNull String name)
  {
    //Some code for null type check added by Kotlin at this place.
    String str = " Hello " + name + " !!!";System.out.print(str);
  }
}
```

As you can see, Kotlin converts the `.kt` file (`CheckInterOperabilityKt.class`) into a corresponding Java class. The `greeting()` function defined in Kotlin is also converted to a Java function. By default, all functions in Kotlin are static. Also, Kotlin is not forcing you to define a `void` in case there is no-return value. (Kotlin has `Unit` in place of `void` actually.) While converting, it will add `void` along with a `static` keyword to the function.

We will now see how we can call the Java code from Kotlin, and vice versa.

Calling the Kotlin code from Java

Let's create a Kotlin function that simply does multiplication of two given numbers in the `KotlinFile.kt` file as follows:

```
fun multiply(a:Int, b:Int):Int{
    print("Calling multiply function From Kotlin....")
    return a * b
}
```

We want to call a Kotlin `multiply()` function into a Java class. As we know, the Kotlin compiler processes this file into a Java class, where it defines the `multiply()` method as a static method of the `KotlinFileKt.class` generated class file, so that it can be accessible with the `KotlinFileKt.multiply()` expression.

 In case you wish to change the Java class file name from the Kotlin source, you need to define it as `@file:JvmName("CustomKotlinFile")` in the Kotlin file. In this case, the Kotlin compiler will generate the `CustomKotlinFile.class` file and the function can be accessed with the `CustomKotlinFile.multiply()` call.

Let's first add the Java class and call the Kotlin function as follows:

```
public class JavaFile {
    public  static void  main(String args[]){
        System.out.print(KotlinFileKt.multiply(3,4));
    }
}
```

This is how the Kotlin function can be called from the Java class. Now let's see how to call a Java function from Kotlin.

Calling Java code from Kotlin

Let's define a function that simply does the addition of two numbers in a Java file as follows:

```
public static int add(int num1, int num2){
    return num1+num2;
}
```

This can be called in the Kotlin file in a similar way to how we called the Kotlin code into Java. Since this is a static function, we can call it with the Java class in Kotlin as follows:

```
fun main(args: Array<String>) {
    var total = JavaFile.add(5,6)
    print("Value from Java is $total")
}
```

The `main` function in Kotlin represents the execution point similar to `public static void main()` in Java.

Smart casts

While working with Java, you may face the scenario where you need to cast the object before further processing. However, even if there is certainty about the type of object that you are passing, you still need to cast the object explicitly in Java as follows:

```
//Java code
public static void  main(String[] args){
    Object name = "Nilang";
    if(name instanceof String){
        greetingMsg((String) name);
    }
}
private static void greetingMsg(String name){
    System.out.print(" Welcome "+name+" ..!!");
}
```

If we try to call `greetingMsg()` without an explicit cast, the Java compiler will show an error because the `name` variable is of the `Object` type. In this case, although the compiler knows that `name` can be only of the `String` type (through the condition `if(name instanceOf String)`), the Java compiler needs explicit casting. In other words, we need to perform casting, even though it is actually redundant.

However, in the case of Kotlin, you are not required to cast explicitly if a parameter is proven to be of a required type. This code can be written in Kotlin as follows:

```
//Kotlin code
fun main(args: Array<String>) {
    val name: Any = "Nilang"
    if(name is String) {
        greetingMsg(name)
    }
}
private fun greetingMsg(name: String) {
```

```
        print(" Welcome $name ..!!")
    }
```

The `Any` type in Kotlin is equivalent to `Object` in Java. In this code, the compiler knows that the input given to the `greetingMsg` function can only be of the `String` type (with the `if` condition) so an explicit cast is not required. This is called **smart cast** in Kotlin.

Operator overloading

Operator overloading is another convenient feature of Kotlin, which makes it more expressive and readable. It allows you to use standard symbols such as +, −, *, /, %, <, >, and so on, to perform various operations on any object. Under the hood, operator overloading initiates a function call to perform various mathematical operations, comparisons, indexing operations with arrays, and lots more.

The classes such as int, byte, short, long, double, float, and so on, have defined corresponding functions for each of these operators. For example: if we do `a+b` on an integer, Kotlin will call `a.plus(b)` internally as follows:

```
var num1 = 10
var num2 = 5
println(num1+num2)
println(num1.plus(num2))
```

Both print statements show the same result. We can define how operators work for custom classes by overloading corresponding functions. For example, we have a class called `CoordinatePoint`, which represents the x and y coordinates for a given point in the graph. If we want to override the operators on this class, then it should be coded as follows:

```
data class CoordinatePoint(var xPoint: Int, var yPoint: Int){
    // overloading + operator with plus function
    operator fun plus(anotherPoint: CoordinatePoint) : CoordinatePoint {
        return CoordinatePoint(xPoint + anotherPoint.xPoint, yPoint +
anotherPoint.yPoint)
    }
    // overloading - operator with minus function
    operator fun minus(anotherPoint: CoordinatePoint) : CoordinatePoint {
        return CoordinatePoint(xPoint - anotherPoint.xPoint, yPoint -
anotherPoint.yPoint)
    }
}
fun main(args: Array<String>) {
    var point1 = CoordinatePoint(2,5)
    var point2 = CoordinatePoint(4,3)
```

```
    //This will call overloaded function plus()
    var point3 = point1 + point2
  //This will call overloaded function minus()
    var point4 = point1 - point2

    println(point3)
    println(point4)
}
```

The `CoordinatePoint` class is our custom class, and the `plus()` and `minus()` functions are actually called when the objects of this class are used along with the corresponding operators. The `operator` keyword is used to associate the corresponding function with the operators.

Apart from arithmetic, Kotlin supports other operators, such as **index access** operators, **in** operators, **invoke** operators, **argument assignment** operators, **equal** operators, **function** operators, and so on. With operator overloading, this code is more compact and concise and of course is clearer as well.

Kotlin versus Java

After going through the feature richness of Kotlin, it would be really helpful to compare it to Java. This is not to prove a particular language is more appropriate than the other, but rather to just list the differences to make the choice easier for different scenarios:

- **Null safety**: Kotlin provides a nice way to define and handle nullable types, whereas Java does not have a similar feature out of the box.
- **Extension function**: Java needs an inheritance to extend the class, whereas Kotlin allows you to define the extension function without inheriting any class. You can define an extension function for custom classes as well.
- **Type reference**: In Java, we need to specify the type of variable explicitly, but Kotlin will handle it based on the assignment so you do not have to define the type in all the scenarios.
- **Functional programming**: Kotlin is a functional language and provides many useful features for functions. Java, on the other hand, has started supporting lambda expressions.
- **Coroutine support**: Coroutines are lightweight threads used to handle asynchronous, non-blocking code. Kotlin support coroutines out of the box. The Co-routines are managed by users. Java, on other hand, supports similar functionality with multithreads managed by the underlying OS.

- **Data class**: In Java, we need to declare constructors, getters, setters, `toString()`, `hashCode()`, and `equals()` manually, while Kotlin does all that behind the scene.
- **Smart cast**: Java needs to check for cast explicitly, while Kotlin does this job smartly.
- **Checked exception**: Java does support checked exceptions, whereas Kotlin does not support them.

Spring supports for Kotlin

Due to its stunning features, Kotlin has rapidly grown in popularity, and many frameworks have started supporting it. The Spring Framework has allowed the development of Spring applications with Kotlin since version 5. Though Kotlin is fully interoperable with Java, you can write an application with pure and fully idiomatic Kotlin code. The diverse range of Kotlin features enhances productivity and combines well with Spring for application development.

As we have seen, the extension function in Kotlin is a non-intrusive way of providing a better alternative to the utility class or creating a class hierarchy for adding new features. Spring has used this feature to apply new Kotlin specific capabilities to existing Spring APIs. It is mainly used for dependency management. In the same way, Spring has also made framework APIs null safe to take full advantage of Kotlin.

Even Spring Boot has first-class Kotlin support, starting from version 2.x. This means you can write Spring-based applications in Kotlin as if Spring was a native framework of Kotlin. The current version of Kotlin released in October 2018 is 1.3, and Spring supports Kotlin 1.1 and higher.

Developing an application – Task Management System

This chapter aims to create an application called **Task Management System** (**TMS**) with Spring Boot and Kotlin. In previous chapters, we created various applications in Java. In this section, we will learn how to develop Spring-based applications in Kotlin with Spring Boot.

With TMS, we will implement the following functionalities; instead of making full-fledged and feature-rich applications, our focus will be on how to leverage Kotlin capability while developing Spring-based applications:

- Task creation and assigning to the user.
- View, update, and delete the task by an admin user.
- Add comments to a given task by the admin and normal user to whom the task is assigned.
- Implement authentication and authorization with Spring Security.
- For simplicity, we will expose the REST service to add users. There will be one admin user and one or more normal users.

Creating a Spring Boot project with Kotlin

The first thing is to create a project structure through the Spring Boot initializer. In all previous chapters, we created a project structure in **Spring Tool Suit** (**STS**—an Eclipse-based IDE). There is another way to create it from the web. Go to the `https://start.spring.io/` URL, and fill in the data as follows:

Make sure you select **Kotlin** as a programming language option along with latest stable Spring Boot version (**2.1.2** as of now). Also select the dependencies as follows:

- **JPA**: Used to interact with the database through **Java Persistence API** (**JPA**)
- **Web**: Add Spring **Model-View-Controller** (**MVC**) specific features
- **Security**: Required to add Spring Security capabilities

- **DevTools**: To make live reload on code changes
- **Thymeleaf**: Designing the views with Thymeleaf templates
- **MySQL**: Java connector to interact with the MySQL database

Click on the **Generate Project** button, and you will see an application structure is downloaded as a ZIP bundle. Just unzip it in your local machine. So far, we have used STS—an Eclipse IDE—as an IDE to develop various applications in previous chapters. However, for a more comprehensive experience, we will use IntelliJ IDEA (a well-known IDE native with support for Kotlin) in this chapter.

IntelliJ IDEA ships in two versions: Community and Ultimate. The former is available free of cost for JVM and Android-based development, while the later is for web and enterprise development, with more feature support. It is available for popular operating systems—Windows, macOS, and Linux. We will use the Community version. Download it from the `https://www.jetbrains.com/idea/download` URL, and install it on your local machine.

To import the project, open the IntelliJ IDEA IDE, select the **File | Open** menu, and select the extracted project structure folder that we have downloaded from the Spring initializer. The very first difference you will see in the Kotlin-based Spring application is the folder structure. The Kotlin source code will reside in `src/main/kotlin` compared to `src/main/java` for standard Java-based applications.

To support Kotlin, Spring requires certain dependencies, which are added automatically to `pom.xml` while generating it from the Spring initializer. You will see the Kotlin specific dependencies as follows:

```xml
<dependency>
    <groupId>org.jetbrains.kotlin</groupId>
    <artifactId>kotlin-reflect</artifactId>
</dependency>
<dependency>
    <groupId>org.jetbrains.kotlin</groupId>
    <artifactId>kotlin-stdlib-jdk8</artifactId>
</dependency>
<dependency>
    <groupId>com.fasterxml.jackson.module</groupId>
    <artifactId>jackson-module-kotlin</artifactId>
</dependency>
```

The `kotlin-stdlib-jdk8` dependency is required for Kotlin 1.2 and higher versions. For Kotlin 1.1, you need to use `kotlin-stdlib-jre8`. The Kotlin-reflect is a reflection feature used in Kotlin.

DB design

To store task-related data, we will use the MySQL database. We will also store user and role information in database tables. The tables and their relationship details look as follows:

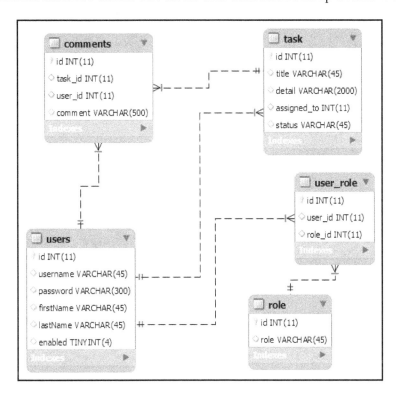

The table details are as follows:

- **task:** This table stores the details about tasks added into the system. It has a one-to-many relationship with the **comments** table.
- **comments:** When a user enters a **task** comment, it will be added to this table.
- **users:** This is a master table to store user details. It has a many-to-many relationship with the table **role**. It also has a one-to-many relationship with the **task** and **comments** tables.
- **role:** This is a master table for roles. Mainly, there are two roles—ROLE_USER and ROLE_ADMIN. It has a many-to-many relationship with the table **users**.
- **user_role:** This is a link table and will store the associated data of **role** and **users**.

Entity classes

We will use Spring Data JPA to interact with the database, so first we need to write entity classes. An entity class will be mapped to a database table, and its attributes are mapped to the table columns. The JPA entity class is a user-defined POJO class, which is nothing but an ordinary Java class with certain JPA specific annotation and is capable of presenting the objects in the database.

We will create a separate entity class for each of the tables except the link table **user_role**, which is handled with the `@ManyToMany` annotation. The details are as follows.

Users

Entity class for the `users` table should look as follows:

```
@Entity
@Table(name="users",catalog="task_mgmt_system")
class User {
    @Id
    @GeneratedValue(strategy= GenerationType.IDENTITY)
    @Column(name = "id")
    private var id:Int? = null

    @Column(name="username")
    private var username : String? = null

    @Column(name="password")
    private var password : String? = null

    @Column(name="firstname")
    private var firstname : String? = null

    @Column(name="lastname")
    private var lastname : String? = null

    @Column(name="enabled")
    private var enabled : Boolean = false

    @ManyToMany(cascade = [CascadeType.PERSIST],fetch = FetchType.EAGER)
    @JoinTable(
            name = "user_role",
            joinColumns = [JoinColumn(name = "user_id",referencedColumnName
= "id") ],
            inverseJoinColumns = [JoinColumn(name =
"role_id",referencedColumnName = "id")]
    )
```

```
    private var roles: Set<Role>? = null

    @OneToMany
    @JoinColumn(name ="user_id")
    private var comments : MutableSet<Comments>? = null

  //.... Getters and Setters
}
```

The `@Entity` annotation is used to declare that the class is a JPA entity. The `@Table` annotation is used to map the class with a specific database table. The attributes of this class are mapped to the respective columns with the `@Column` annotation. The attributes are defined as nullable, as they will be populated at runtime.

The `@JoinTable` annotation is used to declare the link table, and `JoinColumn` is used to define the column reference between tables associated with a many-to-many relationship along with the link table. The many-to-many relationship declaration in Kotlin is a little bit different than in Java. The same configuration is declared in Java as follows:

```
@ManyToMany(cascade = CascadeType.PERSIST,fetch = FetchType.EAGER )
@JoinTable(
    name = "user_role",
    joinColumns = @JoinColumn(name = "user_id",referencedColumnName = "id"),
    inverseJoinColumns = @JoinColumn(name = "role_id",referencedColumnName =
"id")
)
```

The visible difference here is the declaration of the `joinColumns` attribute of the `@JoinTable` annotation. In Java, it is declared with an annotation, while in Kotlin it is defined as an array. Another difference is defining the `cascade` attribute in the `@ManyToMany` annotation.

Role

The entity class corresponding to the `role` table looks as follows:

```
@Entity
@Table(name="role",catalog="task_mgmt_system")
class Role {
    @Id
    @GeneratedValue(strategy= GenerationType.IDENTITY)
    @Column(name = "id")
    private var id:Int? = null

    @Column(name="role")
    private var role : String? = null
```

```
        @ManyToMany(mappedBy = "roles",cascade = [CascadeType.PERSIST])
        private var users:Set<User>? = null
    // ... Getters and Setters
    }
```

In the many-to-many relationship between `User` and `Role` entities, the ownership is with the`User` entity so the `@ManyToMany` annotation in the `Role` entity is defined with the `mappedBy` attribute.

Task

The entity class associated to `task` table should look as follows:

```
@Entity
@Table(name="task",catalog="task_mgmt_system")
class Task {
    @Id
    @GeneratedValue(strategy=GenerationType.IDENTITY)
    @Column(name = "id")
    private var id :Int?=null

    @Column(name="title")
    private var title : String? = null
    @Column(name="detail")
    private var detail : String? = null

    @Column(name="assigned_to")
    private var assignedTo : Int? = null

    @Column(name="status")
    private var status : String? = null

    @OneToMany
    @JoinColumn(name ="task_id")
    private var comments : MutableSet<Comments>? = null

    // .. Getters and Setters
    }
```

The `@OneToMany` annotation is used to declare a one-to-many relationship with the `comments` table. The `@JoinColumn` annotation is used to declare the column reference in the `comments` table.

Comments

The entity class for `comments` table should look as follows:

```
@Entity
@Table(name="comments",catalog="task_mgmt_system")
class Comments {
    @Id
    @GeneratedValue(strategy=GenerationType.IDENTITY)
    private var id :Int?=null

    @ManyToOne
    @JoinColumn(name = "user_id",nullable = false)
    private var user : User? = null

    @ManyToOne
    @JoinColumn(name = "task_id", nullable = false)
    private var task : Task? = null;

    private var comment:String? = null

  // .. Getters and Setters
}
```

The `@ManyToOne` annotation is used to declare a many-to-one relationship with a **task** table. The `@JoinColumn` annotation is used to define the reference column (primary key).

Spring Security

Spring Security is the de facto standard for implementing security constraints in Spring-based applications. In previous chapters, we used Spring Security with an in-memory model while implementing user authentication and authorization. The in-memory model should only be used for testing purposes only. In a real scenario, authentication and authorization details are fetched from other systems to make it loosely coupled with the application code, such as LDAP, OAuth, and so on.

In `Chapter 3`, *Blogpress – A Simple Blog Management System*, we learned how to configure Spring Security with LDAP and OAuth in detail. In this chapter, we will use database tables to store authentication and authorization details. First, let's create a class and define the security configuration as follows:

```
@Configuration
@EnableWebSecurity
@ComponentScan("com.nilangpatel.tms.security")
class WebSecurityConfig : WebSecurityConfigurerAdapter() {
```

```
@Throws(Exception::class)
override fun configure(web: WebSecurity){
    web.ignoring().antMatchers("/js/**")
    web.ignoring().antMatchers("/css/**")
}
@Throws(Exception::class)
override fun configure(http: HttpSecurity) {
    // .... HttpSecurity specific configuration
}
}
```

This is a typical security configuration. The way we declared annotation for Kotlin is similar to what we have done with Java. However, there are differences as follows:

- In Kotlin, we can use a colon (:) to declare inheritance.
  The `WebSecurityConfigurerAdapter` class is a parent class, but with the surprise that it is a Java class. You can extend your Kotlin class from another Java class, and it is absolutely fine. This is how Kotlin is deeply interoperable with Java. Another difference is the parent class is used with the constructor notation (with brackets).
- To override a method from the parent class, Kotlin uses the `override` keyword.
- Since Kotlin does not support checked exceptions directly, the `@Throws` annotation is used to define the exception details.

Next, the access mechanism needs to be configured to various pages in the system. This can be done by overriding the configure method, which basically provides an HTTP specific security configuration. It looks as follows:

```
@Throws(Exception::class)
override fun configure(http: HttpSecurity) {
    http.authorizeRequests()
        .antMatchers("/","/login","/api/register").permitAll()
        .antMatchers("/controlPage/**","/getAllUsers/**",
            "/allTaskList/**","/addTaskComment/**","/viewTask/**")
.hasAnyAuthority(TaskMgmntConstant.ROLE_USER,TaskMgmntConstant.ROLE_ADMIN)
        .antMatchers("/showAddTask/**","/showEditTask/**",
                "/addTask/**","/updateTask/**","/deleteTask/**")
            .hasAnyAuthority(TaskMgmntConstant.ROLE_ADMIN)
        .and()
      .formLogin().loginPage("/login").permitAll()
        .defaultSuccessUrl("/controlPage",true)
        .failureUrl("/login?error=true")
      .and().csrf().disable()
        .logout()
        .permitAll().logoutSuccessUrl("/login?logout=true")
}
```

The noticeable things here are we have configured various URLs accessible for all users, even without login, and only the admin needs to log in. We also have configured the login, success, and failure URLs along with the logout URL. We will talk more about them in the *Defining the Spring MVC controller* section.

Now, we will configure an authentication mechanism. Spring supports various options such as in-memory, LDAP, OAuth, and so on. For this application, we will fetch user details from the database. To implement Spring Security with the database, there are two approaches.

Query approach

Spring Security needs users and their role details to perform the security check. In this approach, we will fetch the user and role details with a SQL query. We will define a query in the application.properties file as follows:

```
spring.queries.users-query= select username, password, enabled from users
where username=?
spring.queries.roles-query= select u.username, r.role from users u inner
join user_role ur on(u.id=ur.user_id) inner join role r on(ur.role_id=r.id)
where u.username=?
```

The first query fetches user details while second queries retrieve the list of roles for a given username. These properties can be read in the WebSecurityConfig class as follows:

```
@Value("\${spring.queries.users-query}")
private val usersQuery: String? = null

@Value("\${spring.queries.roles-query}")
private val rolesQuery: String? = null
```

In Kotlin, the symbol $ is used to print the variable within String without explicitly using the + operator. Since we want to read the property from the application.properties file, we have to use the escape character (\) along with the $ operator. Apart from this, the variables are declared as nullable (with String?) as they will be populated by Spring at runtime.

Next, we will override the configure() method to define the authentication configuration as follows:

```
@Throws(Exception::class)
override fun configure(auth: AuthenticationManagerBuilder?) {
    auth!!.jdbcAuthentication()
            .usersByUsernameQuery(usersQuery)
```

```
            .authoritiesByUsernameQuery(rolesQuery)
            .dataSource(dataSource)
            .passwordEncoder(passwordEncoder())
    }
```

The nice thing about IntelliJ IDEA is, whenever you pass any Java code, it will prompt to convert to Java. On choosing **yes**, it will automatically convert Java code into Kotlin code. The `!!` symbol is a not-null assertion operator, which basically converts any value to a non-null type and throws a `NullPointerException` if the variable is null. It is part of the null safety feature of Kotlin. The `dataSource` and `passwordEncoder` methods can be defined as follows:

```
@Autowired
private var dataSource: DataSource? = null

@Bean
fun passwordEncoder(): BCryptPasswordEncoder {
    return BCryptPasswordEncoder()
}
```

The `dataSource` will be injected by Spring at runtime, so it must be declared as nullable (with `?`). We will use `BCryptPasswordEncoder` to encode the password with the `bcrpt` algorithm, which is considered to be a very strong encoding algorithm.

The `userQuery` and `roleQuery` objects are not necessarily required. If you do not provide them, you need to design the tables with predefined names and columns. The user table must be created with a name—`users` with columns `username`, `password`, and `enabled`, while the **role** table must be created with a name—`authorities`.

This approach has certain restrictions. For example: `userQuery` must return the `username`, `password`, and `enabled` column value in the same sequence and `roleQuery` must return `username` and `role name` in the same sequence. If any change happens in this sequence, it may not work properly.

UserDetailsService approach

Another approach to fetch use and role information is using the `UserDetailsService` interface. It is an abstract way to fetch authentication and authorization details. It has one method—`loadUserByUsername()` that will return user details based on `username`. You can override it and write your own logic to retrieve the user details.

Spring provides a class called `DaoAuthenticationProvider` that basically uses the `UserDetailsService` implementation to fetch user details during the authentication process. The flexibility in this approach means we can define a custom method to fetch user details. We will define a method in the JPA repository for the `User` entity. The JPA is a standard way of interacting with a relational database with Java objects. The repository looks as follows:

```
@Repository
interface UserRepository : JpaRepository<User, Int> {
    fun findByUsername(username: String): User?
}
```

`UserRepository` is a Kotlin interface that extends the Java `JpaRepository` interface. The `@Repository` annotation is used to declare this interface as a JPA repository. The `findByUsername` method is a query method, which will fetch the user. Spring Data JPA has an inbuilt query building mechanism, based on the repository method name.

For the `findByUsername` method, it will first remove the `findBy` prefix and compose the query from the rest of the method name. In this case, it will internally create a query, such as `select * from users where username=?`. This method returns an object of the `User` entity class. Next, we need to provide a custom user service, and for that we will implement `UserDetailsService` as follows:

```
@Service
class CustomUserDetailsService : UserDetailsService {

    @Autowired
    private val userRepository: UserRepository? = null

    @Throws(UsernameNotFoundException::class)
    override fun loadUserByUsername(username: String): UserDetails {
      val user = userRepository?.findByUsername(username) ?:
                    throw UsernameNotFoundException(username)
      return CustomUserPrinciple(user)
    }
}
```

The `CustomUserDetailsService` class is declared with a `@Service` annotation to declare it as a service component. It overrides a `loadUserByUsername()` method, where we can write custom logic to fetch user details. A repository `findByUsername()` method that we have created is used here to fetch user details.

The return type is `UserDetails` that is an interface that actually stores user information, which is then encapsulated to authenticate objects later. We have created a `CustomUserPrinciple` class to provide an implementation of `UserDetails` as follows:

```kotlin
class CustomUserPrinciple : UserDetails {
    constructor(user: User?) {
        this.user = user
    }
    private var user:User? = null

    override fun isEnabled(): Boolean {
        return true
    }
    override fun getUsername(): String {
        return this.user?.getUsername() ?: ""
    }
    override fun isCredentialsNonExpired(): Boolean {
        return true
    }
    override fun getPassword(): String {
        return this.user?.getPassword() ?: ""
    }
    override fun isAccountNonExpired(): Boolean {
        return true
    }
    override fun isAccountNonLocked(): Boolean {
        return true
    }
    override fun getAuthorities(): MutableCollection<out GrantedAuthority>
{
        var userRoles:Set<Role>? = user?.getRoles() ?: null
        var authorities:MutableSet<GrantedAuthority> =
HashSet<GrantedAuthority>()
        for(role in userRoles.orEmpty()){
            authorities.add(CustomGrantedAuthority(role))
        }
        return authorities
    }

}
```

The `UserDetails` interface requires the implementation of certain methods as follows:

- `isEnable()`: This method basically returns if the user is activated or not. In a practical scenario, there must be a separate database column to check if the user is enabled or not. For simplicity, we simply return `true` assuming that all users are enabled. If the user returns `false`, Spring Security will not allow login.
- `getUsername()`: This simply returns the username.
- `isCredentialsNonExpired()`: This is a very useful method when you want to impose a constraint on the user to update the password after a certain time limit. In this method, you need to check whether the password has expired, based on your requirement, and return the value accordingly. For simplicity, if we return `true`, it means password has not expired.
- `getPassword()`: It should return the password.
- `isAccountNonExpired()`: This indicates whether a user account has expired or not. To make it simple, we just return `true`.
- `isAccountNonLocked()`: This is used to check whether a user account is locked. Again, for simplicity, we a just return `true`.
- `getAuthorities()`: This method returns authorities granted to the user. We retrieve roles from a user object and wrap them in a `GrantedAuthority` type. The `GrantedAuthority` is an interface. We have provided an implementation through the `CustomGrantedAuthority` class as follows:

```
class CustomGrantedAuthority : GrantedAuthority{
    private var role:Role?=null
    constructor( role:Role ){
        this.role = role
    }
    override fun getAuthority(): String {
        return role?.getRole() ?: ""
    }
}
```

- We are injecting a user object through the constructor, which can be used to retrieve further details in each of these methods.

The last part is to define the Spring Security configuration. Add methods to the WebSecurityConfig class as follows:

```
@Throws(Exception::class)
override fun configure(auth: AuthenticationManagerBuilder?) {
    auth!!.authenticationProvider(authenticationProvider())
}

@Bean
fun authenticationProvider(): DaoAuthenticationProvider {
    val authProvider = DaoAuthenticationProvider()
    authProvider.setUserDetailsService(userDetailService)
    authProvider.setPasswordEncoder(passwordEncoder())
    return authProvider
}
```

The authenticationProvider() method simply creates an object of the DaoAuthenticationProvider type, configure it with user detail service object and password encoder and return. It is then used in the configure() method to set as the authentication provider. The object of UserDetailService can be injected in the same class as follows:

```
@Autowired
private var userDetailService: CustomUserDetailsService? = null
```

This approach is more flexible in terms of allowing a customized way to fetch user details, which are then used by Spring to perform various security constraints. It simply decouples the logic of authentication and authorization from the mechanism to fetch user details. This makes the system more flexible.

Defining the Spring MVC controller

Our backend layer is ready, and now we will design the controller and view layer. We have decided to user Spring MVC for the frontend, which is the best fit for web-based Spring applications. The declaration of Spring MVC controller in Kotlin is similar to what we have done in Java, as follows:

```
@Controller
class TaskMgmtSystemController {

// Controller methods...
}
```

The Kotlin `TaskMgmtSystemController` class is declared with the `@Controller` annotation, which is used to define the class as a Spring MVC controller. The way of defining controller methods in Kotlin is also similar to Java. For example: a home page can be shown by the following controller method:

```
@GetMapping("/")
fun showHomePage(model: Model): String  {
    logger.info("This will show home page ")
    setProcessingData(model, TaskMgmntConstant.TITLE_HOME_PAGE)
    return "home"
}
```

This method is mapped with the / URL (accessible at `http://localhost:8080`) and returns a home page. As mentioned, we are going to use Thymeleaf templates to construct a view layer.

 If you are not very familiar with Thymeleaf, it is a natural template engine used to produce views, which are processed at the server side. A detail explanation was given in `Chapter 3`, *Blogpress – A Simple Blog Management System*, of this book. You can refer to it to get more idea about how Thymeleaf works with Spring.

We also have defined constants to access predefined values. Unlike Java, we can not define constants in the Kotlin interface. To define constants, we will use a singleton class. In Kotlin, we can create a singleton class by an object declaration feature. This can be achieved with the `object` keyword. The `TaskMgmntConstant` singleton class looks as follows:

```
object TaskMgmntConstant {
    const val ROLE_USER :String = "ROLE_USER"
    const val ROLE_ADMIN :String = "ROLE_ADMIN"
    const val TITLE_HOME_PAGE: String = "Home"
    const val TITLE_LOGIN_PAGE: String = "Login"
    const val TITLE_LANDING_CONTROL_PAGE:String = "Control Page"
    const val TITLE_ADD_TASK_PAGE:String = "Add Task"
    const val TITLE_UPDATE_TASK_PAGE:String = "Update Task"
    const val PAGE_TITLE: String = "pageTitle"
}
```

Though there is no `class` keyword used here, this code combines both `class` and the singleton declaration altogether. Internally, Kotlin will create a single static instance of the `TaskMgmntConstant` class. The `object` declaration can contain functions as well, which can be accessed with the `object` declaration name directly. It is similar to accessing the static variables and methods of the class type in Java.

The `const` keyword is used to define constants. The variables declared with the `const` keyword are compile-time constants, meaning they must be populated at the time of compilation. Because of this reason, they can not be assigned to function or class constructors but only to a string or primitives.

Next, we will see how to define controller methods for other operations as follows.

Showing the control page

When a user does log in, the system will land on a page called the control page. From this page, users can view the task and perform various operations based on the role they have. For example: a normal user can see the task list assigned to it and also able to add a comment for a specific task. The admin user can add a new task, edit, and delete an existing one. This controller method simply redirects the user to the landing (or control) page. The code looks as follows:

```
@GetMapping("/controlPage")
fun showControlPage(model:Model):String {
    logger.info("Showing control page ")
     setProcessingData(model, TaskMgmntConstant.TITLE_LANDING_CONTROL_PAGE)
     return "control-page"
}
```

In the *Spring Security* section, we configured `/controlPage` accessible to normal and admin users. It cannot be accessed without login.

Showing the login page

This controller method will redirect the user to the login page. It looks as follows:

```
@GetMapping("/login")
fun showLoginPage(@RequestParam(name = "error",required = false)
error:String? ,
       @RequestParam(name = "logout", required = false) logout:String?,
model:Model):String {
    logger.info("This is login page URL   ")
    if (error != null) {
```

```
       model.addAttribute("error", "Invalid Credentials provided.")
    }
    if (logout != null) {
       model.addAttribute("message", "Logged out")
    }
    setProcessingData(model, TaskMgmntConstant.TITLE_LOGIN_PAGE);
    return "login"
}
```

It is accessible from the navigation menu. This method also handles an error in the case of invalid credentials and shows an appropriate message to the user.

Showing the add new task page

The **add new task** feature is configured to allow only admin users. It will redirect the user to the add new task page. The code looks as follows:

```
@GetMapping("/showAddTask")
fun showAddTask(model:Model):String {
    logger.info("Going to show Add task page")
    setProcessingData(model, TaskMgmntConstant.TITLE_ADD_TASK_PAGE)
    return "task-add"
}
```

The /showAddTask URL is configured as a navigation menu in the control page.

Showing the edit task page

Only admin users can edit existing tasks. Admin users can see an **Edit** button for each task record on task—list screen. Upon clicking it, this method will be triggered. It looks as follows.

```
@GetMapping("/showEditTask")
fun showEditTask(@RequestParam(name = "taskId",required = true) taskId:
Int,
      model:Model):String {
    val task:Task? = taskRepository?.findById(taskId)?.get()
    if(task !=null){
        val userId: Int = task.getAssignedTo() ?: 0
        val user:User? = userRepository?.findById(userId)?.get()
        val taskDto = TaskDTO(task.getId(),task.getTitle(),
             task.getDetail(),userId,(user?.getFirstname() + "
"+user?.getLastname()),task.getStatus(),null)
        model.addAttribute("task",taskDto)
    }
```

```
        logger.info("Going to show Edit task page")
        setProcessingData(model, TaskMgmntConstant.TITLE_UPDATE_TASK_PAGE)
        model.addAttribute("screenTitle","Edit Task")
        return "task-edit"
}
```

The `taskId` parameter will be sent as a request parameter from the task list screen. First, we fetch the task object from a given `taskId` with `taskRepository` and then copy it to the `TaskDTO` object. You can see we have declared variables with the `val` keyword, which is used to declare constants. Kotlin recommends using `val` in case the variable is not changed after assigning the value. The `TaskDTO` class is a data class defined in Kotlin as follows:

```
class TaskDTO( var id :Int?, var title : String?,
              var detail : String?, var assignedTo : Int?, var
assignedPerson:String?,
              var status : String?, var comments : Set<Comments>?)
```

The **Edit Task** screen looks as follows:

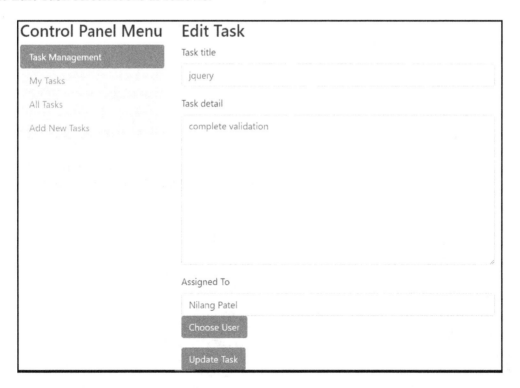

Adding a new task

Only admin users can add a new task. This controller method will insert the task record in the database. It looks as follows:

```
@PostMapping("/addTask")
fun addTask(@RequestParam(name = "title",required = true) title:String,
        @RequestParam(name = "detail",required = true) detail:String,
        @RequestParam(name = "selectedUserId", required = true)
selectedUserId:Int,
      model:Model):String {
  val task = Task()
  task.setTitle(title)
  task.setDetail(detail)
  task.setAssignedTo(selectedUserId)
  task.setStatus(TaskStatus.PENDING.getStatus())
  taskRepository?.save(task)

  logger.info("Goint to show Add task page")
  setProcessingData(model, TaskMgmntConstant.TITLE_ADD_TASK_PAGE)
  model.addAttribute("screenTitle","Add new Task")
  return "redirect:allTaskList"
}
```

The `title`, `detail`, and `userId` parameters (to whom the task is assigned) are provided from the **add task** screen. This method simply creates an instance of the `Task` class, populates its value, and saves it in `taskRepsitory`. Unlike Java, the instance can be created without the `new` keyword in Kotlin. Also, Kotlin defers the type of variable wherever it is possible. For example, we have not defined the type of the `task` variable because it is assigned the object of the `Task` type class so Kotlin understands that it is the `Task` type only.

Instead of redirecting to a specific page, we are redirecting to another controller method with the `/allTaskList` URL pattern, which basically shows a task list.

Updating a task

Updating a task is similar to adding a new task method. Only admin users can update the existing task. This method looks as follows:

```
@PostMapping("/updateTask")
fun updateTask(@RequestParam(name = "taskId",required = true) taskId:Int,
        @RequestParam(name = "title",required = true) title:String,
        @RequestParam(name = "detail",required = true) detail:String,
        @RequestParam(name = "selectedUserId", required = true)
```

```
selectedUserId:Int,
        model:Model):String {
    val task:Task? = taskRepository?.findById(taskId)?.get()
    if(task !=null) {
        task.setTitle(title)
        task.setDetail(detail)
        task.setAssignedTo(selectedUserId)
        taskRepository?.save(task)
    }

    logger.info("Going to show Add task page")
    model.addAttribute("screenTitle","Edit Task")
    setProcessingData(model, TaskMgmntConstant.TITLE_ADD_TASK_PAGE)
    return "redirect:allTaskList"
}
```

The code looks similar to the `addTask()` method. The only difference is we get the `taskId` of the existing task as an additional parameter. First, we retrieve it, update its value, and finally save it with `taskRepository`. This method also redirects to another controller method to show a task list with an `/allTaskList` URL pattern.

Adding a task comment

Normal and admin users can add comments to an existing task. On opening the task in view mode, the screen provides a facility to add a comment. The code of the controller method for adding task comments looks as follows:

```
@PostMapping("/addTaskComment")
fun addTask(@RequestParam(name = "taskId",required = true) taskId:Int,
        @RequestParam(name = "taskComment",required = true)
taskComment:String,
        model:Model):String {
    val currentTask:Task? = taskRepository?.findById(taskId)?.get()
    if(currentTask !=null) {
        val principal =
SecurityContextHolder.getContext().authentication.principal
        if (principal is CustomUserPrinciple) {
            val user = principal.getUser()
            var existingComments: MutableSet<Comments>? =
currentTask.getComments()
            var comment:Comments?
            if(existingComments == null || existingComments.isEmpty()) {
                existingComments = mutableSetOf() // Inmitialize empty hash set
            }
            comment = Comments()
            comment.setTask(currentTask)
```

```
            if(user !=null) comment.setUser(user)
            comment.setComment(taskComment)
            comment = commentRepository?.save(comment)
            if(comment !=null) {
                existingComments.add(comment)
            }
            currentTask.setComments(existingComments)
            taskRepository?.save(currentTask)
        }
    }
    return "redirect:viewTask?taskId=$taskId"
}
```

In this method, the `taskId` and `taskComment` parameters are supplied by the view task screen from where the user can add the comment. We fetch the `Task` object from `taskId` and fetch its comments as a mutable set.

Kotlin provides an API collection (list, set, map, and so on) with a clear distinction between mutable and immutable types. This is very handy to ensure you avoid bugs and design clear APIs. When you declare any collection, say, `List<out T>`, it is immutable by default and Kotlin allows read-only operations, such as `size()`, `get()`, and so on. You cannot add any element to it.

If you wish to modify the collection, you need to use mutable types explicitly, such as `MutableList<String>`, `MutableMap<String, String>`, and so on. In our case, we need to add a comment in the existing set so we used the `MutableSet` type. The comment set is empty while adding the first comment so we create an empty set with the `mutableSetOf()` method. This method is used to create a collection of the `Set` type on the fly.

We also need to add `userId` of the currently logged-in user to a comment. To do so, we make a call to `SecurityContextHolder.getContext().authentication.principal`. The `SecurityContextHolder` class is provided by Spring Security, and it is used to get various security-related information.

Getting all users

This method will return all users available in the system. It is used to create a task screen to fetch a user list to choose for a task assignment. The method is as follows:

```
@GetMapping("/getAllUsers")
fun getUsers(model:Model):String{
    var users: List<User>? = userRepository?.findAll() ?: null;
    model.addAttribute("users",users)
```

```
        return "users"
    }
```

We call it from the model popup in the add task screen. The UI will be rendered by the Thymeleaf template—users.html.

Showing a task list

This method shows the list of tasks to both normal and admin users. The difference is a normal user can only view and add comments, while the admin user can view, edit, and delete operations on a task record. Another difference is a normal user can see a list of tasks assigned to it, while an admin user can see all tasks available in the system. The method should look as follows:

```kotlin
@GetMapping("/allTaskList")
fun showAllTaskList(@RequestParam(name = "myTask",required = false)
myTask:String?,
                model:Model):String{
    var taskLst:   List<Array<Any>>? = null
    if("true" == myTask){
        //get current user ID from Spring context
        val principal =
SecurityContextHolder.getContext().authentication.principal
        if (principal is CustomUserPrinciple) {
            val user = principal.getUser()
            if(user !=null){
                taskLst = taskRepository?.findMyTasks(user.getId() ?: 0)
            }
            model.addAttribute("screenTitle","My Tasks")
        }
    }else {
        taskLst = taskRepository?.findAllTasks()
        model.addAttribute("screenTitle","All Tasks")
    }
    val taskDtoLst:MutableList<TaskDTO> = ArrayList()
    var taskDto:TaskDTO?
    for(row in taskLst.orEmpty()){
        taskDto = TaskDTO(row[0] as Int,row[1] as String,row[2] as String,
         null, row[3] as String,row[4] as String,null)
        taskDtoLst.add(taskDto)
    }
    model.addAttribute("tasks",taskDtoLst)
    return "task-list"
}
```

This method serves two operations, based on the `myTask` request parameter. If it is available then pull the tasks assigned to current users only or else fetch all tasks. Fetching all tasks is available to the user with the admin role. After fetching the tasks from the database, we map them on to an object of the `TaskDTO` class. The **data transfer object** (**DTO**) is the Kotlin data class and looks as follows:

```
class TaskDTO( var id :Int?, var title : String?,
              var detail : String?, var assignedTo : Int?,
              var assignedPerson:String?, var status : String?,
              var comments : Set<Comments>?)
```

In the task list, we show the name of the user to whom the task is assigned. In the `task` table, we store `userId`, so we need to fetch the username by combining the task and user tables. Spring Data JAP provides a convenient way of fetching results of complex queries with the `@Query` annotation.

This annotation is used to define a query using JAP query language (and even native SQL query) and bind it to the method of the JPA repository. When we call that repository method, JPA will execute the query attached to that method with the `@Query` annotation. Let's define two methods with join query on a repository interface as follows:

```
@Repository
interface TaskRepository : JpaRepository<Task,Int>{

    @Query("SELECT t.id, t.title, t.detail, concat(u.firstname,
            ' ',u.lastname) as assignedTo ,t.status FROM task t
            inner join users u on t.assigned_to = u.id",
            nativeQuery = true)
    fun findAllTasks(): List<Array<Any>>

    @Query("SELECT t.id, t.title, t.detail, concat(u.firstname,
            ' ',u.lastname) as assignedTo ,t.status FROM task t
            inner join users u on t.assigned_to = u.id and
            u.id =:userId",nativeQuery = true)
    fun findMyTasks(userId : Int): List<Array<Any>>
}
```

The first method will fetch all tasks available in the system, while the second method will fetch tasks that are assigned to a specific user only. The `nativeQery` attribute indicates that it is a SQL query. Since this query returns columns from multiple tables (**task** and **users** in our case), it returns a list of an array of the `Any` type, instead of a specific entity class object. The `List` object represents the records row, the elements of `Array` are columns, and `Any` means any available type in Kotlin. `Any` is equivalent to `Object` in Java.

It can be then used to populate the `TaskDTO` object in the controller method—`showAllTaskList`. The keyword `as` is used to do casting from `Any` to a respective type. Kotlin compiler uses smart cast so you don't need to explicitly check if the `Any` type given is compatible. For admin users, the task list screen looks as follows:

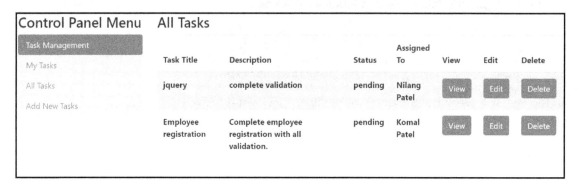

For the normal user, it looks as follows:

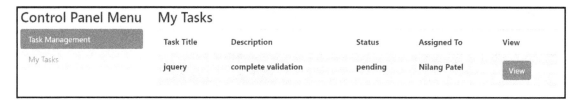

Viewing a task

The **view task** screen will open the task in view mode, meaning it will show the details of the task. It also allows you to add a comment and shows the list of comments added to the selected task. The controller method for viewing the task will populate the task and comment data, and redirects the user to view the task screen. The method looks as follows:

```
@GetMapping("/viewTask")
fun viewTask(@RequestParam(name = "taskId",required = true)
                                taskId:Int,model:Model):String{
    val selectedTask:Task? = taskRepository?.findById(taskId)?.get()
    val user:User? = userRepository?.
                findById(selectedTask?.getAssignedTo() ?: 0)?.get()

    val taskDto= TaskDTO(selectedTask?.getId(),selectedTask?.getTitle(),
        selectedTask?.getDetail(),selectedTask?.getAssignedTo(),
        (user?.getFirstname() + " "+ user?.getLastname()),
        selectedTask?.getStatus(),selectedTask?.getComments())
```

```
    val commentLst:  List<Array<Any>>? =
commentRepository?.findByTaskId(taskId)
    val commentDtoLst:MutableList<CommentDTO> = ArrayList()
    var commentDto:CommentDTO?
    for(row in commentLst.orEmpty()){
        commentDto = CommentDTO(row[0] as Int,row[1] as String,row[2] as
String)
        commentDtoLst.add(commentDto)
    }
    model.addAttribute("task",taskDto)
    model.addAttribute("taskComments",commentDtoLst)
    model.addAttribute("screenTitle","Add Task Comment")
    return "task-view"
}
```

The `taskId` parameter will be sent from a task list screen. First, we fetch the task detail from a given `taskId`. We also fetch the user data from the user ID associated with the `Task` object. For comments, we do the same thing: fetch comments with a given `taskId` from `commentRepository`.

We fetch comments from `commentRepository`, but we could have fetched it from the `Task` object, since they have one-to-many relationships. The reason we do not fetch them that way is, we want to show the username to whom the task is assigned. If we fetch comments from `Task`, it will return the collection of the object of the `Comments` type, which has a user ID but not first and last name. So we might have to make an additional round of database calls to fetch the user first and last name for each comments record. This may result in a poor performance.

As an alternative, we use a JPA query language mechanism, by associating the `join` SQL query with the repository method as follows:

```
interface CommentRepository: JpaRepository<Comments, Int> {

    @Query("SELECT c.id, c.comment, concat(u.firstname,' ',u.lastname)
            FROM comments c inner join users u on c.user_id=u.id inner join
task t
            on t. id = c.task_id and t.id =:taskId",nativeQuery = true)
    fun findByTaskId(taskId: Int):List<Array<Any>>
}
```

It is returned as a List<Array<Any>> type because the data is fetched from multiple tables (**task** and **comments**). We are iterating it and populating the list of CommentDTO, which is defined as a data class as follows:

```
data class CommentDTO(var id:Int,var comment:String,var userName:String)
```

The TaskDTO object is used to show task details while the list of CommentDTO is used to show comments in tabular format in the **view task** screen.

Deleting a task

Only admin users can delete an existing task. The delete option is visible in the task list screen. The controller method of deleting a task looks as follows:

```
@PostMapping("/deleteTask")
fun deleteTask(@RequestParam(name = "taskId",required = true)
taskId:Int,model:Model):String{
    var selectedTask:Task? = taskRepository?.findById(taskId)?.get()
    if(selectedTask !=null) {
        taskRepository?.delete(selectedTask)
    }
    return "redirect:allTaskList"
}
```

The taskId parameter is provided in the task list screen. First, we fetch the object of Task with taskId from taskRepository and delete if it is not null. Finally, we redirect to another controller method with the /allTaskList URL to show the task list screen.

REST call in Kotlin

Let's understand how to make a REST call with Kotlin. We expose the REST API to add users to the system. Basic user details along with role information need to be given. Defining REST controller in Kotlin is similar to Java as follows:

```
@RestController
@RequestMapping("/api")
class TaskMgmntRESTController {
...
}
```

The `TaskMgmntRESTController` Kotlin class is defined as a REST controller with `@RestController` and configures the `/api` URL pattern with the `@RequestMapping` annotation. We will write a function that handles the registration of users as follows:

```
@PostMapping(value = "/register", consumes =
[MediaType.APPLICATION_JSON_VALUE])
fun registerNewUser(@Valid @RequestBody userRegistrationDto:
UserRegistrationDTO,
                                    errors: Errors):
ResponseEntity<List<String>> {
        // registration code...
}
```

This function is defined with the `@PostMapping` annotation so data must be sent with the HTTP POST method. Also, the URL mapping is `/register` so the effective path would be `/api/register` to access this function (method). It consumes the data in JSON format. Spring will populate an object of `UserRegistrationDTO` from the JSON input. The Kotlin data class is as follows:

```
data class UserRegistrationDTO(var username:String, var password:String,
                              var firstname:String, var lastname:String,
                              var roleList:List<String>)
```

The `username`, `password`, `firstname`, and `lastname` attributes are used to insert a record in the user table, while the `roleList` attribute is used to associate the roles this user has. The input data must be given in JSON format with the HTTP POST method from the REST client as follows:

```
{
  "username":"dav",
  "password":"test",
  "firstname":"Dav",
  "lastname":"Patel",
  "roleList":["ROLE_USER","ROLE_ADMIN"]
}
```

The code written in the `registerNewUser` method will be divided into the following two parts.

Validation

A user sends the data in JSON format and it must be validated before entering into the system to avoid any backend errors. Instead of imposing a full list of validations, we will implement a few basic validations. For example, validating an existing username, the role list has invalid values other than ROLR_USER and ROLE_ADMIN. The code looks as follows:

```
if (userRegistrationDto.username != null) {
    var existingUser : User? = userRepository?.findByUsername(
                                    userRegistrationDto.username)
    if (existingUser != null) {
        errors.reject("Existing username","User is already exist with
username
                                    '${userRegistrationDto.username}'.
")
    }
}
if( userRegistrationDto.roleList.isEmpty()){
    errors.reject("No Roles provided","Please provide roles")
}else{
    var validRole = true
    var invalidRole:String?=null
    for(roleName in userRegistrationDto.roleList){
        if(!TaskMgmntConstant.getRolesLst().contains(roleName)){
            validRole=false
            invalidRole = roleName
            break
        }
    }
    if(!validRole){
        errors.reject("Invalid Roles"," $invalidRole is not a valid role")
    }
}
if (errors.hasErrors()) {
    val errorMsg = ArrayList<String>()
    errors.allErrors.forEach { a -> errorMsg.add(a.defaultMessage ?: "")
    }
    return ResponseEntity(errorMsg, HttpStatus.BAD_REQUEST)
} else {
 // .. User Registration code goes here
}
```

First, we check whether the username sent in JSON data already exists in the system. If it does, then return an appropriate message. The second check is about the role list. We have created a predefined role list in the `TaskMgmntConstant` class with the function declaration as follows:

```
object TaskMgmntConstant {
    const val ROLE_USER :String = "ROLE_USER"
    const val ROLE_ADMIN :String = "ROLE_ADMIN"

    //... Other constant declaration

    fun getRolesLst():List<String>{
        return listOf(ROLE_ADMIN, ROLE_USER)
    }
}
```

Let's recall that `TaskMgmntConstant` is singleton class and we can define functions apart from constants. If the `roleList` data sent as a JSON string is different than these two roles, then we show an appropriate message. You can see how a for-loop is used by the `forEach` method with a lambda expression. If any error occurs, we send a validation message with HTTP status 401 (`HttpStatus.BAD_REQUEST`).

User registration

If all validations are satisfied, then we will do user registration along with role mapping with the following code:

```
val userEntity = User()
userEntity.setUsername(userRegistrationDto.username)
userEntity.setEnabled(true)
val encodedPassword = passwordEncoder?.encode(userRegistrationDto.password)
userEntity.setPassword(encodedPassword ?: "")
userEntity.setFirstname(userRegistrationDto.firstname)
userEntity.setLastname(userRegistrationDto.lastname)

var role:Role?=null
var roles: MutableSet<Role> = mutableSetOf()
for(roleName in userRegistrationDto.roleList){
    role = roleRepository?.findByRole(roleName)
    if(role !=null) {
        roles.add(role)
    }
}
userEntity.setRoles(roles)
userRepository?.save(userEntity)
```

```
val msgLst = Arrays.asList("User registered successfully")
return ResponseEntity(msgLst, HttpStatus.OK)
```

In this code, we create the `User` object and populate its value from the `UserRegistrationDTO` object. We also create the mutable role list and populate it by fetching roles with `roleRepository`, based on the role name populated in `UserRegistrationDTO` from the JSON data. Finally, we associate the mutable set with the `User` object and save it in `userRepository`.

Summary

In this chapter, we learned the basics of Kotlin and its various features, and then created an application with Spring Boot and Kotlin. Within a short time span, Kotlin has gained huge momentum and popularity due to its capabilities, such as its interoperability, conciseness, safety features, and support for well-known IDEs.

Spring Framework has lots of features and is widely used in developing modern enterprise applications. With its first class support of various programming languages such as Java, Scala, Groovy, and Kotlin, Spring Framework has become a dominant player among enterprise-application development frameworks.

Spring Framework has a modular design and provides seamless integration in all aspects of the system, such as the frontend, controller layer, security, persistence, cloud support, messaging support, web flow, and lots more. With the invention of Spring Boot, developing Spring-based applications has become easier than ever before.

Throughout this book, we have explored the Spring Framework, showcasing its capabilities by developing a sample application in each chapter. This should definitely build your confidence and encourage you to explore the framework further. However, we recommend you create more sample apps so that you gain more hands-on experience and you really get the most out of the framework.

Here is a perfect way to finish our journey. For further reading, you can refer to the official Spring documentation and forums. Spring has a huge active community, and you can find many personal blogs that will help you to learn and explore the concepts.

Other Books You May Enjoy

If you enjoyed this book, you may be interested in these other books by Packt:

Mastering Spring Boot 2.0
Dinesh Rajput

ISBN: 9781787127562

- Build logically structured and highly maintainable Spring Boot applications
- Configure RESTful microservices using Spring Boot
- Make the application production and operation-friendly with Spring Actuator
- Build modern, high-performance distributed applications using cloud patterns
- Manage and deploy your Spring Boot application to the cloud (AWS)
- Monitor distributed applications using log aggregation and ELK

Hands-On Reactive Programming in Spring 5
Oleh Dokuka

ISBN: 9781787284951

- Discover the difference between a reactive system and reactive programming
- Explore the benefits of a reactive system and understand its applications
- Get to grips with using reactive programming in Spring 5
- Gain an understanding of Project Reactor
- Build a reactive system using Spring 5 and Project Reactor
- Create a highly efficient reactive microservice with Spring Cloud
- Test, monitor, and release reactive applications

Leave a review - let other readers know what you think

Please share your thoughts on this book with others by leaving a review on the site that you bought it from. If you purchased the book from Amazon, please leave us an honest review on this book's Amazon page. This is vital so that other potential readers can see and use your unbiased opinion to make purchasing decisions, we can understand what our customers think about our products, and our authors can see your feedback on the title that they have worked with Packt to create. It will only take a few minutes of your time, but is valuable to other potential customers, our authors, and Packt. Thank you!

Index

CPSIA information can be obtained
at www.ICGtesting.com
Printed in the USA
LVHW062104200919
631724LV00019B/405/P

9 781788 390415